Contents

Acknowledgments

Many people contributed to this account of the New York Zoological Society's first seventy-five years, catching inadvertencies, filling in blank spots, and explaining what occasionally I thought was inexplicable. I list them alphabetically. Dr. James W. Atz was helpful in sorting out the Aquarium's achievements in the 1940s and 1950s; Paul Bransom gave a happy account of animal artists in the Zoological Park in the early days; Dr. Charles M. Breder, Jr., sent revealing anecdotes of Dr. Charles H. Townsend's career; Director William G. Conway was an invaluable guide to the later manifestations of the Zoological Society; Grace Davall drew on more than forty years of association with the Zoo, from Dr. Hornaday's time to the present, to keep me on the right track (except for some points of syntax and punctuation which I insisted on winning); Robert M. Ferguson guided me to James B. Trefethen's Boone and Crockett Club book, *Crusade for Wildlife,* which in turn enabled me to run down details of the actual founding of the Zoological Society; J. Ripley Forbes of the National Science for Youth Foundation made available some documents from Dr. Hornaday's private papers; Dr. Leonard J. Goss, director of the Cleveland Zoo, advised on early veterinary problems in the Zoological Park; Dr. Theodore Kazimiroff produced early maps to illustrate the geography of the park before it was the Zoological Park; Dr. Ross F. Nigrelli reminded me of some early work in pathology at the Aquarium; Director James A. Oliver of the Aquarium made welcome suggestions; and Charles B. Sackett reminisced about my editor predecessor, the talented Elwin R. Sanborn. My best thanks to all of them.

Often there is someone of whom you can say: "Without whose . . . this book could not have been written." My choice is Dr. William Temple Hornaday. His files and scrapbooks and letter books stand in boldly numbered rows on the shelves of the old Department of Tropical Research Laboratory in the Bronx Zoo. Without them . . . well, this history could still have been written, but with what a difference!

W.B.

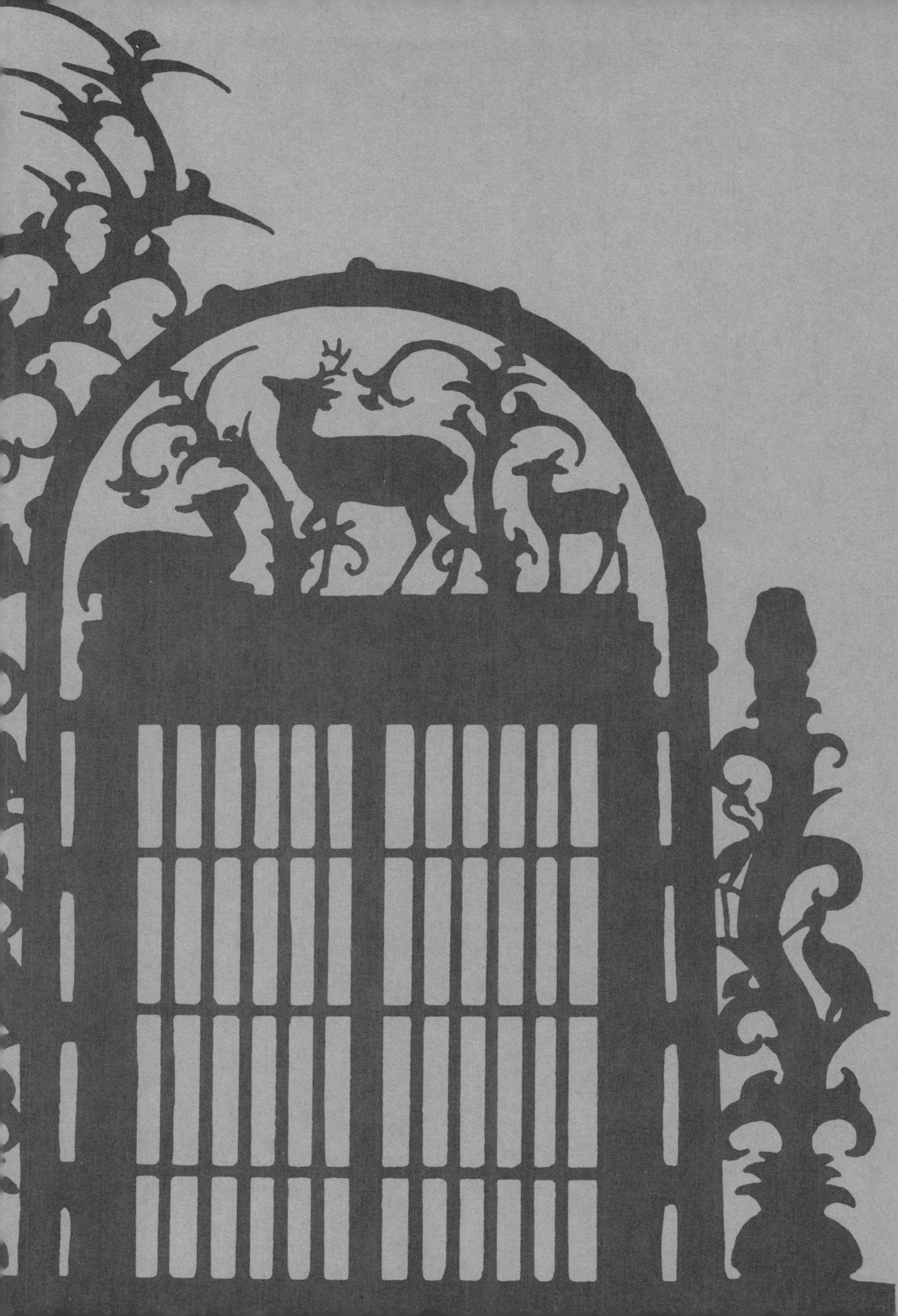

Gathering of Animals

A JOAN KAHN BOOK

GATHERING

An Unconventional

HARPER & ROW, PUBLISHERS

New York

Evanston

San Francisco

London

WILLIAM BRIDGES

Curator of Publications Emeritus,

New York Zoological Society

of ANIMALS

History of the New York Zoological Society

Grateful acknowledgment is made for permission to reprint excerpts from
A Zoo Man's Notebook, by Lee S. Crandall in collaboration
with William Bridges. Copyright © 1966 by The University of Chicago.
Reprinted by permission of The University of Chicago Press.

FIRST EDITION

Designed by Dorothy Schmiderer

CA 5.23.74

Library of Congress Cataloging in Publication Data
Bridges, William, 1901–
   Gathering of animals.

   1. New York (City) . Zoological Park—History.
2. New York Aquarium—History. I. Title.
QL76.5.U62N482   590'.744'74723   74–1793
ISBN 0–06–010472–4

Preface

When I agreed to write a history of the first seventy-five years of the New York Zoological Society, Director William G. Conway sent notes to half a dozen former or retired staff members asking them to help me with anecdotes and reminiscences. They all sent cordial replies but felt sure they could contribute nothing, since I had been on the staff longer than most of them and undoubtedly knew all they knew. . . .

Robert M. McClung, a former curator of mammals, did add a word of advice: "Tell the story from irascible Hornaday on up—the fascinating thing about it all is that the story of the Bronx Zoo is the story of *people* as much as (if not much more than) the story of animals."

At the time I didn't realize how close to the mark McClung had come. I had known Dr. Hornaday as a no longer irascible octogenarian and had a handshaking acquaintance with Professor Henry Fairfield Osborn and Madison Grant in their latter years. I had worked alongside Beebe and Crandall and Ditmars, Mitchell and Leister, Blair and Tee-Van at the Bronx Zoo, and with Townsend and Breder, Coates and Nigrelli and Atz at the Aquarium. I had had many friendly squabbles and amicable agreements with President Fairfield Osborn from January 1, 1935, to my retirement in January of 1966. But how decisively all these personalities molded the Zoo and the Aquarium, especially in the early days, I couldn't realize until I started wiping the dust off archives that had not been disturbed—some of them—since 1896.

Probably all institutions have an autocrat somewhere in their genealogy, perhaps several of them. The New York Zoological Society was particularly well endowed, with Professor Osborn, Mr. Grant, and Dr. Hornaday (and, yes, one should add William Beebe in his own special field). Hornaday was what might be called "the autocrat's autocrat." If the history of the Zoological Park from 1896 until his retirement in 1926 sometimes reads like a biography of William Temple Hornaday, it is because his personality was impressed on every single phase of the operation—sometimes modified by Osborn and Grant, but never effaced. How all these strong-willed men each managed to have his own way most of the time beats me.

One other circumstance has an important bearing on this history. There are many zoological societies in this country, sponsoring and standing behind many excellent zoological parks. But until recent years, when a few of them have begun to participate in serious research, their concern has stopped at the chain-link wire fence around their property. The New York Zoological Society's never did. Exhibition of animals in the Zoological Park (and later the Aquarium) was the first of its objectives, but conservation, education, and research were basic objectives, too. It took them seriously in the beginning, and it still does.

WILLIAM BRIDGES
New York Zoological Park

In an era when the accent is on youth, the New York Zoological Society may perhaps boast that it is young—or certainly that it is not the oldest institution of its kind even in the United States. It is junior by thirty-six years to the Zoological Society of Philadelphia and by twenty-two years to the Zoological Society of Cincinnati. In a wider context, when it was born in 1895 the Zoological Society of London was already a venerable sixty-nine.

Youth implies vigor, and vigor the New York Zoological Society has indubitably demonstrated. Its first avowed object was the creation of a zoological park along lines never before attempted, and its second and third objectives were the promotion of zoology and the preservation of our native animals. Even before ground was broken for the park, it had made and published a national survey of the accelerating destruction of American birds and mammals. Since then the New York Zoological Park has become the most innovative zoological park in the world, while the society has steered the New York Aquarium into a respected position among the world's aquariums, fostered a great laboratory of marine sciences, sent men half a mile down in the ocean, and unlocked secrets of bird and mammal and reptile life in the New World tropics. Its envoys have studied fiddler crabs on the shores of Asiatic lagoons, flamingos on the cold salt lakes of the Andes, whales in the depths off Argentina.

Vigorous? It has sent men to New Guinea for birds of paradise, around the world to study pheasants in their mountain homes, to the heart of Africa for okapis and gorillas and Congo peacocks.

Thrice it alone has exhibited duck-billed platypuses from Australia. It has created a biological research station where the Rockies look down on Jackson Hole in Wyoming. It has raised and administered funds for the protection of wild-animal life in Africa and for studies of mountain sheep in the American West, and sponsored grants for vital investigations of gorillas and lions in Africa, tigers in India, seals in Antarctica.

1

It Began in the Boone and Crockett Club

1

It has—but why go on and on and on? Later there will be more room even for sidelights: how the American bison was saved to flourish in great national herds because of a meeting in the New York Zoological Park's Lion House in 1905, and how California's giant redwoods were befriended in 1919.

It is interesting to speculate whether these things would have happened, what divergent courses the New York Zoological Society might have taken, what manner of men would have controlled its destinies, if champions of "the poor man's monkeys"—that is to say, the Central Park Menagerie—had not held out as long as they did and capitulated when they did.

That story is a very human one, and in it are involved the very human elements of rumor, suspicion, politics, and, it must be said, a slight lack of candor on the part of the founders of the society. . . .

Before taking a running jump at the founding of the Zoological Society, it is necessary to back up a few years, to 1884, when the New York State legislature received a report from its "Commission to Select and Locate Lands for Public Parks in the Twenty-third and Twenty-fourth Wards of the City of New York, and in the Vicinity Thereof." The commission had worked hard for a year, and to it we owe the creation of what are now known as Van Cortlandt, Bronx, St. Mary's, Claremont, Crotona, and Pelham Bay parks, all acquired by the city on December 12, 1888. Of specific interest is the commission's Conclusion No. 13: "That as no park system can be regarded as complete without suitable tracts for botanical and zoological gardens, your Commission has provided for these in the selection of sites."

It did not indicate in which of the new parks it thought these gardens might be located, but it did nudge the legislature toward the creation of a zoological garden:

A park system that failed to include a zoological garden would be wanting in one of the most essential requisites. A proper site secured by the favorable action of our State Legislature, a number

2

of wealthy gentlemen in New York city, who have already signified their intention to subscribe to an enterprise of such a character, would set the ball in motion.

The ball rested on dead center until Andrew H. Green, later to be honored as "the Father of Greater New York," tried to get it rolling. Year after year he sponsored, through various assemblymen, a legislative bill that would create a New York Zoological Society with power to establish a zoological garden and would give New York City's commissioners of the Sinking Fund the authority to endow it with some of the parkland acquired in 1888. Year after year the bill was defeated, for reasons that will appear a little later.

Now to sidestep momentarily. At a dinner party sometime in December, 1887, Theodore Roosevelt and ten guests founded the Boone and Crockett Club. The initial members and those who later became members, to a total of one hundred, were men prominent in many professions and, in the main, of considerable means, but above all they were sportsmen and hunters of big game. They knew only too well what market hunting, game hogs, and unsportsmanlike practices were doing to American big game and the wilderness, and they were determined to stop them by legislation, by publicity and protest against abuses they observed on their travels, and by any other means their prominence and influence could make effective. The club was not a mere social organization; it was a crusading—almost what today we call an activist—group.

One of the men who soon (1893) became a member of the Boone and Crockett Club was Madison Grant, then in his late twenties and a lawyer newly minted by Columbia University but considerably more interested in the pursuit of big game than of the law. Roosevelt thought highly of him, for he was filled with youthful energy and enthusiasm for the principles of sportsmanship that animated the Boone and Crockett Club.

It seemed to Grant and his fellow sportsmen that the big-

Madison Grant.

4

game animals not only of the United States but of the world were doomed unless something were done to protect them against careless, indiscriminate slaughter. Their protests were reminiscent of some that were to be made again in the 1950s and 1960s when new waves of what had come to be called conservation moved concerned men. Indeed, in the Boone and Crockett Club book *Trail and Camp-Fire*, in 1897, Grant issued a warning that has a familiar ring:

It may be confidently asserted that twenty-five years hence, the rinderpest and repeating rifle will have destroyed most, if not all the larger African fauna—including certainly the most beautiful antelopes in the world—and game in India and North America in a wild state will almost have ceased to exist.

Perhaps it *would* indeed have ceased to exist if such Jeremiahs had not lifted their voices.

In the fall of 1894 Madison Grant and his brother De Forest threw themselves into the political reform movement in New York City which ousted Tammany Hall and elected Mayor W. L. Strong. The Grants had long had a dream that New York ought to have a great zoological park that would permit wild animals, particularly those of North America, to be exhibited in surroundings as nearly as possible like those of their native habitats. The National Zoological Park in Washington had been created only a few years before along novel lines—big ranges for big animals and more or less natural habitats. What Washington could do, New York could do better. And so, when De Forest Grant remarked to his brother that their political activities should have given them some influence with the new administration, Madison saw a chance to make the dream a reality.

Theodore Roosevelt was still president of the Boone and Crockett Club while serving as Civil Service commissioner in Washington. Madison Grant wrote to him at the end of November, 1894, and proposed that Roosevelt appoint a committee from the club for the double purpose of seeking legislation in Albany to stop the running of deer in the

Adirondacks by dogs and to establish a zoological park in New York City.

Roosevelt consulted with George Bird Grinnell, secretary of the club, and on December 4 replied to Grant that Grinnell liked the idea but was a little doubtful whether he had the authority to establish a committee without explicit authority from the club. "However," he added with the Roosevelt directness, "I think I will go ahead and do it."

There was further correspondence about who should be on the committee, and it was finally decided that the matter should be laid before the club at its upcoming annual meeting on January 16, 1895. At that meeting Grant moved that the president appoint a committee to introduce whatever legislation was necessary to stop the hounding of deer and to create a zoological park, whereupon Roosevelt appointed Madison Grant as chairman, the other members being C. Grant La Farge, a promising young architect, and the lawyer Elihu Root, then forty-nine and later famous as a statesman.

C. Grant La Farge, of Heins & La Farge, architect of the early buildings in the Zoological Park.

A bill to stop the running of deer was quickly drawn and was introduced but was killed in the assembly just as promptly; it was, however, enacted two years later.

The creation of a zoological park was obviously a more complicated matter than a simple prohibition of unsportsmanlike hunting. As everyone knew, the city was already in the business of exhibiting wild animals, for there had been a small and decidedly smelly menagerie in Central Park since about 1861. But that kind of operation for the entertainment of nursemaids and children and their unfastidious elders was by no means what Grant had in mind. Central Park Menagerie occupied nine acres. Grant wanted the biggest zoological park in the world, even more than the 168 acres set aside in 1889 for the National Zoological Park in Rock Creek Park, and he wanted it to reproduce *naturally* and spaciously the kind of habitats for big-game animals so familiar to him from roaming the forests and mountains of the West. The National Zoological Park went far but not far enough; Grant dreamed

6

of an entirely new concept in zoological exhibition.

Grant's committee—but especially Grant and La Farge, for the middle-aged Root played a comparatively minor role in the agitations of the next few months—began to talk and inquire. They soon discovered that the idea of a zoological park in New York City was already shopworn; that Green not only had been beseeching the legislature for several years but that his current version of the bill to create a New York Zoological Society and establish a zoological park was already before the assembly in Albany. It had been introduced by William White Niles, Jr., the assemblyman for the northern wards where parklands were available, on January 17, the very day after the Boone and Crockett Club meeting. Routinely it had been referred to the Committee on Affairs of Cities.

Grant and La Farge called on Niles, introduced themselves as interested members of the club's committee, and asked about the status of the bill. To Niles it was a welcome intervention, for he soon discovered that they were "very well versed in matters pertaining to wild life." He himself was a zoological-garden enthusiast as a result of having recently visited all the major ones of Europe, and had been glad to accede to Green's request that he sponsor the bill that Andrew Green had drawn up. Not until it was introduced did he discover that there would be strong opposition and, what was more disconcerting, found that all of Green's time was taken up with his scheme for consolidating Brooklyn and other adjacent communities into Greater New York, so that he could not help with horse-trading in the legislature. Niles then talked to several of the incorporators named in the bill and found that they knew nothing at all about it—or said they didn't. He was in a discouraged frame of mind at this point, convinced that even if he got the bill passed the incorporators were not sufficiently interested to make anything of it.

Grant and La Farge were certainly interested and were

William White Niles, who pushed through the New York State legislature the bill creating the New York Zoological Society.

7

thinking in big terms, so he outlined to them the opposition he was meeting in the legislature. There were three charges against the bill:

1. That it was intended to do away with the Central Park Menagerie in the interests of property holders along Fifth Avenue.

2. That the society would breed and sell small animals in competition with pet shops.

3. That it was an attempt to remove the animals in the menagerie to a new location where they would be put under the control of William A. Conklin and William Van Valkenberg, menagerie employees (Conklin, a veterinarian, had been the superintendent) who had been discharged by the reform administration.

These were emotion-charged issues. Miserable as it was, the Central Park Menagerie had an enormous appeal to the submerged masses of people living on the Lower East Side, in the slums and ghettos that the political bosses of the day controlled. Central Park was a green oasis in their drab lives and the menagerie was a focal point of outings either on foot or at the price of a five-cent fare. No wonder that politicians from New York City resisted any threat to the menagerie. And its dissolution, by the terms of Green's repeatedly introduced bill, was almost certain to happen. The bill made it clear:

The commissioners of the department of public parks may make an agreement with the corporation hereby created [the New York Zoological Society] for the use of the animals and other property now constituting the menagerie under the control of said park commissioners, for such price and on such conditions as they may deem proper, or may sell, transfer and deliver such animals and other property to said corporation upon its request.

There it was: ask and it shall be given unto you. It was believed that in all likelihood the proposed Zoological Society *would* request the transfer of the menagerie's animals to its new park, which by the terms of the bill must be in the nethermost wilds of the city, and the populous poor would lose their cheap and nearby entertainment. So the politicians fought the Green bill year after year and always won. In 1890, for example, every New York City assemblyman except the sponsor and one other man voted against it.

Lesser opposition was not as well organized, but it had a certain weight. There was a rumor in pet-shop circles that a zoological society would soon be forced into the business of breeding and selling small animals for revenue—puppies and kittens and the like—and would thus become a formidable competitor for their market. So the pet-shop proprietors spoke up at political clubhouses and were listened to.

Grant and La Farge now had enough background to call on Mr. Green. He denied that there was any basis to the objections as far as he was concerned and said unequivocally that if they could get the bill passed, he would give them control of the new society.

Niles, a shrewd legislator, suggested that Grant and La Farge add their names to the list of incorporators named in the bill. He had made inquiries, he said, and neither Green nor any of the originally named incorporators had well-defined ideas about the establishment of a zoological park. In fact, he felt that unless the names of truly interested and qualified men were included, no adequate use would be made of the privileges granted by the bill when it became a law. Since amendments could be made as the bill passed through successive readings, he undertook to insert the names of Grant and La Farge of the Boone and Crockett Club and of his own brother, Robert L. Niles.

Furthermore, he would strike out the clause directing the Park Department to turn over the animals in the menagerie and substitute a more innocuous one whereby the new society would merely have preference *if* at any time the menagerie's animals were disposed of. It was to read that "nothing herein provided shall be construed as giving the commissioners of the department of public parks authority to sell, lease, transfer or in any otherwise dispose of said animals." In other words, maybe sometime the city would want to get rid of the menagerie, but it would have to be a special transaction that could be considered on its own merits. Nothing could happen just because a new zoological park was set up.

The pet-shop owners were still a force to be reckoned with, however. It is hard to imagine the aristocratic Madison Grant or the busy architect La Farge calling on them and allaying their fears of competition from a zoological society yet to be born, but they did call, and they did scotch the rumors. They gave firm assurance that the new zoological park would have not the slightest interest in breeding and selling domestic animals, or in breeding any kinds of animals except for its own collections.

Many years later Grant wrote:

When Mr. Andrew H. Green was told by Mr. Grant that the bill had been amended in this manner [to make the removal of the menagerie merely theoretical], he flew into a rage and said that the bill had been ruined, demonstrating, as appeared even more clearly at a later date, that his object was to secure the control of the menagerie in Central Park.

Ruined or not, Assemblyman Niles argued for the bill and explained and campaigned in the assembly, even persuading Mrs. Hamilton Fish, wife of the speaker, to exert her influence over her husband to have him support the bill by coming down from the speaker's chair to talk in its favor. He induced Senator Charles L. Guy to introduce the measure in the state senate, and Guy pulled the appropriate political strings. After a "prolonged battle" and "some of the hardest work done in Albany that year," the "Act to incorporate the New York Zoological Society and to provide for the establishment of a zoological garden in the city of New York" was passed on April 26, 1895, and became a law.

It has been noted that there was a certain lack of candor on the part of the activists among the incorporators. The Central Park Menagerie *was* in their minds, or came to be as the Zoological Society's program developed, although they had to

10

be extremely careful not to say so or even imply it. Not that they wanted to do anything right away; the safeguards inserted in the bill were perfectly acceptable and aboveboard. It was just that there was a strong feeling that when the great New York Zoological Park was finally established, its accommodations would be so overwhelmingly superior that the menagerie's out-of-doors animals, at least, would be transferred to its keeping. Furthermore, no one could conceive of the city's maintaining two zoological collections simultaneously. There would be no excuse for the continued "nuisance" in Central Park (and that is exactly what many of the "better class" in New York thought of it), and removal of its animals to the new park up north was seen as both desirable and inevitable. Opposition to the menagerie was particularly strong among the wealthy residents of upper Fifth Avenue opposite Central Park. At one point in 1897, when the Zoological Society was struggling to raise the $250,000 it was obligated to obtain by private subscription for the building and stocking of the Zoological Park, it was suggested to fundraising members of the board of managers that they might appeal to certain men "whose property would be greatly benefitted by the opening of our zoo and the consequent decadence and final absorption of the existing menagerie."

But abatement of the Central Park "nuisance" was certainly an afterthought and a minor one, no part of the original concept of a great zoological park that had been in Madison Grant's mind. If it fitted into the grand new scheme, well, that was all right; it could be considered lagniappe.

Some New Yorkers had quite altruistic grounds for encouraging the society. A Dr. John A. Hinton wrote to it in 1898: "I am very fond of animals—they are better than men. Please relieve the Central Park innocent victims as soon as you can."

Whatever the men engaged in putting the society and the park together may have thought privately about the inevitability of the menagerie's disappearance, they were careful

11

not to encourage action. Rumors of impending changes in the ownership of the menagerie's animals kept popping up in the newspapers for a year or more after the society got its charter, and just as regularly they were knocked down. "The Zoological Society has never planned, or proposed, or suggested, or desired" to absorb the menagerie's animals, the park's director truthfully wrote to one alarmed correspondent.

The incorporators lost no time in getting down to business. Three days after the successful action in Albany, incorporators Andrew H. Green, Charles E. Whitehead (a lawyer), Charles A. Dana (editor of the New York *Sun*), Oswald Ottendorfer (philanthropist and proprietor of the *New-Yorker Staats-Zeitung*), and Wager Swayne (soldier and lawyer) convened and called a meeting of their fellows for 10:30 A.M. on May 7, 1895, in Green's office on the second floor of the Park Bank Building at 214 Broadway for the purpose of organization, adoption of bylaws, and election of officers. Among the Boone and Crockett Club men, there was already a quiet suspicion that despite his promise to give control to their group, Green meant to take it into his own hands. Niles, indeed, had become so dissatisfied with Green's attitude and with the former menagerie employees, William A. Conklin and William Van Valkenberg, who represented Green in legislative matters connected with the bill, that he stayed completely out of the organizational proceedings except to discuss them with Grant and La Farge. Niles had concluded that Green had no larger ideal than to take over the menagerie and install it somewhere else.

Eighteen of the incorporators named in the bill—all men of prominence in the city—duly met on May 7, referred Green's draft of bylaws to a committee, appointed another committee to submit names for a board of managers with thirty-six members and to think about methods of raising funds, and adjourned for a week.

The minutes of all those meetings have been preserved, set

down in an engrosser's flowing copperplate hand, and show that the actual business of electing the first board of managers (now called the board of trustees), adopting bylaws, and recommending the election of two vice-presidents, a secretary pro tem, and a treasurer was accomplished at the meeting of the incorporators on May 14.

The Boone and Crockett Club men had been promised control and they meant to have it. Working through Whitehead, Grant salted the board liberally with club members, including, besides Whitehead, La Farge and himself, Thomas H. Barber, Percy R. Pyne, George Bird Grinnell, Henry Fairfield Osborn, John L. Cadwalader, Philip Schuyler, and Winthrop Chanler. Not all of them entered the board immediately or lasted through the formative years, but they stuck together when matters of procedure and policy came up and ensured that Boone and Crockett Club ideas would prevail.

(Twenty-eight years later Henry Fairfield Osborn wrote that "the real founders of the Society and pilots of its policies" were himself, Grant, Whitehead, Cadwalader, Schuyler, La Farge, and John S. Barnes.)

The managers held their first meeting on May 17. Although at that time Andrew Green and George G. Haven more or less took charge of proceedings and Green was elected president, the club members came out very well. Whitehead and J. Hampden Robb (a banker and former commissioner of the New York City Parks Board) were elected vice-presidents; L. V. F. Randolph, treasurer; Grant, recording secretary; and Grinnell, corresponding secretary. Thus the club held one of the vice-presidencies (Whitehead) and both secretaryships.

Only eighteen of the original incorporators were on the first board, with the other eighteen being prominent men with presumed special interest in the undertaking. Most of the incorporators, in fact, had been willing to lend their names to strengthen the bill in Albany but were not necessarily willing to devote time and money to the development

13

of the society. By 1900, Grant and Whitehead were the only incorporators still members of the board of managers.

The name of Henry Fairfield Osborn, who with Madison Grant and Director William Temple Hornaday made up the team of wheel horses who were to drag the Zoological Park into existence, appeared in the minutes for the first time on May 14, as a member of the board of managers. (Whitehead had suggested him as one of the original members of the executive committee.) As a professor at Columbia University and head of the Department of Vertebrate Palaeontology at the American Museum of Natural History, he was one of the city's foremost scientists. In the early days of the legislative struggles he had walked into Madison Grant's office on Exchange Place and offered his assistance. It was a fateful and fortunate day for the Zoological Society, for Osborn matched Grant in determination and certainty as to the way the society should develop.

Certainty and determination were needed, for there followed a long struggle in the executive committee to beat down the ill-formed plans of President Green and create a great zoological park. Green's vision by no means coincided with that of the Boone and Crockett Club members of the board; at one time when his earlier bills had been before the legislature, he had drawn plans for a zoological garden to be established on some vacant lots near where the American Museum of Natural History now stands, and in the months to come he argued for a narrow and highly unsuitable strip of land along the Harlem River. He battled in the executive committee, too, to have Conklin appointed superintendent of the Zoological Park. But gradually "Green men" faded from the board of managers and on November 6, 1896, Green sent his resignation as president, whereupon the former U.S. Vice-President and current New York Governor Levi P. Morton was elected in his place. Green had no further connection with the society he had sponsored. In 1903, in his eighty-fourth year, he was shot to death on his own doorstep by a

Professor Henry Fairfield Osborn; a portrait painted in 1924 and presented to the Zoological Society by the board of trustees. The artist was Julian Lamar.

man who had mistaken him for someone else.

Theodore Roosevelt, who might be looked upon as the patron saint of the society, since it was his encouragement in the Boone and Crockett Club that gave Madison Grant his impetus, was not present at any of these organizational meetings in the spring of 1895, but—like so many men who get elected to onerous jobs in absentia—he was put on the board of managers anyway. He did not stay put. At its meeting on January 30, 1896, the executive committee voted to ask each member of the board of managers to become either a life member at $200 or a patron at $1,000. Three weeks later T. R. submitted his resignation from the society. He was then president of the Board of Police Commissioners, and he wrote President Green that he had "more demands on my time and purse now than I can honor, and it is a simple impossibility to undertake anything new." The society's minimal demands upon his purse were certainly not unbearable—he was a ten-dollar-a-year annual member—but it is likely that the calls upon his time were the main element in his decision to let the society develop without him. He was soon to become Assistant Secretary of the Navy; Cuba and Roosevelt's Rough Riders were just ahead, and so were the governorship of New York and the Vice-Presidency and Presidency of the United States. With his resignation he drops out of the society's history, except for the gift of a few animals acquired on his expeditions. He could not even find time to attend the opening of the Zoological Park on November 8, 1899, while he was governor; he had a previous engagement in Maryland. Madison Grant, with perhaps a touch of pique, wrote to C. Grant La Farge that "Roosevelt does not seem to be sufficiently interested to attend the opening." Interested he surely must have been, but in the days before airplanes governors could not be in Maryland and the Bronx on the same day.

T. R.'s career touched the Zoological Park most memorably in 1914 when, after his return from his "River of Doubt"

Levi P. Morton, one-time Vice-President of the United States, a governor of New York, and the second president of the New York Zoological Society.

15

explorations in the Amazonian jungles, he presented a large and already old South American tortoise, *Geochelone denticulata,* that he had picked up along the way. "Teddy," as the tortoise came to be called, lived in the Bronx Zoo for forty-eight years and was the oldest animal in the collection, in terms of time in captivity, when it died by accidental drowning in 1962.

The Roosevelt name, at least, was later associated with the Society. T. R.'s son Kermit was an interested and active member of the board of trustees from 1929 until his death in Alaska in 1943.

The charter granted by the legislature had authorized the city's commissioners of the Sinking Fund to turn over to the Zoological Society an unspecified amount of city-owned parkland in an unspecified area—the only restriction being that it must lie above 155th Street and not in Central Park. How much land should the society ask for, and what spot should it choose?

A committee consisting of Green, Osborn and La Farge went to work on those and broader general questions, but the elderly Mr. Green was in uncertain health and not in accord with the views of the younger men, so that he took little active part. Osborn and La Farge carried the burden and the "Preliminary Plan for the Prosecution of the Work of the Zoological Society" they presented to the executive committee on November 26, 1895, offered a new concept of what a zoological park should be:

This new principle will be to place both native and foreign animals of the tropical, temperate and colder regions as far as possible in the natural surroundings. Thus the larger wild animals of North America—Deer, Elk, Caribou, Moose, Bison, Antelope, Sheep—should be shown not in paddocks but in the free range of large enclosures, in which the forests, rocks, and natural features of the landscape will give the people an impression of the life, habits and native surroundings of these different types. We may also present the tropical and equatorial animals to a certain extent in their natural surroundings.

Their "new principle" truly was new in 1895. Some minor "habitat exhibits" had been attempted in the London and Berlin zoological gardens, and large ranges were the glory of the new National Zoological Park in Washington, but cramped pens and paddocks were traditional almost everywhere else.

The committee had in mind a park of some three hundred acres—almost five times the size of the largest in Europe (Berlin's, with sixty-three acres) and nearly double the area of the spacious National Zoological Park (168 acres). Plenty of city parkland was theoretically available; Pelham Bay Park had 1,756 acres, Van Cortlandt Park 1,142. Bronx Park was very large, too, but the New York Botanical Garden had been given the northern portion of it above Pelham Avenue (now Pelham Parkway), and it was understood that the southern part had been reserved by the park commissioners for a large public playground.

To some extent the choice of a site would be connected with the kind of exhibition first attempted. Should the society begin by exhibiting large North American mammals, which would require large and naturally open spaces for ranges, or with tropical animals for which a more condensed open area for heated buildings would suffice? Or should it attempt to exhibit both kinds of animals simultaneously? There were even some timid voices in the Green faction that suggested a temporary zoological exhibit somewhere south of the northern parklands, as a sort of showcase to arouse interest and bridge the interval before a permanent exhibit could be completed.

It was certain that a committee that included Osborn and Grant would have no interest in the timid approach, but it kept an ostensibly open mind and raised the point in its report to the executive committee. Assemblyman Niles certainly had no use for it. He felt that his hard work in the legislature entitled him to speak up about the course the society should follow. While the committee was still trying to make up its mind about what to do first, he wrote a long letter to Osborn urging the largest and broadest views. A small and temporary exhibit would be a waste of money, he felt. He plumped for a commodious plan—not something that would entail enormous expense, which people might feel was impracticable, but a plan that could be modified and scaled down if necessary and yet would represent the committee as having "a realizing sense of the possibilities of the enterprise."

Osborn and Grant hardly needed persuasion to think in large terms. But first they had to recommend a site, and that meant getting expert advice. They called in Arthur Erwin Brown, director of the Zoological Garden of Philadelphia; Daniel Giraud Elliot of the Field Columbian Museum in Chicago; and Frank Baker, superintendent of the National Zoological Park. As experts they were asked to look at Crotona, Van Cortlandt, and Pelham Bay parks and say what they thought about their relative advantages.

The experts braved the rough winter weather to tramp over the sites, unanimously eliminated little 155-acre Crotona Park, and then more or less agreed that Van Cortlandt Park had to be it. Elliot had time to scout only Crotona and Pelham Bay parks, but from what he had been told about Van Cortlandt he was in accord with the others that it had many things in its favor, such as adequate size, accessibility to water from the Croton Aqueduct, and its position in the direct line of the city's expansion. (One of his main objections to Pelham Bay Park was the likely prevalence of mosquitoes in summer.)

The executive committee mulled things over a little longer and on January 6, 1896, recommended to the board of managers that the selection of a site be allowed to rest for the moment, especially since there were now reports that the southern part of Bronx Park might be available after all. More study would therefore be needed. But it was unequivocal about one thing: go for a permanent installation, nothing temporary. Brown and Baker had given the same advice emphatically.

Its final recommendation was that the society should start looking for "an officer of practical experience and acknowledged scientific standing" to take on the rapidly expanding affairs of the society and decide the many practical questions that were coming up. That officer would be the director of the Zoological Park, and part of the reason for letting the site hang fire was that he should have a hand in its selection.

Who first brought up the name of William Temple Hornaday as a possible director for the Zoological Park does not appear in the archives of the society. But Professor Osborn was chairman of the committee charged with seeking a director, and if he made inquiries among his associates at the American Museum of Natural History, Hornaday was likely to be mentioned. Museum people knew him well. As chief taxidermist of the United States National Museum, he had created artistic and lifelike displays that significantly advanced the art of natural-history exhibition. He had a strong interest in living animals, too, and after working for some years with the small collection of caged animals on the Mall near the Smithsonian Institution—animals kept chiefly as models for the museum's taxidermy staff—in 1888 he had advocated the establishment by Congress of the great National Zoological Park in Washington. Congress appropriated $200,000 in 1889 and Hornaday thereupon designed the park and became its first superintendent. He was not given all the authority he needed to carry out his ideas and he resigned after the first year, abandoning taxidermy and zoological-park dreams alike and moving to Buffalo to become secretary of the Union Land Exchange, a large real-estate organization. Nevertheless, many years of his earlier life had been concerned with animals in one way or another and his reputation was still remembered.

Hornaday was then forty-one years old. He was five feet seven and a half inches tall, and wore a mustache and a beard. He had been a farm boy, born near Plainfield, Indiana, on December 1, 1854, and his formative years were spent on another farm in Wapello County, Iowa, and on a smaller family holding near Knoxville, Iowa. He was later to recall, in a fragment of autobiography written in the third person, that it was while he was living on the virgin prairie in Iowa that he received the "first impressions of wild life with which he later became so deeply concerned. It was during a visit to his half-brother, David Miller, who had remained in Indiana, that William Temple saw a case of mounted birds and re-

2

Enter William Temple Hornaday

ceived the first definite stimulation affecting his future career."

For one year, 1870, he attended Oskaloosa College in Oskaloosa, Iowa, which he later praised for grounding him in reading, composition, and elocution, and then two years at Iowa State Agricultural College in Ames introduced him to books on natural history. He determined to become a naturalist, with taxidermy the opening wedge. He wrote:

In furtherance of this ambition, he managed an appointment as taxidermist for the purpose of building up a collection of mounted native mammals and birds for the college museum. This was to be accomplished in spare time, with compensation at nine cents an hour. Entirely self taught and without benefit of instruction, he soon acquired sufficient skill to convince himself that taxidermy was his proper field. He realized, however, that he could not make further progress unassisted and in November, 1873, he joined [Professor Henry A.] Ward's Natural Science Establishment, at Rochester, New York, as an assistant.

He started at six dollars a week. He must have thrown all his characteristic energy into the job, for the following year Professor Ward sent him on a collecting trip to Florida and to Cuba and other islands of the West Indies. In Florida, incidentally, he was the first to report that the big "alligators" that inhabited a restricted area in southern Florida were actually the American crocodile, *Crocodylus acutus*. Two years later he was collecting in South America, and then he took off for three years in India, Ceylon, the Malay Peninsula, and Borneo.

It is ironic that Hornaday, whose name is almost synonymous with the conservation of wildlife in the first third of this century, should have spent so many years in killing animals. He himself, of course, made a distinction between killing for sport or the market (and often overkilling) and killing for scientific study and exhibition in a natural-history museum; schools and museums were the customers of Ward's Natural Science Establishment.

21

"I have never been what you might call a sportsman," he told a reporter in an interview soon after he became director of the Zoological Park. "While I have killed scores of species and hundreds of individuals of large game animals, I have never hunted save as a naturalist, bent on making studies and preserving in one form or another every animal killed that was worthy of a place in a museum."

In 1880 he was a prime mover in the organization of the Society of American Taxidermists, and then in 1882 came appointment to the United States National Museum. His habitat group of American bison was for many years famous in museum circles and much admired by the public. In the summer of 1957 workmen dismantling the exhibit in the Smithsonian Institution found a rusty metal box containing two copies of *Cosmopolitan Magazine* dated 1887, and a message written across the top of the first installment of an article by Hornaday, "The Passing of the Buffalo." The message said:

My Illustrious Successor.

Dear Sir: Enclosed please find a brief and truthful account of the capture of the specimens which compose this group. The Old Bull, the young cow and the yearling calf were killed by yours truly. When I am dust and ashes I beg you to protect these specimens from deterioration & destruction. Of course they are crude productions in comparison with what you produce, but you must remember that at this time (A.D. 1888. March 7.) the American School of Taxidermy has only just been recognized. Therefore give the devil his due, and revile not—

W. T. HORNADAY
Chief Taxidermist, U.S. National Museum

By the time the Zoological Society was ready to be interested in him, Hornaday had written three books. *Two Years in the Jungle* came out in 1885 and recounted his adventures while collecting for Ward's. *Taxidermy and Zoological Collecting* followed in 1892, and in 1894 he wrote a novel, *The Man Who Became a Savage*. It ran serially in a Buffalo news-

Director William Temple Hornaday at his desk in the Administration Building in 1910.

paper, the *Illustrated Express,* before being published in book form in 1896.

With such a career behind him, Hornaday was the man most likely to come to mind when a director for the Zoological Park was being sought. Professor Osborn wrote to him on January 9, 1896, enclosing a copy of the "Preliminary Plan for the Prosecution of the Work of the Zoological Society" and informing him that he was being considered for the position of director. A letter came back by return mail:

Six months ago, a similar suggestion came to me from Pittsburg, where that city is now about to expend $250.00 [*sic*] on a public zoological garden. It did not take me many minutes to reply that with the death of my plans for a really great Zoological Park in Washington, and the lapse of that golden opportunity into a rather moribund affair, my ambition in that direction also died, past all possibility of resurrection! My disappointment over the wreck of that great National possibility was so great that for five years I have believed nothing could ever revive my interest in zoological gardens.

But human nature has its limitations. The magnificent possibilities of your plan are enough to awaken keen interest anywhere. The fact that your Zoological Park will undoubtedly be larger and finer than any other in this country, quite stirs one's blood, and since I have received and studied your plan, I have given the subject of your letter serious thought.

As to my fitness for the position you have to fill, I have some doubt. If it is your desire to secure the services of a man who is technically scientific,—an "investigator," a linguist, and a describer of new species,—then I am not the man for you. I am not another Philip Lutely [*sic*] Sclater [Philip Lutley Sclater, secretary of the Zoological Society of London], and probably never would be; and I do not need to tell you that I am not an Allen [Joel Asaph Allen, head of the Department of Birds and Mammals at the American Museum of Natural History] nor a Merriam [C. Hart Merriam, chief of the United States Biological Survey].

But, I feel that, such as they are, I *have* my powers! I believe I am in touch with the general public, and know how to serve out popular natural history, for the millions, even though I cannot

24

interest and instruct the technologist. I believe that if I have one mental gift that I may prize, it is the creative faculty—the power to originate. Moreover, I believe my practical knowledge of business would be valuable in such a serious business undertaking as your society has before it.

Hornaday went on to agree that Osborn's suggestion of an early interview was a good one.

When you see me, and find out fully about me and my limitations, you may find I am not the best man for the place. And on my side, I am puzzled to know how a society like yours can afford to pay any one officer a salary large enough to enable him to live in New York! To live in New York City, costs, as I am told, $5000. a year, even for very modest accommodations and expenses.

It was a skillfully composed letter. Despite his modest disclaimers of technical skills, he must have known the kind of abilities the new society would need and expect of its operational officer, and he mentioned his possession of them with convincing self-confidence. Osborn's letter of inquiry has not come to light, but presumably it did not specify the salary that went with the job; in his almost throw-away query about the society's ability to pay, Hornaday let it be known what his price would be. It, at least, was not a modest one; an annual salary of $5,000 was very good in those days.

The committee had expressed a desire to interview him in New York. Very well; he could come down any time on twenty-four hours' notice. And then he closed his letter with a teaser designed to whet the appetite of the committee:

I will read over your Plan once more, and then return it. The prospect it opens up is really magnificent,—and when I see you, I have one more idea to suggest as a means for *at once* getting hold of the Public.

(His idea for "getting hold of the Public," on the evidence of a subsequent letter, seems to have been an exhibit "to ilustrate the houses and the house life of the aborigines of North America. I think I see how such a collection can be

25

made a very picturesque, striking and popular feature, at very moderate cost; and it would be 'something new under the sun.' But of course such a feature would be only a mere side issue to the leading features of the establishment." Nothing ever came of the idea.)

Hornaday came to New York and was interviewed a few days after he replied to Osborn, and by the end of January he and the society were in substantial agreement. There was frank talking on both sides. The society's committee confessed its reservations about making a permanent engagement "during a business depression and before any site had been secured," but Hornaday was willing to take a chance when a two-year contract—at $5,000 a year—was offered, and he "expressed his entire willingness to place his whole time and effort at the service of the enterprise."

At this stage the young society had plenty of faith but little money, and felt compelled to hedge just a little. It was agreed that if, toward the end of the first year of Hornaday's engagement, the managers decided it was necessary to postpone or abandon the effort, the engagement might be terminated at the end of that year. In that unhappy event, the managers promised to make it clear to everyone that the abandonment or postponement was in no respect caused by Hornaday.

Naturally enough, by mid-January the committee had made private inquiries about Hornaday from men who knew him and had worked with him. Dr. G. Brown Goode of the Smithsonian Institution (who had encouraged Hornaday in the founding of the National Zoological Park) came through with a good recommendation—as well as a word of caution:

I do not think you can get a better man. Hornaday has strength, intelligence, experience, power over men, both to direct and to secure support, and boundless energy and push.

Then his word of caution:

It would be well however for you to have a definite understanding with him in advance as to how much independence and individual initiative it is intended that he shall have. Probably

26

you will be willing to have him go ahead and do all that he can.

Secretary [Samuel P.] Langley [of the Smithsonian] wished him to subordinate himself more than he was willing to when he had the Zoological Park here, but I think the trouble was due to a lack of definite understanding.

He was with me in the museum for a good many years and I always found him perfectly tractable.

Dr. Merriam went all out:

In my judgment no one in America is better qualified for the position of Superintendent of a great zoological park than William T. Hornaday. [He] is a man of absolute integrity, and his most prominent characteristics are energy, enthusiasm and common sense. He is the father of our National Zoo at Washington, and I believe him to possess more of the qualifications necessary for building up a great Zoological park than any other man in America.

Professor Osborn had not neglected to scan Hornaday's writings in order to gather sidelights on the man, and he seems to have been troubled by some implications he thought he detected in Hornaday's novel. It is difficult today to read anything "leftish" or "Socialistic" in *The Man Who Became a Savage*—indeed, it is difficult enough to read simply as a story. Its hero is an American businessman who becomes disgusted with corruption in high places and low, and renounces "civilization" for a better life among the noble savages of Borneo. It closes with the hero and his wife going off, hand in hand, to make an American flag from pieces of red, white, and blue cloth. However, something in the story bothered Osborn and he let Hornaday know his feelings.

Hornaday reassured him in a postscript to a letter: "I hope you are mistaken in thinking there are 'Socialistic ideas' in my novel; for if there is one thing I abominate particularly, it is Socialism!"

If there were any nagging doubts in the managers' minds about raising the money and getting started, there were none in Hornaday's. Just before he went to work in April he wrote to Osborn:

Overleaf:
The northwest corner of the Zoological Park in 1896. The buildings are outside the park, and the site of Cope Lake is in the middle distance.

27

The more I study over the matter, the more certain I am that the key to the success of this whole undertaking lies in its magnitude. If we set out to give Greater New York the grandest zoological establishment on earth, and make New York believe we can and will do it, with proper support—we will *get* the support! Why not raise $200,000 by subscription, instead of $125,000? If the Society should say $300,000, I believe we could get every penny of it within 12 months from the date of the first subscription!

The new director of the zoological-park-to-be had to wind up his own business affairs in Buffalo. While officially his engagement began on April 1, 1896, actually it was April 6 before he reached New York. He seems to have spent a busy first day giving interviews to the New York press from his office at 69 Wall Street. The next day several of the leading newspapers gave him column-length stories, going into great and laudatory detail about his earlier career but especially about his plans for what the headlines began calling "Finest 'Zoo' in the World," "Greatest on Earth," or "New York's Splendid Zoo."

"I have so many plans and ideas in my head to put into practice that I would be afraid to tell half of them at any one time," he told the *Times*.

His first job was to settle on a site. Unlike the experts who had given their opinions a few months before, he was free to examine the southern portion of Bronx Park, and above all he had the advantage of mentally fitting into the terrain an actual zoological park, the kind of park *he* wanted, not a theoretical one. All his meetings with the board of managers had been harmonious, and he could be certain they had confidence in his judgment and wanted nothing so much as a forceful and forthright director who would show them how to attain what they all wanted.

He spent three spring weeks walking over Van Cortlandt, Pelham Bay, Crotona, and Bronx parks. He saved Bronx Park for the last and was beginning to think that the prospect of an ideal zoological park was more than doubtful. Then—

I shall never cease to enjoy my discovery of South Bronx Park! Nor will I ever forget my unbounded astonishment at finding, within an hour after first crossing its boundary, that there nature has made a marvelously beautiful and perfect combination of ridge and hollow, glade and meadow, rock, river, lake and virgin forest, and that man has mercifully preserved it all from defacement and destruction.

Hornaday was an artist with words; he could paint pictures with them.

As I walked over the ground, again and again, and tried to imagine what would happen there if Noah should arrive with his arkful of animals and turn them loose, I saw the bison and the antelope seeking the rolling 20-acre meadow in the southeastern corner; the deer, elk, moose and caribou scampering for the open sun-lit woods all along the west, where grass and shelter could be found together; the bears and foxes hiding in the rock ledges; the mountain sheep clambering to the top of the highest point of rocks, and the beaver scuttling down into the deep, secluded pool where there are trees to be cut, and dams without number to be built. It really seemed that if the animals of America could be left to choose, each species would promptly find there its own suitable place.

He had found the paradise he was looking for, and so he went home and composed a two-thousand-word "Report on the Character and Availability of South Bronx Park." He drew up a list of ten characteristics the ideal site should have, rated Crotona and Pelham Bay parks impossibly low, and concluded that the Bronx Park site scored ninety-two points against sixty-eight for Van Cortlandt Park. His summary was: "From the standpoint of one whose reputation is at stake on the issue, I have neither doubt nor hesitation in recommending South Bronx Park as the spot best adapted to the creation of a truly great and monumental zoological park."

The executive committee concurred and on May 7, 1896, exactly one year after the formal organization of the New York Zoological Society, it adopted a resolution accepting southern Bronx Park as the site it wanted.

31

Hornaday's report on southern Bronx Park was a detailed and well-reasoned document. Because there were lingering pockets of preference for Van Cortlandt Park among some individuals and newspapers, it was printed in full in the society's first *Annual Report,* for 1896. Also, since this was the society's first publication for general distribution and it was important that the scope of the undertaking be made plain, the *Report* led off with a statement of plans and purposes. It gave plenty of latitude.

First.—The establishment of a free zoological park containing collections of North American and exotic animals, for the benefit and enjoyment of the general public, the zoologist, the sportsman and every lover of nature.

Second.—The systematic encouragement of interest in animal life, or zoology, amongst all classes of the people, and the promotion of zoological science in general.

Third.—Co-operation with other organizations in the preservation of the native animals of North America, and encouragement of the growing sentiment against their wanton destruction.

The statement of plans and purposes was not signed, but from internal evidence the bulk of it was certainly written by Hornaday. In it he rode his hobbyhorses off in all directions: the society's first duty was to exhibit "a liberal number" of the more noteworthy species of North American animals now threatened with extinction; labeling of exhibits was to be done better than it had ever before been done in a zoological park; a library of zoological works must be formed; publications would be issued and lectures held; animal painting and sculpture were to be encouraged; the zoological park was to be considered as a preserve because "Throughout the entire continent of North America, nearly every wild quadruped, bird, reptile and fish is marked for destruction."

Nor did he forget the protection of trees. Most other zoological parks created their landscapes artificially, but

The Society now has before it a series of preliminary plans locating the various buildings, aviaries, fences and walks, and these plans do not involve the cutting of a single tree! The only concession proposed in this direction is that the beavers shall be allowed to cut down several small trees that stand in the bog where it is proposed the Beaver Pond shall be located.

Once the desired site had been selected, the society moved swiftly to have it allocated by the city. Hornaday drafted the application to the commissioners of the Sinking Fund, pointing out that the society had made exhaustive studies of the available sites and had called in experts for advice (not mentioning that *they* had favored Van Cortlandt Park) and was now unanimously agreed on southern Bronx Park. The commissioners were assured that:

It is not sought to establish a mere menagerie, even on a large scale. A Zoological Park in which the larger and more important native animals have free range in large enclosures, where a satisfactory attempt can be made to copy or suggest natural haunts, and where visitors can find enjoyment in the contemplation of fine, healthy animals, amid beautiful natural surroundings, is quite different from even the best fifty acre menagerie.

The application was presented to the commissioners on May 21, 1896, and was referred to a committee and put over for a public hearing two weeks later. It was immediately obvious that it was not going to sail easily and rapidly through the commission. Mayor Strong thought the managers of the new Botanical Garden ought to be consulted about having a zoological park as a neighbor. Controller Ashbel P. Fitch suggested that the dock commissioners join the hearings, inasmuch as the site bordered the Bronx River. The park commissioners of course had to be heard, for they would have ultimate jurisdiction.

No objections developed from the Botanical Garden or the dock commissioners, but snags did appear at the public hearing on June 3. Mayor Strong and City Chamberlain Anson G. McCook spoke up in opposition. McCook pointed out that the Bronx Park site was nearly a mile from the nearest transit point, and New Yorkers wouldn't walk that far. Besides, the land had cost the city $800,000 and he was not sure the people would stand for turning over such a valuable tract to a "private corporation." Mayor Strong was even more vehement: "If we want a great zoological garden, let us get one of our own," he declaimed. "We already have the nucleus of one, and that would make a good start. The residents in the immediate vicinity of the proposed site are protesting against the location of a garden there. I don't think we should get into this business at all."

Most newspapers reported the controversy noncommittally or favored the society, but the *Tribune* thought Mayor Strong had taken the right view. It favored having a zoological park, all right, but did not want to see the wildness of "the most charming of all our pleasure grounds" destroyed—let the society pick a site in Van Cortlandt or Pelham Bay Park.

The *Journal,* however, took an editorial stand that was later echoed by some other newspapers. It simply quoted the mayor verbatim and continued ironically: "In other words, if we want a great zoological garden, let us tax the people several hundred thousand dollars to pay for it, instead of accepting the offer of a number of public spirited citizens to establish it at their own expense. Especially let us put it in charge of politicians, instead of allowing it to be created and managed by scientific experts."

Much of the opposition was trivial and captious. Even after the commissioners of the Sinking Fund had decided to make the grant, two members of the Parks Board continued their sniping, and insisted on inserting a stipulation that the society must agree not to mortgage its animals. As spokesman for the society's executive committee, John S. Barnes replied that he did not know of anybody who would advance money on the mere security of living animals, but that as he was not inclined to "fight windmills," he would agree to such a clause. This infuriated one of the Parks Board men: he shouted that he allowed no one to call him a windmill and stalked out of the hearing room. Professor Osborn and Grant, however, followed him into his own office, explained the story of Don Quixote and the windmills, and so soothed him that he signed the agreement on the spot.

John L. Cadwalader, as counsel for the board of managers, had drafted the contract with the commissioners of the Sinking Fund and the Board of Parks, and the corporation counsel had gone over it minutely and made mutually agreeable changes. His opinion, after comparing the contract with those made by the city with the American Museum of Natural History and the Metropolitan Museum of Art, was that the restrictions placed on the Zoological Society were much more stringent, that the society's freedom of control was much less than that given to the museums, and that the city's interests were amply protected.

The commissioners thereupon held a special meeting on March 24, 1897, and approved a grant of southern Bronx Park to the society.

The negotiations had been tedious and stretched over ten months, and certainly they were never as folksy as Hornaday made them sound in his breezy account of "The Zoological Society's Gifts to the People" published twenty-five years later in the society's *Annual Report* for 1922:

The City government of Mayor Strong hesitated about accepting the partnership in Zoological Society building that the Society proposed. The sledding became so hard that finally the Society said to the City:

"Now, come. In this matter New York is already fifty years behind the times. As an earnest of our good faith, and for the purpose of showing you some good works, the Society will guarantee to expend $125,000 of its own money in permanent improvements, and if you treat us right we will go on and make it $250,000."

The Government was amazed, and pleased, by this very spirited and absolutely unprecedented offer. Nothing like that had ever happened before. The Zoological Park site was at that time nothing but a wild and unkempt wilderness.

"Done!" said Mayor Strong.

The mayor had indeed made an about-face between the first submission of the request for land and the actual grant. In fact, in newspaper interviews he declared that he had been a zoo enthusiast all along. As the negotiations dragged along, strong newspaper support had been building up. Rosters of the society's board of managers and the names of prominent contributors to the building fund were repeatedly printed, and comments were made that a society in the hands of such men as Governor Levi P. Morton, Andrew H. Green, Charles T. Barney, Charles R. Miller, Andrew Carnegie, Edward J. Berwind, Philip Schuyler, Professor Osborn, and Madison Grant could certainly be considered respectable.

Even the prospective neighbors of the Zoological Park, whom the mayor had once asserted were opposed to having wild animals in their midst, had let him down; the North Side Board of Trade and the Taxpayers' Alliance of the North Side enthusiastically endorsed the proposal to place the Zoological Park in Bronx Park, and they let the mayor know their feelings. What else could a politician do but get on the bandwagon?

As the corporation counsel had said, the city drove a hard bargain. The grant of the southern Bronx Park might be revoked if, within three years from the date of commencement of work on the grounds, a zoological park had not been established. The society must pay for the original equipment of buildings and animals, and the buildings would belong to the city. Within one year from the date of the grant, and before entering into possession of the land, the society must raise $100,000, and within three years from the start of work, at least another $150,000. If it failed in any of these financial requirements, the land and any improvements made upon it would revert to the city.

In return, the society was permitted to establish an endowment fund and was given the rights to all income-producing privileges in the park—refreshments, boating, the sale of photographs, and so on—but the income must be used to expand the collections. The city undertook to meet the cost of roads, grading, fences, water supply, and general preparation of the ground before buildings were put up, and to supply police protection. But the first year's cost to the city was not to exceed $60,000.

Admission was to be free on at least five days a week.

The final stipulations of the contract were of the greatest importance to the society. It was given the right to "appoint, direct, control and remove all persons and officers" it employed, but "all regular employees shall be chosen, and their salaries fixed and promotions made, by reason of special fitness and ability." Subject to conditions about giving the Parks Department access to the grounds, getting its approval of building plans and the removal of any trees, undertaking not to mortgage its buildings or animals or to exhibit any of its animals elsewhere, and agreeing to keep the land east of the Bronx River open at all times as a pleasure grounds, it was confirmed that the society "shall exercise entire control and management over all the affairs of the said Zoological Garden."

In a city where and at a time when political patronage was a way of life, those concessions were precious.

By May 18, 1897, a bill had been put through the legislature authorizing the city to sell bonds to the amount of $125,000 to meet the cost of ground improvements. Thus the city was assured of funds to cover its own obligations, but the society's money did not come quite so easily. By the end of the year, only $47,191.01 was in the treasury, including $28 from Director Hornaday representing his fee for an article he had written about the park for *Harper's Weekly*. Members of the board of managers drew up lists of the richest men in town and called on them for contributions. The response was encouraging. Abram S. Hewitt, iron-and-steel magnate and former mayor, wrote to Osborn in January of 1898:

When the original organization was effected I wanted to subscribe but was unable to do so. I am not willing however that any effort to diffuse knowledge among the people and to bestow upon them rational recreation should lack either my sympathy or my support, so far as I can command the means.

He sent a check for $1,000.

The philanthropist-publisher Ottendorfer, whose *Staats-Zeitung* regularly reported everything that happened to the society and who was an incorporator and a member of the first board of managers, had to drop out of the canvass for funds:

I regret to inform you that, owing to ill health, I cannot attend the meeting tomorrow, and for the same reason I will be unable to aid you in raising the fund required. Enclosed please find my check for $5,000, which I contribute to the fund, with my best wishes for the Society's success.

He was the first contributor to qualify as a founder in the membership classes of the society.

The excuse that there were so many calls upon discretionary funds was sometimes heard, then as now. A well-to-do woman living on West Eleventh Street advised the society that there was no need to send someone to see her about membership "while there is so great need to succor the poor Doukobortsi, who suffer for conscience' sake—for the dying in India, victims of the awful famine—for the poor widows under Ramabei's care at Poonah—for so many things."

By degrees, with $1,000 here and $5,000 there as well as the ten-dollar contributions of a rapidly increasing number of annual members, the initial building fund began to build up. George M. Bailey, employed from 1897 to 1901 as a membership solicitor on a commission basis, had fair success from the start. By February 17, 1898, more than a month before the one-year deadline, the first $100,000 was in hand and certified to the Board of Parks. The society had qualified to enter into occupation of its land in Bronx Park.

Raising the money was the responsibility of the board of managers, and it kept plugging away on the next $150,000 it was obligated to have in hand within three years from the start of work. Meanwhile, ever since he was hired in the spring of 1896, Director Hornaday had been busily gathering ideas and applying them to the 261 acres of wilderness on which he had staked his reputation.

European zoological gardens had much longer experience than any in America could offer. On June 18, 1896, the executive committee asked the director to go abroad and acquaint himself with "methods of management, relation to public authorities, means of support, details and plans of buildings and of all equipment connected with the animals, special methods of caging and exhibition, general arrangement of the parks with reference both to exhibition and pleasure grounds, photographs, plans, maps, architect's details, etc."

A travel budget of $500 was provided (his living expenses were to be at his own charge), and he and Mrs. Hornaday sailed for Southampton on June 27 to visit fifteen zoological gardens in England, Belgium, Holland, Germany, and France. He spent only $410.07 of his allowance, and that sum included $11.58 for photographs and albums of views of the gardens he visited. When the Hornadays returned at the end of August, the director was tremendously impressed with the popularity of zoological gardens abroad, and he brought encouraging words for the managers, who were trying to raise money and create an atmosphere of social support for the Zoological Society.

In Antwerp, Amsterdam, and Rotterdam, he reported,

The membership rolls include practically all the people who make up the aristocracies of intelligence, of wealth and of birth. It is considered an honor, as well as an advantage, to belong to those Zoological Societies, and a well-to-do resident who will not become a member is not allowed to enter the gardens, even upon payment of the stranger's fee.

4

Ground-Breaking Began at 7 O'Clock in the Morning

More than one European zoological-garden director had told him, "With such ground, and the money that New York will give you, you can do anything that you choose."

The protracted discussions between the society and the city over southern Bronx Park were in full swing before Hornaday took off for Europe, but there was no serious doubt of the outcome; it might take months to reach agreement, but those were months that would be needed anyway for mapping the site and deciding where to place buildings and ranges and walks—in short, getting ready for action when the application was approved. Hornaday threw all his energies into that task the moment he returned.

Actually, he had not even waited for his appointment as director to take effect before getting started. On a final visit to New York late in March of 1896, he had somehow gotten on the trail of a topographical map of the park area west of the Bronx River. It had been made in 1873 for the Department of Parks, but neither the superintendent of Bronx Park nor the civil engineer who was at that moment resurveying it had known of the map's existence. Hornaday ran it down and had a topographical model made from it. He made his own survey, too. In his unpublished autobiography he wrote:

During the glorious autumn of that year, Mrs. Hornaday graciously offered her services in helping me to make a very useful chain survey of the glades and forests, the ridges and valleys, the bogs and the waters of those coveted 264 acres. [Acreage was variously cited as 260, 261 and 264 in documents of the time.] With a one-hundred foot tape-measure and an armful of home-made surveyor's pins—and a delectable picnic lunch—we made the first interior survey of that tract of land that seemingly had ever been made—there being absolutely no map of that place save a surveyor's boundary plot.

Armed with his topographical model and map, he worked up a map which he called a Preliminary Plan for the general layout of the Zoological Park.

It was a map that could still be used as a guide to many of

40

the original buildings and installations. Baird Court (not yet named) was plotted where it is today, with perhaps a few degrees' shift of axis, although the present main entrance between Cope Lake and the Bronx River was not contemplated; instead, the main entrance was to be at the northwest corner of the park at the junction of Southern Boulevard and Fordham Road. The shift to what was essentially the present Rainey Gate, or Concourse, entrance on Pelham Parkway, was made, however, before the Final Plan was drawn at the end of 1897. But the Preliminary Plan did accurately locate the Lion House, Monkey House, Bird House, Flying Cage, Reptile House, Small Mammal House, Mountain Sheep Hill, and a number of lesser exhibits and installations. Perhaps as a concession to the earlier plans of the parks commissioners to use southern Bronx Park as a gigantic playground, an area roughly where the World of Birds Building now stands was indicated as a Children's Play Grounds. (This was dropped from the Final Plan.)

Hornaday offered his map to the executive committee on November 27, 1896, and that body submitted it to Dr. Merriam and George Bird Grinnell, the editor of *Field and Stream,* for detailed criticism. Neither could find anything seriously wrong with it, but they did make minor suggestions. There was a natural knoll in the center of Baird Court, and Merriam thought it would be a good spot to exhibit prairie dogs, "these mild-mannered and inoffensive animals." Grinnell urged that pronghorn antelopes be allowed to mingle with the bison herd scheduled for a twenty-acre range in the southeastern corner of the park. In general, they were enthusiastic about the plan, and the executive committee thereupon adopted it for what it was—a preliminary plan. It would serve as a starting point for elaboration and refinement, and as something to show the commissioners of the Sinking Fund and the Department of Parks, although their approval would not be required until the society settled on its Final Plan.

Goode of the Smithsonian Institution had spoken of Hornaday as "perfectly tractable," and he was certainly not intractable about his vision of how the park should be laid out. Two days after the land was granted to the society, he wrote to the executive committee to "place on record an expression of my desire that all plans made and to be made by me shall be subjected to the most careful scrutiny of several classes of competent judges, beginning, however, with the Executive Committee itself."

The executive committee took him at his word and submitted his plan to the best landscape and engineering men of the day. On the animal side, Superintendent Arthur Erwin Brown of the Philadelphia Zoological Garden, Dr. Joel Asaph Allen of the American Museum of Natural History, Professor Daniel Giraud Elliot of the Field Columbian Museum in Chicago, and Carl Hagenbeck, the great animal dealer of Hamburg, went over the layout of animal installations and plans for the buildings as they were developed.

The most important action taken as the Preliminary Plan was on the point of becoming the Final Plan was the appointment of Heins & La Farge as the Society's official architects. C. Grant La Farge, one of the incorporators and subsequently secretary of the executive committee, resigned from the board of managers in the fall of 1897 to work with the director on building plans, since by the terms of the charter no manager could receive compensation for his services or be interested in any contract concerning the society's property or affairs. Heins & La Farge ranked high among the architects of the time. George Lewis Heins had been a classmate of La Farge's at the Massachusetts Institute of Technology and they had formed a partnership in 1886. Among their commissions were the original Romanesque designs for St. John the Divine (only the apse was built according to their plans) and the original subway stations for the Interborough Rapid Transit lines.

The first concern of Heins & La Farge was the development of the Glade (as Baird Court was called before it was named for Spencer F. Baird, late secretary of the Smithsonian Institution). Hornaday's idea was to make it a ring—or rather oblong—of major exhibition buildings and to give over the periphery of the park to large ranges for big animals that would not need heated buildings. The area was almost devoid of trees, except for a row of large oaks and maples on the west side, and buildings could be sited there without removing trees—a matter that both the society and the Board of Parks were adamant about. The architects studied the Glade for several months and finally decided on a formal treatment, which was to be the only contrast to the natural wildness of the rest of the park.

Controversy over naming areas in the park—mostly between Hornaday and Osborn—went on for a couple of years, although the only name, apart from Cope Lake and Lake Agassiz, that is consistently used today is Baird Court. It was Osborn's choice in the end, although at first he had suggested Audubon Court. Hornaday had wanted to call it Baird Hill, but Osborn pointed out that the name would not be appropriate when the central knoll was leveled. Then Hornaday came back with objections to the word "court." He had just looked it up in *The Century Dictionary,* and "court" was defined as "A short arm of a public street enclosed on three sides by buildings." Also, the whole area—not just the knoll —was elevated and sharply defined. Therefore. . . . But Osborn did not give in, and Baird Court it became.

At any rate, Hornaday's ear was better than Osborn's. The professor had suggested Lake Cope, and Hornaday changed it to the more euphonious Cope Lake.

(Hornaday later wrote that it had been agreed between the executive committee and himself that "the body of water in the northeastern corner of the Park should be called Cope Lake, in order that certain restorations of extinct North American animals that we talked of might be associated with the name of one of America's greatest palaeontologists." He repeatedly urged Osborn and Grant to commission full-sized restorations of dinosaurs around the shores of Cope Lake, but they never got around to it.)

Various other protuberances and ponds were given names: Merriam's Hill, Allen's Pool, Goode's Rock, Wilson's Hill, but none of these have survived the years. Nor has Audubon Court, the southern area bounded by the Reptile House, the Antelope House, Mountain Sheep Hill, and the Ostrich and Small Mammal Houses. Two names that happily had a little better luck are Osborn's Walk, the road that wandered down from the former Fordham Gate to the present Aquatic Birds Building, and Grant's Walk, which runs along the southern boundary of the park from Crotona Gate to Boston Gate. They are remembered and sometimes used, at least by the few survivors of the late Hornaday era.

Outsiders wanted to get in on the naming. The Literary Society of Morrisania, "representing the more intelligent element of the German citizens of the Borough of the Bronx," petitioned the executive committee to name something for Alexander von Humboldt and Alfred Brehm. One petitioner modestly offered to be satisfied with "a clump of trees or any small object." However, the executive committee felt that the names should be restricted to celebrated American naturalists, and so the petition was acknowledged and nothing more came of it.

Drafting of the Final Plan for the park began in the director's Wall Street office on September 27, 1897, and it was finished and approved by the executive committee on November 9. Mayor Strong approved it on November 13, and the Board of Parks accepted it on November 22.

Not surprisingly, considering the care Hornaday had given to his Preliminary Plan, the Final Plan did not differ greatly in essentials, except that a long, key-shaped seal pool was planned for what is now the north end of Baird Court and a subtropical house was supposed to stand about where the present Administration Building is placed, with a lakeside restaurant just north of it, overlooking the broad reach of the

Audubon Court in the south end of the Zoological Park in 1907.

44

Bronx River that had been named Lake Agassiz. The planned Administration Building was to be small and placed halfway between the Lion House and the original Bird House, and slightly to the west. The Elephant, Small Mammal, Reptile, and Antelope houses were confirmed in their present locations. Roads and paths have, of course, been radically modified over the years, and a southern service road halfway along what is now Bronx Park South has entirely disappeared. The Northwest (Fordham) Gate was closed in 1973, the Southwest Entrance (Crotona) is now used for automobile traffic only, and a new gate has been opened halfway down the west side of the park; other gates are unchanged. There is no trace today of Wheelmen's Rest House alongside the upper stretch of Boston Road—if indeed it was ever built. Bicycles were a popular means of transportation near the end of the century, and in the fall of 1898, while building operations were being carried on in a dozen spots, Madison Grant wrote to Hornaday: "I expect to be at the Park Monday afternoon, as I have an engagement in that part of town, and shall try to ride up to the Park on my wheel." At about that same time, Osborn had to take a little time off from his close supervision of progress. He had been run into from behind by a bicycle at his home up in Garrison, and had suffered a broken collarbone.

Hornaday and the board of managers were looking beyond the bicycle era, however. In their statement of fundamental principles to be observed in planning the park, they noted that "A single-track road for horseless carriages, so laid out as to reach the principal buildings and collections, but without interfering with pedestrians, is not objectionable and will probably become necessary."

To the executive committee, "Final Plan" did not mean *final plan;* it was feeling its way and its own members understood that what it offered the city was a general treatment of the park and that details might be changed later. Many were changed, and there was much pushing and hauling before Baird Court was skewed into its present position to coincide roughly with the long axis of the tract. Five complete studies were made and at various times Heins & La Farge, the Boston landscape architect Warren H. Manning, and H. A. Caparn, a New York landscape architect, were called upon for advice. As it turned out, Professor Osborn's own preference for the axis of the court, for its establishment on a single high level, the walling of its sides, its widening and provision of greater space between its buildings, as well as the planting of shade trees in formal lines, eventually prevailed. Since its cluster of buildings would be the focal point for all visitors, the executive committee felt that it must study the court with deliberate care; it had already decided to construct an off-court Winter Shelter House for Birds and a Reptile House as the first major buildings, and there was no rush about settling details of the court; there was no money for its buildings anyway. It was not until November 30, 1900, that the executive committee decided that its often-revised "Final" really meant final as far as Baird Court was concerned. Nearly thirteen months later, on December 21, 1901, the first building on it, the Monkey House, was opened to the public.

When not embroiled in the Baird Court controversy, Heins & La Farge was hard at work on plans for a heavy schedule of buildings to be constructed immediately or as soon as money became available. Director Hornaday had brought back from European zoological gardens a large number of ground plans and photographs of buildings he considered most advanced and practicable for New York. These he turned over to the architects, who modeled the Lion House after London's, the Elephant House after the Palais des Hippopotames in Antwerp, and the Antelope House along the lines of that in Frankfurt am Main. The Reptile House was borrowed from London, but with improvements. Hornaday exulted:

Our Bird House, Monkey House, sub-tropical House, Small Mammals' House, Winter House for Birds, Administration Building, Bear Dens, Wolf and Fox Dens, Alligators' Pool, Burrowing

Overleaf:
Panorama of the New York Zoological Park drawn by William Adickes, 1913

47

Rodents' Quarters, Squirrel installations, Beaver Pond and Aquatic Rodents' Ponds, all are features absolutely new, both in design and general arrangement.

With its first $100,000 in hand, the executive committee called on the city to spend some of its $125,000 in getting the land ready—erecting fences, laying in sewers, constructing walks, and clearing underbrush—and, knowing that it would take a good deal of time for red tape to be unwound, voted $30,000 of its own funds to begin construction. Even so, it was not until mid-July to mid-August of 1898 that the city approved the working drawings for an Elk House, Bear, Wolf, and Fox dens, Winter Bird House, Flying Cage, and Reptile House. By August 1, the society assumed formal control of the land and put up ten signs around the grounds declaring its occupancy and warning off neighbors who for years had been accustomed to using the forest as a source of firewood. The city appropriated $62,000 as a half-year improvement fund, and the heavy work started. Director Hornaday wrote in the 1898 *Annual Report:*

At that time, the site of the Zoological Park was an unbroken wilderness, to the eye almost as wild and unkempt as the heart of the Adirondacks. It was a jungle of ragged forest trees, brambles, bushes, and tall weeds. There were three extensive bogs, in any one of which an elephant might easily have become entombed. Poison dogwood and poison ivy grew in many places, and a deadly sewer stream flowed for nearly half a mile on the surface of what is now Birds' Valley. Throughout the whole 260 acres there was not a drop of drinking water available, not a seat, sidewalk, nor shelter of any kind other than those which nature had provided. Worse than all else for personal comfort, the tangle of tall weeds, blackberry bushes, and green-briar which grew up from the earth was met by the low-drooping branches of the trees, and the breathing of the forest was seriously obstructed. The heat was intense, and the mosquitoes were very troublesome. It was a rare sight to see in the Park any other visitors than those of the kind parks are best without.

50

Those casual visitors were to be a serious problem for years. The guardian force of the Department of Parks had paid very little attention to the wilderness since the city acquired it, and the neighbors, as Hornaday wrote Captain Hugh Fitzpatrick of the 41st Precinct, "seem to feel that they own the Park and are at liberty to raid it for fire wood." The director carried on a constant correspondence with the police captain, even complaining about the police he assigned. On one occasion a patrolman refused to arrest two men who were caught carrying wood out of the park. "Oh, what in hell is the matter with you? That's only dry wood," the patrolman had told a park workman. Fitzpatrick promised to impose better order and assigned plainclothesmen to the job, as well as increasing the uniformed patrol to eight. Even so, there were further complaints about Sunday visitors breaking off branches of flowering trees, stealing young trees, and digging up plants, and about boys setting fires in hollow trees to smoke out squirrels. The worst single piece of vandalism was committed by some "heartless miscreant" who cut slabs of bark from the so-called Delancey Pine, an ancient 112-feet-tall tree that stood near the Lydig Dam across the Bronx River. (Annual rings showed it was 260 years old when it was cut down in 1912.)

In October of 1898, the society hired from Heins & La Farge the German-born gardener Hermann W. Merkel as chief forester, with the preservation of trees his main job, and soon thereafter he was appointed a special police officer and the park began to be known "as a good place for miscreants to avoid."

For a time the park was so overrun with vagrants, and some of the contract workmen were so unruly, that Madison Grant directed Hornaday to get a fireproof safe for his maps and papers. "I would also suggest that you buy a brace of Smith & Wesson revolvers and keep them in your desk, as you are liable to have trouble unexpectedly some day with some of your employees," he added.

The safe and the revolvers were promptly purchased and one gun was issued to Merkel and the other to a young man who was assigned to sleep in the Elk House office as a sort of night watchman. There is no indication that the weapons were ever used, however, and conditions rapidly improved after Merkel came on the job and especially after Cope Lake was excavated and became a water barrier in the northwest corner.

Grant would have been even more drastic in the precautions. "I am afraid that you have too much confidence in our public," he wrote Hornaday. "For my own part, I would like to see the park shut in with a 10 foot stone wall, and only let people in at our sweet will."

Professor Osborn was in Europe in the summer of 1898. On August 18 Hornaday wrote him a jubilant letter.

On Monday, Aug. 15, at 7 o'clock in the morning, we really "broke ground" for a building in the Zoological Park. Of course for the Winter House for the Birds. The weather was gloriously clear (for a change!), the ground was mellow, and 20 lusty men were lining up for work. The gods are kind to us, and thus far we have found no bed rock. If all goes well, I think Saturday night will see that excavation practically completed. The men are all furnished by contract, with 15¢ per hour.

The working plans for the Reptile House were finished at 10 o'clock this morning, and at 11:05 standard time, were formally approved by the Park Board! The building is all staked out, battenboards up and next week we will do the excavating for the boiler room and foundations.

The weather has been dreadful; excessive rains, breezeless heat, dampness, mould and mosquitoes—just like India in the rainy season.

Pick-and-shovel labor remained cheap for a good while, but skilled labor came high; a year and a half later the United Brotherhood of Carpenters and Joiners of America gave notice that their pay scale would be $3.50 for an eight-hour day. (The rate went to $4 a day in 1903.) The society bowed to the times, and Osborn marked the notice "Approved."

Ground was broken for the Reptile House on August 22, and every few days throughout the autumn of 1898 some other exhibit was started. One contract, let on August 15, must have been of special interest to the director. It was for the Elk House, a commodious wooden structure sheathed in bark slabs and located about halfway down what is now the Crotona Parking Field. Lacking a collection of elk, Hornaday planned to use it as the administrative headquarters in the park, and he moved his offices to it from 69 Wall Street on October 11, although it was not completely sheathed for another month. Most of his days had to be spent in the park in supervision of the construction, but paper work—and there was a vast amount of it, for he seems to have drafted most of the official as well as casual documents—demanded a desk and space to spread out. Now he had it, right on the site.* His first actions after moving were to have a telephone installed in the Elk House (at fifty dollars a year for five hundred local messages) and to notify the Williamsbridge Branch post office that mail could now be delivered to the office of the society, which he described as "a modern building with a red roof" about five hundred feet east of Southern Boulevard and Columbine Avenue (183rd Street).

As consulting engineers, William Barclay and Herbert deB. Parsons had designed the water-supply and sewerage system for the entire park and the steel-pipe framework for the great Flying Cage. George M. Beerbower, taken on as a full-time engineer and draftsman, had spent the summer staking out the buildings and smaller installations shown on

* One of his casual documents was "The Preservation of Health in Cuba." War against Spain was declared in late April, and two weeks later Hornaday had written and printed a four-page pamphlet telling American soldiers how to take care of themselves in a tropical climate. His instructions, based on his own experiences in the tropics, were reasonable: avoid sleeping on the ground, use a hammock, wear a mosquitoproof shirt, don't sleep in wet clothing, wear a hat or pith helmet in the sun. One does wonder, though, about the advice that "A great protection against diarrhoea is a flannel bandage to be worn around the waist." Professor Osborn paid for the printing and distribution of the pamphlet.

the Final Plan. Hornaday himself directed a crew of laborers in clearing weeds and brush from the sites and along fence lines, but so jealous was the Parks Department of its trees that finally one man from the society and one from Parks were detailed full time to supervise underbrush clearance, to make sure that nothing of value was destroyed.

Grapevine communication was not as efficient in the summer of 1898 as it became in later years when the news that "Mr. Grant has just come in the Boston Road Gate," or "Professor Osborn's in the park," or "The director's heading south" was spread from building to building by telephone. Nobody knew where or when Director Hornaday would materialize—certainly not the driver of Wagon 978 at two o'clock on a certain summer afternoon. Hornaday wrote the foreman of the city Department of Parks that he had had occasion to visit the eastern dumping ground and found a team standing at rest with the wagon empty and the driver sitting on a rock about fifty feet away, "idling away the time of the team. The number painted on the side of the wagon was 978, and the team was composed of one gray horse and a bay. I request that this team be discharged tonight for unfaithfulness and neglect of duty on the part of the driver thereof, and as a warning that the loafing and soldiering of certain teamsters must cease forthwith."

By the end of summer fourteen exhibits, fence lines and shelter houses for all the large ranges, and all the buildings on Baird Court were staked out. If the weather had held, as it showed promise of doing when ground was broken on August 15, the Zoological Park might actually have opened in July of 1899, as Director Hornaday was predicting in his more optimistic moments.

Instead, a heavy snowstorm came during Thanksgiving week and most of the work stopped for nearly four months. The society had to spend nearly two thousand dollars on temporary roads of plank and stone to keep the contractors' wagons from miring down after every thaw.

With the winter's end, teams rolled faster; in some weeks sixty were bringing materials into the park and construction was proceeding at twenty-six points. Gangs of laborers swarmed from the Buffalo Range to Baird Court, and the walls of the Winter Building for Birds and the Reptile House shot up and were roofed over. Early in the summer the park was fenced in west of Boston Road, and so were the ranges and corrals.

Good fencing was important to the park, not only to keep trespassers out and animals in, but also because of the way in which it affected the natural landscape. Heavy bars would be necessary in some installations, of course—around enclosures for elephants, for example—but the ideal for ranges for deer and antelopes, wild sheep, and the like was a strong but almost invisible fence. Hornaday had found the ideal in the fencing manufactured by the Page Woven Wire Fence Company of Adrian, Michigan. In *Thirty Years War for Wild Life* (Permanent Wild Life Protection Fund, Stamford, Connecticut, 1931), Hornaday told of the discovery. In the summer of 1888 he was visiting an old friend in Medina, New York, and saw "a new stock fence of strong but springy woven wire, about four feet high. It was graphically advertised to be 'horse high, pig tight, and bull strong.' " It seemed to embody a new principle of hard-steel horizontal wires tied together by upright wires of softer temper, and it had remarkable strength and resiliency as well as being relatively unobtrusive. With a few modifications it could be used to confine large animals in the National Zoological Park then being designed, and Hornaday invited J. Walter Page, the inventor, to Washington for a conference. Out of it came a sixty-inch fence for buffaloes and an eighty-eight-inch fence for elk, deer, and moose. Subsequently Page fence was used throughout the New York Zoological Park and later around many square miles of bison preserves in the West. It was made in many styles, with strands closer or farther apart, and it did the job perfectly. There was no doubt about its being

55

a fence, but it did not leap to the eye. Hornaday was always enthusiastic about Page fence and recommended it strongly to Andrew Carnegie, who at one time consulted him about fencing some of his property.

Other manufacturers tried to get some of the park's business by dubious means. To one of them Hornaday wrote:

If we should find that your fence is particularly well adapted to any one of the numerous wants of our Zoological Park, we will not hesitate to use it. I hope, however, that you will not again be so unwise as to offer to divide profits with me, for however well intended, every such proposition must, by an honorable man, be considered as decidedly offensive. I am not aware that I have ever done anything, either in an official or private capacity, that would lead anyone to suppose for a moment that I would seriously consider, much less embrace, an opportunity to share profits, in an underhand way, which were derived from the Society which has done me the honor to put me in charge of some of its practical efforts.

He closed by saying that he knew of no fencing the equal of Page's.

By late spring of 1899 the July opening date had been given up, but the park was fenced, twenty-two contracts were proceeding simultaneously, the two major buildings were taking shape, and the executive committee and the director were beginning to think about a staff, acquiring animals, and opening officially near the end of the year.

Among the first letters that Hornaday had to deal with when he became director in the spring of 1896 were offers of animals, and his correspondents often betrayed a hazy impression of what kind of critter the New York Zoological Society was. Some who knew of Hornaday as the foremost American taxidermist took it for granted that he would pay well for skins and skeletons and mounted specimens, but an equal number of speculators offered eight-footed hogs and calves, two-headed turtles, a "perfect cross between a cat and a rabbit," a petrified man (guaranteed genuine), a thirty-six-drawer collection of mounted butterflies, and the like. Better-informed hunters and ranchers and dealers in game animals offered to supply live animals of almost any description. To all of them the director replied either that the Zoological Park did not intend to exhibit stuffed animals or "Curiosities" —his file classification of letters about monstrosities—or that it was still far from ready to consider acquiring live animals.

As month followed month and the Zoological Park began to take on a recognizable form, as water mains were hooked up, exhibit areas were fenced, and the first two buildings steadily rose, the director had to think more urgently not only about gathering a collection of animals but also about men to be in charge of them. As director, the first responsibility for the animals would be his, but he needed a competent staff to work under his direction. He and the executive committee were agreed that the society should engage men with scientific training rather than mere "animal keepers," however experienced in rough-and-tumble work. In the beginning he thought "Keeper of Mammals, Keeper of Reptiles and Keeper of Birds" would be sufficient designation for his department heads, but some more imposing form was needed to distinguish them from the working keepers. He consulted with Professor Osborn, who replied that he felt he could take the liberty of granting the title of assistant curator to the head of each animal department. He trusted, he said, that later the excellence of their work might lead the executive

5

The Final Step: Getting a Staff and Animals

committee to consider the advisability of raising the men to full curatorship. Hornaday agreed.

Hornaday's own primary interest was in the larger American animals, the "game animals" that he wanted to preserve at all costs, and he sought an assistant curator of mammals first. For more than two years the society had repeatedly called on men in the Smithsonian Institution and the U.S. Biological Survey for advice about the development of the park, and now they were asked to suggest possible assistant curators. C. Hart Merriam of the Biological Survey responded promptly with a nomination for the mammal position: J. Alden Loring, a young man who had worked for eight years under him as a field naturalist specializing in mammals. He had the great advantage of two years' experience in practical animal keeping in the Zoological Garden of London, and presumably he was at liberty to take the job, since he was struggling to establish himself in taxidermy at Owego, New York.

On April 29, 1899, Hornaday wrote to Loring and offered him the assistant curatorship at seventy-five dollars a month. He would in addition eventually have living quarters in the park, but for the time being he would have to sleep outside "until the Reptile House has been sufficiently completed that we can give you a room there."

Loring accepted promptly and announced that he would arrive ready for work on May 12, just as soon as he finished some taxidermy jobs in hand.

The choice of a reptile man was no choice at all; it simply grew into inevitability. Raymond Lee Ditmars, a twenty-three-year-old reptile enthusiast, was a reporter on the staff of the *Times* in the winter of 1898–99, assigned to the Criminal Courts Building. In pursuit of his hobby he had formed the Harlem Zoological Society with amateur naturalist friends as members, and for a year or two had been an assistant to Dr. William Beutenmüller at the American Museum of Natural History, working with insects. But reptiles and writing about them were his real interests, and since there seemed to be no certain future at the museum, he took a probationary reporter's job. When *The News Bulletin* of the Zoological Society was published in December of 1898, with a photograph of the foundation of the Reptile House and an article by Hornaday expressing his high hopes for it, young Ditmars rewrote the piece for the *Times*.

His story was not signed, but he let the director know who was responsible:

Have received the last Bulletin of the Society, and noted with interest the progress of the Reptile House. Matters have certainly assumed a most satisfactory form when we see a number of buildings in the course of construction.

At present I am on the reportorial staff of the N.Y. Times, and have compiled the matter in the Bulletin into the shape of a newspaper article, which is enclosed herewith.

If there is anything in the shape of press work I can do for the Society, it will be my pleasure to aid you in that direction.

Hornaday and Ditmars were already acquainted; the director had given a talk on "The Buffalo" before the Harlem Zoological Society.

On the bottom of Ditmars's letter in his files, Hornaday penciled: "How would you like to be Keeper of Reptiles?"

It was apparently a note to himself, for five days later he wrote to Ditmars:

I am delighted to find you on The Times, which has always been one of our staunchest and most helpful friends. Your "story" is very good and helpful, and very correctly written.

I have been thinking about you in connection with our Reptile House. Would you like to be Keeper of Reptiles? If so, we had best meet soon, at our Wall Street office, some day when I go down town, to talk over the matter.

It does not appear when they met, but on February 1 Ditmars wrote to the director:

As the time is rapidly approaching for obtaining specimens for exhibition in the Reptile Department of the Zoological Gardens,

I desire the honor of donating to that department, my own collection of reptiles, numbering about 40 specimens, comprising a representative collection of the reptiles found in the vicinity of this city, and a number of the larger poisonous snakes of the United States among which are a large diamond rattlesnake with four young, and several of the largest cottonmouth moccasins in captivity.

In reference to the above would say that I will retain them in my care until the opening of the Reptile House.

As an aide-mémoire for the next meeting of the executive committee, Hornaday wrote out on an ordinary park requisition form:

Please authorize the services mentioned below. Engagement of Raymond L. Ditmars, as Keeper of Reptiles, at $75 per mo., J. Alden Loring as Keeper of Mammals, at $75, and Arthur B. Baker as Inspector at $150 a month.

The executive committee gave him permission to correspond with Ditmars, Loring, and Baker "with the intention, without at present committing the Society, that they will probably be appointed."

Ditmars left no doubt about his eagerness. He replied that he could break in his successor at the Criminal Courts Building in one day and be ready to go to work the next. Construction of the Reptile House was moving along steadily, but it was not until July 17 that he joined the staff, with an allowance of ten dollars a month for room rent until living quarters were ready for him in the Reptile House.

It could be that prior acquaintance induced a slight case of favoritism here, for Loring was not promised an allowance for renting outside until he could live on the grounds.

The job of inspector which Hornaday had in mind for Baker was more or less that of general assistant to himself, helping to oversee the construction going on in every part of the park, keeping an eye on the staff and the animals—anything to make himself useful and take some share of the director's burdens. Baker was employed by the National Zoological Park and Hornaday both knew and liked him, so that while urging him to join up he suggested that he see his doctor about the possible effects of the New York climate on his health. As it turned out, both the doctor and the salary of $1,800 moved Baker not to accept.

Hornaday was thereupon left to struggle on alone with his overseeing tasks, but he soon found that his curatorial staff was both capable and energetic and that Merkel was able to take on many of the construction details. He did not again raise the question of hiring an assistant.

The onerous responsibility of keeping track of all expenditures for work in the park, out of both society and city funds, up to now had fallen entirely on Hornaday. He realized that he had to have a chief clerk to handle time sheets and payrolls, payments to contractors, purchases of supplies, and, as soon as the park opened, not only outgo but income from gate receipts, restaurants, and any other profitable privileges that might be developed. He wanted to divest himself of all the exacting financial transactions that were deflecting him from exhibit planning, and he had a candidate for a chief clerkship in mind: his nephew, H. Raymond Mitchell, who was at that time a chief clerk, cashier, and agent for the Santa Fe Railway in Oklahoma. He therefore wrote a four-page longhand letter to "Dear Ray," offering him the job if he cared to make a change from railroad work. It was a persuasive letter, and the starting salary of $1,200 a year, later to go to $1,500 when he settled into the job, was attractive. Mitchell, who was then twenty-seven years old, accepted after only a few days' thought, came East, and took over the job on May 23, 1899.

Selection of an assistant curator of birds was delayed for a little while. One of Hornaday's Washington associates, W. E. D. Scott, made some tentative inquiries about the job, but Hornaday was dubious. He wrote to Merriam and asked his opinion. Scott, Hornaday pointed out, was older than himself and "fully appreciates himself, and it might be he would

elect to regard me with a feeling of tolerance, which to me would be intolerable. What do you think? Would it be like sleeping with a porcupine to try to get along with him?"

Merriam's reply has not been found, but no more was heard of Scott's application.

Nor did anything come of an approach to Dr. Sylvester D. Judd of the Biological Survey, strongly recommended by Dr. Frank M. Chapman of the American Museum of Natural History. (Chapman himself had been considered, but Hornaday thought he was not experienced in keeping live birds.) The going rate for assistant curators was $900 a year, and Judd replied that he could not consider any position, however desirable, unless it paid at least $1,500 a year.

In the end, it was Professor Osborn who came up with the answer. Since 1896 he had been well aware of one of his special students in the department of zoology at Columbia University, young Charles William Beebe. Beebe was interested in birds—mainly—and insects, and he had a restless energy that brought him to the attention of everyone in the natural sciences both at the university and at the American Museum of Natural History.

(In his obituary of Beebe in *The Auk* in 1964, Lee S. Crandall wrote that "His mother, a woman of intense drive, was determined to see that her son should have the benefit of all available aid in furtherance of his choice of professions and made sure that he met the leaders in the field.")

In 1899 Beebe was twenty-two years old and had a year to go before graduation from Columbia. Hornaday's efforts to find a bird man were hanging fire, or misfiring. So on October 4 Osborn took Beebe up to the Zoological Park and introduced him to Director Hornaday. Again, no record of the meeting exists, except Beebe's statement long afterward that it was his first visit to the park. But Osborn had settled the matter in his own mind, and had assured the young man that a year in the Zoological Park would be more valuable to him than another year of college training. C. William Beebe became assistant curator of birds on October 16. His domain consisted of an almost completed Winter Shelter House for Birds, the incomplete skeleton of a big Flying Cage, and a small but varied collection of water birds and birds of prey.

Hornaday had one other staff position in mind, for what he called a nomenclator—"some person who is sufficiently familiar with mammals, birds and reptiles to be able to promptly identify and correctly label the living creatures that come to us, besides taking charge of the catalogues. It requires what might be called an all-round technologist on these three classes of vertebrates." The salary would be $900 a year, and he made a tentative inquiry of an acquaintance in Buffalo, Lawrence Irwell. That idea soon faded away, however, for he was himself quite competent to assign scientific names to the mammals, and he was to find that Ditmars and Beebe were well versed in the systematics of their own fields.

Between May and October, then, the staff was put together, and Loring, Ditmars, and Beebe entered upon their duties with the titles of assistant curators. Hope of quick advancement to full curatorship may have been held out to them; in any event, for some weeks in 1900, Assistant Curator Ditmars jumped the gun and in correspondence about purchases of reptiles signed himself "Curator of Reptiles." Then that style ceased abruptly and he returned to being plain assistant curator of reptiles. However, both he and Beebe were raised to full curatorial rank in 1902. In addition, Ditmars was placed in general charge of mammals on June 15, 1901, but he never held the title of curator of mammals as well as of reptiles until after Hornaday's retirement in 1926.

Loring had the misfortune to run afoul of Madison Grant within three months of his appointment. Grant had visited the park one August day on one of his twice-a-week-or-oftener inspections, and the next day Hornaday received a letter from him about

what appeared to me to be the very careless way in which Mr. Loring handled the birds and animals. I will be very much obliged to you if you will not put too great authority in Mr. Loring's hands in this matter, until he shows a more serious appreciation of his duties. He may develop into a capable keeper of mammals, but I must say that I am not at all favorably impressed with him at present. Maybe he is a little young for the responsible position in which he finds himself [he was twenty-eight years old], and I am sure he needs the benefit of your strict supervision.

Hornaday later protested in defense of Loring that he *did* work under strict supervision, but when the situation finally erupted at the end of November, 1900, Hornaday was on an animal-buying trip in the West. Grant, with the concurrence of Professor Osborn, suspended Loring and ordered him to turn in his keys and stay away from the park.

The incident that triggered the explosion was minor, but it followed months of dissatisfaction on Grant's part with Loring's feeding and quartering of his animals. Two very young wildcats had arrived on November 24 (one, at least, from Texas) and Loring placed them in the temporary Mammal House, which was dry, warm, and well lighted. Grant ordered them moved to the Buffalo House, which was then used as storage quarters for almost everything except reptiles and aquatic birds. Loring protested that the cats were mere kittens, that the Buffalo House was cold and dark and damp, the day was cold and rainy, and that at the very least the animals should be kept warm and dry overnight.

Grant immediately went to the office of Chief Clerk Mitchell and dictated letters suspending Loring and ordering the cats taken to the Buffalo House.

A full report on the incident was made by Mitchell to Hornaday, who received it a week later in Denver, along with a copy of the letter suspending Loring. The director was outraged and penned a reply to Osborn that left no uncertainty about how he felt. Whether he actually mailed it is doubtful, but it must have relieved his mind to set down exactly what he thought of such an action. The heavy black ink fairly jumps from the pages:

I have been greatly shocked by the Park news in Mr. Mitchell's letter. A blow with a hammer would have felt about the same. It must be a new kind of madness which has let you, and Mr. Grant—and Mr. Niles concurring, so I hear—to attack the Park administration in my absence, and without any sort of warning to me.

The copy of your letter of suspension seems to indicate that there was no specially serious act of delinquency on Mr. Loring's part. I imagine, however, that something very serious must be charged against him to lead you to inflict upon him a punishment next in severity and disgrace to dismissal.

If the animals have not been fed and treated properly, *I* am the one to be investigated, not Loring. He has, in the main, simply carried out *my* definite and *strict instructions*. I am so absolutely certain that you have all made a great mistake in this matter, I go to the limit, and advise you to reverse yourself, and restore the status quo before I reach home.

There was to be no reversal. When Hornaday returned from his trip, Osborn asked for a complete report from Loring, Ditmars, and Beebe on every animal that had died since they entered the service of the society. Loring's report was complemented by statements of the veterinarians who had been called in from time to time.

The two small cats that had precipitated Loring's dismissal were themselves the subject of a veterinarian's report, for one had died on November 27 and the other on November 30 while still in the Buffalo House. The veterinarian gave it as his impression that the Buffalo House was not a good place for cats; it was unhygienic, with little or no sunlight, the temperature scarcely above sixty degrees, the air close and damp, ventilation poor—all in all, "a good atmosphere for pneumonia."

Hornaday worked hard to get Loring reinstated. In transmitting Loring's report on deaths in the collection he conceded the young man's drawbacks: "small stature [he was five feet six and a half inches tall and weighed 138 pounds], youthful appearance and faults of manner are against him." On the other hand, Loring was

able to show any of his keepers how to do good work, he can handle animals better than any of them, and he can shoot and trap animals successfully.

Your attention is called to the fact that we have been attempting to acclimate five important species of North American ruminants which up to this date have not been kept successfully anywhere, either in the Mississippi Valley or on the Atlantic coast. I refer to the Moose, Caribou, Antelope, Mule Deer and Black-tailed Deer. Any failures made with these animals must be charged to the Director, for from the first he has made their management his special care.

I do not know of a man in this country for whom I would be willing to exchange him, and to take a candidate from Europe is to take a leap in the dark.

Receipt of Loring's report and justification of his stewardship was acknowledged by Professor Osborn in one sentence with a further note to Hornaday: "I hardly think it probable that we can bring ourselves to consider Mr. Loring's retention for the best interests of the Park."

With Loring gone, someone had to supervise the mammals. An animal trainer and showman, Arthur Spencer of Wheeling, West Virginia, applied for the job. He was apparently an excellent animal man but was more accustomed to the rough ways of the circus world than to the amenities of a Zoological Park. If a visitor fed a peanut to a monkey or tapped on a cage front with his umbrella to get a dozing animal to move, Spencer yelled at him and ordered him out of the building. Unfortunately he yelled at an influential member of the Zoological Society, and so he too disappeared from the scene in the early summer of 1901. (He wound up as superintendent of Cleveland's municipal zoo.) It was almost immediately thereafter that Ditmars was given general supervision of mammals in addition to his work with reptiles.

Although Loring's usefulness in the Zoological Park was at an end, Hornaday was not willing to see him cast aside completely. Grant was interested in having collections of Alaska's big-game animals made for the American Museum of Natural History and took the lead in raising $5,000 a year for three years of field work by Andrew J. Stone, an explorer and hunter. Hornaday proposed that as an allied effort the Zoological Society send Loring to Alaska to establish friendly relations with the Alaskan Commercial Company and various local men who might capture Kadiak bears, white sheep, the gigantic Alaskan moose, and anything else of great rarity and interest; Loring would himself try to make some captures.

67

The executive committee concluded that this would be a good way to smooth ruffled feelings, and so Loring was dispatched on March 12, 1901.

Loring was barely out of town when wrath descended on him again. As he was leaving, he gave an interview to his cousin, a reporter on the Brooklyn *Eagle,* stressing that he was going primarily in search of Kadiak bears and detailing what he proposed to do on his expedition. The interview was doubly unfortunate, for the National Zoological Park in Washington already had a man in Alaska trying to get Kadiaks, and it might appear that the New York Zoological Park was trying to undercut its sister institution. Apart from that, the interview gave a little too much emphasis to Loring's intrepidity and not enough to the enterprise of the Zoological Society. Letters went speeding after him instructing him to make no contact of any kind with the National Zoo's source of supply and in any future interviews to suppress any reference to himself and his exploits.

Loring had learned his lesson, and his behavior in Alaska was exemplary. He made the contacts the society wanted, and he asked questions and kept his eyes and ears open so that on his return he was able to write two excellent papers, "Notes on the Destruction of Animal Life in Alaska" and "Notes on Mammals and Birds Observed in Alaska" for the 1901 *Annual Report* as well as a lively account of "The Quest for *Ovis dalli*" (the white, or Dall's, sheep) for the society's *Bulletin.* With the aid of natives he actually managed to capture three lambs of the beautiful white sheep, but they all died within a few days. All he came home with on September 15, as a result of his own capturing or purchasing efforts, were a grizzly bear and a brown bear. But he had kept out of trouble and the expedition was officially accounted a success, so that the executive committee was willing to use him again in 1906 to help select a site for the Wichita Bison Preserve and arrange for its fencing.

The gathering in of animals had started in May of 1899,

well before staff positions were all filled. Ever mindful of the fact that he was engaged in a history-making enterprise, the director had planned to have photographs made of the first living animal to arrive, and had some hope that it would be a grizzly bear which the Engineers Club of New York had offered—if one could be bought for fifty dollars.

The offer had been made in December of the previous year, and Hornaday wrote in reply:

That the Engineers Club should be the first in the field with a gift of a live animal for the Zoological Park is a most gratifying augury of future favor with the public. To have received a gift thus early from an organization of zoologists would have been very gratifying, though no occasion for surprise, but to have the first come from a club of engineers is something of which we may be proud. The early action of the club will make its gift "No. 1" in our catalogue of animals and gifts.

The fifty-dollar check came through, but a satisfactory young grizzly was hard to find. Hornaday had already alerted Rudolph Kersting, a free-lance photographer who had semi-official status as photographer of the park's animals and installations, to be ready to get a picture of the historic first animal. But instead of the grizzly the director hoped for, which did not come until October 14 (and cost seventy-five dollars instead of the fifty provided by the Engineers Club, the society paying the difference), the first arrival was a pair of white-tailed prairie dogs from Big Horn County, Wyoming, the gift of an artist and sportsman, A. A. Anderson of New York City. They came on May 12 and Hornaday wrote Kersting not to bother about pictures, as they were "in very poor health, and their arrival was in no way a noteworthy event, save on paper." Nevertheless, they are No. 1 and No. 2 in the Zoological Park's Mammal Accession Book. Despite their poor condition, one survived eleven months and the other nineteen months.

After May 12, animals arrived almost daily, whether the park was ready to receive them or not. With a few exceptions they were not important animals—a star-nosed mole, opossum, skunk, weasel, flying squirrel, raccoons. One was notable: a giant anteater that had been captured in a tree in Venezuela. It cost forty dollars. The little municipal zoo in Buffalo donated three gray wolves, and a seventy-five-dollar yearling woodland caribou came on August 25. Other interesting acquisitions during the summer and fall were four California sea lions, nine American elk (three of them transferred from a herd in Prospect Park in Brooklyn and six presented by George J. Gould from his herd at Furlough Lodge in the Catskills), six pronghorn antelopes, three orangutans, a Bengal tiger (named Dewey for the hero of Manila Bay), and two polar bears, the latter bought from Carl Hagenbeck in Germany.

Later Hornaday regretted in print that he had accepted some animals before proper quarters were available, for losses were high. He did, unfortunately, feel impelled to turn down the offer of an echidna which the Kny-Scheerer Company, a scientific-instruments firm, surprisingly held in its European establishment. The publicity value of the first living egg-laying mammal in the New World would have been enormous. He declined, too, the offer of the United States consul in Honduras to go to the Galápagos Islands and collect some of the big tortoises. Hornaday felt that the cost of an expedition would be too great, and anyway he had exhibited ten Galápagos tortoises in the National Zoological Park and the public took little interest in them.

Temporarily an "Animal Yard" was set up in the center of the park, fenced with boards and fitted with sheds, for none of the permanent installations were ready in early summer. The polar bears came before their dens and big pools were completed and they had to be kept in one of the grizzly-bear dens with a very small pool, where they rubbed all the hair off their backs. Two pythons, one twenty-six feet long and the other twenty-two feet, were held in a drygoods box in the Reptile House, with wire netting and a cloth over the front. Florida otters found a temporary home in turtle tanks in the Reptile House; and with the onset of cool weather in the fall, tropical deer and peccaries were penned up in the new Buffalo House, which had been equipped with stoves and pens. Indeed, for the first two or three years almost any kind of animal could be found almost anywhere.

A glassed enclosure—a greenhouse, Hornaday called it—had been built about where the present Small Mammal House stands, and some of the overflow could be kept there. The three young orangutans that came in September and October needed special care, so Hornaday took them home and Mrs. Hornaday became their foster mother—a role familiar to many a zoo wife since. They went through a series of dietary crises which the director met with what was probably the standard practice of the day. To an inquirer he wrote:

The best food is boiled rice, with a little milk in it, varied with oat meal mush, also with a little milk. I am also feeding them at intervals on corn meal mush and tapioca, all with milk. For variety, we give our orangs ripe apples, and also well-ripened bananas. The safest fruit for apes of all kinds is bananas. If you find hard lumps forming in the bowels, which you can easily determine by feeling of the animal's abdomen, the best thing is to use a syringe at once, by means of which we have twice saved the life of one of our specimens. To this particular specimen we are now giving a teaspoonfull of castoria daily in order to get its digestive apparatus in good working order. One other thing, an orang utan or chimpanzee requires an occasional bath in warm water to keep its skin soft and keep its pores open. In case of sickness, use Mellin's Food.

Hornaday's abiding interest in the American bison led him to press hard for the formation of a sizable herd to occupy the twenty-acre range he had laid out in the southeastern corner of the park. He sent begging letters to Austin Corbin, Sr., who had stocked bison on his Blue Mountain Preserve near Newport, New Hampshire, and to William C. Whitney, who had bison on October Mountain near Lenox, Massachusetts. Noth-

Dr. Hornaday inspects the Zoo's bison herd in 1901.

ing came of these pleas immediately, and the director made inquiries in Texas and Oklahoma that resulted in the purchase of three bulls and a cow from Colonel Charles Goodnight's herd in the Panhandle, and a bull, a cow, and a yearling heifer from Ed Hewens at Camp Supply, Oklahoma. Charles J. (Buffalo) Jones himself selected the animals and accompanied them to New York, where he arrived on October 1. The price was $500 for cows, $400 for bulls. The executive committee urged the director to beat down the cost, but he argued that they were fair prices and that Jones, as an expert, would deliver perfect animals worthy of the park's new range, which offered "everything that buffaloes could possibly desire in this world."

Part of Corbin's reluctance to endow the Zoological Park with buffaloes may have come from an unhappy experience in 1896 when he moved twenty-five animals from Blue Moun-

72

tain to Van Cortlandt Park. They were under the care of the Parks Department, and the city was to get half of any calves born there, for exhibition at the Central Park Menagerie. But several of the animals died—Hornaday thought it was because of the open sewer that ran through the Van Cortlandt enclosure—and Corbin eventually took them away. He kept them isolated from the rest of his animals, but eventually all of them died from what was thought to be gastroenteritis. The Corbin family later was generous in providing buffaloes when the American Bison Society was stocking national herds.

Whitney in 1900 gave the park two bulls, patriotically named Cleveland and McKinley, and in that same year two calves were born and three adult cows came to the park on a two-year loan from David J. Gardiner, so that the big range began to be one of the showplaces of the park.

The director's determination to show big herds of the larger American animals was constantly running into difficulties, and nowhere more so than with pronghorns. Six came from the West in that stocking-up summer of 1899, and four of them died promptly. Ten more were soon acquired; and since it was thought that access to green grass was responsible for the early deaths, they were kept in a bare corral and given mostly dried food—hay and alfalfa shipped in from the West. But they never thrived, and by June of 1900 Hornaday was writing desperate letters to ranchers in the West urging them to send him pronghorns. At that time the park's herd had been wiped out by disease and "sheep-killing dogs," and not a single animal was left on the Pronghorn Range. But the director was still optimistic: "We are going right on buying until we have a fair-sized herd of acclimatized animals." But he never did establish a viable herd; determined as he was to exhibit them, the pronghorns were even more determined to die. They are undeniably difficult animals to keep under Eastern Seaboard conditions, and another major attempt to exhibit them in 1936, when veterinary skills and knowledge of nutritional needs were greater than in Hornaday's time, also ended in failure. In 1900 Hornaday wrote:

The difficulties involved in acclimatizing moose, antelope, caribou, mule deer and Columbian black-tailed deer anywhere on the Atlantic coast, or in the Mississippi Valley has from the first been fully recognized. The great majority of the efforts that have been made to rear these species to maturity, and to induce them to breed anywhere east of the great plains, have resulted in failure and disappointment. Notwithstanding this, the Zoological Society long ago determined to experiment and persevere with these species until at least the majority of them have been successfully established here.

Despite sporadic successes over the years, the early hopes have not been realized.

Beavers were also more or less a disappointment. It proved to be unexpectedly difficult to buy any, although standing orders were placed with twenty trappers at twenty-five dollars a head. The Beaver Pond, a natural bog between high rock ridges, was scooped out and made into a seemingly ideal beaver habitat with plenty of mud and small trees for the construction of a dam and a lodge. It was ready for occupancy when the park opened, but there were no occupants until the spring of 1901, when beavers trickled in from Texas, Colorado, Maine, and Canada. They liked the pond and immediately began felling small trees and building a lodge. The edible bark was soon consumed and branches pruned from other trees in the park were provided, along with bread, grain, vegetables, and a variety of greens. Staff Photographer Elwin R. Sanborn, on a vacation trip to New England in the fall of 1901, discovered a toothpick factory that had an unlimited supply of green birchbark and sent back a trial package. The beavers loved it, and for a time it was an important supplement to their food, tempting them out onto the bank of the pond to feed, even at midday.

The beaver colony persisted after a fashion for a good many years and there was even some breeding, but it was never very successful as an exhibit, simply because under natural conditions—as represented by the Beaver Pond—the animals are normally nocturnal and can seldom be seen during the hours when visitors are in the Zoological Park. Still, they persisted well enough to justify the creation of the pond, and one beaver lived in the collection for thirteen years, three months, and twelve days.

There was one proposed auxiliary use to which the Beaver Pond was never put—as an experimental pond for the study of blind fish. Professor Carl H. Eigenmann of Indiana University, a great ichthyologist, asked Hornaday whether the Zoological Park afforded a place that might be stocked with the fish, and Hornaday offered the Beaver Pond as soon as it was in operation. The stocking was never done, however.

The reptile collection was, of course, ready-made, thanks to the donation of Ditmars's personal collection. He moved it to the park soon after he was engaged, and for some weeks the reptiles were boarded in the Animal Yard until the Reptile House was far enough along to receive them. Ditmars spent the late summer of 1899 in adding to the collection, and his prizes were the two huge reticulated pythons that came on the market. Unfortunately, a cold wave hit the New York area in October and the larger python, lacking heat in the Reptile House, died two weeks before the opening of the park.

Beebe wrote in later years that when he joined the staff, he found that he was in charge of sixteen ducks and herons. Actually, he took over a good collection of water birds and half a dozen owls, eagles, hawks, and vultures. Hornaday had made a brief vacation trip to Florida in February and had engaged C. F. Latham to collect birds in the heronries along the St. John's River and had bought up a few otters, squirrels, raccoons, and a black bear and some crocodilians from Dr. John Vedder in St. Augustine. They all arrived on August 7. About two hundred birds, mammals, and reptiles (as well as plants for exhibit backgrounds) reached the park alive and guaranteed a good show on opening day, although temporary housing during the cold months of fall created plenty of problems and there were considerable losses.

With the arrival of animals, keepers had to be hired to do the routine work. Hornaday interviewed all applicants and weeded them out ruthlessly. Thirty-five years later Rudolph Bell, then the park's cook for the animal departments, told a New York *Sun* reporter how he was hired.

As a boy he worked in butcher shops in the Bronx, then in various circuses, and learned a little about cooking in a lumber camp in Michigan.

Returning to New York, he got a job running a steamroller in the Zoological Park in the spring of 1899. He halted his roller at a gate one day at lunchtime and got talking with William Parker, the gateman.

"They need a butcher here at the zoo," Parker told him.

"What the hell do they need a butcher for? Are they killing their own animals now?"

But Parker convinced him it was a legitimate job, so he turned in his steamroller that night and hunted up Director Hornaday.

"I don't want any circus butchers!" Hornaday barked at him when he told what he had been doing for the past seven years.

Bell hunted up some of the Bronx butchers he had worked for, got affidavits of his competence, and presented them to Hornaday to prove he had been a butcher before he became a circus man. So he got the job.

"You know what we had here when I started? Well, it was comical, to think of it now. Two monkeys, an anteater, and a black bear—on a chain. I used to buy a pound of meat and a quart of milk a day. I'd walk over to Third Avenue of a morning and come back with everything in one paper bag."

It was Bell's pride that there were only two men in the country with jobs like nobody else's. "Me and the President of the United States." He had it all figured out. There was only one President of the United States, obviously. And other

Rudolph Bell, the Zoo's cook, at his daily chores about 1909.

76

zoos didn't have official full-time cooks; their head keepers did the job, each for his own department. Bell cooked for all departments.

Circus-trained men usually got short shrift from Hornaday, but few got the blast he sent a man named Winner who had applied for a keeper's job on the strength of his work with the Ringling Brothers Circus in Wisconsin. The man followed up his first letter with a photograph of himself. Hornaday replied:

Last week I received from Mrs. Winner your photograph, and it gave me a very disagreeable surprise. From it I find that I had a conversation with you. I was then Chief Taxidermist of the National Museum, and visited the show with which you were connected for the express purpose of studying the puma which was in the collection. You were in charge of the animal, and in front of the cage part of the time. Your treatment of me was so rude and ill-natured that I went away without having fully accomplished my object, and feeling that I had been ill-used. I remember your face perfectly, for it was the first and only time that I had ever been so treated by a man in charge of animals.

We would not care to employ in our Zoological Park any man with such a temper as you manifested toward me on that occasion.

Winner countered with the assertion that he was not the man—that he was never in charge of pumas in any show in Washington—but Hornaday was skeptical.

If it was not you, then it must have been your twin brother whom I saw, because your photograph perfectly resembles the face of that man, except the difference in age. Since you say that you never had charge of pumas in any show which visited Washington during those years, and therefore could not have been the man I saw, I am, of course, bound to believe you, and while I regret that I have hurt your feelings by believing that you were the same man, the resemblance was so strong that no other conclusion was possible.

That ended the correspondence for the time being, but Winner cropped up again a year later when he applied for a job in the Buffalo Zoological Park. Probably he did not know that Hornaday was a Buffalo man and had close relations with the Buffalo park's administration. In any event, Buffalo wrote to Hornaday and asked whether he knew anything about an animal man named Winner. He knew plenty. He recounted his contact with Winner in Washington ("He declares he is not the man, but if he is not then it was his duplicate") and remarked that he imagined Winner, if engaged, would be trying to supplant the Buffalo director within a year. End of Winner.

As the man on the site, Hornaday had to have authority to make decisions and keep the work going, but it was a precarious authority liable at any time to be directed or reversed by Osborn or Grant, who had opinions about everything and no hesitation about expressing them. The feverish weeks before opening were probably not made more joyous for Hornaday by Osborn's note saying he thought the wire cages in the Bird House might be a light color, with perhaps an admixture of blue. He wanted to see one cage in this color and another in black, for comparison. Also, the columns between the cages should be ivory white, with an eggshell finish. Also, again, "the water closets should receive an inconspicuous green roof."

At this time it seemed that poor Hornaday could not even clear the ground without permission. Osborn to Hornaday: "Do not cut any bushes of any kind in the Park. Nor move any stone. I was shocked to hear of the removal of stones from one of our brooks. I know you would not approve of either removing bushes or stones—and the only prevention is absolute orders against it."

Hornaday's reputation for tractableness must have been sorely tried, but he justified his stones-and-bushes policy as best he could. Osborn wrote him again: "I regret that you took so much to heart my criticisms regarding the stones and the bushes. Remember that whenever I am emphatic, it is only in the most friendly spirit."

Friendly it may have been, but it was often more emphatic than was comfortable and more restrictive than was practicable. In May of 1899, when the frantic building operations were being complicated by the arrival of animals before holding quarters were ready, Osborn wrote to Hornaday:

I am in very bad humor about the border planting, after this please do not allow one stroke of work done on any plan until it receives my official approval in writing. I would give a great deal to be relieved of the responsibility of deciding all these matters, but as long as I am responsible, I feel it very keenly.

I am much disappointed in the Prairie Dog enclosure, the fence is so high and shuts off so much of the view, that the *natural* effect is entirely lost. The next plan of this kind must be an improvement and give less of the suggestion of a prison.

Hornaday fended off the prairie-dog complaint:

When the fence is in position and the walk is built and the fence is painted the color it is to have, the entire effect will be totally different from anything you can get now. Visitors will look over the fence and not through it.

No detail was too small to escape the professor's scrutiny—and comment. Hornaday was an indefatigable writer of reports and his style came under Osborn's tutelage. "City" with an initial capital should be used "unless it is used as an adjective," and "itals and quotation marks are not *both* necessary when referring to publications. I much prefer italics."

The director could not even have his own undisputed way about exhibit labels. Grant warned him that he was uncertain about the text on some labels, and was it necessary to include the authority after the scientific name? (That is still a moot question. Many zoological parks do not include the authority —i.e., the name of the person who described and named the species—but the New York Zoological Park does.)

Oddly enough, Hornaday professed a layman's dislike and distrust of scientific names. After he published "Notes on the Mountain Sheep of North America, with a Description of a New Species" in the *Annual Report* for 1900, he became embroiled with Professor Elliot about the scientific names he used, and he wrote to the Field Columbian Museum scientist:

Whatever may be the name of the Big Horn according to the senseless and ever-oscillating dictates of "priority," to about 75 per cent of all Americans who are interested in the animal, and know any Latin name for it, it is *Ovis montana,* and will so remain to the end of the chapter. [It didn't; today it is *Ovis canadensis.*]

But considering the very general disrepute into which the scientific names of the higher animals have fallen, they are today of less value and less real utility than English names. In my opinion, the first man of standing who will lead off in discarding them altogether will be a public benefactor.

At this distance in time, one may charitably suppose that both the chairman of the executive committee and the secretary were feeling as fine-drawn and harassed as the director and that their sniping was a reflex of nerves at too tight a stretch. Not only was Professor Osborn carrying on two jobs, at Columbia University and at the American Museum of Natural History; he was also constantly engaged in writing various of the more than a thousand titles he published during his lifetime. All his days were allocated: Monday was his museum business day, Tuesday his Columbia day, Wednesday, Thursday, and Friday were his book days, and Saturday was his park day. But however busy he was, he read the newspapers and found much to comment about. In the month before the opening, the New York press had whipped itself up to a frenzy of interest in "The Greatest Zoo in the World," and almost every day saw news and feature stories about the animals, the progress of construction, the delights that were to be revealed shortly. It was, as they say, publicity you couldn't buy for a million dollars. Nevertheless, it was not what Professor Osborn wanted. Enclosing a newspaper clipping, he wrote to Hornaday:

I know *you* are not responsible for the tone of this article, but it serves to show that hereafter *everything* in the Park must be in the name of the Society. The terms "I" "We" "This Curator" and "The Curator" and "Our Forester" *must all* be replaced by the "Society." Last night's Post has an article describing "Dittmars'" work in the same style. Probably he also was innocent in the matter. We cannot hold our Members together, we cannot secure the money for the prosecution of our work, unless the members of the Society feel that they are getting the credit.

Forty years later, when Professor Osborn's son, Fairfield Osborn, was president of the society, a somewhat similar edict went forth: it was not to be "the Bronx Zoo" that had acquired this animal or that; it must always be "the New York Zoological Society." The reasoning was the same: members of the New York Zoological Society must be made to feel that *they* were responsible for whatever triumphs came along. At this second go-around, the president and his curator of publications reached a reasonable compromise: press releases would say that the *society* had acquired the animal, but that it was being exhibited *at* the Bronx Zoo (or the Aquarium). Professor Osborn's instructions to Hornaday had little effect. Newspaper reporters are seldom interested in writing about such an abstraction as "the Society." They insist on pinning their stories on real, live, colorful people, and on a concrete, visitable place.

The big excitement of the early fall of 1899 was the escape of a European wolf, the female of a pair captured near Moscow and delivered in a shipment from Carl Hagenbeck in September. She broke off the metal overhang of her den and fled during the night. It was a great story for the humorists on the New York newspapers, and interviews with people who were supposed to have seen the animal were filled with excruciating (but not excruciatingly funny) Negro and small-boy vernacular. The official account was that the wolf was a three-months-old baby and that nobody should get alarmed. But after she had been at liberty for four days, the *Journal* gave a different version:

In order not to alarm the people the size, age and power of the wolf were dragged down to almost a harmless nursing age. But the secret leaked out yesterday through laborers at work about the park, and the news spread about the district, quickly causing much alarm.

The wolf is of Russian breed and the native pack is very ferocious. Farmers are already fearful, and old guns, rusted and neglected, have been taken from cob webbed corners, bathed in kerosene and loaded to the muzzle. Small parties of men have wandered through the woods and fields with a big following of dogs to capture the wolf. Every boy in the neighborhood who possesses a gun is on the hunt for Mrs. Wolf.

Eventually the wolf was sighted in St. Mary's Park in the Bronx. After a policeman fired at her and missed, she ran into the open cellar door of the park attendant's house. In his excitement, the attendant entered the cellar, too, and the quick-thinking policeman slammed the slanting door shut and stood on it. Fortunately he eventually recovered enough presence of mind to get off the door and let the attendant out while keeping the wolf in, and presently three keepers arrived from the Zoological Park with a portable cage and recaptured her without difficulty. Hornaday sent the park attendant a check for five dollars and a note of thanks.

The immediate aftermath was a claim from a Bronx resident that the wolf had killed several of the rabbits he had penned in his back yard. The director was having no part of that yarn, however. He gave the citizen a long discourse on the habits of wolves, saying that a hungry wolf *never* kills a number of animals for the mere sake of killing, and that it finishes eating whatever it has killed. Furthermore, this wolf was famished when recaptured and obviously had eaten nothing in the five days she was at liberty. In his opinion, the rabbits were killed by a vicious dog. That ended that episode, but the subsequent history of the Moscow wolves was not untroubled. In November a boy put his hand under the guard rail into the wolf den and was bitten on a finger. Four days after the opening of the park, the male killed his female companion, and he himself died of "fits" the following spring.

For the newspapers of New York City, the Zoological Society and the Zoological Park—its progress, its greatness, its superiority to all other "zoos" in the world—were matters for serious and generously lengthy reporting. The animals were something else. They were fair game for the funnymen on the papers, and when a two-story house across the street from the park burned down one night, the *Press* reported it in a dialogue between a lion and a lioness (neither of which the park had at that time), in which they wondered whether the acrid smell was caused by the tigress curling her hair again. Another paper imaginatively reported that "In five minutes after the fire started the entire zoo was bellowing, braying, barking, roaring, squeaking and making all sorts of noises, all of which indicated terror."

Sea lions escaped from their pool that fall, and one of them had a vacation in the Bronx River for three weeks before it was recaptured. The escape of a Bornean sun bear had a less happy ending. It did not get out of the park, but Hornaday attempted to recapture it by force of personality and was bitten in the hand. As he wrote to the curator of the Buffalo Zoological Park, "I learned that it is not a particularly wise move to grab a bear by the scruff of the neck and ram its head into a noose which is about to slip off. It was like trying to lasso an eel or a greased pig. The animal died of exhaustion after we had succeeded in making the ropes hold."

Dr. W. Reid Blair, who was the park's veterinarian at the time, had a different version. He said that after the director's hand was injured and he was hurrying away to have it dressed, he called back: "Shoot the bear and give every man a steak!"

One unique exhibit, to quote a headline, inhabited the

park until shortly before the opening. A column-long story in the *Sun* described the life of a hermit who had lived for the past twenty years in the deep woods of Bronx Park. He was said to be known as Crazy Billy, and he lived in a tiny cave formed by slabs of rock. He seems to have been a conscientious sort of hermit, for he insisted on working at gardening or cutting firewood when neighbors offered him food or clothing, although he would accept gifts of tobacco without repayment. He survived the blizzard of 1888 by wearing many layers of clothing. The police, it was said, finally ousted him from his hideaway when the Zoological Society expanded throughout the grounds, and he took up residence with compassionate neighbors in the little cluster of houses known as Bronxdale.

There is no record of the hermit in the Zoological Park's archives but confirmation of his existence came by chance in the spring of 1973. Miss Grace Davall, curator emeritus of the Zoological Park, happened to mention Crazy Billy to Miss Emma Beardslee, a lifelong Bronx resident then ninety-six years old. As a child Miss Beardslee had lived on Boston Road before it was incorporated in the park.

She did not remember anyone called Crazy Billy, she said, but when Miss Davall identified him as a hermit who was supposed to have lived in the woods around Bronxdale, she remembered him perfectly and recalled that he wore many layers of cast-off clothing summer and winter for fear that his spare garments would be stolen.

Her one contact with the hermit stuck in her mind. One day when she was about ten years old she was sitting on the garden fence at her home, eating a white turnip, and the hermit came along.

He was on his way to Livingston's Grocery to buy crackers and cheese. That's all he ever bought.

I thought he might like a white turnip for a change, so I offered him one and said he could use my knife to cut off the top and scrape the meat out. It's delicious that way.

85

But he just smiled and thanked me. He took the turnip and said he had a knife.

After he walked on, my older sister came running out and scolded me for talking to him. She said he stole children, and now I would be the next. But when she went inside and told my father what I had done, he came out and told me not to be afraid. He made my sister listen, too. He said the old man was a good man and didn't steal children, and anyway he would always be my friend because I had given him a white turnip.

By mid-July of 1899, 250 men were working in the park, and the construction litter and confusion were so great that a midsummer opening was obviously impossible. Even a tentative late-October date seemed uncertain. An election was coming up, and the *Telegram* seized upon the political situation as a peg to hang a joke on: "There is probably no truth in the rumor that postponement of the opening of the Bronx Park Zoo was due to the fact that the Elephant and the Tiger [the Tammany Hall symbol] have important political engagements just now."

More prosaically, contractors were slow and work on the exhibit decoration in the Winter House for Birds was running behind schedule. Louis Agassiz Fuertes had been approached about painting murals of birds in flight as cage backgrounds but had to turn the commission down because of other work. Finally Robert Blum, a New York City artist, was engaged to paint background scenes of Florida's swamps and New Jersey's Shrewsbury River and the nearby long bulwarks of the Navesink Highlands. He created some much-admired scenes in tints of blue and gray, but five days before the opening, which had finally been fixed for November 8, it was discovered that two-thirds of his backgrounds lacked two to three inches of joining up with the metal molding at the base of the cages. He was called back to work frantically to paint a transition strip in time for it to dry before the birds were installed.

At any rate, the staff's gray uniforms with dark green piping had arrived on time. The director had ordered them from Browning, King & Co. six weeks in advance, and had sent sketches of the kind of caps he wanted. Those for Hermann Merkel, Loring, Ditmars, and Beebe were to bear two pairs of miniature shoulder straps on the crown, and his own was to have an eagle made of gold cord.

Assistant Curator Beebe revolted against the regimentation of a uniform, but he came to see its wisdom. Writing to an official of the Buffalo Zoological Park who had asked his advice about putting employees in uniform, the director reported:

A rather interesting illustration of the value of a uniform came to my notice shortly after they were received. One of our Curators, who came to us from Columbia University, first viewed the uniform with indifference. It happened that the men under him received theirs before his was finished, and they began to wear them. After the lapse of a week the Curator in question came to me and requested that the completion of his uniform should be hastened as much as possible because he had found, much to his chagrin, that his colored helper in a uniform commanded more respect from the crowd of visitors in his building than he did with no badge of office. He said that the orders of his colored boy were obeyed without question, whereas when he admonished a visitor, or made a request, he was looked at in surprise and his words were usually disregarded.

Fears that the New York City public would not know how to reach the Zoological Park were apparently unfounded, for all through the fall months uninvited visitors strolled through the grounds and got in the way of the workmen. On a Sunday in late October there was a crowd estimated at twenty thousand, even though all they could see were the buffaloes and elk on open ranges. Hornaday repeatedly urged the public, via newspaper stories, to stay away and let the workmen get on with their jobs, but by this time he had an enthusiastic press behind him, and repeated guesses at the opening date—October 25 and November 5, 8, and 10 were announced at various times—made people believe there was more to see than there actually was.

By the first week in November one thing was certain: the *Popular Official Guide to the New York Zoological Park As Far As Completed* was not going to be ready by opening day, even though it bore the opening date of November 8 when it did come out. Hornaday had written the 108-page volume entirely himself, a feat that in view of all his other duties and responsibilities would seem impossible. He needed help to see it through the press and luckily he got it from a bright young man named Elwin R. Sanborn whom he had found sketching animals in the park. On September 25 he wrote to Sanborn, later to become the society's staff photographer and editor, asking him to "help me in the publication of a Guide Book to the Zoological Park, which must be completed by October 25, dead or alive." At that time October 25 was the putative opening date, and to add to Hornaday's distress Professor Osborn was holding up the copy. He insisted on reading every word of it, and he kept the copy and kept it until Hornaday warned him on October 7 that unless the printers received the manuscript by October 10, they could not deliver the books by the twenty-fifth. But the chairman of the executive committee was not to be hurried, and publication on November 17 missed the opening by nine days. Hornaday sent his own first copy to Andrew Carnegie, from whom he had high hopes of major contributions to the building fund.

It had been a wilderness fifteen months before; it was a wilderness still beyond the twenty-two islands of accomplishment linked by graveled roads and walks, but there were 843 animals of 157 species behind its five and a quarter miles of fence, and it could proclaim itself the New York Zoological Park at last. And it did, proudly, on the afternoon of Wednesday, November 8, 1899.

At three o'clock the procession of carriages and hacks drew up at the Northwest Gate, bringing guests who had reached the Fordham station of the Harlem Division on the special train that left Grand Central at 2:15. Director Hornaday, wearing his cap with the gold eagle, his assistant curators in their gray and green uniforms in military rank behind him, threw open the gate and the first carriage rolled through. It bore the Honorable Levi P. Morton, onetime Vice-President of the United States, former governor of New York, and now the New York Zoological Society's second president. His health was precarious (although he lived until his ninety-sixth birthday, in 1920), and his was the only carriage admitted that day; the other guests dismounted to walk the short distance through the leafless trees to the Aquatic Birds House, where the opening day's brief ceremonies were to take place.

Nearly three thousand engraved invitations had been sent out ten days before, to every city commission and board that had expedited—or in some cases hindered—the society's work, to members of the board of managers, to scientific men in New York, Washington, and Europe, and to the generous donors of animals and money. Frank Baker of the National Zoological Park was there, and so were Professor Joel Allen and Frank M. Chapman from the American Museum of Natural History and Professor William Stratford from the College of the City of New York. Money came to see what it had bought: Oswald Ottendorfer ($5,000), Percy R. Pyne ($5,000), William E. Dodge ($5,000), J. Pierpont Morgan, Sr. ($5,000), Jacob H. Schiff ($5,000), William C. Whitney

6

Opening Day: November 8, 1899

(elks and $5,000), Collis P. Huntington ($5,000), Henry A. C. Taylor ($5,000), Samuel Thorne ($5,000), Mrs. John B. Trevor ($5,000), John L. Cadwalader ($2,500), Morris K. Jessup ($2,500), Philip Schuyler ($2,500), Edward J. Berwind ($2,500), Charles W. Harkness ($2,000), James B. Ford ($1,500), A. Newbold Morris ($1,000), Charles T. Barney ($1,000), Mrs. William H. Osborn ($1,000), Henry W. Poor ($1,000), William C. Schermerhorn ($1,000), Lispenard Stewart ($1,000), and Joseph Stickney ($1,000). As well as money, it was some of the best society New York could boast, and a good indication that social acceptance had been achieved by the New York Zoological Society and it was on its way to the status proclaimed a few years hence by the statement in a society magazine that "Not to be in the New York Zoological Society is not to be in society."

Mayor Robert A. Van Wyck had sent his regrets, but the city was represented by Controller Bird S. Coler, Parks Commissioner August Moebus of the Bronx, and the president of the Department of Parks, George C. Clausen.

Even Director Hornaday received a formal invitation to the opening. In what was obviously the standard letter sent to all special guests, he was requested to "occupy a seat on the platform," and was directed to enter the south door of the Bird House on or before 3 P.M. and to present his invitation to the watchman.

It was an overcast day, with a cold northwest wind, and the speechmaking from the bunting-draped platform in front of the Bird House was mercifully short. President Morton walked to the railing around the platform and introduced "the man who has done more than any other for the establishment of this Zoological Park, Professor Henry F. Osborn."

Professor Osborn told the crowd around the platform, now swelled to some two thousand by the arrival of ticketless visitors and neighbors:

Unlike the small closed zoological gardens of Europe, this is a free Park, projected upon a scale larger than has ever been at-

tempted before. Nature seems to have shaped these two hundred and sixty-one acres for the express purposes of a Zoological Park. Two hundred thousand years ago the great Ice Sheet cut its giant grooves through Bird Valley where we are standing, and through Beaver Valley yonder, on either side of the broad ridge of granite which the engineers are now levelling for the imposing buildings of Baird Court. The Ice Sheet left behind the famous "Rocking Stone" as a memorial of its visit, and there followed the forest of oak and beech, whose noble offspring are the glory of the Park. Then wandered in the Mastodon, Buffalo, the Elk, Moose, Deer, and Beaver, the Indian, and finally our Dutch and English ancestors as the enemies and exterminators of all. The Mastodon is beyond recall, but before long his collateral descendant, the elephant, will be here; and this afternoon, as you wander through the ranges, you will see restored to their old haunts all the other noble aborigines of Manhattan.

Opening day ceremonies at the Aquatic Birds' House on November 8, 1899. The speaker cannot be positively identified, but if the photographer had a feeling for priorities it was Professor Henry Fairfield Osborn.

91

Then, perhaps remembering Hornaday's idea of "getting hold of the public" by an exhibit illustrating Indian homes and home life, he added, "Later we shall find a place upon the Buffalo Range for the Indian and his tepee." Despite this promise, the idea was never worked out.

Professor Osborn made the obligatory acknowledgments of gifts to the Building Fund, to the city's officials, and to the scientists and professional men who helped to create the park. Controller Coler, responding on behalf of the mayor, referred to New York's now firmly established tradition of public cooperation combining with private generosity to establish such institutions as the Metropolitan Museum of

Art, the American Museum of Natural History, the great New York Public Library now being built, the Museum of Arts and Sciences in Brooklyn, and the Botanical Gardens elsewhere in Bronx Park. "They are or will be show-places which attract visitors," he said, and he hoped that when the pleasures of the Zoological Park "shall be experienced in the future by the millions of visitors who will come to this Park there will be realized also the feeling that it is a pleasant thing—a glorious privilege, in fact—to be a New Yorker."

Two days later the *Commercial Advertiser* poked a little gentle fun at the controller. Under the headline "The Tiger's Sylvan Retreat," it remarked:

The rural citizen coming to view the wonders of New York will no more be left to wander down on the Bowery, into McGurk's and the resorts of knock-out-drops men. He will no longer leave us and return to the corner grocery of his village, emporium of wit and reason, with a fixed belief in the wickedness of the great city. Our Zoological Garden is open, and Controller Coler has said that now we may put a better face on the matter of our city's morals.

Nor are outlanders solely to be benefited. Prof. Osborn declares that what our museums are doing for art and natural science the zoological park and its fair botanical companion up in the Bronx will do for nature. Nature shall not look upon the millions in Manhattan and adjacent regions and think that they do not love or understand her. Nature shall not weep that her charms are known and beloved solely by those that have bank accounts and places of resort in summer. Nature will take the humble mechanic and the lowly crossings sweeper gently by the hand, lead them up to the zoological garden and introduce them to her children, the bear and the lynx and the staring owl. Nature makes her children to prey one upon the other, but how she must weep for joy when she sees man, most destructive of animals, setting the example of peace and good will; feeding the caged beast, and only gently prodding him with the peaceful weapon of civilization, the umbrella. Nature comes to instruct—she will stay to learn.

Parks Commissioner Moebus spoke last and promised to

93

further the good work in every way as long as he was in office. And then, at about 3:30, President Morton said: "Ladies and Gentlemen: I now take great pleasure in declaring the New York Zoological Park, and all its collections, open to the public."

It was a pity that Director Hornaday was not called upon to say a few words, for the emotions that must have been boiling up in him in the realization of how gloriously his dream was coming true would surely have produced some highly colored rhetoric. But it was a chilly day and the committee of managers which put the program together perhaps was too well aware of the director's liking for oratory. The park and all the collections were open; it was time to look at them.

Newspaper coverage of the opening was extensive and congratulatory. The reporter from the *Sun* described the tour that followed the speeches:

Prof. Osborn invited the company to pass from the aquatic bird house to the reptile house and the bear dens as soon as the front rail of the platform was removed. In a few moments the rail was lifted away and the procession was admitted to the inside of the bird house. Outside, clustered about under the eaves of the house,

Interior of the Reptile House a few days after the opening on November 8, 1899.

the visitors had already seen a number of cages containing five specimens of owls, jays and other birds, but inside was a revelation.

In the centre cage was a collection of handsome storks, penguins, geese, ducks, and other water fowl from many climes, while about the walls were other cages containing more interesting birds of allied kinds. Many visitors lingered to see these, but most of them followed Mr. Morton, Mr. Coler and Mr. Moebus down the walk through Bird Valley to the reptile house.

From the sea lion pool to their left came a constant barking, while to the right they passed ranges in which were caribou, moose and elk, and cages and dens in which wolves and foxes were confined. Just beyond these, but not immediately in sight, was the pool for seals and other aquatic mammals, the prairie dog village and the collection of small mammals.

The great Flying Cage was not completed by opening day. This scene, taken in December, 1899, shows the Ducks' Aviary in the foreground.

96

Police Captain Fitzpatrick led the way to the reptile house and Mr. Ditmars, the snake expert of the park, was there to greet the visitors. Mr. Ditmars led President Morton and Mr. Coler through his domain.

Mr. Morton was much interested in the reptiles, from a cage of tiny snakes recently hatched, whose mother was caught in the park, to the 175-pound python and the 12-foot alligator which lay in big cages at the other side of the room. In each cage was shrubbery, and Mr. Ditmars explained that it was intended to show each kind of reptile surrounded by his natural conditions. Many of the snakes are climbers, and were coiled among the branches of small trees. An interesting part of this exhibit is a row of cages in which are scores of snakes native to The Bronx, which have been caught there by the workmen. They are all harmless.

The procession went next to the bear dens, passing the outdoor

The Buffalo Shelter House and the herd in October, 1899, just before the opening of the Zoological Park.

alligator pool. The official party left the park in carriages by the Boston Road entrance, going by the buffalo range. As they passed a mounted keeper rounded up the herd of buffaloes for their inspection.

Most of the visitors remained and spread themselves over the park to see the other exhibits. Some went to the curious rocking stone just north of the bear dens [south of the bear dens, actually], some continued north from there to the beaver dam, while others visited the many ranges of deer, elk and antelope. Although the collection of animals is yet only a small part of what it is to be, there is already enough to keep one busy sightseeing on more than one visit.

The visitors straggled out of the park before the early sunset, and no doubt the director, the staff, and the keepers were not far behind. Assistant Curator Ditmars and his keepers had worked until after midnight to get the Reptile House ready, and Hornaday's desk was piled high with unanswered correspondence for which he would be apologizing for weeks to come. Madison Grant said good-bye and announced that he was leaving the next morning on a moose-hunting expedition in the Maine woods.

The Zoological Park quickly returned to normal after opening day—normalcy being the sounds of hammers and saws, the rumbling of steamrollers, and the creaking of wagons hauling stone and lumber and animals. After the long weeks of intense pressure to open, when so many things were happening at once that he felt he was "like a blacksmith hammering cold iron," Hornaday could return to his desk in the Elk House, catch up on his mail, and resume the battle that was to go on for some twenty more years—to add building after building, exhibit after exhibit, until the Final Plan of 1897 was essentially completed.

Contributions to the Building Fund were coming in at a satisfactory rate, and in fact the $150,000 which the society was obligated to raise within three years from the start of work was all in hand and certified to the city by June 17, 1901, nearly seven weeks before the deadline. There had been one pleasant windfall. In the outpouring of public enthusiasm after Admiral George Dewey's victory at Manila Bay, a movement was started to reward the hero and to crown his fame with a permanent marble arch to replace the plaster arch over Broadway at Madison Square. A public subscription was opened and some $65,000 had been contributed when it was learned that the admiral had, in all innocence, transferred to his wife a residence presented to him by his admirers. Public sentiment turned sour and the Dewey Arch idea was dead. The contributions presumably would be returned to the donors, but Hornaday had a better idea. He wrote to Madison Grant suggesting that the donors be asked to transfer their subscriptions to the society's Building Fund. It was a rather delicate situation, for the subscription committee hesitated to admit it had lost steam. Nevertheless, it rather grudgingly released its donors list to George M. Bailey, the society's membership solicitor, and against stiff competition from some other worthy causes that sought pieces of the pie, Bailey managed to get $9,250 transferred to the society. With the help of this fillip, the statutory $150,000 was at-

7

Check Your Camera at the Gate

tained and the society thereupon gained title to its land and could not be dispossessed except by failure to maintain an animal collection upon it.

Money was coming in—but it was being spent as fast as it came, and sometimes a little faster. Hornaday was impatient. The great Flying Cage had not been completed in time for the opening, but now it was rising rapidly and a number of other installations were in progress. Still, most of them were of secondary importance compared to the big buildings that were needed for big animals, and the director wanted lots of money quickly. Ten days after the opening of the park he wrote to his old friend Andrew Carnegie:

Won't you, for the sake of auld lang syne,* tell me *why* it is that you scatter your favors broadcast over the earth (and in some cases scatter pearls before swine), all unmindful of the fact that our Zoological Society is in great and urgent need of some of the help which you so lavishly bestow upon strangers?

He reminded Carnegie that the Zoological Park was now open, a third of the way toward completion (a considerable exaggeration), and said that the Building Fund was in a sad state. The park needed three large buildings and one small one: a Lion House, an Antelope House, a Monkey House, and a Library Building.

From the beginning it has been my fond hope that the "Model Millionaire" would set the example for the other leading men of New York by giving a completely equipped building. Yes, I know that you have given us $5,000—as much as anyone has given. But of our Managers, no other is giving away millions, and almost

* Hornaday and Carnegie had met for the first time on January 10, 1879, at a dinner party at the residence of the American consul in Singapore. In his unpublished autobiography, Hornaday remarked that he was "fresh from the steaming and fragrant jungles of Borneo" (where he had been collecting for Ward's Natural Science Establishment), and Mr. Carnegie was amused and interested by the adventures of his fellow guest. Hornaday's dilemma at the moment was how to ship two live baby orangs from Singapore to Madras—he feared they would not survive unless they were watched over by some responsible person—and Mr. Carnegie and his traveling companion, John W. Vandevorst, volunteered to convoy the babies and see that they were properly cared for. "They reached Madras in fine fettle."

forgetting us! If you could see how our buildings are crowded with eager people every Sunday when the toilers can come, and note how eager they are to enjoy our beautiful wild creatures, surely we would fare as well at your hands as the people of Emporia and Tucson. *Do* give us a chance to place over the door of the finest Lion House on earth the words—"Gift of Andrew Carnegie."

It was a persuasive, not to say presumptuous, letter, but Carnegie was able to resist it and his reply was a good-natured refusal:

I cannot expect you to understand how one feels that he must not be expected to do everything. You give one a large choice, "Lion House, Antelope House, *Monkey House,* and *Library Building.*" Don't quite like the connection.

In the next few years Carnegie did make large contributions to the endowment and special-purpose funds of the society, and so did Mrs. Carnegie; the largest was a gift of $100,000 in 1914 to start the society's Pension Fund. But he never did endow any specific building.

At the time Hornaday wrote to Carnegie, the building funds were large enough to meet normal obligations. But the city's red tape was badly snarled and allocations of city money were often so late that the society was compelled to spend its own scanty reserve on jobs properly chargeable to the city, against eventual reimbursement. An overdraft was in sight, and Osborn, Morton, William White Niles, Charles E. Whitehead, and John L. Cadwalader signed a note for $17,000 to secure a loan from the Atlantic Trust Company.

The city had no patent on red tape. It is difficult to believe that officers of a society engaged in such a mammoth undertaking as creating a great zoological park from scratch would have time to compile or even read an itemized, day-by-day list of petty-cash expenditures. But compiled it was by the chief clerk, and duly examined and approved by the secretary of the board of managers. For the sixteen months from May 1, 1899, to September 1, 1900, $153.81 was expended from

petty cash, and the six-page typewritten report did not overlook even the two-cent stamp that was occasionally the only
daily outgo.

When Hornaday got back to "routine" work after the
opening, his first act was to send out a press release to inform
the public that thenceforth admission would be charged on
Mondays and Thursdays: twenty-five cents for adults and
fifteen cents for children under twelve; all other days were
free. Bicycles and cameras had to be checked at the gate, for
five cents each. And, "as is customary in zoological gardens
throughout the world, no photographing is permitted and
permits to photograph can not be purchased."

His press release contained one surprising statement. The
society, he said, "notes with some satisfaction that while
twenty-five hundred copies of its programme were distributed
on the opening day, only one copy was thrown away in the
Park." It was perhaps the last time he could boast of the
orderly neatness of visitors, for in the next few years he was
to wage a continual and mostly unavailing war on littering,
and to document his campaign with Monday-morning photographs of discarded newspapers, sacks, fruit skins, and bottles
that are shocking even today. New York's current litterbugs
could learn a few things from study of those photographs.

"Human swine," one of Hornaday's choicer epithets for
the "degenerates" who litter the park, inspired a quatrain in
the *Sun*'s celebrated column of humor and comment, "The
Sun Dial."

> I'll never see a little pig
>   Disport itself in play
> But that I'll think of Bronnix Park
>   And William Hornaday

Both the opening of the park and the follow-up announcement of admission days got abundant press coverage, and the
Zoological Park even received the blessing of religion. "To
the Christian visitor," said the *Christian Herald*, "it will be
a reminder of that era, yet to come, which Isaiah foresaw,

when these animals will dwell together, not, as in this case, caged and separated by strong barriers to keep them from devouring each other, but sharing with men the gentle influence which is to subdue all ferocity."

The ferocity of amateur photographers was certainly not subdued, however. News that they would not be allowed to take snapshots stirred up a storm of protest in letters to the director and to the newspapers. It was a public park, wasn't it? The city put up the land and a lot of money, didn't it? What right had a private society, etc., etc.

The fact, of course, was that the sale of photographs was one of the privileges specifically reserved to the society in the grant of southern Bronx Park, along with the proviso that income derived from such privileges had to be used for the increase of the collections, and the executive committee had adopted the restriction as a firm policy.

But in view of the ill will the policy engendered and the flimsiness of most of the arguments for keeping photography tightly in the society's hands, it is a matter for wonder that it was not relaxed for almost forty years. The official explanation was that revenue from the sale of photographs was needed for the development of the collections, but Director Hornaday had several other stock answers to protests. He cited the restrictions on photography in European zoological gardens, asserted that the society's own photographers could take better pictures than amateurs could get, that the park was often too crowded to permit the use of cameras with tripods, and that the officers and employees of the park objected to the presence of cameras not subject to control, for "Many circumstances arise in the care of a very large number of wild animals when photography might prove detrimental."

Hornaday was never noted for questioning the rightness of his opinions, but it must have strained his conscience to pretend that revenue from the sale of photographs was important to the society. For one thing, the society had very few pictures to offer the public in those early days, although Mr.

103

and Mrs. Edward F. Keller and G. E. Stonebridge held the title of official photographers and did begin taking pictures in the late fall of 1899 and the following spring. Rudolph Kersting also was a "semi-official" photographer and contributed some excellent negatives. Prints in various sizes were offered at twenty to forty-five cents each, the income being shared by the photographer and the society, and even at these modest prices they were not selling well. Hornaday wrote to Kersting in May of 1900:

People who go about taking pictures merely for the sake of increasing their collections have been very clamorous both in the newspapers and elsewhere, and yet not one of them has ever bought one of the many beautiful photographs which we have for some time been offering for sale. Persons of the class referred to do not care in the least about our animals or about the Park, and care nothing about pictures save those which they themselves make. With such people we do not care to bother, and will not admit them.

Some misguided amateurs did more than protest; they sneaked cameras into the park and "increased their collections" whenever they could get away with it. In the spring Hornaday issued a notice to all police officers assigned to the park, requesting them to ask anyone carrying a camera to show his permit—for newspaper and magazine photographers and animal artists were given letters authorizing them to use cameras. Anyone who had no permit was to be escorted to a gate and the camera deposited with the gatekeeper. The police were especially warned to look out for cameras that were being handed over the fences, particularly on Sundays.

Of course administrative and accounting problems were involved in confiscating cameras at the gates. People went in at one gate and out at another, or forgot to claim their property, or lost their deposit slips. Cyril Newman, who went to work as a clerk under Manager H. Raymond Mitchell in 1906, recalls that at one time there were scores of unclaimed cameras in a Service Building storeroom.

As time went on and the society's photographic collections grew, a certain amount of revenue did of course flow from the sale of pictures to magazines, encyclopedias, book publishers, and the like, although the photographic department was never self-supporting. Its primary purpose, then as later, was to provide illustrations for the society's own publications, but publishers found it a convenient source of good live-animal illustration and willingly paid reproduction fees ranging from $2.50 to ten dollars.

Writers who needed photographs to illustrate articles they were selling to magazines were not always happy about having to buy them: the publicity, they thought, should be enough compensation. Hornaday had a brisk run-in with one such man:

In recalling our interview of yesterday, I am reminded of a fact which I meant to have spoken of at the time, but from which my attention was diverted. You said that you would explain to Harper Brothers our "graft" in connection with our business of selling the rights to reproduce our photographs. So far as I am aware, the word "graft" is applied exclusively to thieves and blackmailers, and never to honest men doing a legitimate business. Your use of it in the connection in which you used it yesterday is therefore decidedly offensive. If you regard us as "grafters," our relations must terminate here. We are not disposed to treat with people who are in any way dissatisfied with our methods of doing business, or inclined to criticize them.

The writer contritely explained that "graft" was merely a common slang term for "business" and that he regretted that offense was taken where none was intended. He was forgiven and continued to write about the park for several years.

Apart from the income, there is perhaps some slight justification for Hornaday's intransigence on amateur animal photography in his belief that supplying *good* photographs of wild animals to artists and sculptors and publishers was a duty and an important function of the Zoological Society. Animal photography in the wild was not the developed art it is today,

Harvesting ice on Lake Agassiz in 1906. In the Zoo's icehouse it preserved foods until well into the spring.

and captive animals were the best and often the only subjects for the nature photographer. When they could be photographed against a natural background such as the Zoological Park provided for its hoofed animals and bears, for example, they could be very good photographs indeed. Hornaday took great pride in them. He set the highest standards for the photographs he selected from those taken by the Kellers, Stonebridge, and Kersting, and rejected prints that were not perfect. The park's animals had to be perfect specimens—he was always stressing that quality to collectors and suppliers, although he didn't always get what he demanded—and he wanted them represented at their very best. An amateur or commercial photographer might, for instance, take a picture

106

of a bison while it was shedding. And Hornaday knew, as perhaps the hopeful amateurs did not, how much work on the part of photographers and keepers was involved in posing animals exactly right, against the best possible background.

Animals confined in buildings might have to be photographed against a simulated background, but it, too, had to be the best. After the Lion House was opened in 1903, Carl Rungius was engaged to paint scenic backgrounds in the outdoor cages. He was to become one of the country's most celebrated animal artists, and his canvases predominated in the Gallery of Wild Animal Paintings which the society began to form in the next decade.

Farsighted in so many things, Hornaday could not see beyond his nose when photography was concerned. In 1901 he turned down a chance to have the park's animals brought to "the principal vaudeville theatres and music halls of America and Europe" by means of that flickering, grainy novelty, motion pictures. The American Mutoscope and Biograph Company (later combined as Biograph, whose director general from 1908 to 1913 was the subsequently famed David Wark Griffith) asked permission to take pictures of the animals and promised that titles and credits would appear on the screen by means of a stereopticon.

But the simple bait of publicity could never attract Hornaday; the park was already getting plenty of that from newspapers and magazines. He wrote back:

From our point of view, the advertising which the Park would receive from biographic pictures would not compensate us for the effort that would be required to enable you to get satisfactory negatives. It is part of our business to furnish photographs for reproduction in various ways, and to compose groups to be photographed for publication, and we prefer, always, a *cash* consideration. We would be willing to put certain animals through their paces, in order that you might get pictures such as you desire, for $25. for each series, but no less. If the pictures are worth anything at all to you, surely they are worth that.

107

Unfortunately the American Mutoscope and Biograph Company was not eager twenty-five dollars' worth, and the Zoological Park lost its chance for a place in the very earliest motion-picture history.

But only by a few years, it seems, and then under circumstances that were resented by Hornaday. In the spring of 1905 he received a letter from Madison Grant quite innocently informing him that the American Mutoscope and Biograph Company wanted to make experimental motion pictures in the park. Dr. Hermon C. Bumpus (director of the American Museum of Natural History) was interested and requested the loan of some of the park's animals, chiefly reptiles, and a "small amount of Mr. Ditmars' time." Grant explained that he had talked the matter over with Professor Osborn and they both thought it would be of general interest and scientific value to have the pictures taken, and probably the society could arrange to have "a set" loaned to show at the annual members' meeting. Would Mr. Hornaday please give Mr. Ditmars the necessary permission and arrange to have pictures made of the moving limbs of lizards, and perhaps of the swimming motions of a marine turtle?

It was not calculated to do so, but it was a letter certain to inflame the director. He and the American Mutoscope and Biograph Company were old acquaintances—enemies, as he saw it—and apart from that he resented getting instructions through Grant; there was never any real break in relations between them, but some chemistry was at work: while Hornaday could, and did, take almost any kind of instruction from Professor Osborn with fair grace, he could not at that period give in to the society's secretary so easily. Without replying to Grant he wrote directly to Osborn.

For the past three years the Biograph people have been trying to "work" the Zoological Park for moving pictures of Sea Lions, Bears, etc. I have offered to meet them on a business basis. Thus far the company, or companies, have been too close-fisted to put up any money.

Now they are about to accomplish by shrewd strategy, through Professor Bumpus, what they are unwilling to secure by open, fair dealing with the proper officer. I am in receipt of the letter which Mr. Grant wrote me certifying to the triumph of the Biograph Company over the undersigned, through Professor Bumpus. For five years I have been discharging for the Society the difficult and thankless task of managing its photographic privileges, and protecting it from being torn to shreds by grafters who, vulture-like, seek to fatten upon it. If I am not managing that trust successfully, then take it boldly out of my hands; and I will very willingly surrender it. If I am to continue in that task, however, I hope you will not permit any Biograph Company to set me at naught, either through Professor Bumpus, Curator Ditmars, or any one else.

Back came a conciliatory letter from Professor Osborn. "I will try to straighten out the biagraph [sic] tangle, although I must submit that you are *far too suspicious!* No one will be allowed to drive a wedge between you and me, or is trying to do so. This business matter should certainly be adjusted through you and not through anyone else."

Undoubtedly Osborn and Grant discussed Hornaday's tantrum; there were no society secrets between them. When Grant returned to the charge, it was through Professor Osborn, who he suggested should take up the Mutoscope matter with Hornaday. Grant felt that it was "highly desirable to have a series of moving pictures and radiographs for our next annual meeting, so do not let Mr. Hornaday's prejudice against the Museum stand in the way of this."

The upshot was that Hornaday was instructed to inquire of the five leading motion-picture firms in New York about their charges for filming in the park and the conditions under which the films might be made available to the society. It must have been a bitter pill for Hornaday to swallow—to ask how much the society would have to pay the companies rather than negotiating for the companies to pay the society—but he wrote the letters. He got back various estimates, from $624 down to $340 for a twenty-minute film. The $340 bidder was the Vitagraph Company, which proposed to keep the rights to the film and show it in sixty-seven theaters across the country while giving one showing at the annual meeting for nothing.

There was no further correspondence, nor do programs of the annual meeting in 1906 exist, but it is probable that during the summer of 1905 the Vitagraph Company did take movies of *Feeding the Sea Lions, Polar Bears at Play, Apes Playing and Walking,* and *Feeding the Bears*—all lively subjects Hornaday had suggested in his letter of inquiry.

The motion-picture battle may have been lost, but not the snapshot war. In later years the unadmitted but practical reasons for excluding visitors' cameras was that amateur photography would have been in competition with the colored postcards, picture books, sepia prints, animal stamps, and the well-illustrated guidebook published by the society and sold at all the gates. That a visitor might want to carry away his own souvenir photograph of his wife and children squinting into the sun with wild animals in the background was never considered; people were supposed to come to the park to look at animals, and if they wanted a souvenir they could buy much better photographs from the park's collection than they could possibly take with their own little box cameras—or so Hornaday and Mitchell believed. Or at least said.

From the beginning all park privileges (later called facilities), including the sale of photographs, were firmly under the control of Chief Clerk (later Manager) Mitchell, and he was well aware of the potentialities of postcard sales to a captive market. Sales flourished, fed annually by new pictures from the current crop of negatives, and indisputably brought in much welcome revenue, however dubious the philosophy behind them.

Restrictions on photography were relaxed after Mitchell retired in 1939. By this time amateur photography had advanced far beyond the Brownie-camera stage and there was no holding back the hordes of eager—and often exceedingly well-equipped and competent—amateurs. It could be argued that if the park had welcomed photography and made it easy by selling film or even renting simple cameras, the net income over the years might have been far greater than that produced by postcards and animal stamps.

One admirable service the facilities department performed was keeping the official guidebook constantly revised and in print. Twenty-four editions to a total of half a millon copies were published between 1899 and 1938, and the numerous revisions and updatings were all supplied by Hornaday. The guidebook sold for twenty-five cents up to 1915, then went to thirty cents, forty cents, and finally fifty cents. It was a great success with the public—if not, in its earliest form, with Mr. Grant, Professor Osborn, and Professor Elliot. By 1904 they were complaining about some of Hornaday's scientific names and about typographical errors allowed to remain in hurriedly prepared new editions, so that Hornaday wrote to Grant: "I have little hope that I can ever make the book as you and Mr. Osborn and Mr. Elliot think it ought to be. I think the best plan to pursue will be to wholly discard this book, and have another written by you to take its place." Grant did not take advantage of the opportunity thus offered him, however, and the Hornaday version was entrenched (with the typos cleaned up) until 1939, when Ditmars as curator of mammals and reptiles and Lee S. Crandall as curator of birds wrote a completely new, expanded, and— truth to tell—much better one. It, too, had a long publication life and was not superseded until 1968, when William Bridges, then retired as curator of publications emeritus, wrote *The Bronx Zoo Book of Wild Animals,* which was published in an initial edition of fifty thousand copies. Hornaday would have hated that title, with its flaunting of the disreputable words "Bronx Zoo."

Before the park opened, the director had thought there would never be enough work for a full-time photographer and

111

that a good picture collection could be built up by the efforts of free-lance talent, particularly the Kellers. They came in on call and took excellent pictures of animals, architectural details, construction scenes—whatever Hornaday wanted— but sales were slow and the Kellers had to make a living. Gradually park work got pushed aside for more profitable commissions and it sometimes took a month to get two or three enlargements.

The photographic situation reached a crisis in the summer of 1900 with complaints and cross-complaints about slowness in getting prints, the quality of prints, and minimal income. Hornaday finally drew up an agreement with the Kellers to buy their existing park negatives outright and be done with it, leaving it to a commercial company to make prints on order. By the end of August the Keller negatives were delivered and signed for by Elwin R. Sanborn, "Curator in Charge of Negatives."

Sanborn, whose first appearance in the society's records was Hornaday's plea for his help in getting the guidebook ready for the printer the previous September, had been put on the payroll on October 1, 1899, as a clerk and gatekeeper at fifty dollars a month. As such he was a sort of first lieutenant to Mitchell, helping with the purchase of supplies, handling gate receipts and the sales of guidebooks and photographs, and supervising the lunchroom that had been established in the eastern end of the Reptile House as a stopgap until the Rocking Stone Restaurant (or, as it was at first called, Public Comfort Building No. 1) was erected. His assumption of the title of curator was certainly unofficial and merely descriptive of his function as caretaker of existing negatives. When he retired at the end of 1934 his title was editor and photographer. At that time his functions were divided: his assistant, Edward R. Osterndorff, officially became photographer, while his editorial chores were assigned to William Bridges as editor and curator of publications.

By internal evidence of the negative accession catalogue,

some 275 negatives were turned over to Sanborn by the Kellers and a few naturalist-photographers who had given their work to the society. Except when they can be dated accurately by the entry—e.g., scenes at the Reptile House and the Bear Dens on opening day—or approximately, as when they show some named and notable animal, they can be attributed only generally to 1899 or 1900 or early 1901. But in March of 1901 the orderly procession of negatives began to be dated routinely and successively by month, and so it is in March that Sanborn may be presumed to have started working as staff photographer. In fact, the establishment of a "photograph department" under Sanborn is announced in the *Annual Report* for 1901. In the same *Report* he is listed as assistant editor as well; Hornaday remained the titular editor of all society publications until he accorded the title to Sanborn in 1909.

Sanborn was thirty-two years old when he became the society's photographer. He was a slight, wiry man with spring-steel energy, a passion for perfection in photography, and a dapperness in dress that made him almost a dandy. Legends have gathered about him. According to one of them, he kept eighteen complete changes of clothing in his darkroom on the second floor of the Service Building after it was erected behind the Reptile House in 1901. He learned animal photography by doing it, and although there is no way of knowing how many flawed negatives were discarded, certainly the thousands that gradually accumulated in the society's collection were consistently of excellent quality, many of them superb and unsurpassed to the present time.

Those were the days of glass negatives and of large and heavy cameras; in the early years Sanborn used 5 × 7, 8 × 10, and even 11 × 14 view cameras. Emulsions were comparatively slow, and when extra light was needed it came from an explosion of flash powder that gave not only light but also a cloud of gray smoke. It was sometimes tricky stuff to handle, but no serious accident occurred until the winter of 1926–27, when a charge exploded in the darkroom and

Sanborn was so badly burned that it was several weeks before he could return to work.

Limited by ponderous equipment, animal photography could not strive for sequences of exciting shots of the kind that are routine with today's fast films, lenses, and strobe lights, but action pictures were not what the society wanted; its photographs were supposed to show exactly what the animals looked like—preferably broadside—and so needle-sharp and in such a pleasing composition that an artist or taxidermist had all the detail he needed. Sanborn gave the photographic collections that kind of pictures, and there are some people even today who think a photograph of an animal should show the whole animal in a normal, natural, recogniz-able attitude.

When Sanborn retired, there were 14,216 negatives in the society's collection (Mrs. Dorothy Reville, the photo librar-ian, reports that since then the number has more than quadrupled), and they record virtually every species of mam-mal, bird, or reptile that came to the Zoological Park during its first third of a century, as well as the aquatic collections of the New York Aquarium, buildings and scenes in the park, and several of the society's expeditions. In the fall of 1907 Sanborn accompanied H. R. Mitchell when the society stocked the Wichita National Forest and Game Preserve in southwestern Oklahoma with bison and photographed the arrival and liberation of the nucleus herd of fifteen animals. In 1928 he photographed Dr. Charles Haskins Townsend's expedition to the Galápagos Islands.

In a privately printed memoir of early days in the Zoolog-ical Park, Charles B. Sackett, in later years the printer of many of the society's publications, described Sanborn as "an extremist in everything," whether it was the collecting of clocks which he kept so well regulated that dozens of them chimed or rang at the same instant, or the cultivation of flowers. On one occasion Sackett was spending a weekend with the Sanborns at their home in Norwalk, Connecticut, and was present when Mrs. Sanborn made a casual comment that it would be nice if there were some flowers under a front window. Sanborn said nothing at the time, but "While we were driving down Monday morning, Sanborn was silently slumped in his seat and finally he started to speak, as if to himself. 'Flowers, flowers—so she wants flowers. I'll give her so many damn flowers she'll be sick of them.' "

He did. Sackett said he bought thousands of bulbs, planted them all over his yard, and then bought an adjacent lot to plant more.

Sackett believes Sanborn had no formal education beyond that of the grade schools in Bradford, Pennsylvania. If so, it is all the more remarkable that he became such a meticulous editor of the society's technical journal, *Zoologica,* and of the *Bulletin* which began to appear four times a year in 1903 and bimonthly in 1910. He wrote comparatively few full-dress articles for the *Bulletin,* but he contributed many of the short notes about new arrivals and happenings in the Zoological Park. They are so numerous and detailed that a history of the animal collections during his years as editor could almost be compiled from them alone.

Sanborn died on December 19, 1947, at seventy-eight. He was an unpredictable individualist to the last, for although he had originally refused to join the Zoological Society's Pension Fund, in his will he left his entire estate to that fund.

Hornaday thrived on fights. "War," "fight," and "campaign" were key words in his vocabulary, and he entered the twentieth century with a campaign he was destined to lose: to have the New York Zoological Park called by its full name, and not "The Zoo," in all newspapers.

He wrote identical letters to the editors of sixteen daily newspapers in the city.

The nicknames "Bronx Zoo," and Bronx Park Zoo, as applied in print to the New York Zoological Park are undignified, offensive to the Zoological Society, and injurious to the Park. They are totally unnecessary, and therefore inexcusable. At this late date,

Typical Monday-morning litter in the Zoological Park in 1914 at the height of Director Hornaday's "Rubbish War."

115

the only persons for whom "Bronx" need be tacked to our name in order that they may know our locality, are newly arrived immigrants, and the harmless imbeciles in our asylums for the insane. If there is now in this city any reading individual who does not know the difference between a "Zoo" and a "Zoological Park," any one of our buffaloes will take pleasure in pointing it out.

Usurping the privilege of the buffaloes, he pointed out the difference himself in a letter to the *Press*.

A "Zoo" is a zoological garden, of small area, where animals are kept in small pens, instead of in wide ranges full of trees, rocks and green grass. *There is no "Zoo" in Bronx Park!* It is not fair that the Zoological Park of Greater New York, 261 acres in extent, should begin life under the name of "the Bronx Park Zoo," "the Zoo in Bronx Park," or even "the New York Zoo."

Say to your men who write, that those who take the trouble to say "Zoological Park" are the ones who will be most welcome to such favors as the Zoological Park can bestow.

The *Press* promised to be good and for a time did spell out the full name in the body of its stories, but "New York Zoological Park" requires twenty-four units of type—letters and spaces—and "Bronx Zoo" takes nine, and "The Zoo" only seven. Type, as printers often say, is not made of rubber, so what would a copyreader do when he came to write a headline about the New York Zoological Park? He would call it The Zoo or the Bronx Zoo, of course.

The *Press* could not resist having a little fun. It published a poem:

> My name is William Hornaday—
>   A trifle pedagogical.
> DIRECTOR I! With ALL to say!
>   My Park is Zoological.
>
> By heaven! Should you dare to say
>   "The New York Zoo Society,"
> There'd be a little hell to pay
>   Anent your contrariety!

But the Zoological Park was such a good source of news and light feature stories that most newspapers seem to have made at least token efforts to go along with Hornaday's obsession, even though inevitably concessions to type's rigidity would have to be made. Then would come another blast.

The record reveals only one newspaper that gave Hornaday an argument. Usually his protests were addressed to "The Editor" and were opened by the mail boy and routed to the city editor, who had direct charge of the reporters actually writing stories about the Zoological Park. One letter found its way to the titular editor of the *Mail and Express*, Henry L. Stoddard, who wrote back:

Your present communication is the first we have heard formally, or otherwise, of your objection to the use of the term "Bronx Zoo." It is a popular expression used by ninety-nine out of every hundred people who refer to the Zoological Park, and I question very much whether the more dignified name of Zoological Park can take its place in the popular mind. However, I have sent your letter to our City Editor, with instructions to bear your request in mind.

It might be thought that the man who cited the doctrine of *vox populi, vox Dei* in support of his preference for *Ovis montana* as the eternal scientific name of the bighorn sheep would see the justice of Stoddard's point. But Hornaday did not give up his fight, and "Bronx Zoo" did not attain respectability until after his retirement. His successor as director, Dr. W. Reid Blair, did not oppose the inevitable.

As Hornaday wrote in the *Annual Report* for 1900, "the first year of the actual existence of a Zoological Park, or Garden, is necessarily its year of greatest trial." Curators and keepers had to adjust themselves to their positions, animals to their strange environment on their way to becoming "acclimated," which Hornaday defined as the state when individuals have settled down in captivity "and seem willing to act rationally in the very important matters of eating, drinking, and exercising." "Willing to act rationally" was a characteristic Hornaday approach to animal psychology; the "rational" animal behaved as the director wanted it to behave. If it caused trouble and obstinately died, the only reason was the innate cussedness of that individual.

In the first year of the Zoological Park the curators adjusted well enough, and so did most of the animals (a notable exception was the black-tailed jackrabbits, which insisted on hurtling into the fence and breaking their necks whenever a visitor approached their corral), but the greatest success was with the public.

More than half a million people came and enjoyed themselves, despite rough and muddy paths and the paucity of refreshment services and toilets. There were four of the latter, plus one near the Flying Cage for the use of workmen grading and finishing Baird Court, and it caused a problem which Hornaday settled in his usual forthright way. Workmen in the southern part of the court got in the habit of resorting to a nearer toilet, which was reserved for visitors, and the director informed the Baird Court contractor that all his men must enjoy only their own facility; otherwise he would be forced to have them arrested for disorderly conduct.

The Zoological Park was by no means standing still during its first full year of operation, but to a director and a staff impatient for buildings in which to display their animal treasures it was a frustrating time. The Flying Cage did manage to get finished by June of 1900 and Assistant Curator Beebe immediately stocked it with nearly a hundred water birds of some twenty-five species, all of which exhibited "evident happiness." As well they might, for the Flying Cage was 150 feet long, seventy-five feet wide, and fifty feet high, and contained not only living trees but a flowing stream. But the badly needed Monkey House and Lion House and homes for the antelopes and nonaquatic birds were still only in the blueprint stage, or not even that far along. The Rocking Stone Restaurant was being built on a knoll slightly northeast of

The Rocking Stone is a forty-ton glacial boulder of pink granite. Seventy pounds' pressure, applied at certain points on its surface, will cause it to rock about an inch. The Rocking Stone Restaurant is in the background. Today the World of Darkness building stands just at the right of the picture.

the huge glacial boulder that contributed its name to the structure, but in Hornaday's scheme the restaurant was a sideline that did not count; it was merely for human beings and he wanted houses for wild animals.

The Rocking Stone boulder could, if pressure were applied in the right places, be made to sway an inch or so. Before the Zoological Park opened, newspapers reported that it was one of the famous sights of Bronx Park. It was said that it was even mentioned in guidebooks to New York City published abroad, so that over the years more foreigners than native New Yorkers had sought it out. The natives made up for their indifference after the rash of publicity, however, and one

119

Sunday in 1899 so many people came to see and make it rock that a park attendant was stationed beside it to lecture about it and show visitors where to push. Perhaps it really was celebrated, for in 1952 a letter came to the park from a woman in upstate New York inquiring whether it was still in place and whether it still rocked. It was, and it did. The letter, incidentally, revealed that the technical, or at least ancient, name for such balanced stones is logan (or loggan) stones, and that a few others are known in parts of the world where glaciers came to rest. It was an obvious symbol for the major park restaurant built within a hundred feet of its site, and a photograph of the stone with two five-year-old girls pretending to push it adorned the cover of the Rocking Stone Restaurant's menu for some years.

The year 1900 was mostly a holding and settling-in operation in preparation for the big building push of the next few years. The forestry department under Hermann Merkel cut and stored fifty-two tons of ice during the winter, sawing thick slabs out of frozen Lake Agassiz (which in recent years has never frozen so solid), and raised eleven tons of root crops, 2,500 heads of cabbage, 4,500 roots of celery, 4,279 heads of lettuce, 2,500 ears of sweet corn, 100 bundles of cornstalks, 354 pumpkins, squash, and melons, and two tons of clover hay—all off the nursery in the northeast area beyond the Bronx River, or the grassy fields that were not earmarked for animal installations. Beebe rejoiced in the accession of nine Canada geese he trapped on one of the ponds after they came down for a feed during migration. Ditmars ran into feeding problems with some of his large snakes and developed a technique for force-feeding them.

Mr. Ditmars prepares a string of dead rabbits, pigeons, or other food animals, and with the aid of several keepers, and the exercise of much skill and judgment, forces the whole collection down the serpent's throat. If the food is persistently disgorged, it is immediately re-introduced.

Modern herpetologists are likely to look askance at such

rough tactics, but in 1900 animals got what was good for them, and anyway—officially—it worked:

Strange to say, food thus thrust by force into a serpent is properly digested, and assimilation appears to be as perfect as when it is brought about by more natural processes.

It was in the fall of 1900 that Assistant Curator Ditmars was involved in the most dangerous incident in his long professional life. A snake figured in it, but only indirectly.

Following his habit of preserving for study purposes some of the rarer reptiles when they died, Ditmars had just coiled the body of a snake in a jar of formalin when the vessel

Dr. Ditmars devised the ramrod method of force-feeding large snakes. Dead rabbits, pigeons, and other small food animals were tied together and forced down the reptile's throat. What it did to the snake's throat tissues, to say nothing of its psyche, can be imagined.

slipped out of his wet fingers. It struck the edge of the sink, the bottle splintered, and a piece of glass slashed his left arm and severed an artery.

A tourniquet was applied but it was a bloody scene when a doctor arrived by horse and buggy, and he judged there was no time to waste on sanitation or even washing his sweaty hands. He took emergency measures and sent young Ditmars home, where infection promptly set in. For some weeks it was touch and go; medical advice was to remove the arm, but Ditmars's sister Ella refused to give permission; she felt he would rather die than live with one arm. Drainage tubes were inserted and he recovered near the end of the year, enough so that he could return to his duties in the park, but the accident left him with a permanently stiff left wrist.

All in all, the development of the park was proceeding smoothly in its first year. At the end of October Hornaday took a well-earned vacation and business trip. The executive committee sent him to the Northwest to investigate sources of animals in that region, Alaska, and British Columbia. He carried a large supply of the society's publications for distribution en route, so that "without seeming to do so, the existence of the Society and its Zoological Park will be thoroughly advertised." One wishes that newspaper clippings of interviews along the way had survived.

It is easy to sympathize with Hornaday's impatience to add major exhibition buildings. By the end of 1901 only the Monkey House (officially called the Primate House on its stone lintel)* had been added to the opening-day nucleus of permanent brick-and-stone structures, and many desirable animals were constantly being declined because there was no room for them. Captain Thomas Golding of the *Afridi,* who liked animals and generally sailed back from the Far East with a personal cargo of monkeys, birds, reptiles, and small mammals he had picked up at modest prices, brought a young and rare Sumatran rhinoceros that the society was not able to resist even at the sizable price of $3,250. Its purchase at that time was a mistake, however, for it had to be caged in the Monkey House, the only heated building available. With regret but a nice profit, the society a few months later sold it to Ringling Brothers Circus for $5,000 and spent the proceeds on a pair of Nubian giraffes.

As early as 1904 the park could have had birds of paradise, probably the first live ones in the United States, if it had had a place for them. An English dealer offered a greater, two lesser, and two king birds of paradise for the reasonable enough sum of $1,500, but a house for perching birds was still a year away and the offer was turned down. No animal dealer was more assiduous in offering animals than Carl Hagenbeck of Hamburg. Although the park depended upon him heavily when more buildings began to be opened, at first he received a discouraging number of declinations.

Keeping the existing buildings filled was no problem. In August of 1900 and again in the spring of the following year, Assistant Curator Ditmars and Keeper Charlie Snyder collected reptiles in South Carolina and came back with several hundred snakes, lizards, and turtles, many new to the collection. Like all efficient collectors, they organized the local boys and men, paying them five cents for medium-sized snakes

8

Disaster in the Ape Collection

---

* The inscription on the lintel now reads simply "Monkeys." President Fairfield Osborn had the change made in the 1950s, on the ground that while some people might know what a primate was, everybody knew a monkey.

123

and ten cents for large ones; they boasted of getting a six-foot chicken snake for a dime. The Reptile House could have been filled to overflowing with rattlesnakes merely by accepting a small fraction of the number offered by mail. Sometimes the offerings were more exotic, however; a man in Small, Idaho, wanted to know what the park would give for a snake in his possession that was two feet long, with a head at each end. "When thrown into water, it holds both heads out of the water. It is rather torpid." This singular serpent might have been worth the offer of a five-dollar bill, one would think, if only for the interesting anatomy to be discovered after its death. Perhaps suspecting a hoax, Hornaday did not answer the letter. (Ordinarily he dictated and signed all correspondence involving the mammal, bird, and reptile departments, and it was several years before he allowed his curators to answer direct or to initiate correspondence.) He had already had an unsatisfactory experience with another two-headed snake, although it was one with both heads at the same end. To an inquirer he wrote:

The two-headed snake was at the Zoological Park on deposit only, and after it had been here about two weeks its owner came and took it away. We do not know whether or not it is now alive. While here, it practically ate nothing, because when one head attempted to eat, the other head attacked it! I imagine that, by this time, the creature is dead.

In the bird department, Beebe was being chided for making only desultory efforts to breed waterfowl and pheasants, thus adumbrating (a favorite word of his in books he wrote many years later) the restlessness and disdain for routine that within the next decade were to start him on a lifelong series of expeditions and field studies and sever him from active management of the department. By the spring of 1901 Hornaday felt something had to be done about young Beebe. (There must have been verbal communications between director and underlings, but everything of importance was put in writing.) He sent a letter:

It is my opinion that you are not sufficiently interested in your work as a whole. I fear that you are interested in outside matters, which should not be allowed to divert your attention from your legitimate work. You have no time for photography during working hours, and no matter what the object, I wish you would suspend it entirely during working hours.

You still come to the Park late every morning, and leave shortly after four o'clock. With the increase in your salary that was made on January 1st, this becomes more unsatisfactory than heretofore, and if you cannot hereafter report for duty promptly at 8 o'clock every week day, and remain at the Bird House until 5 o'clock, I will be obliged to reduce your salary to $80 per month. I see no reason why you should not render the same hours of service as the other officers of the Park.

Presumably Beebe reformed, for he stayed on the payroll at $100 a month.

Salaries all down the line had been raised as of January 1, 1901. Assistant curators jumped from $75 a month to $100, and keepers from $50 to $60. This largesse brought an immediate gratified response from the keepers, all of whom signed a memorial to Hornaday:

We wish to express our appreciation for the increase in salary. It is our desire to state, that in our sincerity to our duties, we shall strive to make the Zoological Park what it intends to be, namely the most successful and finest institution of its kind in the world.

In August of 1901 the profusely gabled frame structure known as the Service Building was completed at the edge of the forest behind the Reptile House. One can imagine the relief with which Hornaday and Mitchell, Merkel and Beerbower, and assorted secretaries and assistants moved out of the tight confines of their Elk House headquarters and expanded in a building where everyone actually had a whole room to himself. It must have been a satisfaction to the elk herd, too.

There were other small accomplishments. The second section of the Bear Dens was finished by a clever combination

125

of natural rock ledge and concrete, and a forty-foot cedar off the south end of the dens was ringed with raccoon-proof fence and officially named the Raccoon Tree. It made a good show for many years.

These were not the longed-for big buildings, but all impatience will be assuaged if one is patient enough. In 1902 the city approved a bond issue of $500,000 to be dispensed in 1902 and 1903; thus work could be pushed vigorously on the Lion House, Antelope House, Bird House (the main Bird House, for perching birds), and the Ostrich and Small Mammal Houses, all to be opened between early 1903 and mid-1905.

The Primate House was an enormous success from its opening three days before Christmas in 1901. Winter weather held the crowds to manageable size, but on good Sundays and with the coming of spring the building's central hall was jam-packed and peanut shells lay in windrows in the cages. Sporadic attempts were made to bar unshelled peanuts from the park, and one of Hornaday's more vigorous ultimatums in 1909 produced such newspaper headlines as:

MONKEYS BEWAIL
FORBIDDEN PEANUT

and

DOTING MOTHER CUDDLES
STARVING BABY MONKEY
HIT BY PEANUT FAMINE

A sketch, probably by Dr. Hornaday, of his first conception of the Primate House.

The Primate House opened with an impressive array of animals—114 specimens of forty-two species—including a couple of large gelada baboons whose "endless grimaces are quite beyond description." No doubt there were numerous crowd stoppers among the other baboons, the lemurs, Old World and New World monkeys, and the two anthropoids, an orangutan and a gray gibbon, so that nobody but the staff missed what was to have been the dazzling centerpiece of the show: five droll young orangs and a lively young chimpanzee playing and romping together.

126

Disaster had struck the ape ménage in October. For want of a better place to keep them, during the summer they had been held in an open-air cage set in the middle of the generously large Galápagos-tortoise yard in front of the Reptile House. Suddenly they sickened, and despite heroic medication the chimpanzee and four of the orangs promptly died. The cause of death was easily determined on post-mortem; their colons were found to be loaded with *Balantidium coli,* an organism causing rapid emaciation and death.

It was assumed that these particular apes had been infected before they came to the park. Sally, the one surviving orang, was isolated and treated, and for the next three months all primate quarters were repeatedly disinfected to make sure the colitis did not spread.

Assistant Curator Ditmars turned out to be the hero of the Case of the Ailing Apes. On January 2, 1902, he was

Interior of the Primate House in 1901.

127

supervising the cleaning of the Galápagos-tortoise quarters in the Reptile House. While excreta were being swept up, it occurred to him that parts resembled feces of the orangs just before their death. The veterinarian's assistant put a sample under the microscope and found that it was swarming with *Balantidium coli.*

What had happened thereupon became distressingly clear. Apes are not fanatically cleanly animals; they scatter food, and if a choice piece fell outside their cage they would reach out and retrieve it. The ground was, of course, infected from the droppings of the tortoises, and the *B. coli* was readily transferred. As for the tortoises, they had long been adjusted to the organism and were presumably immune. However that may be, they lived perfectly well with infusoria that were fatal to the apes.

Outbreaks of diarrhea in anthropoids today have been attributed to *B. coli* in situations where the only consistent finding was tremendous numbers of balantidium organisms in the feces. They are reduced by prompt treatment, without fatalities. A veterinarian now may suspect that some other factor was involved in 1902, but there is no way of knowing for sure.

(Incidentally, the name of the house variously referred to as the Primate House and the Monkey House caused some slight confusion among the public. A man in Plainfield, Connecticut, wrote Hornaday that he had recently visited the park and had seen the word "Primates." Did this refer to "the Monkeys" or to "the Snakes"? None of his reference books could tell him, so would the director please explain by postcard?)

The Monkey House was a bonanza for the imaginative young men on the newspapers. The early years of this century imposed few restraints on stories about animals—the more unlikely they were, the funnier they were considered to be. Thus the *Tribune* could print a story headed "Fire in the Monkey House. Chimpanzee Helps Put Out Blaze in

His Cage." Hornaday could not let that pass. He wrote to the *Tribune* that while the *Sun* might think such a fabrication worthy of its columns, he didn't like to see the *Tribune* place itself in the same class. The facts were that someone threw a match in the cage of a ring-tailed monkey—not a chimpanzee— and that a keeper put the fire out. The monkey did *not* empty its pan of drinking water on the blaze.

Week in and week out, the New York newspapers gave Hornaday plenty of exercise writing letters of correction or denial. The *World* published a straightforward, laudatory story about the park but closed it with the comment that the Central Park Menagerie's animals were infested with fleas. Readers overlooked the important three words "Central Park Menagerie" and wrote abusive letters to Hornaday. *He* thereupon wrote to the *World* setting the record straight, and denied that there were fleas on any animals in the New York Zoological Park. As a result, more letters came to him from readers whose dogs had fleas, asking whether his anti-flea know-how could be applied to their pets.

During the summer of 1902 it was obvious that the Lion

The Lion House was opened in 1903. Dr. Hornaday thought it was much overdecorated.

House was soon going to be ready for occupancy, and stock had to be acquired. It would be a costly matter, for Hornaday wanted a representative collection of the big cats of the world. Without special contributions from wealthy members of the society, the Animal Fund could not do it alone. He circulated a list of desiderata with approximate prices and—surely to his pleased surprise—found a taker in Andrew Carnegie.

In midsummer he wrote to Charles T. Barney, who succeeded Professor Osborn as chairman of the executive committee:

I have just received the following from Mr. Carnegie. The "Baba" referred to is Mr. Carnegie's little daughter, five years old, who is greatly interested in animals, and, incidentally, somewhat interested in the undersigned. I should tell you that I first met Mr. Carnegie in Singapore, twenty-three years ago, and he says that he has read a great portion of my "Jungle Book" to his little girl. She remembers my tiger and elephants, and the manner in which she now presents us with a $1,500. lion is thus described by Mr. Carnegie:—

"Baba was asked what she wished to give to Mr. Hornaday, the elephant and tiger man, as she calls him. Her reply was, the biggest hairy-headed lion in the world, Papa! I read her this list, and of course she chose the dearest! I will make her promise good. Get it!"

In August Hornaday and William White Niles sailed for Europe with a letter of credit for $13,000—which they overspent by a mere $145. Hagenbeck had been saving his choicest animals for a year in anticipation of the stocking of the Lion House, and there were good things to be picked up in various British and continental zoological gardens. From Hagenbeck they bought three lions, a pair of Bengal tigers, two black leopards, a jaguar, a clouded leopard (which died in transit), and half a hundred other mammals, birds and reptiles— $10,609 worth. Other zoological collections yielded snow leopards and a cheetah for the Lion House, so that with the odds and ends of feline stock already on hand, the success of the opening was assured. Hagenbeck shipped his animals promptly but the finishing of the interior of the Lion House moved more slowly than had been expected, and once again the park was faced with a housing crisis. Everything had to be quartered in the Elk House until the animals could be moved into the Lion House as cages were completed.

Never one to overlook a good story, Hornaday immediately upon his return from Europe wrote an account of his trip for the Zoological Society's *Bulletin* and, naturally, quoted Baba (Margaret) Carnegie's exclamation about "the biggest hairy-headed lion in the world."

The newspapers went mad over the story. For childish prattle to come up with such an evocative phrase was alone enough to catch attention, but when the tiny tot bore the magic name of Carnegie. . . .

Every newspaper wrote stories about the lion and pestered the director for advance news of its arrival. The Union Bureau of News in Germantown, Pennsylvania, told Hornaday it was greatly interested in this gift of an "immense lion" and begged for a description of it "together with a photograph, and if possible one of your self."

Even Hornaday began to realize that he had launched a greater sensation than he intended. Privately he explained to the executive committee that actually the Carnegie lion (named Hannibal) was not as large and impressive as Sultan, the gift of Nelson Robinson, or as costly. Hannibal actually cost $1,250, Sultan $1,500. These facts were not made known to the press, naturally, and the superiority of Hannibal was taken for granted when the European shipment arrived on October 17. He was indeed a magnificent animal, eight years old and with a luxuriant mane, and could pass for "the biggest hairy-headed lion in the world," at least to an undiscerning newspaper reporter's eye.

The stories about Baba's lion went on and on until everyone was worn out. Three weeks after the arrival Hornaday wrote to Madison Grant:

131

Charles J. (Buffalo) Jones presented a lion to the Zoological Park in 1910. Spectators of its unloading, apart from the workmen, are, left to right: Paul Bransom, the animal artist; Director Hornaday; Dr. W. Reid Blair, the veterinarian.

You have undoubtedly observed that a newspaper can, upon occasion, act as foolishly as an individual human being. The exploitation of the fact that Mr. Carnegie gave, in his little daughter's name, the purchase price of a lion, was carried to such ridiculous and disgusting extreme by certain newspapers, that their treatment of the fact has proven intensely annoying to all parties concerned. It has so annoyed Mr. and Mrs. Carnegie that Mrs. Carnegie has just written to me commanding that the lion shall stand as Mr. Carnegie's gift and that her little daughter's name shall be used no longer in connection with it.

So Baba's lion faded from the news, but there was no lack of other good stories. In July a puma escaped and was at liberty for the better part of three days. To Charles Sheldon, who had sent the puma from Chihuahua, Mexico, Hornaday wrote:

[The puma] is today the most celebrated puma in North America, having rampaged through the columns of the New York press ever since last Sunday morning. The animal reached the Park last Saturday night in good condition. At eleven o'clock [on Sunday morning] the creature was to have been set free in the big cage. Between nine and ten, however, the puma took a notion to escape, gnawed through two of the wooden slats in its box, and went free. The newspaper accounts are not nearly as sensational as they might have been. We assured the press and the public that the animal was perfectly harmless, and could easily be captured alive. He was seen three or four times during the interval of three days and nights. All this while the papers contained numerous accounts and pictures, and as an advertisement, the puma was literally a "howling success." Last night the creature showed itself on the eastern border of the Zoological Park, in a small settlement where lived a man who was once a cow-puncher in Texas. The puma was tired of freedom and desired the society of human beings. The first man to whom it applied for reinstatement in the Zoological Park, was frightened and threw a pan of oats in its face. It then retired in disgust to the bushes. Cowboy Joslin was notified immediately, and procuring a rope, he sought the creature which was actually "crying" for him! After he had answered its cry several times, it actually came out of the bushes, and after various manoeuverings, he managed to get within ten feet of it, when he threw a noose at it and caught it around the neck. It struggled quite hard at first, but was soon subdued, and after he once got his hands upon it, it quieted down. He attached a collar and chain to its neck, and with two dogs trotting beside, and three policemen and a large miscellaneous following, he actually led it a mile and a half to the Zoological Park.

Hubert's Dime Museum tried to rent the animal for exhibition downtown, but Hornaday knew how to capitalize its publicity value in the park. He exhibited it in a cage by itself, with a special label.

One of the most celebrated of the animals gathered for the Lion House was a jaguar named Señor Lopez; it could almost be called the notorious Señor Lopez in the light of its subsequent history. The animal was presented to the Zoological Park by William Mill Butler, the vice-consul of Paraguay at Philadelphia and manager of the Paraguay Development Company, and the events of its transportation were entertainingly described by Mr. Butler in a diary he kept from its arrival in Asunción to its delivery in Liverpool for later transshipment to New York. Accounts of any animal's pre-exhibition history are so rare, and Mr. Butler's account is so graphically detailed, that it is worth while transcribing generous selections from it:

Tuesday, December 31, 1901. The last day of the year proved an eventful one, as it saw me with—not an elephant, but a tiger on my hands and a very much alive one, too. Before leaving home, I had promised my friend, Mr. William T. Hornaday, director of the New York Zoological Park, to see what I could do in the way of procuring him some wild animals from Paraguay. On my arrival here [Asunción] I had consulted with a dealer in animal skins. He promised to make inquiries and if possible to get me a pair of Paraguayan tigers. I heard no more about it until this morning when I received a note saying: "I have on board the steamer "Albatross" a nice tigre [jaguar; 'tigre' was the local name] of six months old, in a wooden cage. It is a very fine and big tigre. I should like to know where I have to let him, because I have to disembark him to-day. Always at your orders."

Although I had wished to obtain the animal—in fact a pair—for Mr. Hornaday, I must confess I was a little startled to learn that I could not only obtain a "tigre," but that he was, in fact, at my door, so to speak, and was a very fine and big "tigre."

In the afternoon we went aboard the "Albatross" and were soon face to face with the wildly gesticulating Captain of the boat, who wished to get the "tigre" off his hands. The beast was confined in a strong wooden cage—the same in which he had been trapped. The deck hands grimaced as we approached to get a look at the animal, which resented our curiosity by growling and spitting and hitting out with its paws. The dealer in animal skins, Mr. S., encouraged us to look again and praised its many fine points, for it was really a splendid specimen.

The next thing was to find an iron cage, and Mr. S. knew a man who had one and who would part with it for $300 or $400 paper, equal to $33 to $44 gold. We got it for the former figure, and then the next thing was to get the "tigre" ashore and make the transfer, from one cage to the other. This feat was accomplished by half a dozen strong men, under Mr. S.'s direction, in the front yard of the Immigration Office, and in full view of several hundred people who gathered to see the show.

The men turned the iron cage sideways, so as to get the opening (which in this one is on top) next to the door of the wooden one. Then they lashed both of them together with ropes, cautiously removed the pieces of wood which confined the captive, and gave him a chance to go into his new prison. For quite a while he was sullen and refused to budge. The spectators made suggestions; some of the men prodded him; others brought some meat and put it into the iron cage. Still the jaguar refused to move, and it was a question of what next, when to the relief of all concerned, amid a great shout from the spectators, the big yellow cat jumped into its new quarters and snarled defiance all round.

We had locked the iron doors leading to the yard, as a matter of precaution; now that all danger was over, the people begged to be allowed to come in and obtain a closer view. We had difficulty in controlling the children who, all unconscious of danger, would have gone to play with the animal, as they might with a strange dog.

Wednesday, Jan. 15—Left Asunción for home on river steamer "San Martín."

My great anxiety was for "Lopez" in his iron cage (for so we had named him), as the day was hot and the upper deck almost like a furnace in his vicinity, for they had put him amidships just behind the funnel where the heat from the boiler-room arose and was added to that of the sun. When I saw him, after we had started down the river, he was panting hard. I got the deck hands to give him a bath by means of buckets of water and this he received gratefully, shutting his eyes each time the water dashed over his head. I also insisted that his cage be put in a better place, away from the furnace heat, and when this was accomplished he recovered and towards evening seemed all right again.

Thursday, Jan. 16—The weather was cool today. Lopez seemed to enjoy the change, rolling over in his cage and, no doubt, purring inwardly with delight.

135

Friday, Jan. 17. The tiger had another comfortable day, the weather being ideal. One fool mariner wanted to feed him some cooked meat, as a special attention. We stopped him. At 6.30 we arrived at La Paz, where many people flocked aboard to see the "tigre." Totally ignorant of the ways of tigers, some of them would have stuck their noses into the cage had I not stood guard and warned them off in terrible Spanish.

Monday, Jan. 20—In Buenos Aires, gave an order for a tarpaulin cover for the tiger's cage to shield him in cold weather.

Friday, Jan. 24. In Montevideo, Wilson & Co.'s man (they are the steamship agents) notified me that he had a tiger for me on a lighter and desired to know what he was to do with it. I informed him that the animal was entirely in charge of his company and that my contract called for its delivery on board the steamer "Liguria." He diplomatically reminded me that his duties did not include feeding the tiger, but he was anxious—more than anxious—to add this to the attentions which he would shower upon the handsome animal, if I would only say the word. I said it.

Saturday, Jan. 25. After breakfast Wilson & Co.'s man gave me a lot of interesting details about the present health of the tiger, the large amount of meat he was devouring and the water he was drinking. Should he buy another kilo of meat for him? He should.

At 4 p.m. we had the pleasure of going aboard the anxiously expected Pacific Liner, "Liguria," bound for Liverpool. Then we watched for the lighter containing our baggage and the tiger. What a sensation he created as they hoisted him up the ship's side, cage and all high in the air, and deposited him upon the little extra deck over the entrance to the saloon.

Wilson & Co.'s man reminded me of his great services in bringing the animal aboard in such fine condition. I gave him three dollars Uruguayan and he went away happy, hoping I would come along again soon with another tiger.

Tuesday, Jan. 28. Warm day. Had an extra canopy put over Lopez's cage and ordered a bath for him, but when the ship's butcher (who is to feed and look after his tigership) asked, "Fresh or salt water, sir?" I was puzzled for a moment. Then I recollected that we do not hear of tigers bathing in the ocean, but only in fresh water streams, if they bathe at all. Besides, no salt is put on the raw meat with which Lopez is fed; therefore, a fresh water bath.

Sunday, Feb. 2. Lopez continues in good condition. At noon the butcher gave him another fresh water bath. (Fresh water being less plentiful than salt, the ablutions are administered with much discretion when not too many are about.)

Wednesday, Feb. 5. At breakfast, for the first time since starting out from Montevideo, the stewards put the wooden racks or "fiddles" on the tables, so that our plates would not slide off upon the floor. The tiger does not seem to like the rough weather. He has a sullen look on his face and a far-away light in his eyes. I guess he would rather be back in the Chaco killing cows for a living than bounding about upon the ugly black waves which he does not understand. He refused to eat his breakfast.

Thursday, Feb. 6. Lopez looked ugly again this morning and still refused to eat. He had some blood on his jaws and must have cut his tongue or mouth biting the iron bars of his cage, as I have seen him do. The butcher declares the animal is seasick.

Friday, Feb. 7. Discovered the reason why the tiger has been so bad tempered and why he has refused food the past two days. He has broken off a tooth in biting the bars of his cage. When the butcher threw some meat to him this morning he took it up into his mouth, began to chew, dropped it like a hot potato, and turned about in his cage snarling with pain.

The news that Lopez had broken off a tooth in his endeavors to get out spread like wildfire through the ship, and all kinds of anxious inquiries were made. Some wished to be assured for the eleventh time that the cage was perfectly safe. One or two, with an eye to the commercial side of the affair, desired to know whether this would not make the animal fetch a lower price. I assured them that the tiger was not for sale, and a tooth more or less would not make a fatal difference, especially as the tooth would grow again.

This afternoon, Lopez, being unable to eat, I consulted the ship's physician and asked him if he had any cocaine. He said, "Yes, but only a small bit." I then inquired it if would be pos-

Anna Hyatt Huntington modeled these figures of Señor Lopez and presented them to the Zoological Park in 1937.

sible to get a solution for the tiger's tooth. He agreed to give me some in the morning.

Saturday, Feb. 8. At 8 o'clock this morning the Doctor, the Chief Steward, the butcher and I met in solemn conclave at the tiger's cage, on the roof over the entrance to the dining saloon. I had the sponge all ready tied to the end of a stick and the Doctor gave me the solution of cocaine in a blue bottle. First, however, I proposed that we see if the patient would eat some finely cut beef, and to our great relief he did. It is true, he made a wry face, now and then, but he got the meat all down and never growled. Everybody below was happy that the tiger had recovered and could bite again.

Sunday, Feb. 9. The tiger ate a good breakfast, and the butcher made him a new bed of hay. We have a good supply, for in addition to what I bought at Buenos Aires, we got several bundles from the keeper of the flock of sheep which we took from Montevideo to Rio.

Tuesday, Feb. 11. (Near the Canary Islands.) Lopez was ugly this morning, and with just cause. In changing the water in the bucket on the inside of his cage, the butcher has always simply poured in fresh water and let it overflow; but the weather is so cool now that the tiger does not relish having the water run all over his parlor floor and wet his feet. He lifted one foot after another, in a comical way, and when he shook all four he turned and uttered a fierce growl and made a dive for the butcher, who, if he did not bear a charmed life would have been dead several times already by this time. He will, however, be careful about wetting Señor Lopez's feet again.

Wednesday, Feb. 12. The sea is running very high and the vessel is rolling badly. This afternoon, when the shaking-up we were getting was at its worst, I climbed up to the top of the ladder to get a look at him. There he was lying asleep, with his paws propped against the bars of his cage so he would not slide about.

Sunday, Feb. 16. In the Bay of Biscay. Lopez is very well and ate his breakfast with his usual relish. His tooth does not trouble him at all now.

Wednesday, Feb. 19.—Bleak, dreary, foggy Liverpool! Wet slush in the streets along the dock; cold, shivering people looking at us as the "Liguria" is being drawn alongside by means of ropes and winches.

Then came our transfer to a tender which was to take us to Princess Landing Stage. It offered us no protection against the cold drizzle.

This was not the worst, however. The Customs authorities would not let us take the tiger aboard the tender with us, and the so-called agent of the Pacific Steam Navigation Company, instead of being helpful to us, was even more discourteous than the Customs officers. I explained in vain that we were expecting to sail for the United States in four hours; that we did not want to land the animal, but only to transfer it; and so forth,—but all appeals were useless. The tiger must go back and remain on the "Liguria" until we obtained a permit from the Board of Agriculture in London allowing him to land!

I saw it was useless to argue the matter further, and, slipping a half-crown into the boatswain's hand, I got him to promise to have the cage covered up again right away, so that Lopez might not take his death of cold in the raw air.

Arriving at Princess Landing Stage, I set out for the establishment of a famous animal dealer. Having thought the situation over, I asked him if he would board and lodge the tiger for me until milder weather, say the beginning of May, and then forward him to the New York Zoological Park?

He would, and nine pounds sterling was the price agreed upon and receipted for.

And—now, mark you—could he immediately take the animal from the "Liguria" and bring him to his place?

He could! So I wrote out an order and handed it to him, and considered the incident closed.

Thus ended Mr. Butler's diary and the immediate history of Señor Lopez. The jaguar spent the rest of the winter in the establishment of the Liverpool animal dealer, William Cross, and in May was shipped to the Zoological Park without incident. He was the first inhabitant of the Lion House, taking over the first finished cage weeks before the others were ready. He quickly became a favorite with the keepers and the few visitors who were allowed in to see him. Hornaday told about him in the *Bulletin:*

From the day of his arrival at the Zoological Park, "Lopez" has never been one of the snarling kind. On the contrary, he constantly manifested what was considered a playful disposition. "Lopez" seemed anxious to play with anyone who came near his cage, and had a trick of rolling on his back, with his paws in the air, quite after the manner of a good-natured house cat.

Such an amenable animal deserved companionship. When a nearly full-grown female jaguar became available in Hamburg, she was purchased and installed in the Lion House alongside Señor Lopez. Each animal showed interest in the other and seemed to be perfectly friendly. After two days, the director decided it was safe to put them together in Lopez's cage. The connecting door was opened, the female confidently and casually walked through, and the next instant Lopez sprang, seized her by the right side of her neck and hung on with a series of savage bites. Keepers beat him with poles and an iron scraper, but he persisted, dragging the female to the far corner of his cage. When he finally let go of her she was dead, her neck vertebrae crushed.

It was a shocking exhibition to those who watched it. "The murder," Hornaday wrote, "was fully premeditated. As a consequence of this act of treachery, 'Lopez' will live in solitude the remainder of his life."

(As it turned out, it was a fairly long life. Señor Lopez did not die until 1914. In his heyday he was modeled by Anna Hyatt Huntington, the sculptor, and in 1937 she presented to the park the two stone figures of Lopez that now stand on the slope from the Fountain Circle to Baird Court.)

William Mill Butler, too, was shocked, and wrote Hornaday that he could not understand the "crime." He recalled visiting the animal with Hornaday, and its rolling over and putting out its paw to Hornaday. That same afternoon the Butlers had gone on to visit Robert Wilcox and his wife, the popular versifier Ella Wheeler Wilcox, and Butler had gotten

140

into a warm discussion with her. She didn't like zoological parks and wished she could open cage doors and let all the animals out—if they could be magically transported back to their native homes. Butler tried to persuade her to visit the Zoological Park and see how happy and contented Señor Lopez was, but now he feared she never would.

With the opening of the Lion House, an early dream of the society became a reality. The building incorporated two rooms at the north end, both set aside for the use of animal artists: the studio in the northeast corner into which any of the big cats could be shifted through a tunnel connecting all the exhibition compartments, and a locker room for easels, modeling clay, and other artists' tools in the northwest corner.

The society's interest in animal art and artists seems to have originated with Ernest Seton Thompson (who soon afterward changed his name to Ernest Thompson Seton), the animal artist and writer. In the society's first *Annual Report* for 1896 he offered a "Communication Regarding the Needs of Artists in the Zoological Park" in which, in the form of a letter to the secretary of the society, he pleaded for special privileges for artists to allow them to work all day, and a model room where the animal would be well lighted. He had worked, he said, in zoological gardens in America, England, and France; everywhere artists were at best merely tolerated.

Hornaday supported him in the body of the *Report:*

We propose to encourage and facilitate the production of high-class drawings, paintings and sculpture of wild animals. Although our magnificent series of large game animals is rapidly passing away, the walls of nearly if not quite all the great art galleries in America are absolutely destitute of representations of them. It is proposed that the Society's library building shall contain studios and workrooms for zoological artists and students, where the earnest worker shall have every facility and encouragement that it is possible to afford him.

He added that a studio had already been planned for the Lion House.

Now it existed. In the spring of 1903 the artists Daniel C. Beard, Eli Harvey, A. Phimister Proctor, Carl Rungius, and Ernest Thompson Seton had been invited to a luncheon at the Zoological Park to advise the director on specifications for the ideal animal studio, and the result was a room twenty-one by twenty-six feet, about half of it occupied by a wide-screened cage for the models. On July 9, 1903, it was formally opened to the artistic fraternity. Seven painters and sculptors, including Rungius, showed up and Baba Carnegie's "biggest hairy-headed lion in the world" was the first model for William M. Carey, the senior animal painter present. After Hannibal, a magnificent young Malay tiger named Princeton was offered to the artists. Princeton, who had cost $100, was the gift of fifteen-year-old Henry Fairfield Osborn, Jr., later to become more intimately identified with the society as Fairfield Osborn, its president for twenty-eight years from 1940 until shortly before his death in 1969.

The feelings of artists generally seem to have been expressed by an artist named J. M. Gleeson, who wrote to Hornaday:

Verily the world do move. Five years ago I had occasion to make some animal drawings and went to Central Park to do them. The policeman on duty treated me as tho I was going to steal something and the secretary Mr. Hollis treated me still worse. "We run this Zoo *our way* and don't care how they do these things in Europe or Phila., etc." So I went to Phila. to make my drawings.

I shall not be able to accept the courteous invitation to attend the opening of the Studio. I wish I might, for it is a wonderful thing. I believe it is one more debt the world owes Mr. Seton. It is a good thing and a great event.

Artists were welcome anywhere in the park, and Hornaday subsequently sent a general order to all employees that "artists, sculptors, zoologists and students generally" were to be given special attention, and "Whenever possible, seats should be offered."

Paternalism extended even to finding living quarters for

artists. Hornaday made a deal with the proprietor of the Parkway Hotel opposite the Northwest Gate to grant a special rate of eight dollars a week for room and board to artists working in the Zoological Park, and was able to assure them that "the place seems respectable, although of course there is a bar-room attachment."

The society not only offered studio facilities to animal artists; it employed them. Carl Rungius engraved the vignette of a pronghorn that adorned the society's certificate of membership, and Charles R. Knight designed the society's seal with its magnificent head of a bighorn sheep. While the Aquatic Birds House was being planned, A. P. Proctor was engaged to model the animal frieze on that building and also on the Reptile and Primate houses, the eagle over the south door of the Bird House, and somewhat later the antelope heads over both doors of the Antelope House. Eli Harvey, then beginning to make a name for himself in art circles in Paris, was called to New York to carve the "sentinel lions" at each entrance to the Lion House, and the frieze and panels on that rather overdecorated building. (Hornaday disliked heads over both doors of the Antelope House. Eli Harvey, good face on things and say it was the most beautiful building of its kind in the world.) In 1907 a competition among sculptors for the decoration of the new Elephant House ended in a dead heat between Proctor and Knight, so Proctor was assigned the sculpture on the south side and Knight that on the north. In 1911 Knight modeled the zebra heads at each end of the Zebra House.

Harvey's sentinel lions were especially praised by connoisseurs, although Engineer George Beerbower gave warning that their tails were in such a position that they were sure to catch water where they rested on the base, and in winter the water would freeze and the tails might break off. (They haven't—yet.)

Proctor borrowed a brown pelican and a blue heron from the park and took them to his studio up the Hudson while he

A. P. Proctor, the sculptor, working on one of the decorations of the Elephant House.

144

was designing the decorations for the Aquatic Birds House. (Three of Proctor's four pelican figures were rescued when the old building was reconstructed in 1964 and are now a pleasing decoration on the west wall. The fourth figure was broken.) Sculptors in particular seem to have made good use of the park's animals; George Grey Barnard asked if he could rent a white pelican for a figure he was making for a monument in Cairo, Illinois, and Assistant Curator Beebe lent him one. Beebe also supplied Stanford White with photographs of a snowy owl for studies White was making while he was decorating a building for James Gordon Bennett, the owl-bemused publisher of the *Herald*. Harvey modeled a nine-foot-high figure of Ivan, a celebrated brown bear in the park's collection, and it was cast in bronze for Brown University. Gutzon Borglum, who many years later was to carve the gigantic heads of Presidents on Mount Rushmore in South Dakota, made studies of eagles in the park.

The Zoological Park still attracts animal artists, and such outstanding men as Roger Tory Peterson, Don Eckelberry, Arthur Singer, and Guy Coheleach work there from time to time. Peterson estimates that in his early days he made at least a hundred sketches of Jimmy, the sedate shoebill stork—he was the only bird that would stand perfectly still for hours.

There is contradictory evidence about the relation of the Zoological Park to one piece of animal art once well known to millions of Americans: the representation of a magnificent bison shown on the "Buffalo nickel" first minted in 1913. Was it modeled from an animal in the New York Zoological Park or from one in the Central Park Menagerie?

James Earle Fraser, the sculptor of the Indian head on the obverse and the bison on the reverse, said he worked in the Zoological Park—which would seem to be good enough evidence for anybody, except that he also said the animal was named Black Diamond. The Zoological Park had no bison named Black Diamond—but Central Park Menagerie did.

Fraser's most extended statement about the circumstances

145

of his design is quoted on an exhibit in the National Cowboy Hall of Fame in Oklahoma City. In 1911 Secretary of the Treasury Franklin MacVeagh asked him to design a coin to replace the Liberty Head nickel, "And, in my search for symbols, I found no motif within the boundaries of the United States so distinctive as the American buffalo, or bison. With the Indian Head on the obverse, we had perfect unity in theme."

The profile of the Indian, Fraser said, "is a composite of three Plains Indians, Iron Tail, Sioux; Big Tree, Kiowa; and Two Moons, Cheyenne. The Indians had come to visit President Theodore Roosevelt and stopped off in New York. During this time, I was able to study and photograph them. The three had combined features of the hardy, virile, type of Plains Indians."

As for his buffalo model:

He was not a plains buffalo, but none other than Black Diamond, the contrariest animal in the Bronx Zoo. I stood for hours watching and catching his forms and mood in plastic clay. Black Diamond was less conscious of the honor being conferred on him than of the annoyance which he suffered from insistent gazing upon him. He refused point blank to permit me to get side views of him, and stubbornly showed his front face most of the time.

The same attribution also appeared in a news story in the New York *Herald* on January 27, 1913, in which the sculptor explained that his animal model was a "typical and shaggy specimen" which he found grazing in the New York Zoological Park. If "grazing" was not merely a reporter's graphic embellishment, it would imply that the animal *was* in the Zoological Park, where the bison herd was free to graze on a large and grassy range; Central Park Menagerie's bison were closely penned and had no access to grass.

Despite Fraser's testimony, it must be admitted that most of the available evidence points to the Central Park Menagerie. The New York Zoological Society still receives occasional letters asking whether Black Diamond was in its herd and whether it was the model for the coin. The same confusion existed more than half a century ago.

In November of 1915 a correspondent wrote to Hornaday from the Metropolitan Club in Washington:

I see in the paper a notice of the death of the big bison "Black Diamond," or "Toby" as he was familiarly known. It has been stated that "Black Diamond" was the model for the buffalo on the ten dollar bill, also the five-cent nickle [sic]. If that is so it does not do him justice and was enough to make him ill. Was Black Diamond in Central Park collection of animals or was he in the Zoological Park? The paper stated he was confined in Central Park.

Hornaday usually replied to every letter, however trivial its subject, and it is surprising that his letter books contain no reply to this inquiry. He did have something to say to the publicity agent of the Lehigh Valley Railroad who wrote to him about the same time. The railroad man asked about the origin of the name Black Diamond, which he described as "the buffalo recently put to death at the New York Zoo because of advancing age." In the best P.R. man's tradition he included a plug for his organization. "The 'Black Diamond' is the crack train of the Lehigh Valley Railroad. It made its first run just about 20 years ago, but I am happy to report that instead of giving out with age, it is running stronger and better than ever before."

Hornaday answered:

The buffalo named "Black Diamond" was a Central Park animal, with which we have had nothing to do. I do not know how it came by its name; but I suppose the name was bestowed by Billy Snyder, the head keeper. If "Black Diamond" was as fine an animal as we are asked to believe, then I cannot understand why he should be sold to a butcher at a cut price. [The carcass was sold to August Silz, a game dealer.]

The director was not averse to a little modest horn-blowing of his own, for he went on:

I do know that "Black Diamond" was *not* the buffalo that served as a model for the buffalo on one of the ten-dollar bills in our U.S. currency. I know all about the genesis of that engraving. I happened to be in Washington, and at the National Museum, on the very day when the glass front of the big buffalo group was taken out in order that the magnificent male bison which forms the central figure of that group might be photographed at the request of the Secretary of the Treasury, and used "in preparing the design for the new ten-dollar bill."

The "big buffalo group" he referred to was, of course, the one he had mounted in the 1880s while he was chief taxidermist of the museum.

Evidence for the Central Park Menagerie mounts with correspondence between Hornaday and Martin S. Garretson, secretary of the Bison Society. On January 7, 1918, Garretson wrote to Hornaday:

The Bison Society is endeavoring to collect for its records pictures and photographs of all noted and historical Bison, and for this purpose will you kindly give me some information; as to where I can obtain a good photograph of "Black Diamond," the Buffalo that was formerly in the Central Park Menagerie? This is the animal I believe that was used as a model for the buffalo on our Nickels.

Hornaday to Garretson:

Regarding the buffalo bull "Black Diamond," we have no information whatever. Judging from the character of the buffalo on the nickel, I should say from its dejected appearance that the animal was an inmate of some small menagerie and had lived all its life in a small enclosure. Its head droops as if it had lost all hope in the world, and even the sculptor was not able to raise it. I regard the bison on the nickel as a sad failure, considered as a work of art.

Garretson agreed that the animal did not look very happy, but he attributed the drooping head and tail to the sculptor's need to compress the animal into the tight circular space allotted him on the coin.

148

A member of the American Numismatic Society made the same criticism of the pose of the animal. The public had other complaints; the molded surfaces were too high, the coins did not stack well, and they were too thick to be slipped easily into coin-operated slot machines. The Secretary of the Treasury was satisfied, however, and announced that the slot-machine people should modify their machines.

It does seem curious that the sculptor confused the record. Could it be that he had inspected Black Diamond at the Central Park Menagerie, found him unsuitable, and subsequently chose a better animal at the Bronx Zoo, with the dramatic name of Black Diamond sticking in his mind when he talked about his model? Of only one thing can we be sure: in its time, this was the most widely distributed figure of a bison. On January 27, 1913, twenty-five stamping machines at the Philadelphia Mint began turning out three thousand buffalo nickels a minute and all three mints kept stamping them until 1938.

The animal artist who was longest and most closely associated with the Zoological Park is Paul Bransom, the illustrator of books and magazines whose imaginative yet realistic work has been familiar to nearly three generations of Americans. He began sketching in the Zoological Park in 1907 and was such a constant and talented student that Director Hornaday gave him the use of an empty room in the southwestern corner of the Lion House as his own private studio. In his eighty-seventh year Mr. Bransom wrote his memories of "those wonderful golden years when the Bronx Zoo was young—and *we* were young!"

They evoke a time that is long since gone and betray a sensitive artist's appreciation of the opportunities the new Zoological Park so gladly offered.

While I occupied that room I illustrated the special [Macmillan] edition of Jack London's "Call of the Wild" with illustrations on practically every page of the work; also some commissions for *Century Magazine*—but, of course, all good things come to an end and my studio in the Bronx Park ended when Will Beebe returned from some expedition with a lot of gear for which there was no room except my studio. However, I did keep my locker in the room designed to draw and model animals at the opposite end of the building. Sometimes there would be an animal sequestered in that "model" cage—for some reason or another—but I never saw anyone working there. Perhaps it was because, in that cage, the light was always *behind* and *above* the model, which was always in silhouette. I recall Mr. Eli Harvey used to come up to the Zoo occasionally to model. Also, Mr. [Frederick G. R.] Roth had a locker in the room, but he always did his work out in the main Lion House (where the light was on the animal). Mr. Roth was (in my opinion) the finest animal sculptor America has produced. The only other artist in constant attendance at the Park whom I can recall at the moment was a lad in knee breeches named Alvord Fairbanks. He was always quietly drawing somewhere around the Park. I tried to make his acquaintance, but he was a "loner" and shyed away from all attempts to become acquainted. [Fairbanks was a fourteen-year-old prodigy from Utah who won a scholarship from the Art Students' League for his model of Sultan, the lion.]

The Park was a glorious place in those early days. Monday and Thursday were pay days with few people present, and those few were of the most understanding type. It was a joy to draw and actually paint anywhere in the Park without a horde of kids swarming all over you; they always asked the same questions, mainly "How much are you going to get for that?" or "I have an uncle who's n'artist—but *he's* good!"

As the park became more crowded each year I began to retreat to the buildings which were noted not only for their beautiful inhabitants but for their unique odors. The public usually rushed through without noticing me at all—and I always got a big seat all by myself going home on the subway. It has all been my good fortune to share in the great feast of knowledge and beauty which is available at the Bronx Zoo for the receptive heart. While only a portion of this great experience may have become manifest in my work so far, I am confident that it will bear abundant fruit in some future experience. Nothing is wasted.

In my fifteen summers at Jackson Hole, Wyoming, where elk are plentiful, I was always amused by the reaction of two fellow

150

artist friends, both of whom were born and raised in Wyoming, when on fall afternoons, returning home after a day's sketching somewhere in the valley, there would be heard the high, thin bugle challenge of a bull elk far back in the mountains. My companions would grab me by the arm with excitement, saying "Listen! Do you know what that is?" Instantly the years slipped back to those magic hours, so long ago, when I would stand spellbound at the fence of our huge elk range, watching one of our three magnificent bull elk exercise his lordship over a herd of about twenty beautiful cows, while the other two rival bulls constantly bugled their raving complaint. Yes, bugling elk was a very common sound at the Bronx Zoo in those days. [They still bugle. The Zoological Park's herd of Roosevelt elk was a gift of Madison Grant and came from the Madison Grant Forest and Elk Refuge in California, and the bugling of the mature bull in early morning and late afternoon is one of the wild, eerie sounds of the zoo in September and October.]

Another wonderful sound I hear in nostalgic memory is the full-throated chorus which always responded to the Park's noonday whistle—I refer to the cries from the old wolf dens where the wolves, coyotes, foxes and Esquimaux dogs gave full vent to their feelings every day at noon only.

Other artists apparently felt the same way as Bransom about the lighting inadequacies of the Lion House studio and it was never utilized to the extent that Hornaday had intended. Artists tended to work in the open air, despite gratuitous criticism by the public, and the studio became a storeroom and then, in the mid-1940s, was turned into an Animal Nursery. For some years it was the domain of Mrs. Helen Martini, wife of the Lion House keeper, and there she had spectacular success in hand-rearing baby lions, tigers, black leopards, and numerous other small fry.

The Eskimo dogs mentioned by Bransom were the one exception to Director Hornaday's rule against exhibiting domestic animals in the Zoological Park. He relaxed his prohibition in 1902 when Commander Robert E. Peary returned from one of his attempts to reach the North Pole. The explorer brought back a walrus, a six-month-old female musk

Jimmy, a sedate shoebill stork for many years resident in the Zoological Park, had one quality much appreciated by young animal artists: he would hold perfectly still for hours.

151

ox, and two adult Eskimo dogs and two pups. For the sake of having the walrus (the first in any American zoological park) and the musk ox, Hornaday was willing to take the dogs. He put them on exhibition but merely for the sake of their association with Peary, whom they advertised by frantic and almost constant barking day and night. Peary deposited several more dogs after subsequent trips until Hornaday put his foot down. Eventually he got rid of all of them, selling some for $2.50 each and shipping others to a New England farm where Peary was breeding them. Only old Bridge, the leader of the dog team on the 1902 expedition, was quiet and well behaved. He remained on exhibition until he died in 1908.

The dogs did serve the cause of art, if not of zoology. Bransom used them as models for his 1912 illustrated edition of *The Call of the Wild,* and he also made illustrations in the same book from the Tlinkit Indian house and totem pole in the park.

The best way to encourage animal art is to pay hard cash for the work of animal artists. Apart from engaging artists for sculptured ornaments on buildings and cage backgrounds, the society started its own animal art collection as early as 1898, when Hornaday raised $400 among members of the board of managers to buy fifty black-and-white wash drawings by Ernest Thompson Seton. They were the best of the illustrations he had made for Mrs. Mabel Osgood Wright's book, *Four-footed Americans and Their Kin,* and were intended to be the nucleus of a collection for a school of animal painting and sculpture that would make "New York and the Zoological Park the center of the world for such work." They were never used for teaching purposes, however, and eventually were merely filed away in the library of the Zoological Society.

A more ambitious art-encouragement policy had its beginning when Hornaday made the acquaintance of Carl Rungius. He told about it in his unpublished autobiography:

On a cold February night-fall in 1895 as Mrs. Hornaday and I were hurrying down Fifth Avenue, we saw in the brilliantly lighted window of Avery's Art Gallery, a big and bold oil painting of unusual size and commanding importance. It looked as if a section with a wild animal in it, had been cut out of the Maine Woods and framed as an exhibit from the workshop of Nature.

Promptly we crossed the street and parked ourselves in front of the new revelation. One look convinced us that it was something new and different. It was a life-size picture, boldly and confidently painted, of the head and shoulders of a young bull moose going through a tall and dark pine forest.

It was signed by a name both new and strange—"C. Rungius."

In the warm shelter of the Galleries the attendant gave us information.

"That was painted by a young German artist named Carl Rungius. He studied animal painting under good masters in Berlin, and now he has come over here to live permanently, and paint America's big game animals."

A masterly young painter interested in American big-game animals—it was a combination to arouse all of Hornaday's enthusiasm. He wrote to Rungius, and they met as soon as the Hornadays moved to New York in the spring of 1896, beginning a lifelong friendship. By 1910 the idea of forming a great collection of paintings of large American animals was taking shape in Hornaday's mind and Rungius was at the center of it. The executive committee was only mildly interested, but Hornaday had a good friend in Emerson McMillin, a wealthy industrialist, and he not only "broke the jam," as the director put it, by presenting two Rungius canvases, "Wary Game" (a band of white mountain sheep) and "The Old Prospector" (a grizzly bear), but he also put up $1,500 to commission the first of Rungius's many large paintings. This was "The Mountaineers," a portrait of bighorns on Wilcox Pass in the Canadian Rockies.

The Rungius paintings were so impressive that Madison Grant and Professor Osborn caught the art enthusiasm and agreed that the society should raise an art gallery fund.

153

Seven men offered to put up $250 a year, so that money was assured to pay Rungius to produce one large painting a year, with occasional purchases from other artists. Eventually two large rooms on the second floor of the Administration Building were turned into an art gallery, one of them mostly filled with Rungius's work alone. Mrs. Frederick Ferris Thompson later gave "Portrait of a Lioness" by Rosa Bonheur and over the years the gallery acquired important paintings by Charles R. Knight, Louis Agassiz Fuertes, R. Bruce Horsfall, and A. Radclyffe Dugmore. For three decades the gallery was a repository of the best animal art produced in the United States, although it was little visited except by members, who received the handsomely illustrated catalogue published by the society in 1930. Until 1929 the Administration Building was inhabited only by the director and his secretary and thereafter until 1940 it had only one other occupant, the young assistant to the director and curator of educational activities, Claude W. Leister. Except on rare formal occasions there was little traffic in the spacious lounges downstairs or the "Gentlemen's Smoking Room" and the library, which shared the second floor with the gallery. In 1940 the curators of the animal departments were routed out of their quiet offices in the exhibition buildings, the department of publications and photography was tucked away in a corner, and the Administration Building suddenly became crowded. The gallery did not survive the demand for space, and the paintings were dispersed. Some now hang on the walls of curatorial offices or among the trophies in the Heads and Horns Museum, others were put in storage, and eight of the largest are now exhibited in the Grand Teton Lodge at Moran, Wyoming.

The society's cash encouragement of animal art did much to stimulate that kind of painting; the acquisition of every new picture was well publicized. Animal art is a *genre* still not fully appreciated by the art museums, at least in the United States, but it is notable that since 1960 there has been a Society of Animal Artists in this country, to which many eminent artists belong, and which regularly holds exhibitions at the Grand Central Art Galleries in New York and elsewhere. The Zoological Park may even claim some small share in its existence, for the society was organized in 1960 by Patricia Allen and the late Guido Borghi as a result of the acclaim given to the "Animals in the Bronx Zoo" show at the Burr Galleries in New York in 1958.

If a well-designed and -engraved bookplate may be considered even a minor art form, the Zoological Society may be credited with patronizing it, too. In 1910 Captain John S. Barnes, a member of the board of managers, offered to provide a bookplate for the society's small but rapidly growing library. He himself designed it, reproducing more or less faithfully the entrance to the Lion House (which is the same at both north and south ends), and in 1911 commissioned the engraver A. N. MacDonald to execute it. It was much admired and bookplate collectors for years asked for copies. The original plate from which it was printed has disappeared, and now the society's library has only a collotype reproduction printed in 1943.

The Zoological Society's engraved bookplate.

155

The Zoological Society had been conceived in a reform year in New York City politics, and in 1902 reform was again in the saddle and looking around for abuses to put to rights. There was a glaring one: the aquarium down at Battery Park at the southern tip of Manhattan. Why not let the Zoological Society manage it along the same scientific and nonpolitical lines as the Zoological Park?

Well, for one thing, the Zoological Society was not sure it wanted to take over Augean stables that could be cleaned only by an enormous amount of work and money. And as some members of the board of managers pointed out, it was a long way from the Bronx to the Battery.

New Yorkers of today who know the old aquarium building only as a more or less circular empty stone shell in a Battery Park acre christened Castle Clinton National Monument must summon all their imagination to see it as it once was—the social center of New York City. Its vicissitudes have been briefly described in a historical souvenir booklet the New York Aquarium published in 1957 when it opened the "new" aquarium at Coney Island:

As in the lives of human beings, institutions are formed and influenced by so many remote and indirect factors. It is not really far-fetched to trace the ancestry of the Aquarium in New York City right back to June 22, 1807, when the British fired on the American frigate *Chesapeake*. . . . For if that warlike act had not occurred, the people of New York would not have held mass-meetings in denunciation of the British, the "fortification fever" would not have swept the city and, in all probability, the Federal Government would not have constructed the [South-] West Battery (or Castle Clinton as it was later called) at the Battery, at the point where the guns could sweep both the East and the North Rivers. [This last statement is inaccurate; the guns could cover the North, but not the East, River.]

Castle Clinton never fired a shot in anger and the fortification fever abated, as fevers do. The War of 1812 over, Castle Clinton became a white elephant. The Government had built it with a vast amount of expense and labor on an underwater foundation

9

The Society Takes Over the Aquarium

of rough stone dumped a few hundred feet offshore. What to do with it now that peace had come?

The City of New York was willing to take it, and as Castle Garden it was opened as a "place of resort" on July 3, 1823. Even in those days the City Fathers had a good sense of timing, and the grand opening on the eve of the national holiday gave the ex-fort a marvellous send-off in its new role. Undeniably the growing, bustling city did need such a place of resort for public entertainment of the crowds that then, as now, would turn out for any spectacle. In later years New Yorkers were fond of boasting that Castle Garden was the largest public hall in the world. The boast may even have been true, for it did seat 6,000 persons and on occasion it could be made to hold 10,000.

Between 1823 and August 3, 1855, Castle Garden frequently needed all the sitting-and-standing room it was asserted to have. Starting off as a setting for fireworks extravaganzas, band concerts and balloon ascensions, it graduated to the demonstration of scientific marvels when Morse showed off his new electric telegraph in 1842. There had been and were to be a series of enormous public receptions—Andrew Jackson was honored at Castle Garden in 1833, President Tyler in 1843, President Polk in 1847, Henry Clay in 1848, and, to climax everything in the city's experience of enthusiasm, the great Hungarian patriot Louis Kossuth was received there in 1851.

An old print of the scene in Castle Garden when Jenny Lind made her American debut.

146. Castle Garden & Bay. N.Y.

All these glorious nights except Kossuth's, which was still to come, paled to insignificance on the night of September 11, 1850, when P. T. Barnum climaxed *his* career by presenting Jenny Lind, the "Swedish Nightingale," in her American debut. The torrent of enthusiastic words written and spoken about that event seems in volume to have rivalled Niagara Falls after the spring thaw.

It is hard to understand, at this distance, why Castle Garden began to wane in popularity after the Lind and Kossuth triumphs. The city was moving uptown, as it has done countless times since, and people were perhaps looking for their entertainment nearer the heart of things. At any rate, in 1855 Castle Garden became an Emigrant Landing Station. Before the Federal Government got around to building a more commodious (if not more conveniently located) Immigration Station on Ellis Island in 1890, a hopeful stream of 7,690,606 immigrants flowed into, through, and out of the old ex-fort, ex-place of resort.

Castle Garden in 1890, the year in which it was abandoned as an immigration station. The outlying buildings were torn down before it became an aquarium.

158

By 1891 the city had its white elephant back in its hands. There is no clear record of what city agency decided to fill it with fish, but it can be surmised that the idea originated in Tammany Hall as a patronage scheme. The *Tribune*, in its story of October 25, 1902, announcing the agreement by which the Zoological Society would take over the Aquarium, specifically referred to its operation under Tammany:

The early history of the New-York Aquarium was a disgrace to the city government. Under several Tammany administrations the old Castle Garden was being transformed from a depot for immigrants to a place for public amusement. For many years workmen tinkered about the place, erecting tanks for fish, only to see the tanks burst when the water was let in. The public could not be admitted to the building and the place was a monument of useless expense.

In one of the city's more enlightened moments, the Department of Public Parks late in 1896 hired Dr. Tarleton H. Bean as superintendent of the Aquarium. Bean was a well-known ichthyologist and the first man of ability to be connected with the Aquarium. Being a mere fish man, naturally he did not last; a new administration turned him out in 1898 and gave his job to "Captain Jim" Jones, a politician whose interest in fish was confined to shore dinners. Then *another* administration came along and President William R. Willcox of the Parks Board decided it was time to see whether the New York Zoological Society could repeat at the Battery what it was being so brilliantly successful at doing in the Bronx.

Willcox proposed to Professor Osborn and Madison Grant that the society manage the Aquarium, but at first they were reluctant, for it had long been notoriously mired in politics. The Parks Board man had two persuasive arguments, however; legislation and the contract it would authorize the city to make with the Zoological Society could be worded to assure the society of complete control without political

159

interference, and above all its management would put the Aquarium on a scientific basis and promote closer relations with the city's educational system. It was an appeal that an Osborn and a Grant could not resist.

In April, legislation was introduced in Albany and passed without any of the travail that had accompanied the creation of the Zoological Society seven years before. On October 13, 1902, a contract between the city and the society was signed, transferring management of the Aquarium to the society and providing an annual maintenance fund of not less than $45,000. The actual formal transfer took place at the Aquarium on October 31 at three o'clock in the afternoon, following a celebratory luncheon at the Down Town Association. Mr. Willcox spoke of the educational values that would be developed by the society. Professor Osborn, perhaps feeling that some of the membership might think the society was overextending itself at a time when major efforts were still needed at the Zoological Park, was careful to mention that "The Society did not seek the care of this Aquarium; Park Commissioner Willcox was the first to suggest it." He did add that "we appreciate this transfer as a sign of approval on the part of the City of our management of the Zoological Park."

Politicians—not the membership—were the only ones to raise an eyebrow. An alderman told Hornaday that it looked to him as if the society had "gone into politics" by accepting the Aquarium and that Tammany believed the transfer was merely a device for discharging the old employees and replacing them with Willcox men. The park's director assured him that this was not so, but the alderman predicted that when Tammany came into power again it would make trouble for the Aquarium. Actually, the society's charter-granted control was watertight—Grant had seen to that—and the Aquarium kept free of politics.

Although he was not called on to make a speech, the central figure in the small party of officials who met in the dim, gas-lighted Aquarium that October afternoon was Charles Haskins Townsend, the new director. Born in Parnassus, Pennsylvania, in 1859, the son of a minister, he was then forty-three years old. He was slender and short (a member of his staff in later years thinks he was about five feet four inches tall); in 1902 he wore a heavy mustache and was almost entirely bald. Despite a quick temper, he was usually genial and by no means as hard to get along with as his brother director up in the Bronx.

Considering the diversification of the Aquarium's activities that the executive committee had in mind, Townsend was an ideal man for the job—a keen naturalist from boyhood. His family had intended him for the ministry, to continue the family tradition, but as he wrote in *The Condor* in 1927, he was "too fully occupied with the natural world to consider the supernatural." A dentist in his home town taught him a little about taxidermy (his early efforts in that line went down the Conemaugh River along with most of Johnstown, Pennsylvania, in the 1889 flood) and taxidermy led him to Ward's Natural Science Establishment in Rochester in 1879 when he was twenty years old—the same first step that Hornaday had taken. After three years he moved on to a very junior position on the staff of the Academy of Natural Sciences of Philadelphia, where he "dabbled in ornithology and other zoologies, with great personal satisfaction, but to little scientific effect." He was still trying to find himself when, in 1883, he met Professor Spencer F. Baird, then U.S. Commissioner of Fish and Fisheries as well as secretary of the Smithsonian. Within a week he was on his way to the salmon hatchery on the McCloud River in California and his uncertainties were over; for the rest of his life he was to be concerned in some way with water and its inhabitants.

For the next eighteen years Townsend held various posts in governmental and fisheries work and when the society hired him (at $3,500 a year) he was chief of the Fisheries Division of the U.S. Fish Commission. The Smithsonian had sent him

Dr. Charles Haskins Townsend, director of the Aquarium. The mustache he wore as a young man did not long survive.

161

to the Arctic Ocean as naturalist on the U.S.S. *Corwin* in 1885 and he was the naturalist aboard the *Albatross* on most of its deep-sea exploratory voyages between 1886 and 1889. The fur seals of the Pribilof Islands were one of his specialties, and for several years he made the annual summer inspection of the rookeries for the American government. On one trip in 1892 along the west coast of Mexico he discovered a new fur seal that Professor C. Hart Merriam of the U.S. Biological Survey named *Arctocephalus townsendi* in his honor. (It was later reduced to a subspecies, *Arctocephalus philippi townsendi*.)

Hornaday had proposed Townsend for the Aquarium job. On April 7, 1902, he wrote to Professor Osborn:

If you are still looking for a man to be Superintendent of the Aquarium, let me mention and strongly recommend my old friend C. H. Townsend. He is capable, vigorous, experienced, knows administrative work thoroughly, and is as fine a man personally as could be found in a years search. No man in Washington has a cleaner record.

(A few years later Hornaday looked upon his "old friend" as one of his worst enemies; they differed on the management of the Pribilof fur-seal harvest and Hornaday never forgave Townsend for his opposing stand. In one of Hornaday's scrapbooks about the fur-seal controversy there is a newspaper clipping about Townsend's retirement from the Aquarium in 1937, mentioning that he had brought about a world seal pact that saved the species from extinction. The item is ringed in blue pencil and two slashing exclamation points stand beside it.)

Director Hermon C. Bumpus of the American Museum of Natural History also recommended Townsend, and on April 29 the executive committee invited him to take the directorship. He accepted promptly, but the formalities of transfer to the society would obviously take some weeks or months and Professor Osborn considered it a "bonanza" (since the society would not have to pay his salary during the interval) when

Secretary of State John Hay asked him to do one last job for the government—to represent it at The Hague in the arbitration of a fur-seal dispute between Russia and the United States. Townsend went to The Hague and later visited half a dozen European aquariums, picking up ideas that might be useful in New York. The assignment as one of the arbiters was to rise up to plague him and embarrass the Zoological Society later on (see pp. 202–206).

Above all, the new director of the Aquarium was a practical man who knew how to make things work, and he needed all his practicality to transform the interior of the old fort. Floor pools and exhibition tanks had always been lined with white tile and the general impression was of a dim and dingy bathroom. Writing to Townsend to congratulate him on the unanimous vote of the executive committee to hire him, Professor Osborn mentioned that "I have already explained to you my ideas and ideals regarding the administration of the Aquarium." Those were the days when Professor Osborn had time to take a close look at every detail of the society's operations, and one can imagine that the director had been fully and forcefully briefed. The Osborn aims were: make the Aquarium more popular, more useful, of greater educational advantage to the city, more attractive, more varied in its exhibits, a center of scientific work.

In his first report to the executive committee, Townsend gave an accounting of the first twenty-five days of his stewardship. He had bought a typewriting machine, figured how to convert a floor pool to a fish hatchery and rearing pond, started hiding the glaring white tiles behind bluffs of natural rock, enlarged the skylights over the tanks so the fish could be seen, made openings for transparent labels over the tanks, and talked the Street Cleaning Department into hauling the Aquarium's coal-furnace ashes and garbage away (at a saving of $500 a year). He closed with a mild suggestion that the gas illumination be replaced with electric lights.

He could have done more if money had been available.

163

The city had put up $5,968.64 for the final two months of 1902, and at the end of the first two weeks Townsend figured he would have a margin of $200 at the end of the year. As it turned out, he had a credit balance of only $8.67 on December 31, 1902. Still, rejuvenation was under way, the city had appropriated $46,500 for 1903, and the newspapers were giving the Aquarium the same kind of enthusiastic support they had given the Zoological Park three years before. The *World* summed it all up quite simply in the first sentence of a two-page picture spread on Sunday, November 23: "The New York Aquarium is the best and biggest in the world."

Up in the Bronx, as more buildings went up or were staked out, and paths and roads were permanently paved, the form of the Zoological Park began to coalesce and take on the unity the executive committee had aimed at when it approved the Final Plan in 1897. There was still plenty of tangled wilderness and rough, unimproved ground, especially on the east side of the Bronx River, but the inner oblong of major buildings was impressive and—a remarkable thing in such a young institution—the grandeur of the concept was being heightened by adornment purely for visual pleasure.

The most prominent ornament was a large stone fountain that had once stood on the grounds of a wealthy resident of Como, Italy. Some time in the 1890s an Italian antiquarian had bought it, moved it to Rome, and set it up in a "quiet nook" where it was admired and photographed in 1901 by William Baumgarten, who seems to have been a New York contractor. He was never able to discover who the sculptor was or the name of the original owner, but he did have reason to believe that it dated from the late seventeenth century. The *Herald* published Baumgarten's photograph of the fountain, and John D. Rockefeller's brother William became interested and offered to buy it for the Zoological Park. At a total cost of about $25,000 it was bought and transported in numbered boxes, and Baumgarten's workmen reassembled it on the east side of Baird Court in front of the spot where the Heads and Horns Museum now stands. It remained there from 1904 until 1910, when it was moved to its present site in the center of the Concourse Parking Circle.

The Lydig family made a contribution, too. David and Philip Lydig had owned all but a small part of the tract occupied by the Zoological Park, and since 1802 successive Lydigs had preserved the original forest and kept untouched the glades and ponds and waterfalls that so entranced Hornaday when he made his first inspection. The current Philip Mesier Lydig offered a memorial Lydig Gate as early as 1899, and two years later Mrs. Frank K. Sturgis, the daughter of

Autocrat vs. Autocrat

Philip and his wife, Catherine Suydam Lydig, provided $3,000 for the purpose. Philip had specified that the gate should be in the southern part of the park, but a site was chosen at the top of a flight of steps leading up to the Buffalo Range from Boston Road. There were to be two massive stone pillars linked by a fanciful wrought-iron arch, and the Lydigs after some demur approved the plans and the site. Not so Hornaday. He wrote to Madison Grant:

I consider it [the site] one of the worst that could possibly be selected. It is apropos of nothing, and it is contrary to all rules of landscape architecture to place a building, or any object worthy of special attention, at the top of a long flight of steps, and accessible only after a fatiguing climb, when the mind of the visitor is least likely to be concerned with memorial monuments.

He had a better point than he knew, for as the park developed and the southeastern, or Boston Road, gate became the busiest entrance after completion of a spur of the rapid-transit line to 180th Street in 1905, the Buffalo Gate lost much of its usefulness, although it was still kept open as a carriage and subsequently automobile entrance for more than four decades. In 1951, when the Boston Post Road was closed to motor traffic and incorporated into the Zoological Park, people no longer entered by the old Buffalo Gate, and today few fatigue themselves by climbing the steps to inspect the bronze memorial plaques on the Lydig Gate of 1903. The iron arch itself rusted away and was taken down in 1941.

The rapid-transit spur to 180th Street poured millions of visitors into the Zoological Park between 1905 and 1951, but in the latter year it was dismantled and the subway point nearest the Zoological Park became the West Farms station at 177th Street (now designated East Tremont Avenue–Boston Road), necessitating a slightly longer walk. According to the Rapid Transit Authority, the spur became uneconomic in its later years, so that the park—and the public—perforce had to accept its demolition. At any rate, the society won an earlier battle with the subway authorities, who in 1904 proposed to extend the line *through* the park, entering at the present Boston Road Gate, traversing the Buffalo Range, and by viaduct and open cut emerging on Pelham Parkway.

Hornaday characterized the scheme with his usual pungency: "It needs no great wisdom to point out that an elevated railroad, operating at least 300 trains per day, is one of the surest and most far-reaching park-destroying schemes that the ingenuity of man could devise." There was so much outcry from the society and civic organizations that the line was curved to the east and gave the park a wide berth beyond what used to be called West Farms.

Although they had nothing to do with the purposes of the Zoological Park or indeed of the more general ones of the society, an Alaskan Indian totem pole and chief's house were erected in the park in the fall of 1904. Edward H. Harriman had found them abandoned by the Tlinkit Indians at Cape Fox during his Alaskan expedition in 1899 and had offered them to the society. He was willing to pay the shipping and erection expenses, and in those days few gifts were rejected.

Inevitably, there was a conflict of opinion as to where they should be set up. Hornaday proposed two sites: on the east side of the Bronx River at the upper end of Lake Agassiz, or on the east side of the Aquatic Mammals Pond almost in the center of the park. Grant and Professor Osborn rather favored the Lake Agassiz site, but Hornaday preferred the other. By the summer of 1904 he had talked them into his view, and the house and pole went up according to approved Tlinkit traditions. "It is," Hornaday said, "absolutely necessary that an Alaskan Indian house and totem pole should front on water and be backed by forest." The Aquatic Mammals Pond (now the Wildfowl Pond) met one condition, and the grove of tall trees to the east, surrounding the wild-turkey enclosure, met the other. The carved pole and the painted house were a striking and incongruous feature of the center of the park until June of 1942, when they were given to the Museum of the American Indian–Heye Foundation at Broadway and 155th Street. No one then could foresee the day thirty years later when the society would buy another totem pole to form an accent at the south end of the rebuilt Alaskan brown-bear exhibit.

July 4, 1905, saw the opening of the new Bird House, the third major structure on Baird Court, and in the society's *Bulletin* Curator Beebe boldly asserted that "From an aesthetic and utilitarian point of view, there is no doubt that it excels most other buildings of its kind in the world." Within a year he was going to be called upon to defend that statement.

Beebe had contributed most of the ideas for the interior design (Heins & La Farge were the architects), and the spacious quarters he provided for small perching birds were entirely within the park's original policy of giving its animals plenty of room. There were many innovations. The building had a roof of thick ribbed glass, and many panels could be raised for ventilation. The center of the north hall was given over to a flying cage thirty-six feet long, fifteen feet wide, and almost twenty feet high. Palms in tubs and hanging baskets of flowering vines were installed, "thus happily combining a profusion of flowers with brightly-colored song birds."

When the July, 1905, issue of the *Bulletin* reached England, there was an outraged reaction from two conservative correspondents of *Avicultural Magazine,* the journal of the Avicultural Society. They had only scorn for such an unconventional approach to the keeping of small birds. As one of them wrote, "The New York experiment is simply grotesque and can only have been conceived by someone entirely unacquainted with birds."

In the first place, the writer asserted, you can't introduce new birds into large aviaries already occupied by a number of species; the newcomers are often so dazed they refuse to eat, and die. Anyway, greedy species eat all the food and more timid birds starve. Everyone knows that the New York climate is given to violent fluctuations, and the glass roof

would cook the birds in summer and freeze them in winter. As for the glass giving diffused light for living plants, that idea would be "a very pretty one if it were only practicable." Mice and rats would invade the earth provided for the plants. The New York upstarts planned picture labels to identify all the species in the large cages, did they? The public would never be able to figure out what was what.

Furthermore, the New York Bird House had its values all wrong: "In a public institution like the Zoological Gardens, the interests of the visitors should certainly be considered in the first instance, that of the birds next."

Curator Beebe replied by return mail when *Avicultural Magazine* reached him. He conceded the terrors of the New York climate, but pointed out that the building had thermostats to regulate the heat in winter and that the glass roof was whitewashed to break the force of the sun in summer. Mice *had* been a problem, but traps, terriers, and sparrow hawks had almost eliminated them. There had been not the slightest difficulty in introducing new birds, and as for identification:

Overleaf:
The Bird House and the
Seal Lion Pool about 1907.

169

I have found that most of the American public possess a large share of that curiosity which is so pronounced a characteristic of many of our more humble brethren of the earth. I have often seen people pass rapidly by several cages, each of which contained a single species, giving but a glance at the label. But in the case of the great central cage, where some 150 birds live happily together, the task of identifying some interesting member of the fifty-odd species offers itself as a fascinating game. The result is that considerable knowledge of several species of birds is gained.

His most vociferous critic had the last word.

[Mr. Beebe] states that the American public pass by separate cages containing but a single specimen or species, and are most attracted by collections of large numbers. That I can well believe. But I fancy that elsewhere the case is somewhat different. We all know that life in America, and especially in New York, is much more strenuous than it is in Europe. The American public want to see as much as possible in a short time, either owing to lack of time or to the habit of doing most things more quickly and on a large scale. We in Europe are habitually less in a hurry, and more interested in details than in admiration of huge numbers.

But perhaps this was not the last word. Beebe, the birds, and the American public had it after all, for the Bird House *was* a resounding success until newer and more dramatic methods of exhibiting birds came along in the 1960s and 1970s. It even extended its use of glass in 1906 by the addition of the so-called Glass Court for American songbirds to the southeastern corner of the building.

Along with new buildings, the first years of the century brought a lessening of the occasional tension between Hornaday on the one side and Professor Osborn and Madison Grant on the other. It was largely attributable to a prickliness on Hornaday's part, for he was always inclined to see snubs where none existed. It rankled him that he had not been made a member of the Boone and Crockett Club—after all, he had probably killed more big game than all the club members put together, and his conservation credentials were certainly first-class. Thus when the club planned to hold a luncheon meeting in the Rocking Stone Restaurant, he informed Grant that he did not expect to attend as official host; Beebe or Ditmars could do the honors. Osborn promptly squashed that fit of pique, however, pointing out that as director of the Zoological Park Hornaday could not let his personal feelings guide his official actions. Hornaday acceded, attended the luncheon, and some years later was made an associate member of the club.

It has been remarked by a British critic that "conventional Americans have been brought up to think it bad manners to express opinion, with the result that they sound bland." No such charge could ever have been made against Osborn, Grant, or Hornaday. They had strong opinions about everything; and if those of Osborn and Grant were perhaps the more heavily weighted because of their positions on the board of managers, Hornaday was no kowtowing employee; he might have to give in before the heavy artillery, but he always spoke his mind before, during, and sometimes after his capitulation.

Grant felt that Hornaday's taste was sometimes questionable, especially in matters of landscaping, and that he and Osborn would have to keep a close watch on him. This was often difficult to do in the very early days when so much was going on simultaneously and the man on the scene had to make dozens of decisions every day. When he could, Hornaday scrupulously consulted with Professor Osborn by letter or telephone, but even though the mails were astonishingly fast in those days, action might have to be taken immediately. Telephoning was precarious; the American Museum of Natural History was poorly equipped with telephones and Hornaday complained of wasted hours trying to reach Osborn or, when it was a matter of informing the museum's taxidermy department that an important animal had died and could be picked up, the official who had to be notified.

And so Hornaday often went ahead and did what he

thought was right, and bickered with the chairman of the executive committee later. His correspondence often gives the impression that he felt himself a much-abused man, and his resentment could take an almost childish form, as in the great Monkey House paint controversy. Hornaday had ordered some of the cages in the new building painted, against the wishes of Osborn and the architects, Heins & La Farge. On his next visit to the park, the professor noticed the paint and ordered that the remaining installations be left unpainted. That "interference" brought a hurt letter from Hornaday to the chairman:

I note with much interest the fact that you have finally decided to sustain the Architects in their claim to superior judgment and authority regarding the interior of the cages in the new Monkey House. Of course I accede to your decision as final, and I have nothing more to say on the subject, except this: This victory of your Architects will mark the beginning of a new era in my relations with the Park, and with them. Hereafter, whenever they wish to commit further blunders in their work, they will not meet with the slightest opposition from me; and henceforth my relations with them will be on a very different basis.

Professor Osborn probably knew that boilers have safety valves for letting off steam, and that writing such letters as this was Hornaday's safety valve. In any event, he could not have taken Hornaday seriously very long, for less than two weeks later he received a two-page letter from the director blasting the architects for specifying glass partitions between the floor cages in the Monkey House ("thin glass, and will be easily broken"), and beaded lumber in the rear, "so carefully provided with innumerable grooves to catch the greatest possible amount of dirt." Either because he was tired of the squabbling or more likely because he recognized the force of Hornaday's arguments, Osborn instructed Heins & La Farge that most of the director's points should be accepted.

In fact, while Osborn was temperamentally inclined to rule by fiat and to nag Hornaday on matters that the director, as

174

an animal man, was better equipped to cope with, he was usually fair and considerate, especially after the first five years, when his own paleontological work and writing took virtually all his time. There was a noticeable slackening off of peremptory letters and hotly worded replies between Hornaday and Osborn, and between Hornaday and Grant, by that time. Of course they may have been in constant acerbic telephonic communication, but enough genial notes survive to indicate that after the first rush was over, Osborn had begun to feel that Hornaday had been so well indoctrinated in the Osborn-Grant principles that he could be trusted to go ahead without much close supervision. After one minor blowup in the summer of 1902 about the location of a soda-water pavilion in Beaver Valley (Hornaday wanted it left there because it was a good moneymaker; Osborn wanted it out because it spoiled the vista) , Osborn wrote to the director:

I sometimes imagine myself as a centre with five lines of conflicting interests radiating off in different directions, the ends of which are Messrs. Hornaday, LaFarge, Heins, Caparn, and sometimes but rarely Grant. Everyone desires to go on his own basis, and finish up the Park in his own style and according to his own ideas of beauty or fitness. So in the present case everyone is totally opposed to everyone else, and judging by your letter, it remains for me to do as I have to do in all these cases, to try to bring about that happy union of conflicting and aesthetic senses which will produce the best results for the Park.

He penned at the bottom of another letter in a somewhat similar vein, "A *director* as well as a *chairman* must join the order Pachydermata."

Run-ins between Hornaday and Grant were rarer, perhaps because the latter had learned to work through Professor Osborn when he had suggestions to make (Hornaday strongly and vociferously objected to getting Osborn's orders "second hand" through Grant) , or perhaps because Grant's work as the paid secretary of the society was taking more and more of his time. By the end of 1901 the executive committee had realized that the charter of 1896, so hastily cobbled on the model of Andrew H. Green's original bill, was not altogether satisfactory. It stated, for example, that "No manager of said corporation shall receive any compensation for his services, nor be interested, directly or indirectly, in any contract concerning its property or affairs."

Grant, as the secretary of the society, had to do an immense amount of work connected with membership and fund raising, and was certainly entitled to compensation, which the charter provision precluded. Furthermore, Section 2 had restricted the society to the establishment of a zoological park, advancing the study of zoology, furnishing "instruction and recreation to the people," and limited it to holding animals, plants, and specimens appropriate to these objects. This was much too restrictive, and so two modifications were introduced in Albany and were passed without opposition. One struck out the words "No manager of said corporation shall receive any compensation for his services" and the other broadened the scope of the society acceptably:

> Said corporation shall have power to establish, maintain, and control zoological parks, gardens, or other collections for the promotion of zoology and kindred subjects, and for the instruction and recreation of the people. Said corporation may collect, hold, and expend funds for zoological research and publication, for the protection of wild animal life, and for kindred purposes, and may promote, form, and co-operate with other associations with similar purposes, and may purchase, sell, or exchange animals, plants and specimens appropriate to the objects for which it was created.

The bill as amended was signed on March 13, 1902, and Grant, who had given in his *pro forma* resignation as secretary the previous December, resumed—or, rather, continued—his work as official secretary. He never had actually ceased to carry out the secretary's duties.

Unlike Osborn, Grant avoided head-on collisions with

Hornaday, but he had his own ideas about landscaping and planting, at least. He studied the forested areas of the park and concluded that the characteristic trees were tulip, oak, and beech, and since they were now approaching maturity, he felt that replacements should be planted. He wrote to Osborn—not Hornaday—about this, suggesting that if poplars and maples were planted, slow-growing trees should also be put in. "Hornaday, of course, is inclined to look for immediate results, and is not offended by the maple." Grant's own preferences were for beeches, hornbeams, lindens, tulips, and oaks, and he opposed elms on Baird Court; New England was full of them, and they were monotonous.

In the perspective of three-quarters of a century, it is too bad that Grant's dislike of elms did not permanently carry the day. European lindens were planted around Baird Court at first, but by 1907 they were pulled out and replaced on Professor Osborn's orders by native elms of three and a half to four inch caliper. The disaster of the Dutch elm disease was far in the future and elms were considered faster-growing and more graceful.

Grant's dendrological theories were so close to those of Chief Forester Merkel that little conflict arose. Merkel was given a more or less free hand under the general keep-it-natural policies of H. A. Caparn, the landscape architect, and Herbert Parsons, the park's consulting engineer; and the nursery that Merkel established on the east side of the Bronx River provided literally thousands of young trees, shrubs and bushes. George Skene, who joined Merkel's staff on January 1, 1904, and in the next forty-two and a half years became successively gardener, head gardener, and general foreman of maintenance, recalled after his retirement in 1946: "Much of the massive planting that today is so natural a part of the Zoo's landscaping that it seems always to have been there, actually was planted about 1905."

Quite apart from its decorative, windbreaking, and screening purposes—screening against the tall apartment houses be-

177

ginning to rise south and west of the park—the planting of hundreds of trees became necessary in the summer of 1905 because the forest suddenly began to be thinned by the chestnut blight. There is no indication that it started its depredations in the Zoological Park and spread from there, but it was discovered and first identified there in midsummer. Merkel noticed that leaves on the chestnuts were withering and that branch after branch was dying. He sent a specimen branch to the Department of Agriculture in Washington and got back word that it was Cytospora, a fungoid growth, that was killing the trees. Orders were immediately issued to cut and burn all diseased branches and to spray with copper sulphate or Bordeaux mixture (there were 486 chestnuts in the Park at the beginning of 1906, and Merkel hoped four hundred could be saved). But the spread of the disease could not be arrested and in a very few years chestnuts throughout the eastern United States were gone. Shoots do come up from the roots of otherwise dead trees, but they are doomed when they are little more than saplings.

It was in the earliest years of the park that a device soon to become familiar to visitors to zoological and other parks throughout the country came into being. This was the Bronx Park basket, a little container formed and painted, for the sake of unobtrusiveness, to resemble a tree stump about three feet high. Hornaday invented it. On one of his western trips he had encountered A. L. Adams of the Steel Basket Company of Cedar Rapids, Iowa, and made sketches of a sheet-metal stump he thought Adams could sell widely among institutions and individuals—if he could make the dies for stamping them out of heavy-gauge iron. Adams worked hard at it. His first designs were merely three-foot-high columns, randomly crimped to resemble bark and painted mottled bark color; the flare of roots at the base of the "stump" defeated him for more than a year, but by the summer of 1902 he had the problem licked and was producing stump baskets in quantity. Merkel came up with an

The "Stump Trash Basket" designed by Director Hornaday. The metal shell was crinkled and painted to resemble a stump.

improvement, suggesting that an inner receptacle be designed, so that it could be lifted out of the permanently placed stump and the litter contents dumped in a wagon.

Adams proposed stamping Hornaday's name on the basket, but Hornaday declined the honor:

I do not think it would be wise for you to place my name on the baskets. They should bear no name save your own, because the presence of your name will help to advertise the manufacturer, which is the desirable thing. If you wish to give it, in your catalogue, another name,—for convenience,—it would not be a bad plan to call it the "Bronx Basket," or, the "Bronx Park Basket." There is no objection whatever to your saying in your catalogue, or circulars, that it was designed by me, if that would help it any. I will place one of these baskets in the backyard at my house, where it will be a great comfort to my wife, in connection with the lawn; and it will also serve as a very pleasant reminder of our meeting on the other side of the continent.

Subsequently the Zoological Park ordered a dozen baskets, which its own painters finished off to look like bark. None of those prototypes exist in the Zoological Park nowadays, and in any event in the early 1930s they were superseded by even more realistic poured-concrete stumps with a closed top and a generous "knothole" through which trash could be deposited. They were so designed that a draft space was left around the base and the trash could be burned *in situ* instead of being lifted out and carted away—and smoky, evil-smelling stumps they were, too. (A city ordinance now makes such trash burning illegal.) Almost all have now been replaced by lightweight metal or plastic trash barrels lined with disposable plastic bags that can be tossed onto a pickup truck.

As one stirs through the archives of those early days when Hornaday was at the peak of his vigor and thrusting the park's development ahead on a dozen fronts at once, the multiplicity of big and little problems he tackled single-handedly and simultaneously gives an impressive measure

An "improved" version of Hornaday's metal "Stump Trash Basket." It was cast in concrete and designed so trash could be burned.

179

of the man's capacity for work. He had a competent staff, but it was a one-man operation nevertheless. Raymond L. Ditmars, as the assistant curator in charge of mammals, was surely diplomatic enough to fend off the ASPCA when it forwarded a complaint by a woman that the Zoological Park's sea lions were always barking and therefore must be unhappy. But Hornaday handled the complaint himself: "As a matter of fact, these sea lions are of the species known as the Barking Sea Lion, and when they are in the best health, they bark the loudest."

On second thoughts, perhaps Ditmars would *not* have had the self-assurance (or the gall) to proclaim a species so conveniently named the "Barking Sea Lion." He might less convincingly have tried to explain that barking is merely the normal conversational mode of the California sea lion (*Zalophus californianus*) and has nothing to do with its well-being.

Letters to the newspapers and aggrieved visitors, notes to the staff, formal orders to keepers and watchmen and gatemen, poured out of Hornaday's office in the Service Building in an accelerated stream during those early days. He was never at a loss for a phrase or a decision. Then as now, visitors delighted in feeding the animals, and a Japanese bear died as a result of injudicious feeding. Hornaday wrote:

In peach-time, some kind friend who loves animals and thinks the Park people are too particular, gave him [the bear] four large peaches. Two weeks ago poor Jappie's skin went down to the American Museum. Moral: if you must kill a captive animal, a gun is more merciful than peaches, candy, peanuts, and tobacco, and far more respectable.

He was not to be taken in by a hard-luck story, either. A lad named William Brown wrote to him:

Kind Sir. While visiting your Zoological Gardens today in Bronx Park I met with an occurrence which I assure you does not benefit me in the least, as I am a young man with out a very high standing in life with a mother and a sister relying on my support and a few dollars spent foolishly on things that could be avoided if your Park Keepers were a little more careful.

As I was walking along the Public Path in your Gardens I happened to be crowded to the wire fencing and the wire being connected in such a fashion that my trousers caught on it and consequently tore them in a manner which leave me to go to the expense of either buying a new pair or stay in the house after working all day, and as I am in no financial standing at present I cannot afford to buy a new pair.

Now Dear Sir what I want to know Is there any possible way that I may recover my loss. I would deem it a great favor on your part if you would assist me in doing so and by so doing you will favor not only me but my aged Mother.

The director informed William by return of post that it was up to visitors to look out for themselves while in the Park.

Generally Hornaday enjoyed full cooperation from the local police precinct, but individual policemen were sometimes a sore trial. A man and his wife picnicking on the bank of the Bronx River were narrowly missed by a shot fired by a policeman at a blue heron wading in the shallows. Another man, apprehended while felling a spruce tree in the park, claimed he had been put up to it by a policeman who wanted the tree for a flagpole. Hornaday wrote all particulars, including the name of the policeman, to the precinct captain, but the woodsman couldn't or wouldn't identify the police officer when the matter came to trial.

People, including the park's own personnel, took nearly as much of the director's time as the animals. Rudolph Bell, after Hornaday's early misgivings about hiring a circus man as cook for the animal departments, turned out to be an excellent chef but less admirable in other ways. He got a stiff note from Hornaday warning him against "lewd, obscene language." "Tax Payer" wrote an anonymous letter to the director, asserting that Bell was sneaking out at quitting time with meat, fish, rice, apples and other fruits. It was never proved on him, though. Bell was later called on the carpet for allegedly taking a pair of fallow-deer antlers to Noah's Saloon to be raffled off. He denied it, and the matter was dropped, although it was something of a mystery how antlers that could have come only from the park found their way to a saloon known to be frequented by the cook.

Bell's behavior, if not his language, may have improved over the years. In any event, he was soon high enough in Hornaday's estimation to be appointed a deputy game warden (along with John J. "Jack" Rose, a carpenter) and to be sent out on Sundays under Merkel's supervision to rid the wilder parts of the park and lower Westchester County of poachers and pothunters. An area just west of the park was locally known as Little Italy, and in the tradition of their native land the inhabitants had always considered it their right to shoot robins, thrushes, bluejays, or any other wild bird large enough not to be obliterated by a shotgun blast or rifle bullet. Hornaday declared war on them in both the spring and fall migrating seasons, and on one Sunday raid the park's wardens arrested fifteen men, one of whom had forty-three songbirds in his bag. The wardens found and destroyed countless snares set for small birds in the park and made special efforts to round up squirrel hunters, who had almost wiped out the park's wild-squirrel population by the fall of 1903. Fortunately the courts cooperated by handing out fines of as much as fifty dollars and ten days in jail, and Hornaday jubilantly reported in 1906 that Bell and Rose had swept through lower Westchester every Sunday since April 1 without finding a single bird hunter.

If any shooting was to be done within the boundaries of the Zoological Park, the park's own personnel would do it. Its armament was limited for the first few years to the brace of Smith & Wesson revolvers Madison Grant had advised Hornaday to buy. (A night watchman accidentally shot himself in the leg with one of them, was treated at Fordham Hospital, and carried home in a pushcart.) Rats, mink, and weasels were attracted by the surplus animal food in buildings and on the ranges, and vermin squads were formed after Hornaday advertised in *Recreation* for shotguns and small-caliber rifles its readers could spare. He gave firm assurance that the guns would not be used for killing game, any time, anywhere. When possible, the weasels and mink were trapped and put on exhibition, but sometimes they were too bold and wary and had to be shot. Merkel saw a mink dragging an eighteen-inch fish out of the river and Hornaday directed Bird Keeper Sam Stacey to go gunning for it. Starlings were increasing to pest proportions as early as 1903 (they were the descendants of sixty birds brought from Europe and liberated in Central Park in 1890), and Hornaday predicted that they would soon become as great a pest as the house sparrow.

The worst problem, however, was with packs of dogs. The Zoological Park was only partially fenced, particularly along its northern border, and the Park Commissioner made captious objections to rigging a dogproof fence in sight of Pelham Parkway or even under the bridge across the Bronx River—for dogs were slipping into the park across the ice in midwinter and killing deer on the open range. The only solution until the fence controversy was settled was to send out nightly patrols of eight men armed with shotguns and rifles. A private census revealed seventy-one dogs—all unlicensed—belonging to seventy houses in the neighborhood, and the ASPCA was called in. It collected a "wagonload" of dogs in Bronxdale alone.

It would be hard to say whether Hornaday on balance considered New York's newspapers blessings or bêtes noires. A little of both, perhaps, depending on how they handled the news from the Zoological Park. They could certainly be depended upon for straight reporting of such image-building news as the annual meetings of the Zoological Society's members, generous gifts to the society's funds by prominent citizens, or the opening of new buildings, but they were entirely unscrupulous about making up stories out of nothing or manufacturing a crisis where none existed—at least not what Director Hornaday was willing to call a crisis. The *Herald* rebuked him for the loss of his "nose for news" in an article headed "Mr. Hornaday as a Press Censor," citing a Hornaday editorial in the January, 1905, number of the *Bulletin* in which he had warned members of the Zoological Society that "about ninety per cent. of the published stories of fearful adventure by and with the animals of the Zoological Park are fictitious." The director claimed editorially that since the inception of the Zoological Park there had been only three really exciting incidents within its boundaries: the escape of a black-tailed python, the escape of a black bear that bit two persons before it was recaptured, and the escape and subsequent killing of a snow leopard. That animal, he said, was "murdered at midnight by a conjunction of rattled men, when it might easily have been caught if anyone present had done one thing with good judgment."

Oh, yeah? was the tenor of the *Herald's* reply. What about the puma that escaped in 1902 and inspired terror in the heart of every mother in the neighborhood? Or the operation on the eye of a deadly cobra—wasn't that an exciting incident? Or the buffalo bulls that fought until one of them was fatally injured and had to be shot? Weren't those newsworthy stories?

It must be admitted by anyone who scans the director's private card file of "Important Events" for 1902–14 that quite a number of escapes and near escapes occurred in those early days and that the crises, real or fictitious, reported in the newspapers were probably far from the complete total. On the other hand, Hornaday did have a good case against the press in its handling of the second puma escape, this one in 1905. According to his editorial, it was a small puma "about as dangerous as a cross fox terrier" and it was herded into a shifting box alongside its cage within fifteen minutes. Animal dramas, however, were likely to increase as the square of the distance from the scene. Thus in newspapers in London and

Paris, the puma became a lion that bounded over a keeper's head when he opened the cage door, and streaked for the forest. Fifty men armed with "guns and agricultural equipment" were said to have chased the lion into a dark corner behind the Monkey House, and finally recaptured it through a combination of baited trap and fire hose. Hornaday's private file showed that nothing of the kind happened. He fulminated against such exaggerations; he never became hardened to them.

The Incident of the Flies brought a quick jab from him. On one of his visits to the park Professor Osborn complained about an excessive number of flies in the animal buildings. It was midsummer and manure removal was still at a fairly primitive level, so the director consulted with the veterinarian and dishes of water poisoned with arsenic were placed at strategic spots, particularly in the Small Mammal House. The arsenic killed the flies—but did it also kill a number of animals that ate the dead flies?

Mammal Keeper William Caldwell said it did and told newspapers that when he came to work the next morning a red fox, blue fox, bush-tailed wallaby, nine-banded armadillo, angora guinea pig, and an opossum were dead and a sun bear and giant anteater were in convulsions.

The director rebutted that story vigorously. Three—not six—animals had died about the time the arsenic water was put out, but their death was not caused by poison. As for Keeper Caldwell, "Ex-keeper Caldwell is a combination liar, and incompetent."

Sometimes newspaper stories were merely silly. The *Evening Journal* enlivened a dull day by reporting that the Zoological Park's giraffe was suffering from a midwinter sore throat. The Tonsiline Co. of Canton, Ohio, saw its chance—a giraffe was its trademark—and dispatched a four-ounce bottle of Tonsiline with full directions for use, asking only to be informed if the remedy was as effective as it was sure it would be. Less commercially minded, a man in Schenectady wrote:

185

I see that all medicine you have used has failed. I send you a bottle of medicine that never failes if you follow the directions in this letter. if it don't help the animal I dont want any Pay for it and if it does give me what you think is right. I am the only man that makes the medicine

Hornaday wrote and thanked them all, but explained that the giraffe did *not* have a sore throat.

In those days, attack was commonplace and the director's usual method of defense was a fierce counterattack. He employed it in the great Smells Battle of 1908.

It started with a well-meaning letter to Hornaday from a realtor named John J. Murphy, a former secretary of the Citizens Union.

I am a resident of the Bronx, and often visit the Zoo. I have seen many animal collections, in various parts of the world, but have seen none which, in my judgment, surpasses the New York exhibit in the perfection of the appointment of its completed parts. It is because I have noticed a defect which I think to be remediable that I write you. I refer to the offense odors, which make a stay in some of the houses unendurable. As long as there seemed to be no help for this, I did not think it worth while to write you. At the present time, where the smell is very bad some kind of "disinfectant" is used which is almost, if not quite, as offensive, as the smell it is intended to cloak. I have been aware of the existence, for some time of a perfectly odorless deodorant, which would, in my judgment, do away entirely with the cause of offence. I have used it in my home for a couple of summers with the best results.

If you are interested in a possible solution of the evil of which I speak, I will be glad to talk with you about it some day, though I have none but a public interest in the matter, not being the owner or in any way interested in the sale of the article to which I refer.

The director's reply gave no hint of the volcano that was about to erupt.

Of course I was greatly interested by the contents of your letter, and first of all I will be glad to know *which* buildings you found

186

objectionable in odor. We have ten large buildings, and before we can discuss the question intelligently, it is necessary for me to know the particular buildings to which you refer.

I will remark, however, that the Small Mammal House contains so many civet cats secreting their peculiar musky odor, that there is no means whatever by which that odor can be wholly eradicated. In some of the Zoological Gardens of Europe, those animals are not kept, on account of that odor. We have, however, resolved to keep representatives of this group, and reduce this disagreeable feature to its lowest terms. We have tried here about *twenty* disinfectants, each of which in its turn has been presented to us as "the best one." Notwithstanding this, we are now trying another.

Murphy took the bait:

While the Small Mammal House is the worst, several of the others are very bad and none but the reptile house is free from offence. Hence I don't think the somewhat optimistic tone of your question, warranted by the facts.

As the simplest way of bringing the matter before you clearly, I have handed your letter to one of my fellow club members [The National Arts Club, New York], Dr. James C. Bayles, who first called my attention to the odorless deodorant of which I wrote. Dr. Bayles was formerly President of the Board of Health.

As he takes an intelligent interest in such matters, I have asked him to write to you. He can tell you scientifically how the material works.

Retribution came by return of post. Hornaday replied to Murphy:

I am simply amazed by your letter, wherein you say that "while the Small Mammal House is the worst, several of the others are very bad, and *none but the Reptile House is free from offense.*"

So far as I am aware, that is the most comprehensive unjust statement ever made about the Zoological Park. I am glad that you have made it thoroughly sweeping, for that will enable every person who has ever visited the Park to fix the value of your opinion. Fortunately, also, it is only an opinion, of a single individual, and not necessarily a statement of fact.

In this connection it is a satisfaction to recall the fact that hundreds of persons have taken pains to speak to me, and to other officers of the Park, of the unusual cleanliness of our buildings, and above all the absence from the Monkey House of the usual offensive odors that prevail in such houses in European zoos. Because of this fact our Monkey House has been reproduced in Rotterdam in all its essential details.

I assure you that such a thoroughly unjust opinion as you have recorded in your letter is not calculated to advance with us any cause in which you may be interested.

In the benighted days of 1908, mail delivery was swift. Murphy replied the next day:

No good can come from the continuance of a correspondence which has reached the point of imputing interested motives to one of the parties. I would leave you to enjoy the keen satisfaction which undoubtedly arises in the official mind from the crushing of one more critic who has dared to offer a suggestion concerning a matter which is not his business.

I have written to Dr. Bayles to whom I transmitted your previous letter, withdrawing my suggestion that he communicate with you.

He was too late. Dr. Bayles had acted immediately after being shown the director's first letter and with restrained enthusiasm asked for Hornaday's "approval and cooperation in an effort to determine whether the cage of the civet cats, for example, can be deodorized." The subject of unpleasant odors, he said, "is one which greatly interests me as a matter of scientific experiment."

There was certainly nothing in Dr. Bayles's letter that the director could seize upon as a peg for a diatribe, but he took another swipe at Murphy nevertheless.

The fact that you are in touch with Mr. J. J. Murphy shall not prejudice me in the least against your evident desire to do us a great service, although I must say that his last letter is quite sufficient to make any one in my position view with positive repugnance anything emanating from him.

He went on to explain to Dr. Bayles that the odorless powder he proposed to use on the excreta of the civet cats did not meet the requirements; it was not the excreta but the animals themselves that offended: "Every inch of their fur and skin surface is a natural scent-sachet for the retention and diffusion of the odors from their scent glands."

He feared, too, that Bayles's powder might be licked off their fur by the cats, and they would be harmed by it.

By the time of his next letter, two days later, Bayles had been shown the letter in which Hornaday slapped Murphy down, and the doctor tried to calm Hornaday.

I much regret that Mr. Murphy should have said anything meeting your disapproval. He is a charming man, of the highest principles; but he is an Irishman, bubbling over with fun, and his sense of humor sometimes leads him into unintentional indiscretions in correspondence. That nothing could have been further from his purpose to offend you I am quite sure.

Bayles was able to assure Hornaday that the deodorizing powder was quite harmless; he had himself taken into his stomach and intestinal tract much larger quantities than any animal would be likely to ingest. He promised to come up to the park the following week and see what he could do about deodorizing a series of cages.

Presumably he did so, but the correspondence broke off at this point and results of the experiment were not recorded. Bayles's powder was no panacea; civets still stink.

In between times, if he had nothing else to do, the director of the Zoological Park could have made a career settling bets and arguments. A Harvard student wanted to know whether the giraffe was extinct, or nearly so; there had been much discussion about this among his friends. If Dr. Hornaday didn't know, would Hagenbeck, the circus man, have any ideas?

Lake Forest College in Illinois checked in with a query about the ability of anthropoid apes to wiggle their ears. Hornaday replied: "I am very sure that none of the anthro-

189

poid apes have the power to move their ears; nor, for that matter, the gibbon. I do not believe that any of the higher monkeys have that power."

Dogmatism became Hornaday—he could put a good face on almost anything—but on rare occasions he was willing to express merely a mild and reasonable opinion. A New York man wrote a pleasantly observant filler in one of the newspapers about a robin he had watched as it hunted for worms, turning its head sideways before dragging a worm from the grass. Did Hornaday think it was listening, or looking? The director inclined to the latter. "I have been greatly amused by this trick of the robin, and also astonished by the keenness of the mental faculties, whatever they are, which enables one of these birds to discover a worm in the thick grass of a lawn. I have, myself, tried to see worms through the grass, as robins do; but never found one."

Nor could anything be less dogmatic than his reply to a correspondent in the State Historical Department of Iowa, who wanted to know whether Hornaday believed snakes swallow their young in time of danger. He replied:

It is impossible either to verify or disprove the question about snakes swallowing their young. Many credible persons say that they have seen this phenomenon. The worst of it is that no naturalist ever has seen this thing happen, and so far as I know, all Herpetologists believe that the like never occurs. As for myself, I am really inclined to think that it does occur, under certain conditions, which naturalists know nothing about. So many persons have said that they have seen it that I really believe it; but my opinion in the matter amounts to nothing.

The question still pops up in the morning mail of herpetologists in zoological parks and natural-history museums, despite decades of being knocked down by experts less impressed than Hornaday by letters beginning something like "My grandfather once saw a snake swallowing its young, and he remembers it as clearly as if it were yesterday."

Hornaday was adhering to the generally safe principle

that except for certain patent impossibilities, it is unwise to be adamant about the capabilities of a given animal. Thus, when he had agreed to be umpire to a controversy in Pennsylvania as to whether snakes can hiss, he replied that some can and some can't, citing the hog-nosed snake, pine snake, and bull snake among the hissers, and went on:

In conclusion, I wish to enunciate a principle which is worth remembering in connection with all observations upon animal life. It is this: it is hazardous, and often unwise, to make any general statement regarding the things which animals of any given class can or "can not" do. The animal world furnishes as many exceptions to general rules as can be found in the affairs of men. For myself, I am exceedingly chary of saying what animals "can not" do.

Two days later he went out on a limb and sawed it at least partly off. To another Pennsylvanian he wrote:

I never saw a crow which was able to talk, and I do not believe there is any way by which a bird of that species could be taught to articulate. Pray do not on any account permit anyone to operate upon the tongue of the bird, because it could not possibly accomplish the object desired. There are birds of several species which seem to talk,—of this, the Magpie is a conspicuous example,—but the articulation of words is quite another matter.

He was writing, of course, long before the days of the celebrated Deacon, a mascot crow in the Zoological Park's Children's Zoo, which spring after spring perched beside the entrance and greeted children with a well-articulated "Hello!"

Or sometimes for the novelty of it, "Good-bye!"

In the first decade of this century, so much was happening at the Zoological Park and both Professor Osborn and Madison Grant were so immersed in its problems that they had little time to spare for the Aquarium and *its* problems—which were many and serious.

The Zoological Society had accepted the management of the Aquarium with the explicit understanding that the city would provide funds for its repair, improvement, and maintenance, and it had no intention of putting its own money into an operation it had undertaken more or less as a favor to the city. Since the city was legally obligated to provide no more than $50,000 a year for maintenance (and in practice rarely appropriated more than $45,000), which was supposed to pay everything from salaries to the purchase of live specimens and the cost of the gas lighting, Director Charles H. Townsend had to be a careful housekeeper. His yearly report of Aquarium Maintenance Fund expenditures typically ended with something like "Balance unexpended . . . $25.14."

The city did make a gesture toward improvement and repair, appropriating $30,000 for 1903 and $40,000 for 1904, and the interior of the old building began to be less gloomy. Visitors could actually see the fishes. The director was by nature optimistic, and in the April, 1903, number of the *Bulletin* he wrote: "The New York Aquarium, while having many serious defects, is by no means ill-adapted to the purpose for which it is now used." The summer before, he had visited the principal aquariums of Europe and was "inclined to the opinion that a circular building, with an exhibition hall, like that of the New York Aquarium, is more satisfactory than one whose collections are arranged along narrow corridors." He changed his mind during the next few years; and after a succession of plans had been drawn up, showing how the existing building could be enlarged to permit more and bigger exhibits as well as offices and a laboratory, the director and the executive committee concluded that what they wanted was an entirely new building, and one that was *not* circular.

11

Lively Times at the Aquarium

For a few halcyon months it seemed they were going to get it. By 1911 the society was resolved to put itself behind an effort to gain for New York an aquarium truly worthy of the city, and it commissioned a grandiose model that was put on display in the American Museum of Natural History. One may suppose that Townsend had given a great deal of thought to the internal design and that he aimed at spectacular tank exhibits; nothing less could have lived up to the colonnaded exterior that would have put to shame the public edifices of Washington, to say nothing of those of New York. The city fell under the spell and approved a corporate stock issue of $200,000 for the foundation and wings of the new building. The society was so bemused by the city's generosity that in its *Annual Report* for 1911, while admitting that no part of the $200,000 had actually been expended as yet, it announced that in the spring of 1912 it intended to ask for an additional $600,000 in construction funds.

"The Aquarium of Our Dreams," Director Townsend called it in a sad, retrospective article in the *Bulletin* four years later. The Board of Estimate and Apportionment had looked the other way when the $600,000 was asked for, and in 1913 the city said quite positively that it was not going ahead with a new building. The bubble burst, and all the society got was the beautiful white model and $26,250 to reimburse the architects for their preliminary work. The rest of the initial $200,000 went back to the city treasury.

Townsend had every right to be disgruntled. The Aquarium was the most popular "museum" in New York; in 1909, the year of the Hudson-Fulton Celebration, it had 3,803,501 visitors—64,795 of them in one day. He wrote in the *Bulletin:*

Other museums in New York are endowed with millions of dollars, but it seems that the Aquarium does not appeal to those who make bequests. Under present conditions the institution cannot have any growth. It has the misfortune to be housed in an unsuitable building, which it long ago completely filled. Like the crab

193

and the lobster, the Aquarium cannot grow without shedding its old shell. Other museums have room for new exhibits, but the Aquarium has not. When especially attractive specimens arrive, those of less interest must be fed to the sea lion or the porpoise to make room for them.

The main hall of the Aquarium in 1905.

It was a complaint he was to repeat time and again in the next few years, often with harrowing details. At the time of new-moon tides, sea water rose so high in the boiler and pump rooms that the stokers had to wear hip boots while shoveling wet coal into the furnace from half-submerged wheelbarrows. Sometimes the pumps were flooded and the fires extinguished, so that there was no heat or circulating water until the tide fell. Four days' coal was all the Aquarium

194

had room to store, and when the Commissioner of Parks ordered the unsightly coal shed removed, the margin dropped to two days. In the winter of 1917 the building had to be closed to visitors for several days and "the living collections would probably have been lost had it not been for twenty-five tons' emergency supply [of coal] long hidden in an underground pipe conduit."

Dr. Townsend [Washington and Jefferson College in Washington, Pennsylvania, awarded him an honorary Sc.D. in 1909] must have felt that the Aquarium was the permanent poor relation of the Zoological Park. But, as everyone knows, true worth will always be recognized and rewarded, and the Aquarium's day was coming.

In 1921 the executive committee decided that conditions at the Aquarium really were intolerable, that the city was not going to act, and that after nineteen years perhaps the society owed something to its foster child. It voted $75,000 for new pump and boiler rooms and larger exhibition tanks, as "a gift from the Society to the City of New York." Then, as promptly as if all along it had been waiting for such a gesture, the city voted $86,000 of corporate stock for enlargement of the second story along the front of the building and the addition of a third story.

The society's money was expended promptly and the Aquarium director's annual report for 1921 was a proud showcase for photographs of the new pump rooms and boiler room. The city's part of the work proceeded more spasmodically; it was not until 1926 that the second and third floors were finished, the second given over to water distribution tanks and shops and the third to offices, a library, and a laboratory. Now the collections could be expanded by about a fifth, and the new offices allowed Dr. Townsend and his small staff to move back into the Aquarium from the basement room in Pearl Street they had occupied while reconstruction was going on.

The society's seeming neglect of the Aquarium for so many

195

years is understandable in the light of its primary obligation to the Zoological Park. Osborn and Grant did not neglect to keep an eye on the Aquarium's general operations, however, and admonitions were directed at Townsend from time to time, just as they were to Hornaday. Inevitably Townsend got a call-down when newspaper stories mentioned Aquarium employees by name. The director was ordered to instruct his men that they must always speak about the work of the New York Zoological Society, not about their own roles in its affairs. The managers of the society, Grant wrote, "are much annoyed."

In its earliest days the Aquarium collected local fishes by seining Lake Agassiz in the Zoological Park.

One of the director's first acts had been to put his working force into smart gray uniforms with a gold seahorse design on the cap. He worked his men hard, and tankmen and attendants were no more exempt from smartening the place up with paintbrushes than ordinary seamen would have been on the ships in which he had spent so much of his earlier life. Perhaps reflecting the training of his ministerial family, he had a quotation from Habakkuk (I:15) painted in gilt letters around the interior of the Aquarium's dome: "They take up all of them with the angle, they catch them in their net, and gather them in their drag, therefore they rejoice and are glad."

With several of the city's most important newspapers located in Park Row, within easy walking distance of the Aquarium, the fish were natural subjects for frequent news and feature stories. Townsend carried on no protracted quarrels with the press as Hornaday did, but occasionally he had to set the record straight, as when the *World* in 1905 reported: FISH GOING BLIND AT THE AQUARIUM.

Striped bass, "the veteran fish of the finny boarding house, several having taken lodging there shortly after the place opened," were the chief sufferers, the *World* said; fully 25 percent of them had been made blind by the glare from the white tiling after skylights were installed over the tanks. "The average visitor to the Aquarium is unable to distinguish the blind fish from those with proper sight. The visionless eyes look sound and healthy and have the true fishy stare, but the sightless fish do not travel as fast as the others."

Dr. Townsend was unruffled. He put a little note in the next issue of the *Bulletin* assuring the society's members that the fishes were *not* going blind and that there were only five cases of blindness among two thousand fishes—and four of these were caused by injuries during capture and were temporary.

It was true, as Dr. Townsend had said, that new exhibits could not be added until the building was enlarged, but even in the lean and constricted years there was a crowd-pleasing change and variety in the tanks. Some fishes managed to survive for years in the brackish and often foul water pumped from the harbor, but in 1903 city money built an underground reservoir for pure seawater in Battery Park just outside the Aquarium's walls, and in 1908 a new 100,000-gallon reservoir was added. Gradually the Aquarium became able to exhibit brilliant tropical marine fishes from Bermuda (they were shipped in tanks on the deck of a steamer, and often became seasick in rough weather but recovered by the second day), and even such interesting invertebrates as sea anemones and jellyfish and an octopus. The Aquarium had been under the society's management for less than a year when it exhibited a manatee from Florida—the only one exhibited in the United States at that time. It lived for five months, and 526,700 people saw it and marveled at its capacity for food. Dr. Townsend seems to have had some of Hornaday's feeling that an animal should eat what its keeper thinks is good for it, for he reported that the manatee "turned up its nose at lettuce and other wholesome garden vegetables, insisting on a diet of salt-water eel-grass and pond weed."

No project was too ambitious for the new director. Visitors were always asking whether the Aquarium had any white whales, remembering the two belugas that had been exhibited in the large central pool in 1897, one living five days and the other seven weeks. Dr. Townsend placed orders with beluga fishermen on the St. Lawrence but they were never able to fill them. (It was not until 1961 that the Aquarium again exhibited white whales; they have been continuous attractions at the Aquarium at its new home on Coney Island since that year.)

The director himself went to Cape Hatteras in 1914 to select Atlantic bottle-nosed dolphins (often called porpoises) from the beach where a considerable porpoise fishery was then carried on, and to ship them to New York in water-filled tanks. Five survived the trip and gave a lively show in the central floor pool, which was thirty-seven feet in diameter and seven feet deep. Unfortunately it had to be filled with seawater pumped directly from the harbor, and in the summer of 1915 the water was so brackish and foul-smelling from raw sewage that the dolphins died; one lived twenty-one months but at last expired "from sheer filth infection."

But where pure seawater from the reservoir could be supplied to the exhibition tanks, the Aquarium was now able to offer a collection of tropical marine fishes unrivaled in this country. John T. Nichols of the American Museum of Natural History recognized this accomplishment when he named a new angelfish *Angelichthys townsendi* "in appreciation of the untiring efforts of Dr. Chas. H. Townsend to show beautiful coral-reef fishes to the public."

The director had bad luck with the new species named after him by admiring colleagues. *Angelichthys townsendi* turned out to be a naturally occurring hybrid between the queen angelfish (*Holacanthus ciliaris*) and the blue angelfish (*Holacanthus bermudensis*). Thus the name has no validity and in the future will be found only in the lists of once-used scientific names that ichthyologists regularly prepare to help them understand just what fishes their predecessors have been writing about.

The director, at least, rejoiced when a Humboldt penguin was presented to the Aquarium in 1915. It lived in one of the floor pools by day (when it was not hopping out and following its keepers around the building), and at night it was kept in an open pen on the gravel roof. It was the first of what was in later years to be a succession of sea birds—pelicans, cormorants, gulls, and the like—that Dr. Townsend insisted on keeping in the floor pools even though they were (to put it mildly) untidy in their habits, given to making noisome messes, and generally unsuitable for exhibition in a closed and not too well-ventilated building. His successor, Dr. Charles M. Breder, Jr., always felt that Townsend was

199

"at heart an ornithologist and he gave me the impression that he rather disliked fishes." Cage birds were his hobby and he had a good collection and an excellent ornithological library at his home near Mamaroneck in Westchester County.

The Aquarium almost had a spectacular exhibit in the summer of 1918. Fishermen a mile off Manhattan Beach at Coney Island caught an ocean sunfish (*Mola mola*) on their sea-bass hooks in seventeen feet of water. It took them an hour to hoist it to the surface, and then they simply tied it to the stern of their motorboat and towed it to Sheepshead Bay. Several more hours passed before the Aquarium was notified and got there with a truck and a tank, and by that time the fish was moribund. It was, of course, only a baby—adults may weigh 1,800 pounds—but in the Aquarium's tank it would have been of great interest to fishermen, for they sometimes encountered large ones basking on the surface. Often they were so sluggish that they paid no attention to being prodded by oars.

Another Aquarium "first" was a freshwater manatee from the upper Amazon. At the time of its arrival in 1916, the species had not been exhibited before in the United States. When it died in 1919, Dr. Townsend wrote: "It had an attack of indigestion. Having two stomachs to consider, and one of them not an exact duplicate of the other, it is not difficult to see that its digestive processes must have been complicated." (Was it really an abnormal specimen? It is normal for the manatee stomach to be compartmental, with three chambers.)

For many years one of the major handicaps of the Aquarium was its lack of its own collecting boat. Nowadays it is commonplace for aquariums in distant parts of the world to exchange specimens by air shipments, but in the first decades of the century exotic fishes came by ship, if at all, and for the most part the New York Aquarium depended upon its own collecting efforts, seining locally or buying interesting specimens from commercial fishermen. The task of keeping the

exhibit tanks filled became much easier when its own boat was launched in Brooklyn on May 20, 1920. Named the *Seahorse,* it was 35 feet long with a beam of 11 feet, and its well for the holding of live specimens was 10 feet long, 10 feet wide, and 2½ feet deep. Powered by a 25-horsepower engine, it cruised off the New York and New Jersey shores twice a week and in its first season brought back more than three thousand fishes of sixty species, plus many invertebrates. Dr. Townsend had designed it along the lines of what he said were Norwegian fishing boats—although at least one Norwegian said privately that he had seen a model of its prototype in the Bergen Marine Museum and that it had been outmoded for three hundred years. Nevertheless Dr. Townsend loved it, "went to sea" on it whenever he could get away, and delighted in taking old Navy cronies with him. On one memorable cruise, rough weather blew up and an admiral who was a passenger was very seasick indeed, but Townsend weathered the storm by holding on tight and puffing at a little cigar.

201

Dr. Townsend's rule over the Aquarium was interrupted in 1910–11 when Professor Osborn summoned him to the acting directorship of the American Museum of Natural History. Director Hermon C. Bumpus of the museum was "allowed" to take a leave of absence and Townsend was available to sit in temporarily, since the Zoological Society by then had "decided to relax its efforts in the improvement of the old Aquarium building, believing that a new building had become a necessity." Dr. Raymond C. Osburn of Columbia University was made assistant director of the Aquarium, to act under the general supervision of Townsend, and since nothing much was happening down at the Battery except the routine day-to-day operation—and for that matter, the director of the museum had comparatively little to do either, with Professor Osborn in the presidential saddle—the inter-institutional borrowing worked out all right. Dr. Townsend sat in the museum director's office until February of 1911, when the Bureau of Fisheries begged for his services for one more voyage on the *Albatross,* this time an exploring and collecting expedition to the Gulf of California organized jointly by the Zoological Society, the Museum of Natural History, the New York Botanical Garden, and the United States National Museum. Dr. Townsend may be supposed to have been happy to get back aboard the familiar old *Albatross,* and the voyage was happily successful. Everyone shared in the spoils and the Zoological Society got some lizards and six elephant seals, the latter from a herd on Guadalupe Island that had been thought to be extinct. By June 15, 1911, Dr. Townsend was back at the Aquarium.

Many times in the next couple of years he must have taken refuge in memories of those congenial and uncomplicated weeks aboard the *Albatross,* for he was soon to be caught up in controversy that left permanent enmity between him and Hornaday.

Nothing is duller than a rehash of old quarrels decades later when all the principals are gone, but the Hornaday-

Townsend clash was of epic proportions and involved the Zoological Society too closely to be passed over. At its center were the fur seals of the Pribilof Islands in Alaska, which were in a bad way around 1910. Pelagic, or ocean, sealing indiscriminately killed females and males of any age, and on land the motherless pups starved to death. International treaties put an end to pelagic sealing, but the harvesting of surplus males on land continued. Hornaday, with the backing of the Camp-Fire Club, was determined to have a five-year moratorium declared on land sealing; allied with him— and even more violently aggressive and outspoken, if that is possible—was Henry Wood Elliott, a naturalist, champion of the fur seal, and onetime associate of the Smithsonian Institution. Hornaday, Elliott, and the Camp-Fire Club challenged the might of the United States government and reserved some of their bitterest attacks for the advisory board of the Fur Seal Service. Townsend was a member of the advisory board.

Both sides agreed that pelagic sealing was bad, but harvesting the surplus of non-breeding-age males on land was another matter. When Townsend was in governmental service he had spent years in the Pribilofs, making censuses and examining the logbooks of sealers to determine what and how many seals they had taken; Hornaday had never been in Alaska. Townsend and his fellow zoologists on the advisory board believed it would be safe, even beneficial, to the land herds to remove the young males and minimize the fighting for possession of the females, which often led to trampling, injury, and death of the pups. The board saw no reason why the United States government should not have the revenue that controlled killing would permit.

The jockeying and name-calling by Hornaday and Elliott, the Hornaday-produced pamphlet appeals to save the fur seals, the letters to Senators, the Secretary of State, and even to President Taft, were unremitting. Not that Hornaday attacked Townsend by name—as he did some members of the advisory board—but the "Barren Work of the 'Experts' of the 'Advisory Board' " (a heading in one pamphlet that was never circulated) left no doubt about his feelings for his fellow director in the service of the Zoological Society.

Even Professor Osborn and Madison Grant got caught up in the fray, with Osborn publicly differing with "my friend Dr. Hornaday," and tensions reached a point at which the society decided it was time to call a halt. A "peace agreement" was declared between the society and the Camp-Fire Club, both directors were ordered to cease firing, and Hornaday's pamphlet entitled "The Last Fight for the Persecuted Fur Seal: New Light on an Amazing Situation" was withheld from circulation after it had been printed and was ready for distribution to the United States Senate.

It was said in Chapter 9 that Townsend's stint as an arbiter for the State Department at The Hague just before becoming director of the Aquarium was to be vexatious to him and an embarrassment to the Zoological Society. The dispute, between Russia and the United States, concerned a sealing vessel, the *James Hamilton Lewis,* which had been seized by Russia in her territorial waters and for which the United States asked $50,000 compensation. Townsend's role in the dispute was a minor one; he was to be called upon to testify about general sealing activities of the time and to provide statistics when needed. In the end, the award was made to the United States, and Townsend probably looked upon it as just another completed chore.

But in 1911 a House of Representatives committee under the chairmanship of John H. Rothermel of Pennsylvania began holding hearings to investigate the fur-seal industry of Alaska, and the policy of permitting killing (on land) under lease to a commercial company was under debate. The nationality of the owners of the *James Hamilton Lewis* and their relation to a commercial company engaged in Alaskan sealing became one line of questioning thrown at Townsend, and Henry W. Elliott was permitted to put a series of what to an outsider seem highly irrelevant and unfair questions through the chairman of the House committee. Townsend's differences with Hornaday and the Camp-Fire Club came into focus. Under questioning he said that he had been a member of the club but resigned "when I found it plunged into this seal business."

Elliott himself annotated in red ink the transcript of Townsend's testimony that Hornaday carefully pasted in his "The Saving of the Fur Seal Industry" scrapbook, and he was free with such comments as "Liar!" and "He dare not tell what he knows to the Committee with Elliott's eye on him." It is hard to see how Townsend could have answered some of the questions; they were entirely outside his frame of reference at The Hague.

Charges that Townsend had been party to presenting a fraudulent claim against Russia and that he received compensation for his testimony at The Hague out of the award were widely publicized in a majority report of the Rothermel Committee. A minority report of three of the seven members completely exonerated him. The society's executive committee thereupon asked William White Niles as its counsel to make an independent investigation. On the basis of the Niles report, it was "the unanimous opinion of this Executive Committee that the honesty and integrity of Dr. Charles H. Townsend have not been impugned in any way" and that "the attack on him is unjustifiable, malicious and untruthful."

And what was happening to the fur seals all this time?

Some years after his retirement, Dr. Hornaday wrote a fifteen page memorandum: "The Inside Story of the Fur Seals Salvage War," which concluded:

The Rothermel investigation lasted from May 31, 1911, to March 14, 1914. In the course of it several reputations were badly damaged. The amount of crookedness revealed was amazing. The report of the Committee was strictly partisan. The republican members voted guilty as charged, the democratic members voted not guilty. Within a very short time after the Committee's report was made to Congress, Congress passed the pending 5-year close season bill, thus making our victory complete.

In due course of time and diplomatic procedure, the Department of State completed an excellent treaty with England and Canada, Japan and Russia, which at once put a stop to the wicked and wasteful killing of seals at sea.

We won! All three of our original demands; but the cost to me in old friendships forever broken up was great, and even today is painful to contemplate. I have many ex-friends who never will forgive me for having started that fur-seal salvage campaign, nor for having been successful in gaining the ends desired. The seals are now back to about a million head, and presently will be 2,000,000 but no one thanks Henry W. Elliott, or the Camp-Fire Club, or me for having brought it about.

Dr. Townsend preserved a great many reports and special publications on the fur seals of the Pribilofs in the archives of the Aquarium, but he compiled no scrapbooks or letter files defending his position; when the battle was over, it was over. Only a permanent bitterness toward Hornaday survived. Years later when a member of his staff happened to be reading one of Hornaday's books and inadvertently left it lying on his desk, he angrily ordered it out of the building. "Never let me see you looking at a thing like that again!"

He had little of Hornaday's instinct to compile, document, and release his thoughts in writing. He produced no books except the *Aquarium Guidebook* in 1919, a rewritten edition in 1937, and a treatise—a pamphlet, really—on "The Public Aquarium: Its Construction, Equipment and Management," published by the U.S. Bureau of Fisheries in 1927. He did, however, produce a steady flow of observational papers in the early years. In the Zoological Society's *Annual Reports* he published "Notes on the Manatee" in 1903, "Notes on Certain Pinnipeds" in 1904, "The Cultivation of Fishes in Natural and Artificial Ponds" in 1906, "Pollution of Streams —an Appeal to Anglers" in 1907, and in 1908 "Observations on Instantaneous Changes in Color Among Tropical Fishes," the first of four papers he devoted to these interesting transformations as he had seen them in the Aquarium's tanks. Long afterward, in the late 1920s and middle 1930s, he combed hundreds of whalers' logbooks to write about "The Galápagos Tortoises in Their Relation to the Whaling Industry" and "The Distribution of Certain Whales as Shown by Logbook Records of American Whaleships." During World War II the Navy made use of the four-color maps he had prepared, showing where whale catches had been concentrated, to give submarine commanders an indication where their sonar was most likely to be confused by whales instead of detecting enemy submarines.

Single-handedly Dr. Townsend wrote many complete issues of the society's *Bulletin,* starting in 1903 when the Aquarium was allowed to blow its horn in one of the four numbers of the year. The *Bulletin* became bimonthly in 1910 and three years later the Aquarium was allotted two issues a year, although by this time he was getting writing help from Assistant Director Osburn and others.

How much editing his writing required it is impossible to say now, although in 1905 Hornaday complained to Madison Grant that Townsend's *Annual Report* copy needed two days' hard work—paragraphing was bad, capitalization was erratic—and suggested that it be sent back to the Aquarium's director to be rewritten. His *Bulletin* notes and articles were certainly well written and popular, as when he published a series of short notes on the habits of fishes:

"Are Fishes Killed by Freezing?" Answer: Almost never.
"Do Fishes Sleep?" Answer: Yes, at night, and sometimes in daytime, too.
"Do Fishes Hear?" Answer: Some kinds certainly hear sounds made under water.
"Have Fishes Memory?" Answer: It is natural to conclude that they have some power of memory, but there is nothing to show that memory is accompanied by mental processes of associating ideas.

Miss Ida M. Mellen, who joined the Aquarium staff in 1916

as secretary and stenographer, soon disclosed a talent for popular writing. She set the *Bulletin's* readers straight about the plural of "fish":

There are few people, even among those who spend their lives studying fishes, who always spell correctly the plural of fish.

The rule is that in referring to fish for the table, one should say fish, but in referring to specimens used for scientific study or as living exhibits, *fishes* is correct. Yet we may hear an expert stoutly aver that one should never speak of living specimens as fish, but only as fishes, and almost immediately thereafter refer to "forty goldfish," confident that this is the right usage.

Life at the Aquarium was not always as serene as pleasant etymological discussions might indicate. When warships in New York Harbor fired their big guns during the Hudson-Fulton Celebration in 1909, the concussion broke tank fronts and windows and blew out the gaslights. A great dynamite explosion at Jersey City on February 1, 1911, shattered twenty-three skylights and windowpanes; glass rained down on several hundred visitors, fortunately without injuring anyone. Damage was even worse on July 30, 1916, the day of the Black Tom explosion set off by German saboteurs at a munitions dock on the New Jersey shore; sixty-four roof skylights and a large number of ceiling skylights were broken, again without injury to visitors, and the Aquarium billed the Commissioner of Parks for the repairs.

Apart from Townsend's own writings, scientific work at the Aquarium was slow in getting started, even though Professor Osborn had enjoined him, when he took the directorship, to make the Aquarium a center for scientific studies. The one exception was practical work on fish pathology. In 1915 the society appointed Dr. George A. MacCallum of the College of Physicians and Surgeons of Columbia University as pathologist to the Aquarium, and in the next three years he produced five papers on trematodes and nematodes found in the collection. They were considered so important that the society established a special journal for their publication.

Zoopathologica appeared sporadically from 1916 to 1928, eventually comprising two volumes with contributions by MacCallum, R. C. Shannon, and C. T. Greene of the Bureau of Entomology, U.S. Department of Agriculture, and Miss Mellen, who contributed a paper on the treatment of fish diseases. After 1928, *Zoopathologica* was discontinued and pathological work was reported in *Zoologica*.

MacCallum's work had to be done in his Columbia University laboratory, for apart from such observational notes that Townsend himself could take by standing in front of the tanks while he was studying color changes among fishes, little more *could* be done at the Aquarium; there was no proper laboratory or other facility for scientific work until the third story of the building was completed in 1926.

For that matter, it is doubtful whether Dr. Townsend was greatly interested in the kind of scientific work that required a laboratory. Several of his associates in the 1920s and 1930s have recalled his attitude in almost identical terms. Dr. Charles M. Breder, Jr., who succeeded Townsend as acting director in 1937, said in a personal communication:

> Dr. Townsend considered himself a "naturalist" and indeed he was just that in the full old-fashioned sense. He became annoyed whenever anyone who worked with live animals was referred to as a biologist, or even more so if the word used was "scientist."
>
> He would pull himself to his full height and declare, "We are naturalists! Naturalists describe and only scientists explain." Frequently he would add for my particular benefit, "That means you, too, Breder." I still cannot quite explain that bit.

With a director who boasted to a newspaper reporter when he retired that he had never used a microscope, any modern scientific work that sprouted in the Aquarium soil had to fight for growth. Yet Townsend was quite willing to encourage off-premises research; in 1912 he was supplying unlimited numbers of killifishes to Dr. Jacques Loeb of the Rockefeller Institute for his research, eggs and embryos of salmonoid fishes to Professor C. F. W. McClure of Princeton for studies on the origin and development of the lymphatic vessels, and materials to Dr. George G. Scott of the College of the City of New York for work on the blood of fishes and on respiration. It was just that he didn't want any of this "science" stuff going on underfoot.

However, Professor Osborn and Grant wanted the Aquarium to become a center for science, and a laboratory seemed to be what "scientists" wanted, so when the layout of the third story was being designed Townsend included a laboratory—at the extreme end of the floor from his own office.

Early in that initial planning-for-expansion year of 1921

210

the Aquarium lost by death its aquarist, W. I. DeNyse, a competent man who had been brought in during the superintendency of Dr. Bean. Word went out that an aquarist was needed and young Charles M. Breder, Jr. (he was then twenty-four), applied for and got the job. Breder had been scientific assistant and fisheries expert for the U.S. Bureau of Fisheries since 1919 and was well qualified to manage a big collection of fishes, although his primary interest was in research; in fact, he applied mainly because he had heard the Aquarium was about to build a laboratory. Dr. Townsend showed him the blueprints of the third floor with adequate laboratory space indicated, but disillusionment set in quickly. Townsend and his aquarist used words very differently. Breder wrote in a personal communication:

Dr. Charles M. Breder, Jr., who succeeded Dr. Townsend as director of the Aquarium.

You can imagine my feelings when I found out after a month or so that what was being built were rooms in which I was supposed to hold daily demonstrations for grade school youngsters on how to set up a home aquarium. This he considered laboratory work.

It was not an auspicious beginning for a dedicated research man, but the story has a happy ending; Breder not only supervised the collection but he pursued *his* kind of research, published voluminously, and Townsend eventually became reconciled to it. He could hardly be otherwise when Breder's scientific publications laid the foundation for the Aquarium's international reputation for research.

211

Back in the 1930s, the staff of the New York Zoological Park idled away a summer luncheon hour by estimating how long it would take, and how much it would cost, to see *in the wild* all the species of animals any New Yorker could see in the Zoological Park by the outlay of five cents for a subway ride. The consensus was that it would take ten years and cost $250,000.

In the 1930s the airplane had made most parts of the world accessible and the estimate of ten years may have been a little high. But in the park's first decade, anyone trying to match its captives against their congeners in the field might have found an allowance of ten years' travel by ship, railroad, horse, camel, or afoot rather inadequate, for in 1909 the collections broke the 1,000 species mark (the total was 1,117) and many of them were rarities and "first-timers"—first-timers in America, at least. Rarities, in the zoological-park sense, are rare simply because they can be found only in the wildest and most inaccesssible parts of the world.

They, as well as many of the commoner animals, came to the Zoological Park by purchase from the professional animal dealers such as Carl Hagenbeck of Hamburg, William Cross in Liverpool, Louis Ruhe and William Bartels in New York, Cecil French in Washington. Hagenbeck was the preeminent dealer of the time and maintained a worldwide collecting organization with such a volume of sales that he was able to finance major expeditions, as when he sent agents to the northern border of the Gobi Desert and, with the help of nearly two thousand Kirghiz horsemen, captured fifty-two colts of the Przewalski or Mongolian horse. Twenty-eight survived to reach Hamburg in the fall of 1901 and several pairs went to the Duke of Bedford for his great collection at Woburn Abbey, at $5,000 a pair. Hornaday was not enthusiastic about wild horses, but Professor Osborn was deep in paleontological studies of living and extinct horses, and he wanted the Przewalskis badly enough to talk several members of the society into sharing the cost with him. A deal was

12

Man
in the Zoo

worked out whereby the society would send Hagenbeck two pairs of bison worth $1,800 for the last pair of Przewalski horses he was willing to dispose of, and so at nine o'clock at night on the next-to-last day of 1902 the horses were hauled from the New York docks to the Zoological Park.

Before they arrived, Hornaday issued what was a more or less standard warning: "Unfortunately, even the rarest animals are not immortal, and as usual in all such cases, we advise all persons specially interested to see them as soon as possible after their arrival."

The male seemed to be a satisfactory animal, but the female was thick-legged, stiff in the lower joints, and inclined to lean against a fence for support. Professor Osborn was not pleased with her. His dissatisfaction was soon transmitted to Hagenbeck, but Hornaday had some hope that she would improve as she matured. As far as he was concerned, wild horses the Przewalskis might be, but they were still horses and he proposed to handle them as such. By spring the female was shaping up a little better and keepers made strenuous efforts to halter-break the pair so they could be led around the grounds and trained to pull a carriage. After a few weeks Hornaday had to confess to Professor Osborn that it was no use. "The longer the men worked with them, the wilder and more obstinate they became."

The female never did improve satisfactorily, and after long correspondence Hagenbeck in 1905 shipped a replacement pair; the original defective animals were sent to the Cincinnati Zoological Garden, Hagenbeck's American depository, where Director Sol A. Stephen was his agent. There was no need for the public to hurry to see the new animals, for the male lived until 1919 and the female until 1923, and they produced six foals. Interfamily breeding raised the total offspring to twelve, and a nice herd was in the making until Hornaday exchanged stallions with the Philadelphia Zoological Garden, in order to bring in new blood. Unfortunately, he decided that the Philadelphia animal was not pure-

213

blooded and refused to allow it to breed, so that the herd
gradually died out.

Amateur collectors of mammals, birds, and reptiles of
North America were so numerous, and their offers to trap
and supply anything so incessant, that they almost constituted a minor industry. Not that the would-be collectors
always had the bird in hand, so to speak, when they wrote to
Hornaday and asked what the society would pay for such
and such an animal; often they merely asserted their expertise
in capturing the local fauna. With few exceptions such as
beavers, which were desperately needed to keep the Beaver
Pond stocked, the director declined all such speculative offers.
Too often when he did set a price on an animal said to be
already in hand, word came back in a week or two that unfortunately it had died just before being shipped. Or it
arrived dead, despite the detailed instructions for crating,
feeding, and watering animals that the park printed and
sent to prospective suppliers.

(Hornaday had his own prescription for shipping. To a
woman who offered a chipmunk he wrote: "All that is necessary is to place your specimen in a box about the size of a

Webster's dictionary, with wire netting over the top and plenty of hay in the bottom." A box the size of Webster's Unabridged Dictionary would have been just about right; the chipmunk arrived safely. Not so an Anolis lizard that a New Jersey woman tried to mail in an ordinary envelope.)

It was many years before the spate of inquiries by farmers, hunters, eager boys, and small-town businessmen slowed to a trickle in Hornaday's files. It is not hard to understand the volume of such correspondence. By and large across the country, animal life was abundant and economically worthless—until word got around that those fellows in the New York Zoo would pay good money for raccoons, squirrels, owls, eagles, coyotes, foxes, garter snakes, black bears, hawks, skunks, herons; in short, anything that the farmlands and prairies and forests provided. Nothing was further from the truth, of course, for so many gifts of common species poured into the Zoological Park that Hornaday's letters refusing offers became almost a standardized explanation that the park already had far more than it wanted, and thank you very much. There were few if any state laws prohibiting the shooting or capture and keeping of the common mammals and birds, and countless farm homes kept wild pets or perhaps got attached to an eagle or hawk shot down and then nursed back to precarious health.

For real rarities, the Zoological Park had to depend upon professional suppliers in the main, and usually they made firm offers or quoted on a precise list of wants sent out by Hornaday. Hagenbeck was one notable exception; in almost impeccable English he flooded Hornaday with sales pitches for animals he had at Stellingen, his vast grounds in Hamburg. In fact, his collection was so varied that the park could almost have been fully stocked by that one dealer alone. He did play a large part in stocking the new Lion House and, when it came along in 1903, the Antelope House.

One of the most assiduous amateur-professional collectors and suppliers was Mrs. C. F. Latham of Grant, Florida, who specialized in Florida birds and had excellent success in crating them so that they arrived in New York alive. Several times in 1902 and early 1903 she offered to send Carolina parakeets at the society's own price, but Hornaday turned her down.

I would not feel justified in making an offer for Florida parrakeets, because the species is so nearly exterminated. We could not hope to induce these birds to breed in captivity, and therefore perpetuate the species, and I think it would not be right to encourage the capture of any of the few living specimens that now remain. The species is so nearly extinct in Florida that unless it is carefully preserved, it will soon totally disappear.

But its breeding in captivity apparently was not impossible, for in 1902 the Smithsonian Institution possessed four Carolina parakeets that were rearing young. Other dealers offered them in 1903, and Hornaday noted at the bottom of his letter to Mrs. Latham that one Nicholson had quoted them at five to ten dollars. But Hornaday rightly did not want to contribute to their extinction, even though it was coming rapidly and inexorably. Thirteen birds were sighted just northeast of Lake Okeechobee in the spring of 1904 and some may have been seen in 1920. Still later sightings were rumored but doubtful, and the species may be said to have become extinct when the last bird, a male named Incas, died in the Cincinnati Zoo on February 21, 1918. Cincinnati gave two to the New York Zoological Park in the summer of 1911 but both were dead by the spring of 1913.

Some reference books give 1914 as the date of death for the last Carolina parakeet, but the Cincinnati Zoo's record for the 1918 date is explicit. The error may have arisen from confusion with another "last of the species." The last passenger pigeon, a female named Martha, died in the Cincinnati Zoo on September 1, 1914. The New York Zoological Park never exhibited a live passenger pigeon, although about 1914 Dr. Hornaday bought a mounted pair for a hundred dollars, including the display case. The usual price at the time was

216

fifty dollars for a single mounted specimen, and they were not uncommon.

Just before Christmas in 1903 the mail brought an international reply postcard that surely set a record for informality in the offer of an important animal. It was addressed to "Administration of the zoological garden New York," and the other half of the card was prefranked in the amount of ten pfennig:

Pless, Upper Silesia, the 7 Decbr. 1903

For 30 years Auerochsen/: Bison europaeus. Sm.:/originating from Russia are reared in this dominion a forest comprising 10000 hectares.

As there will be an opportunity this winter for catching of these extremely rare animals, we offer you one of the Auerochsen—a bull—aged 3 or 4 years, at the cost of 4000 Marks/:£200:/. Animal will be delivered in his traveling box franco to the railway-station of Pless. We beg to kindly answer as soon as possible.

FOREST ADMINISTRATION OF PRINCE OF PLESS.

Hornaday was not quite so offhand in his reply as to make use of the other half of the postcard; he pondered, but apparently not much more than overnight, and on December 21 wrote a letter to the Pless Forest Administration:

The New York Zoological Society has concluded not to purchase at present, specimens of *Bison europaeus*. During the present year the Society's expenditures for the purchase of collections for new buildings have been very heavy, and in the near future three more buildings must be filled with more new animals. We have not yet begun to form a collection of wild cattle and bison.

In view of Hornaday's intense interest in the American bison, it is surprising that he did not jump at the chance of exhibiting the European species, which had not been seen in any American collection. But he knew, or thought he knew, the state of the society's finances and that the funds available for animal purchases would not permit such an outlay at the moment. He was too hasty. In all likelihood he reported the matter to Professor Osborn as a more or less routine

217

decision—no record of this exists—but in any event consultations were held among wealthy members of the society over the Christmas–New Year's period and Hornaday was instructed to buy the European bison (or wisent) and to get a pair, if he could. On January 7, 1904, he cabled the Forest Administration to disregard his letter of December 21, that several gentlemen had put up the four thousand marks, and that he hoped the specimen selected would be a fine animal.

At the same time he wrote to Hagenbeck asking him to arrange for the crating and shipping of the Pless bull, and immediately got word back that Hagenbeck happened to have two splendid wisent cows, one of which he could supply for $1,300. Thus a pair was assured. Norman James of Baltimore, Charles Sheldon of New York, and Dr. Leonard C. Sanford of New Haven put up the $3,900 it would cost to have the pair delivered in New York, and they arrived in April of 1904, "very thin and weak, and much bruised on the hind quarters." They quickly perked up in a special corral near the Buffalo Gate of the park and the male lived eight years, the female thirteen. It was hoped, of course, that they would breed, for American bison in the collection were beginning to reproduce satisfactorily. Nothing ever happened, however, and it was supposed that the male was sterile.

He was. The gamekeepers of the Prince of Pless had seen to that.

What had happened was never put on published record, but Hornaday was explicit in a letter he wrote to Lorenz and Heinrich Hagenbeck on July 3, 1919. At that time World War I was just over and Hornaday was campaigning for a complete embargo on everything German or originating in Germany. The Hagenbeck brothers had written to him offering, among other animals, some wisents. Hornaday replied:

Your offer of a pair of European bison arouses recollections of past years. It was the Prince of Pless who sold to us, through your father, a male European bison (of poor quality) who had so shrewdly been operated upon by the Prince that it had been rendered impossible for him to procreate, and the scurvy trick was not detected until after the transaction had been closed. With charming impartiality Herr Pless furnished two other male bison, similarly maltreated, to two German zoological gardens.

No more wisents came to America until 1956, and the Zoological Park did not receive a pair until 1959. They came as a gift of the Zoological Gardens of Amsterdam, were in perfect condition, and have bred often—as have pairs in other American zoological parks.

The park had acquired a taste for first-timers. Hornaday knew well the romantic story of efforts to bring live musk-oxen out of the forbidding Barren Grounds north of Hudson Bay, for his friend Charles J. (Buffalo) Jones had made one of the earliest attempts in March of 1898, and had actually captured five calves. For two days Jones and a single companion shepherded the calves southward, fighting off packs of wolves as they traveled. When the wolves were finally left behind, the exhausted men slept for a few hours—and awakened to find that Indians had crept into their camp and cut the throats of the calves, in the belief that all other musk-oxen of the Barren Grounds would follow Jones out of the country. A Swedish Arctic expedition captured two calves on the east coast of Greenland in 1899, but they went to Woburn Abbey in England and the Berlin Zoological Garden, and none had been seen alive in the United States until a solitary calf showed up in San Francisco in 1902.

In March of the previous year, Captain H. H. Bodfish of the whaler *Beluga* was icebound in the Arctic Ocean north of Great Slave Lake, and to keep his men busy he sent out a musk-ox expedition. Thirty miles from the coast they encountered a herd with four calves, all of which they captured. Almost immediately their sled dogs killed two calves, and the remaining pair was harnessed to sleds and driven back to the ship, where another attack by dogs finished off the third. Bodfish managed to get out with a single calf, and when it

The Zoo's first musk ox, Olive, in 1902.

reached San Francisco it attracted enormous publicity that boosted the asking price to $3,000. As Hornaday wrote, "If the Western Union Telegraph Company did not declare an extra dividend because of the musk-ox telegrams that went hurtling to and fro across continents and under seas, it was not the fault of the senders." Unfortunately for the owner of the musk ox, the telegrams were all phrased to find out how much less than the asking price he would take. American zoological gardens were few, and nobody wanted to take an expensive chance on an animal acclimated to the fierce blizzards and winter storms of the Far North. After months of fruitless bargaining, the owner showed up in New York and offered the musk ox to the Zoological Society for $1,600.

William C. Whitney, with a long history of interest in bison, elk, and mule deer, agreed to put up the money, and so Olive, as the young female was called, came to the park on March 22, 1902. Fears for musk-ox longevity in a temperate climate were well founded. Olive lived only until the middle of August. Subsequently the Zoological Park received other musk-oxen and in 1925 single calves were born to two females in the collection, the first ever bred in captivity.

Showmanship is undeniably a part of the zoological-park mystique, so perhaps Hornaday cannot be blamed for offering only a token fifteen dollars for a live Haitian solenodon in 1917; it was certainly not a crowd-stopper. *Solenodon paradoxus* is a long-snouted, bare-tailed creature hardly larger than a big rat. Still, it was an authentic rarity, for scientific knowledge about it was virtually a blank between 1833, when a skin and a skull in the St. Petersburg Academy were described as belonging to a new species of insectivore, and 1907, when A. Hyatt Verrill brought out three specimens from Haiti and the Dominican Republic where he was making collections for the American Museum of Natural History. But as Hornaday wrote to Verrill, the park's policy was being revised and he was not going to be in the market for great but unspectacular rarities which nobody appreciated except the staff. He didn't really want a solenodon, so Verrill's specimens went to the museum for study and preservation.

As so often happens when someone does break the log jam, animal "rarities" tend to turn out to be not so rare after all. Nine more solenodons came out of Haiti between 1907 and 1910 and three were presented to the Zoological Park. They all died within a week. Twenty-five years later a native Haitian collector offered one to American zoos for $30,000— with no takers—and in 1935 the Zoological Park bought a pair at a more modest price.

The kind of spectacular rarities Hornaday wanted were not easy to come by, although he tried hard enough to get some of them. In 1901 and again in 1902 he gave commissions to travelers and collectors in the Orient to bring back Père David deer and the "particolored bear," or giant panda, offering "$500 in Spanish silver" for the latter, $250 for the former. It is doubtful whether the deer still survived in China in 1901, for the herd in the Imperial Hunting Park near Peking had been wiped out during the Boxer uprising in 1900, and a living giant panda did not come out of China until 1936, so these early probings were no more than that. The Duke of Bedford did have a thriving herd of Père David deer on his four-thousand-acre Woburn Abbey estate, however, and Hornaday tried unsuccessfully for years to get a pair away from him, at first offering in exchange a pair of pronghorn antelopes ("They are likely to become extinct in a few years") and in 1909 appealing to his sense of duty: "If Germany *should* invade England—as so many staid Englishmen fear she might or could do—the herd might easily be butchered to make a soldier's holiday, as was the herd of 200 in the Imperial Park south of Peking." As further insurance, he proposed that the duke establish a few pairs on the newly created Wichita National Bison Range in Oklahoma, but Bedford had a ducal disdain for Germany's threat and was not to be stampeded. It was many years before any of the deer were released from Woburn Abbey's grounds and not until 1946 that the Zoological Park received two pairs via the London Zoo's Whipsnade establishment.

Hornaday's showmanship sometimes failed him—or so it seems to later-day zoo men envious of his opportunities to acquire zoological treasures—as when he turned down a pregnant specimen of the almost extinct Tasmanian wolf, or thylacine; it went to the National Zoological Park and promptly gave birth. Professor Osborn was unhappy about that missed opportunity, so Hornaday bought for $125 the next thylacine that came from the Hagenbecks a few months later.

But his foresight did not equal his sense of showmanship on one occasion, and the result was the most bizarre incident in the history of the Zoological Park. That was the Ota Benga episode.

Ota Benga was an African Pygmy from the (then) Congo Free State who for just under a month in the fall of 1906 was attached to the Zoological Park. "Attached" is used deliberately as a noncommittal term; "employed" in the park was the word Hornaday used in print. Less biased publications asserted that he was "exhibited" in the park.

Perhaps it would be best to give first the official version as printed in the October, 1906, issue of the *Bulletin*.

On September 9, a genuine African pigmy, belonging to the sub-race commonly miscalled "the dwarfs," was employed in the Zoological Park. His name is Ota Benga, and he was brought to America by Mr. Samuel P. Verner, the American explorer and collector. His height is four feet eleven inches, he is about twenty-three years old, weighs 103 pounds, and has been married twice. His first wife was stolen by a tribe of hostile savages, and his second wife died from the bite of a poisonous snake.

Ota Benga is a well-developed little man, with a good head, bright eyes and a pleasing countenance. He is not hairy, and is not covered by the "downy fell" described by some explorers. His skin is as free from hair as that of a typical European. He has much manual skill, and is quite expert in the making of hammocks and nets. He is happiest when at work, making something with his hands.

The story went on to explain that Verner had found Ota Benga in 1904 on one of the southern tributaries of the Congo River, where he was a captive of the cannibalistic Baschilde tribe.

Knowing that this tribe sometimes sacrifices their slaves, and sometimes eats them, Mr. Verner, prompted solely by the instincts of humanity, ransomed Ota Benga, and attempted to convey him back to his own country. The attempt . . . failed, because of insurmountable difficulties.

Verner at this time had the idea of bringing a party of Pygmies to the United States and exhibiting them at the

A Père David's deer buck.

223

Louisiana Purchase Exposition in St. Louis in 1904. He and Ota Benga became friends and when "palavers" were held with a Pygmy tribe about going across the ocean, Ota Benga was in favor of it and swayed the others. The "ethnological exhibit" at the exposition was a great success and Verner was awarded a Grand Prize.

Verner subsequently returned the entire party to its tribal home in the Congo, but could not deliver Ota Benga to his own Badi tribe because they were at war with the cannibalistic Baschilde. According to the *Bulletin's* story, "The pigmy then begged to accompany Mr. Verner to America, and even threatened to drown himself otherwise. Finally the explorer decided to give him the desired opportunity."

In the late summer of 1906 Verner reached New York with Ota Benga and a young chimpanzee. What long-term plans he had for the Pygmy does not appear, but he approached Hornaday about boarding the chimpanzee in the park and somehow Ota Benga got included in the deal.

In his manuscript draft of the *Bulletin* article, the director gave a detail or two which he edited out of the printed account. Ota Benga, he wrote, "is now on exhibition every afternoon . . . and he can be seen during his working hours at the Primate House, working with the Chimpanzees and the Orang."

The Pygmy worked—or played—with the animals in a cage, naturally, and the spectacle of a black man in a cage gave a *Times* reporter the springboard for a story that worked up a storm of protest among Negro ministers in the city. Their indignation was made known to Mayor George B. Mc-Clellan, but he refused to take action. Hornaday thereupon wrote to him:

We are glad to learn that you have declined to seriously consider the absurd matter relating to Dr. Verner's African pigmy. The whole episode is comic-opera material, and nothing more.

Briefly stated, the pigmy matter is a newspaper sensation, created out of nothing, by a very bright reporter on *The Times*.

He personally aroused the negro ministers and invited their indignation. The *Times* reporter personally conducted the ministers to the pigmy, but none of them have ever seen the pigmy in a cage, either as an exhibit, or as a helper to the keepers.

No one, he wrote, except the committee and the reporter had "in any manner criticised my action in placing Dr. Verner's interesting little African where the people of New York may see him without annoyance or discomfort to him."

Was Ota Benga "exhibited"—like some strange, rare animal? That he was locked behind bars in a bare cage to be stared at during certain hours seems unlikely; that he did for the first few days enter a cage in the Primate House to play with the chimpanzee that had accompanied him from Africa is certain; also it is certain that a "label of information" about him was hung on the front of the cage while he was in it. At this distance in time, that is about all that can be said for sure, except that it was all done with the best of intentions, for Ota Benga *was* interesting to the New York public that had not been privileged to see Verner's family of Pygmies in St. Louis.

After the uproar generated by the *Times*'s bright young man, Ota Benga was immediately withdrawn from official exhibition (or employment) and the label was stowed away, but the dust did not settle quite so quickly. The committee of ministers engaged a lawyer to rescue Ota Benga from his cage, but by that time he was no longer allowed to enter it, and he stayed out. "As an exhibit," Hornaday wrote to Professor Osborn, "he has fallen into innocuous desuetude."

Verner missed all the excitement, or at least direct participation in it. After depositing Ota Benga and the chimpanzee in the Zoological Park, he had taken a train for his family's home in the mountains of North Carolina and was out of touch when his ward most needed his guidance, firm hand, and ability to communicate in the Baluba language.

A week after the *Times* story set off the explosion, Hornaday wrote to Verner:

225

Ota Benga, the African
Pygmy, whose brief
exhibition (or, as Dr.
Hornaday preferred to
call it, employment) in
the Zoological Park in
1906 created a tremendous
furor.

I regret to say that Ota Benga has become quite unmanageable. He has been so fully exploited in the newspapers, and is so much in the public eye, it is quite inadvisable for us to punish him. Finding himself immune from punishment, the boy does quite as he pleases, and it is utterly impossible to control him. Whenever the keepers go after him in his wanderings, and attempt to bring him back to the Monkey House, he threatens to bite them, and would undoubtedly do so if they persist. I see no way out of the dilemma but for him to be taken away.

It is my suggestion that he be turned over to Dr. Gordon and placed in the Colored Orphan Asylum. They have been insistent that they are the proper ones to take charge of him.

Daily letters, interspersed with telegrams, flowed between Hornaday and Verner during the next few days. One piece of Verner's advice which Hornaday did not act upon was that, if Ota Benga "should become too nervous, a dose of some sedative might do good, as I frequently found in the ecstatic frenzies which sometimes occur among the natives in Africa; tho I never had to use any for him."

Two of Verner's letters contained long messages to Ota Benga in Baluba, which Hornaday was instructed to read to him phonetically. He read them, and Ota Benga listened, but communication between them was less than complete. One message apparently asked Ota Benga whether he would be willing to journey to Asheville and enter a school there, where Verner would meet him. He may have said "Yes"— in Baluba—but Hornaday could not understand Baluba and had no way of sending him to Asheville anyway, since he could be controlled only by someone who could talk to him. Verner appreciated that point, but he wired back that he could do nothing immediately, since a terrible storm had washed out roads and isolated him in the mountains. Hornaday wrote to him:

Of course we have not exhibited him in the cage since the trouble began. Since dictating the above, we have had a great time with Ota Benga. He procured a carving knife from the feed-

227

room of the Monkey House, and went around the Park flourishing it in a most alarming manner, and for a long time refused to
give it up. Eventually it was taken from him. Shortly after that
he went to the soda fountain near the Bird House, to get some
soda, and because he was refused the soda, he got into a great
rage and started to disrobe on the spot! Finally, he disrobed to
such a point that the watchman rushed up and seized him to hold
the remainder of his clothes upon him. This led to a great
fracas. He fought like a tiger, and it took three men to get him
back to the Monkey House. He has struck a number of visitors,
and has "raised Cain" generally.

In the midst of the uproar, the manager of the New York
Hippodrome wrote Hornaday asking permission to give a
theater party for Ota Benga. In the same mail came a letter
from a manicurist (who described herself as "colored") asking to be allowed the pleasure of manicuring Ota Benga's
nails. Both requests were declined, with polite notes saying
that the boy had received so much notoriety that it was
thought best to keep him "somewhat in the background."

Verner kept sending telegrams saying that the flood was
still high but that he would arrive as soon as he could. Hornaday telephoned the director of the Colored Orphan Asylum
and was told that the institution would be happy to accept
Ota Benga. Then the asylum backed off when Hornaday
passed on Verner's stipulation that he should be allowed to
take the boy away when he reached New York.

What finally became of Ota Benga?

In his letter to Mayor McClellan, Hornaday had pooh-
poohed the whole matter by saying: "When the history of the
Zoological Park is written, this incident will form its most
amusing passage."

One may suspect that Hornaday did not really find the
Ota Benga incident all that amusing, even in retrospect, and
certainly the terminal history of the young man gave no cause
for mirth. He committed suicide in 1916.

He appeared briefly in the archives of the Zoological
Society between 1906 and 1916. He departed from the Zoolog-

ical Park in the last week of September, 1906, and presumably he was taken away by Verner, since no one else was able to talk to him and control him. Eight months later Verner was back in the Congo Free State as general manager of the American Congo Company, and Hornaday wrote to him that a young man had recently called at the park, asking for "my advice and possible assistance in getting hold of Ota Benga for exhibition purposes. He informed me that Dr. Gardiner is willing to let him have Ota Benga, but only on condition that he shall not bring him back. The Doctor admits that they would be glad to get rid of the young man for whose possession and presence they were once so desirous."

Hornaday did not say so, but it may be taken for granted that he did *not* encourage any scheme to put the Pygmy on exhibition again, anywhere.

It would appear that when Ota Benga left the park he found shelter with the Colored Orphan Asylum, for there is no hint of any other institution that was desirous of his "possession and presence." Then a colored Baptist association in New Jersey became interested in him. His subsequent history was told by the Lynchburg, Virginia, *News* in a story about his suicide. It was headed "Pined for Native Home," and it attributed "Otto Bingo's" act to "a yearning desire to return to his people on the East Coast of Africa."

The young negro was brought to Lynchburg about six years ago by some kindly disposed person and was placed in the Virginia Theological Seminary and College here, where for several years he labored to demonstrate to his benefactors that he did not possess the power of learning, and some two or three years ago he quit the school and went to work as a laborer.

After leaving the college he went into a colored home near the school, and since that had earned a livelihood by working in a tobacco factory and by day labor. For a long time the young negro pined for his African relations and grew morose when he realized that such a trip was out of the question because of the lack of resources. Finally, the burden became so heavy that the young negro secured a revolver belonging to the woman with whom he lived, went to the cow stable and there sent a bullet through his heart, ending his life.

Part of the suicide story was reprinted in the May, 1916, issue of the society's *Bulletin,* and Hornaday wrote a paraphrase of it to Verner, who was then attached to the Panama Canal Commission in Cristobal, Canal Zone. Verner wrote back:

The news of Ota Benga's sad death inexpressibly shocked and grieved me. His case is strangely like that of the devoted companion of David Livingstone, Skeletu, who jumped overboard from the ship on which he was travelling with the great explorer, apparently rendered suddenly insane by the marvels of civilization as they grew upon him.

He was the first of the pygmies that consented to come to America, and so was the first that ever left his native wilds to see what the white man's country was like.

[After the Pygmies were returned to Africa from St. Louis] he said he wanted to go back to America, and with some misgivings I permitted him to come. I did not think that Ota would ever take an education in the conventional sense of the word, but I believed that I would be taking other trips to Africa, so that he could go back again if he wished. After Ota started on his school course he became interested in it and so attached to his friends in the work that when I offered him the chance to return to Africa with me on my next expedition, he would not go. Later on I offered him an opportunity to work here on the Panama Canal, but he still stood firm on his first position.

I never did thoroughly understand his mental attitude, but he was one of the most determined little fellows that ever breathed. Possibly he was trying all the time to prove that he was not a "pygmy," as that term, even in Africa, always conveys the idea of difference from and inferiority to other people. I never called him one, to himself. To me he was very human, a brave, shrewd, even smart, little man, who preferred to match himself against civilization than to be a slave to the Baschilde. All honor to him for that, even though he died in the attempt.

230

One can think of any number of animals that a young zoological park would like to exhibit, but there was only one absolute necessity. An elephant. And the Bronx Zoo* was elephantless for most of its first five years.

It was not for want of trying that the zoo that set out to be the greatest in the world was lacking the most spectacular of all zoological exhibits. As soon as the Antelope House was well under construction (it was opened on November 12, 1903, on the site of the lodge of the old Lydig homestead), and accommodations for elephants (for want of better) were thereby assured, Dr. Hornaday placed a standing order with the Hagenbecks for an African elephant of any size and an Indian elephant standing at least seven feet at the shoulder. One baby African elephant was captured for the Zoo but died while still in Africa. Then an Indian elephant was found that met all the specifications and a price was agreed upon with the native owner, but at the last moment he was seized with belated affection for the creature and swore he could not part with it for less than double the original agreement. The Hagenbecks decided affection couldn't be purchased at such a price.

Another Indian elephant was on the point of being shipped when it gave a rampaging demonstration of bad temper and the deal was called off. Then Gunda came on the market.

If anyone had suspected Gunda's potentialities (and Dr. Hornaday said long afterward that he did), it is likely that the Zoo's first elephant would have lived out his stormy life in the forests of Assam instead of in the Zoo. For Gunda was a killer.

It was a proud day when he arrived, on July 2, 1904. He had been caught wild a few months before and he came close

13

Good Elephants- and Gunda

* There comes a time when enough deference has been paid to Hornaday's obsessive conviction that "zoo" and "Bronx Zoo" are dirty words. This is it.
  In partial appeasement of his shade, however, from now on he will generally be referred to as "Dr. Hornaday," although an honorary degree of Doctor of Science was not bestowed upon him by Western University of Pennsylvania, at Allegheny (now part of Pittsburgh), until June 12, 1906, a couple of years later than the time when he figured in the first of these elephant chronicles.

enough to fulfilling the Zoo's requirements to be entirely acceptable. A seven-foot elephant had been ordered, and Gunda stood only six feet seven inches at the shoulder, but he had attained the impressive weight of 3,740 pounds and possessed a pair of handsome tusks already sixteen inches long. The exact date of his birth was of course unknown, but it was estimated on the basis of size and development that he was seven years old in 1904. Colonel Oliver H. Payne had the honor of presenting the first elephant to the Zoo, at a cost of $2,340.

"He is, if anything, a little too fat and vigorous, and is unnecessarily mischievous about pulling and breaking everything that is loose," Hornaday wrote to a member of the board of managers. It was a considerable understatement.

With Gunda came an Indian attendant, Kodah Bux. Hornaday didn't care for him:

Just at present, the native Mahout who accompanies the animal here for two or three months, is giving us more trouble than the elephant! Being a Mohammedan, he is under the usual Musselmanic disabilities in regard to eating, and, absurd as it may seem to you, we are at the point of putting up a shanty for him amongst the trees south of the Antelope House, in order that he can kill fowls, say "Bismala" as he cuts their throats, and cook them together with his rice, with his own sacred hands. We have endeavored to feed him at our own Rocking-Stone Restaurant, but while he cannot speak a word of English, he succeeded in making me understand that he has grown very thin and weak because he cannot eat the unholy fare of the chef at our Rocking-Stone Restaurant!

A week later Hornaday wrote Hagenbeck that Kodah Bux was sailing for Hamburg the following Saturday. "He is one of the laziest, surliest swine I ever saw come out of India, and is worse than useless."

Kodah Bux had been supposed to stay at the Zoo long enough to train Gunda for riding, but he would do no work himself and his advice was unintelligible, so his return to

Interior of the Elephant House soon after its opening.

232

India via Hamburg was no serious loss. Actually he was not needed, for Gunda accepted training without difficulty and in six weeks had been broken in as a riding elephant and was carrying clusters of happy children around the Zoo on a big howdah. In his spare time he operated a "bank," an open-top box placed high on the wall of his stall. When visitors tossed pennies into the compartment, Gunda would pick them up, drop them in the box, and pull a rope that rang a bell. Theoretically the bell was the signal for Gunda's keeper to reward his thrift with a chunk of bread. If the keeper was busy and didn't answer promptly, Gunda kept up a continual clangor.

He turned out to be a dishonest banker. Some days the bell rang almost continuously and the till at night showed deposits of only half a dozen pennies; he was surreptitiously filching pennies out of the box, dropping them, redepositing, and claiming his reward. Thereafter the box was studded with

234

long nails so that a penny once deposited could not be picked out again by Gunda's trunk.

And there were other mysterious doings at Gunda's bank. Hornaday wrote identical letters to Gunda's two keepers:

I regret to inform you that a thief has been stealing money from the Elephant's Bank. Last week the elephant put into the bank (for me) a nickel, and it is not to be found in the money which you have just sent me for the last week's collection. The week before that I put a silver quarter into the bank; that also disappeared. To my certain knowledge a number of nickels and silver pieces are given to the elephant every week, yet during the last two weeks the bank has been robbed of every one of these pieces.

I wish you to say nothing about this to outsiders, but do your utmost to catch the thief. If you can catch him in the act, I promise you to make short work of him whoever he may be. If neither of you succeed in catching him, I will have to try a hand at the game myself.

Gunda's early docility did not last. His keepers began to lose control of him and could regain it only by lashing his trunk with a whip. This sometimes occurred when visitors were in the building, and letters protesting against the seeming cruelty poured in. Hornaday answered them calmly, explaining that an elephant out of control was a very dangerous animal and that punishment was sometimes necessary. In 1907 he had a large sign painted and hung outside the elephant stalls.

TREATMENT OF LARGE ANIMALS

On account of their size, *unruly* elephants are dangerous animals. Male elephants often become obstinate, and hard to manage. Every elephant (and every bear) must be made *afraid* to attack his Keeper. The voice of the Keeper *must* at times be stern and commanding. Whipping an elephant *does not hurt him;* but he *thinks* that it does. If an elephant seriously misbehaves, he must be punished, *immediately.* When Kartoom jabs Sultana with his tusks, he must be whipped. When Gunda refuses to obey his Keeper, he must be *forced* to obey.

235

Visitors are assured that no animal in this Park is ever punished unless it is very necessary, and never with any undue severity; but they CAN NOT be permitted to become uncontrollable, and attack their keepers.

WILLIAM T. HORNADAY

Within a year after he arrived Gunda knocked down a keeper—who managed to scramble out of the compartment without injury—but by 1911 he was seized by recurring periods of sexual excitement, or musth, during which he was increasingly excitable and dangerous. His temper, always uncertain, manifested itself particularly against Curator Ditmars, Keeper Dick Richards, one of the Zoo's painters, and one of the messengers. There was no explicable reason for his dislike of these particular persons; it was just one of those "I do not love thee, Dr. Fell" antipathies so familiar to every zoo man. Walter Thuman, who with Richards shared the keepers' work in the new Elephant House of 1908, was the only keeper for whom Gunda showed affection—and even then it was little more than tolerance. As a rule he would obey Thuman's commands promptly enough.

It was all the more unexpected, then, in 1913, when Gunda turned on Thuman and nearly killed him. The keeper spent three months in a hospital and after his return was transferred to another building, for Gunda's hatred now concentrated on him and he would no longer willingly obey anyone. A normally docile elephant will stand quietly, or move out of the way, while its stall is being cleaned, but Gunda was so erratic and his swipes with trunk or tusks so quick that the only recourse was to chain him to the floor with shackles on the left front foot and right hind foot. He could move a yard or two but the keepers could work around him with safety.

Then in June of 1914 the Gunda controversy began.

The *Times* started it by recalling that a year before, a citizen had written to the American Society for the Prevention of Cruelty to Animals protesting the chaining of Gunda.

236

The ASPCA had investigated and asked Dr. Hornaday, if Gunda was vicious, what justification there was for keeping him chained. Should he not be destroyed?

The director had returned "an aggressive reply," the *Times* reported, and now the ASPCA had received more complaints and was preparing to investigate again—for Gunda was still chained.

The *Times* had always been a supporter of the Zoological Park and of the director, and its news story was certainly legitimate, for letters of protest about cruelty to Gunda were being received by the newspaper as well as the ASPCA and the matter was of general public interest. But Hornaday took the news story as "An Attack on the Zoological Park," as he headed the violent letter he immediately wrote to the *Times*.

Ever since the Zoological Park was opened I have warned the Zoological Society that the day would come wherein we would be attacked. "Be thou as chaste as ice, as pure as snow, thou shalt not escape calumny."

Because of his uncertain and dangerous periods of rage, Gunda had to be chained in his stall—an action that caused a great public outcry.

237

In our most extravagant moments, however, we never dreamed that one of the leading newspapers of New York City would promote an attack on the Zoological Park, keep it up day after day, and print such letters as those of the remarkable Charles H. George [one of the protesters]. It is rather odd,—and a pity, too,—that it should have been the *Times* that started the movement that now seems very likely to lead to the shooting of Gunda at an early date, in response to the clamor of poets and editors and others who are so tender-hearted that they can not bear to have him live any longer!

Won't it be a spectacle for gods and men when Gunda, munching hay in the most comfortable animal room in the whole Zoological Park, hears the roar of the elephant rifle that sends a steel bullet rushing through his skull and brain in the name of The Merciful, The Compassionate? When it is done, I shall insist that those who are now attacking the management of Gunda shall be compelled to come to the death chamber, and see it done. As for myself, I will ask to be excused.

I think that Gunda's days are numbered; and when he is finally shot to death we will erect a tablet in his memory bearing this inscription: "Shot to death in response to the demands of tender-hearted friends who wanted him to be free to turn completely around in his room."

One thing I will say to those who are flooding that mischievous elephant with bathos and literary bouquets. There are exactly two alternatives, and only two. Either let him alone where he stands, give him a chance to recover from his present spell of ill temper (which possibly may come to pass), or shoot him to death where he stands. If the editor of the *Times* prefers to have his blood now, I shall not do anything more than file strong protests against it, and denounce it as being, at this time, unnecessary, and therefore cruel.

The controversy raged all summer. It was the eve of World War I, but the letter columns of the *Times* found plenty of room for the friends of Gunda, each one with a different solution to the problem. A woman in Hempstead, Long Island, was convinced that "This elephant would never have developed murderous tendencies if a mate had been put in the

238

cage with him." Another correspondent recommended that he be given a place to take cold baths. "Animal Lover" contributed the brilliant idea that somebody should come up with a plan for giving Gunda more liberty.

Even the ASPCA was taken to task; while it was "a source of gratification" that it was coming to the relief of "poor Gunda," it would be more gratifying if the ASPCA did something to relieve the plight of the draft horses in New York City. Another correspondent wished the ASPCA would forget Gunda and look into the licensing of cats.

A German animal trainer would take off the chains and have Gunda eating out of his hand in four days; a Westchester woman offered to take care of Gunda's stall if she was given a keeper's salary, a long-handled scraper, a shovel, and a fire hose.

On July 10, according to the *Times,* an anonymous poem was found written on the wall alongside Gunda's stall:

> The times are out of joint!
>   Oh, Lord, how long will fools rush in
> Before this clamor ends?
>   Must I be shot to death to please the throng?
> Lord, save me from my friends!

This was variously interpreted as a sly slap at the *Times* and as a parody of another poem previously published as a letter to the editor, with the refrain "The time is long, Lord God, the time is long!" The latter poem purported to be a lament by Gunda for having to spend the rest of his life (estimated by various correspondents at sixty to eighty years) in chains.

Not all poets took Gunda's plight so lugubriously:

> By thunda!
>   I wonda
> If 'tis a blunda
>   To chain Gunda.

By late July the uproar over Gunda had risen to such a

crescendo that the *Times* ran a whole page of Gunda correspondence—this on top of five and a half columns it had previously devoted to the subject. It is likely that never before or since have the "Letters to the Editor" columns of the *Times* been so lively.

A few excerpts—

The editors, poets, and correspondents of The Times have proved beyond all doubt that our friend Gunda thinks exactly as do human beings. Therefore we must ascribe the same motives to his present publicity campaign that we would ascribe to similar courses of action by men and women. The conclusion, then, is obvious that Gunda intends either to run for Governor of New York, or else to go on the vaudeville stage.

What a pity it is that those who lavish their sympathy on Gunda because his feet are tied with chains do not know of the real and needless suffering of cattle and hogs before being slaughtered?

Why is it we are hearing so much about Gunda? Why should we wander up to the Bronx and concern ourselves about the limited existence of the elephant Gunda when there are so many frail little human Gundas in New York? By frail little human Gundas I mean the young girls who come to this part of the country in an effort to enter into the economic struggle and who are quartered in spaceless hall bedrooms where they drag out their unmated womanhood unthought of and neglected.

Many correspondents ("Engineer," for one) made suggestions for alleviating Gunda's presumed discomfort, such as confining him in a pit of several acres' size, with access to running water and an overhead walk from which the public could view him in safety. Another advised partitioning Gunda's stall so he could be confined in one side while the other was being cleaned. A mechanically operated outer door was also proposed, although how it would help to turn Gunda out of doors in the middle of winter was not discussed.

Dr. Hornaday did admit, on being pressed by a *Times* reporter, that it would be possible at the cost of perhaps a thousand dollars to rig up a mechanically operated door.

However, he did not intend to make the Zoological Park over for the sake of one bad elephant. . . .

The war in Europe warmed up, the world (or at least New York City) had other things to think about, and by autumn correspondents were only occasionally writing to the *Times*—but now to ask what had happened to Gunda. Had he been forgotten?

No, not forgotten, but a hundred-foot cable had been rigged, and Gunda, though chained to it by a sliding ring, had comparatively great freedom out of doors. Curator Ditmars even made a movie of him and it was shown at the Brooklyn Academy of Arts and Sciences with great acclaim.

Came winter, and Gunda's recurrent period of musth returned in aggravated form. He refused to eat, lost weight, and was so dangerous that again he had to be closely chained. The executive committee made the only possible decision. Gunda would have to be destroyed. Carl Akeley, the famous African explorer and sportsman, brought his elephant gun to the park on the morning of June 21, 1915, and the ill-starred career of the Bronx Zoo's first elephant was abruptly terminated.

The urbane writer of "Topics of the Times," an editorial-page column which had frequently mentioned the Gunda affair, had the last word—in print, at any rate:

Gunda has been shot. The chains no longer were trusted, and Gunda is a "good" elephant at last. The Times was his friend and tried to help him. For his sake it came to a near-quarrel with the estimable Dr. Hornaday, but fortunately it never denied that able scientist's superior knowledge of elephants, and war was avoided.

As the *Times* said, Dr. Hornaday did have a superior knowledge of elephants. He also had responsibility not only to the elephant but to its keepers, while his critics had nothing but emotions born of ignorance. Gunda was not "suffering" by being chained. In a state of sexual excitement he was an irresponsible and highly dangerous animal, and if the director can be blamed at all it was for publicly calling Gunda a "bad" and "mean" elephant—thereby leading many people to the conclusion that he was being chained as a punishment—and for not stressing again and again the cyclical and unpredictable nature of musth.

When Gunda arrived in 1904 the search for an African counterpart was being carried on vigorously, and it was just a matter of time before a suitable one would be found. The Hagenbecks provided an African elephant for $2,500 about a year later. It was a male, named Congo, and he had a special distinction: a European zoologist saw him in Hamburg and pronounced him to be the type of a new pygmy race, *Elephas africana pumilio*. As such, he would be the first pygmy elephant exhibited anywhere in the world.

American zoologists did not go along with this designation and for some time Congo was the center of a mild scientific controversy. When he was finally destroyed and his body was deposited in the American Museum of Natural History, he was listed in the museum's records merely as an African forest elephant.

One of the arguments for Congo's status as a pygmy was based on the observations of R. L. Garner, a zoologist and collector who had spent many years in the French Congo, where Congo was captured. He said there were two types of elephant in the Lake Fernan Vaz basin: one was definitely the large African elephant, known to the natives as *njagu*, and the other was much smaller and was called the *mesalla*. The *mesalla* he described as a "malicious" animal in the wild, so aggressive that few native hunters would venture to attack it.

Garner pointed out another curious characteristic of the *mesalla*—one which, as far as the Zoo's records show, no one seems to have checked against Congo: "One observant white man . . . has assured me . . . that when running he [*the mesalla*] gallops with his front feet and trots with his hind ones."

242

An elephant that trots at one end and gallops at the other would surely be enough of a curiosity to be entitled to a special name, and it is really too bad motion pictures were not made of Congo's gait, in case he was a true *mesalla*.

Small he was—three feet eight inches at the shoulder when he arrived and only six feet eight inches ten years later—and his size made him an object of interest to visitors, every one of whom inevitably exclaimed over the "baby elephant," even when he had attained his presumed full growth and had a formidable armament of 23½-inch tusks. Their error was pardonable, however, for after 1908 Congo shared a stall and corral with a big Indian elephant named Alice, which energetically "mothered" the small elephant. She seldom let him stray far from her side, pushed him inside the Elephant House when she thought the weather was dubious, and squealed with rage when he was taken away from her.

Stubbornness was Congo's chief trait on the negative side, but it never created any particular problem except at the periodic weighings. Early in his career Congo took a dislike to platform scales—which seemed unsafe because the platform swayed slightly under his feet—and it used to take the efforts of half a dozen men to pull the little elephant onto the boards. The chief difficulty was keeping his head up; if he could get his head down, he generally plunged his tusks into the ground and they were a most efficient anchor.

In the latter years of his life, Congo developed trouble with one of his hind legs. The disease became progressively worse, so that in the late fall of 1915 it was decided to destroy him. Once more Carl Akeley brought his elephant gun to the Zoo.

Congo may not have been a pygmy, but he was always small; Khartoum went to the opposite extreme. He was a wrecker of buildings, a foe of steel bars, a giant among giants. He rivaled in height the famous Jumbo of the Barnum and Bailey Circus, and he was certainly one of the tallest elephants ever exhibited in an American zoo if not the tallest.

When Khartoum arrived from the Blue Nile in June of 1907, he was about four years old. Nothing about him indicated the record he was to make for himself; he was four feet nine and a half inches tall and weighed 1,235 pounds. He began to put on weight and size at a commendable rate, but these took on special importance for the Zoo staff only near the end of his life, when it seemed he was about to eclipse the celebrated Jumbo.

Long before a natural death came to him in 1931, he had made himself notorious by his grudge against masonry and structural steel. It was not, apparently, that he resented confinement in stall and corral, for both were large and commodious and he had plenty of room for exercise. He just liked to push, batter, bump, shove, and jolt.

Khartoum amused himself in the summer of 1918 by pushing against the steel girders of his corral fence until those heavy bars, set three feet deep in concrete, swayed and staggered out of alignment. He bent his yard gates, shattered stall doors, and flouted Zoo manners by throwing hay at visitors. It was not viciousness, just high spirits.

Small boys may be forgiven for running wild on the first warm days of spring, but not an elephant, even though boys and elephants are motivated by the same urge. Khartoum's behavior on an April day in 1922 was typical of him. When the Elephant House doors were opened he began to run, flapping his ears and tearing up clods of earth and tossing them on his back. It would have been fine if Khartoum had stopped at that, but his besetting sin was too much earnestness. He found a bulge in the iron fence railing—a bulge he had created the summer before—and with one blow of his battering-ram head straightened the protuberance. Then he charged the gate of heavy railroad iron and bent it three feet at the top, stripping the heavy bolts of their threads. The keepers managed to get him back inside just in time. At one time or another most of the walls and fences that confined him had to be replaced or repaired. Three-inch iron spikes studded his doors and the fences and effectively stopped battering blows—except in spots where he had set the tip of his trunk against the spikes and broken them off.

And yet Khartoum never attacked his keepers or displayed any of the vicious traits that eventually caused Gunda to be put to death. One Sunday afternoon in 1922 he broke a ninety-pound section of railroad iron from his corral fence and it flew into a crowd of onlookers, bruising one woman as it fell. But that, of course, was pure accident, for apart from a few wisps of hay Khartoum never attempted to throw anything. He was simply a lovable, playful giant.

It was in the late 1920s that the Zoo staff began to look hopefully at Khartoum and wonder whether he was going to set a new record for height. The mark to shoot at was Jumbo's, and the Zoo thought it knew what that was.

As long ago as 1912, Dr. Hornaday had published in the society's *Bulletin* a short note headed "The Real Height of Jumbo." He wrote:

Inasmuch as Jumbo, the great African elephant brought to America by Mr. P. T. Barnum in 1882, was probably the tallest elephant that ever lived in America, his standing height has been a question of more than passing interest. When Jumbo was shown in Washington, D.C., in 1883, the writer secured from Mr. Barnum a card of permission to measure, "provided Mr. [James A.] Bailey consents." When that card was presented to Mr. Bailey, his indignation was as colossal as the great pachyderm. *"Measure Jumbo? In-deed!"*

So far as we know, Jumbo went to his death, in front of a locomotive, with his exact height unknown. Professor Ward's men measured him dead, and declared his height to be eleven feet four inches; and for twenty years the matter rested there.

Recently Mr. Robert Gilfort, of Orange, N.J., has given me Jumbo's exact standing height. In the year 1883 Mr. Gilfort was a performer in the Barnum Show, in which there was also a "pole-jumper" named Elder. The chief stage property of the jumper was the long, straight pole with which he did his leaping.

While the show was in Madison Square Garden, New York, Mr. Gilfort and his colleagues decided that they would ascertain the actual height of Jumbo. In the course of his free exercises between the acts, the pole-jumper casually leaped to the side of Jumbo, and carelessly stood his pole up close beside the animal. Mr. Gilfort, being quite ready, carefully noted the point on the pole that corresponded with Jumbo's highest point at the shoulders; and when measured it proved to be ten feet nine inches.

Jumbo died two years after the measuring and the pole vaulter's figures are probably as nearly accurate as will ever be known, for the eleven feet four inches of Ward's men could be accounted for by the "flattening" of the carcass many hours after death.

On December 30, 1930, Khartoum was measured in his stall and found to be ten feet eight and one half inches at the shoulder, just half an inch under Jumbo's living measured height. He was growing very, very slowly—but he was still a comparatively young elephant, about twenty-seven or twenty-eight years old, and there seemed to be no reason to believe that he would stop growing for yet awhile. Next year . . . !

But before the next measuring period came around, Khartoum was dead. On an October Sunday morning in 1931 his keeper found him in a state of collapse on the floor of his stall, and he died before the veterinarian could bring him succor. The veterinarian measured him immediately after death. He taped the shoulder height at ten feet ten inches. One inch taller than Jumbo! But too late.

By 1908 the Zoo was top-heavy with African elephants; it had three Africans and one Indian. So when the animal exhibitors Thompson & Dundy let it be known that their Coney Island concession had Indian elephants for sale, it looked like a good chance to redress the balance. The Zoo's veterinarian, Dr. W. Reid Blair, was dispatched to Luna Park to see what could be had.

There were several elephants at bargain prices, and Dr. Blair's choice wavered between a fifteen-year-old that bulked a comfortable 4,500 pounds and a slightly smaller elephant. One of Thompson & Dundy's keepers, Dick Richards by name, volunteered some advice.

"If it was me, I'd take Alice," he said, pointing to the fifteen-year-old. "She's got all the marks of a good elephant and she's a fine animal."

Actually there was nothing that pointed strongly to one animal over the other, so Dr. Blair bought Alice for nine hundred dollars. She was crated and delivered to the Zoo on September 3 and about two weeks later she began to make history.

(Not until thirty-two years later did the story of the secret diplomacy behind the Zoo's purchase of Alice come out. Richards confessed that Thompson & Dundy had "rigged him up to it." Alice had been used as a riding animal at Luna Park, he said, but she was always pulling up and eating plants in the ornamental flower borders and was liable to panic and bolt at sudden noises. "She was the least useful elephant in the herd, so they told me to put up a good story and get rid of her.")

The new Elephant House was not quite ready for occupancy, and temporarily the elephants were quartered in the Antelope House. Alice was destined to be a riding animal, so she was taken on a daily walk around the grounds to get her accustomed to her new surroundings. On a Friday afternoon in mid-September she was plodding past a caged puma when the cat let out its unearthly scream. Alice trumpeted in sudden fear and bolted for the nearest shelter, which happened to be the Reptile House. She went in, taking much of the door with her.

"Evidently she thought it was a barn, and possibly she hoped to find within it the three companions she had left in the big and gloomy elephant-barn at Coney Island," Dr. Hornaday wrote afterward.

Instead she found about fifty visitors, who duly panicked. Her two keepers soon persuaded her to leave the building and tried repeatedly to steer her back to the Antelope House, but just as often she rampaged back into the comforting darkness of the Reptile House. She was inside when Dr. Hornaday arrived and he ordered her chained in the front hall for the night. He and the keepers sat up all night with her, feeding her and making soothing noises, and by early morning they figured she was under control and slacked off one of her two chains. That was a mistake. She could now reach a row of lizard exhibits in glass cases and she smashed them, then placed one foot on a guard rail and broke down a section.

"By great effort" she was dragged or driven out of the building and by the combined strength of the Zoo's working force her hind legs were tied together; then she was thrown, thus hog-tied, and anchored with chains to trees in front of the Reptile House.

She remained prone for most of the day. Dr. Hornaday's gift for playing down an awkward situation was never better demonstrated than when he reported that "During the day, the Saturday crowds of visitors inspected her briefly and with mild interest, then went their way to see other animals."

248

Mild interest, indeed! Only that for a roped and chained elephant lying athwart the sidewalk, in front of a splintered door?

A telephone call was made to Coney Island. Dick Richards was located, and by three o'clock in the afternoon he reached the park by subway. In *Life with Alice,* his little book published by Coward-McCann in 1944, Richards wrote that he simply walked up to the elephant's head and said, "Alice, you old fool! What's the matter with you?"

She recognized her Coney Island friend, "chirruped" to him, and searched his pockets for sugar. When Richards had Khartoum brought up from the Antelope House and stationed nearby as a lure, and her bonds were released, she struggled to her feet and followed Khartoum and Richards back to her own stall quite docilely. The Zoo hired Richards a month or so later and he was Alice's keeper and best friend from that day until her death in 1943.

Inevitably the fracas in the Reptile House produced a lawsuit. As Alice burst through the door and visitors fled to the far side of the building, one woman fainted. Reptile House keepers carried her into Curator Ditmars's office, sat her down

249

in a chair, and revived her. A week later her husband lodged a claim for five hundred dollars against the city, which Dr. Hornaday rebutted with seven numbered arguments, the last of which was:

7. On the occasion referred to there was no good reason why any person should faint. Persons who are liable to faint at the sight of an elephant, or other wild animal, should not visit places where wild animals are kept. If a visitor faints, or falls down, at the unexpected sight of a wild animal in a zoological park, they alone are responsible.

When the Elephant House was opened in the fall of 1908, it took thirty-one men to drag Alice to the new building and into her corral, alternately pulling and checking her return flight by dropping an anchor tied halfway down the cable. It wasn't that she was mean or unduly stubborn; she was just timid and slightly scatterbrained. Dr. Hornaday put it even better: "Alice suffered, I merely believe, from curvature of the brain."

Less than a month after taking up residence in the Elephant House, Alice was the center of a typical Hornaday storm.

On a December afternoon, prima donna Emma Eames of the Metropolitan Opera Company visited the Zoo and happened to enter the Elephant House just as Dick Richards was having one of his periodic arguments with Alice. All Mme. Eames and her companion could see was that a keeper was yelling at an elephant and banging it with his heavy hooked stick, while the elephant kept backing off and trumpeting in what the Metropolitan's soprano interpreted as terror.

Mme. Eames was understandably upset by what she took to be an exhibition of unwarranted brutality, and she hastened to Hornaday's office to protest. The director listened to her account of the events, and after she and her companion left he investigated further, then wrote to Mme. Eames: "Much as I shrink from recalling to your mind your distressing experience today in our Elephant House, it is yet my plain duty to place before you the keeper's reasons for the occurrence."

After the interview with her, he continued, he went to the Elephant House and interviewed Richards. There followed what purported to be a verbatim question-and-answer session with the keeper. Richards said it was the regular day to give Alice her oil bath (oil was brushed into the skin on the theory that it was necessary to keep the skin from cracking), and soon after Alice obeyed orders and went down on her side, she decided to get up. He left her alone for a few minutes and then ordered her to lie down on the other side. She refused. "I saw that if I didn't make her mind right then, she never again would lie down for me! I simply had to conquer her, or there would be no living with her."

"Did you punish her severely?"

"I left only one mark on her,—on her ear when I was trying to pull her down with my hook."

"Did she trumpet loudly?"

"Oh, yes; she yelled 'bloody murder'—just as they all do when you are trying to make them mind."

"Visitors who were present have complained that you were terribly severe with her."

"Well, to hear her holler, it may have looked that way; but I never left a mark on her skin only once."

Such is the keeper's statement.

> The toad beneath the harrow knows
> Exactly where each tooth-point goes.

That elephant has been sent to me as a punishment for all my sins against wild animals.

If my Nemesis becomes the means of spoiling your pleasure in the Zoological Park, that will make it a little easier to shoot her when her last hour comes!

It was a remarkably restrained letter, considering how violently Hornaday usually reacted to criticism, and the incident might have ended there except that the story of Mme.

Eames's protest got into the newspapers. Hornaday thereupon wrote to the soprano again:

It is not often that I offer to anyone who is displeased with me a statement in my own behalf, but since reading your communication in this morning's *Herald* I have decided to give you a few final facts.

The particular newspaper reporter who in some manner heard on the street a story about your protest to me, called me up on the telephone to ask me about it. I declined to say anything and referred him to you.

He said, "Well, it is said that there was a regular scene in your office. They have given their story and I want yours. It is *said* that you ordered Mr. [Antonio] Scotti [a Metropolitan Opera basso] out of your office. Is that true?"

I said, "It is *not* true at all; I did *not* order Mr. Scotti out, nor anyone else."

"Is it true that Mr. Scotti said that if he could have got into the elephant's cage with a revolver, he would have shot the keeper?"

"Yes, the man who was with Madame Eames did say so; but he was a little excited and didn't realize what he was saying."

"Is it true that the gentleman refused to give his name?"

"Not at all. There is no truth whatever in that statement."

"Did Madame Eames introduce him to you?"

"She did; but I did not catch his name."

"Was it Mr. Scotti?"

"I do not know."

"What was it that Madame Eames complained of?"

"Cruelty to the elephant."

"What was the keeper's excuse?"

"Absolute necessity. I have since written Madame Eames giving her the keeper's explanation."

Mme. Eames apparently was willing to let the matter drop, and her secretary wrote to Hornaday thanking him for his "kind letter" of explanation. She wanted it made clear, however, that she did not give the story to the *Herald;* it must have been someone close to Hornaday. "Madame Eames did not speak of the incident to anyone except her mother who certainly would not give it to a newspaper, & Mr. Scotti could not have done so as he was not with Madame Eames."

The secretary pointed out what was undoubtedly true; the reporter had gotten wind of the affair somewhere and had alternately called Mme. Eames and Hornaday, saying the other party had talked, and what's your version?

Who the singer's companion was did not come out. Despite the newspaper story, Mme. Eames's secretary said Scotti was not with her—but the companion was undoubtedly the person who lodged a strong complaint with the American Society for the Prevention of Cruelty to Animals, for almost immediately Hornaday received a formal complaint notice and a demand from the superintendent of the ASPCA that such cruel practices be stopped. Hornaday's fury boiled over again and he drafted a scorching letter to the president of the ASPCA demanding that a public hearing be held at which the complainant must appear and be faced by responsible people who knew the facts. Fortunately he submitted the letter to Madison Grant first, with the comment that "I feel sure that the ridiculous individual who accompanied Madame Eames to my office is the party who made the complaint. He left my office vowing vengeance, and this is his plan for getting back at me." Grant toned the letter down considerably and was able to report a few days later that the ASPCA president had replied in a most conciliatory way and evidently did not want a row.

So the Eames incident faded away, but it was by no means the only complaint about the treatment of the Zoo's elephants that Hornaday had to answer in the next few years. His defense was always the same—that for their own safety, the keepers had to dominate their charges, and that elephants understood nothing except a resounding thwack on the trunk or ears, and anyway such blows didn't really hurt them. They were the arguments he finally had painted on the sign "Treatment of Large Animals."

They were not valid arguments, and the only excuse for them is that Dr. Hornaday thought they were. He was not a brutal or callous man himself, but he was convinced that wild animals had to be mastered for their own good, and especially such large and potentially dangerous creatures as elephants and bears. That there might be other and gentler ways of handling an animal never entered his mind, and in that respect he was a man of his time. All elephant keepers were rough-and-tumble characters—they thought they had to be—and in Richards's case, rough treatment came naturally; he was a showman in the tough tradition of the circus and Coney Island. He gave the orders, and he *had* to be obeyed. Over the years he did work out an understanding with Alice so that force seldom had to be employed, and a curious kind of affection developed between them. Late in both their lives Richards entered Alice's stall one day to practice a stunt he expected to put on for the members of the Zoological Society at their annual garden party that afternoon. Alice was expected to kneel down so that Richards could sit on her trunk, whereupon she would wrap it around him and rise to her feet, lifting him high in the air.

Alice remembered the stunt and went through the first moves perfectly, but Richards was no longer the young showman he had been; as Alice rose, he slipped and fell to the concrete floor, breaking a leg.

Alice was terrified. If she had been a mean elephant, it was a perfect opportunity for her to trample him to death. Instead she trumpeted in the shrill tones of terror and backed away, into the farthest corner of her stall. Other keepers came running and carried Richards out, but Alice paced and shrilled for hours, and into her actions it is easy to read dismay over the mishap to her trusted friend.

Once settled in the Elephant House, Alice drifted into placid middle age. She made a good, tractable riding animal for several years, but the story goes that at last she tired of work and began scraping her howdah against trees and buildings, finally dumping a whole load of paying guests onto the ground when the howdah girths broke. So the Zoo retired Alice from the riding track.

For fifteen or twenty years her life was uneventful and colorless. Then on the night of February 4, 1936, icy water

backed up in the drains of her stall and she panicked. She battered open the locked but unbarred door to her outside corral and made her way into the snowy yard. The corral gate was unlocked because workmen had been repairing the fence the day before, and sometime between midnight and morning Alice walked out into the Zoo, a completely free elephant.

Her subsequent movements could be traced by tracks in the light snow. She turned southward and found her way through the service yard to the porch of the cookhouse where, twenty-five years before, she had been accustomed to getting a reward of bread at the end of her day's duty on the riding track. The ancient breadbox was still there, still filled with stale bread. Alice lifted the lid and helped herself, then retraced her steps toward the Elephant House. Only this time she did not go through the gate and the swinging door back to her flooded stall; she walked through the public door— glass, storm sash, framework, and all.

Dick Richards found her at seven o'clock the next morning backed up to a steam radiator.

An elephant's memory is proverbial; Alice remembered the way to the breadbox after twenty-five years. How much longer could she remember?

255

Early in 1941 the Zoo was putting on a series of Sunday-morning radio shows, and one was devoted to the Elephant House with Alice as the star. Dick Richards had recalled that exactly thirty years before, he taught Alice to answer the telephone—or pretend to. Would she still remember a trick she had not performed in thirty years?

Richards rummaged in the basement and found the same old telephone he had used in 1911. He rigged it up again out in the corral, and as the finale of the show, after a big buildup about an elephant's memory, Alice was put to the test on the CBS network, coast to coast.

Richards turned the telephone crank, the bell tinkled, and the keeper called "Alice, it's for you!"

But instead of lumbering over and taking the receiver in her trunk and holding it to her ear, Alice just stood there and gazed into space. Twenty-five years she could remember, but not thirty.

On a spring Sunday in 1941, Alice sagged on unsteady legs and went down. She tried hard but could not again stand upright, so a diesel-operated derrick was summoned, ropes were slung around her body, and she was hoisted to her feet.

Two weeks later she went down again, and again the derrick was summoned. After four go-downs, it was obvious that things could not continue like that and it was reluctantly decided that the next time would be the last. She would have to be destroyed—if she did not die a natural death.

She somehow kept going for almost two years more. But on August 27, 1943, she was found lying helpless in her stall, for the second time in a week. She seemed to have given up, for she made no attempt to rise or even to eat the delicacies Dick Richards pressed upon her. And so, quietly and painlessly, she was put to sleep with an overdose of anesthetic.

Her passing left the Zoo with two young Indian elephants and one African, and there have been several others since. They were all good elephants. But there was only one Alice.

In 1905 there was a "business as usual" air about the affairs of the Zoological Society. When the important events of the year were summarized in the *Annual Report* there were fat paragraphs about the new Bird House, "cunning and murderous dogs" that killed seven deer, the astonishing growth of alligators from egg to a length of five feet in four years, the woes of the Aquarium's modernization program—but not a word about one event in the park that had truly national significance. That was the organization of the American Bison Society by thirteen men and one woman, in the reception room of the Lion House, on December 8, 1905.

The omission was not mysterious. The Bison Society was born *in* the Zoological Park, and Dr. Hornaday was its reluctant first president, but the Zoological Society and the Bison Society were quite separate organizations—parallel in their concern for the bison but separate in all other ways. There was a feeling on Hornaday's part, at least, that they should keep their distance; working together for the preservation of the bison, by all means, but each under his own banner so that they would not become confused in the public mind.

The American Bison Society is generally credited with saving the bison from extinction in the United States, and at the end of its first decade its current president, Professor Osborn, was able to write: "The Society has accomplished the main object for which it was established ten years ago: not only is the American bison no longer in danger of extinction but it is firmly reestablished in all parts of this country."

Nevertheless, the New York Zoological Society was in the business of trying to save the bison well before the American Bison Society was born and had already offered a nucleus herd of fifteen animals from the Zoological Park's own collection if the government would set aside and fence a suitable range in the Wichita National Game Preserve at Cache, Oklahoma. The offer had been accepted.

It would be truer to say that credit must be shared between the American Bison Society and the New York Zoological

14

The American Bison Society Is Formed

Society. And it is high time to pay full tribute to a man whose name weaves in and out of the early *Reports* of the Bison Society and yet, somehow, seemed never to carry the weight of its older, graver officers: Ernest Harold Baynes.

The Bison Society did acknowledge its debt to him, handsomely, in its combined *Reports* for 1924–1925–1926, after his death.

> With profound sorrow the American Bison Society now records the passing from earth on January 21, 1925, of Ernest Harold Baynes, honorary member, the first proposer of the Society, one of its active founders, and its first secretary.

The society placed a memorial tablet to him on a boulder near the summit of Croydon Mountain in the Blue Mountain Forest Game Preserve in New Hampshire.

In 1904, at thirty-six, Baynes was an energetic writer and lecturer. He was looking for a half-wild place in which to settle down and write, and he found just what he wanted on the fringe of Austin Corbin's game preserve in New Hampshire, where Corbin had long maintained a large and virtually wild herd of bison. Baynes had met Hornaday, and he gave the Zoological Park's director as a reference when Corbin asked for testimonials to his sobriety, seriousness, and ability to pay the rent on a small house in the preserve. Hornaday gave him an A-1 rating and Baynes began studying the local wildlife, almost immediately turning out a book, *Wild Life in the Blue Mountain Forest.*

Corbin's bison were, of course, the most prominent animals in the preserve—he had 160 head—and Baynes began writing and lecturing about them, chiefly in and around Boston. The idea began to grow on him that the only way to save the species from extinction was to put under government control the existing herds in private hands. He wrote to President Theodore Roosevelt along those lines and got back an enthusiastic letter. Baynes thereupon began to campaign actively for some kind of society to work for the preservation

Ernest Harold Baynes, who first had the idea of forming the American Bison Society.

258

of the bison and extended his lecturing to such influential groups as the Boone and Crockett Club and the Camp-Fire Club of America in New York. He impressed the Boone and Crockett Club's secretary, Madison Grant, and the Camp-Fire Club's president, Dr. Hornaday. In fact, after the Camp-Fire Club's dinner meeting, and in what he later regarded as a weak moment, Hornaday promised that if a society were formed, he would become its president.

It is impossible to be sure now what other commitments Hornaday made to Baynes at that time, but it is likely that some involvement of the Zoological Society in Baynes's project was discussed—always providing, of course, that the executive committee approved.

In February of 1905 Hornaday wrote to Professor Osborn: "I have a great thing to propose to the Zoological Society, through you, in connection with the preservation of the Buffalo from extinction, but it is too long a matter to offer you upon paper now."

Ideas, no matter how great, have a way of being laid aside when practical concerns clamor for attention, and Hornaday dawdled over reporting an interest on the part of the executive committee until Baynes prodded him: "If you have not already made any definite arrangements with the New York Zoological Society concerning the movement to preserve the Bison, I think that after all perhaps it will be best to have a special organization—a national one."

By this time Baynes was getting dubious about Hornaday's anxiety for action and he took things in his own hands, asking President Roosevelt if he would be honorary president of a national society for the preservation of the bison. Roosevelt would be glad to, provided the names of the other officers were submitted to him and approved.

This was a major step forward and Baynes then suggested to Hornaday that if the Zoological Society was still holding back, perhaps a bison society could be organized at a meeting of the Camp-Fire Club.

259

Hornaday was noncommittal about that. But he did reply that "In view of my silence I think you were quite justified in going ahead with the formation of a national society." He explained how busy he had been with plans for new buildings, and "As for myself, I shrink from becoming a member of any more societies, and attending any more meetings, or paying any more dues."

The fact was that Hornaday had grabbed the ball and was off and running on his own.

On March 7, 1905, he wrote to Charles Payne, an old friend in Wichita, Kansas, saying he was going to ask the Zoological Society to place a herd of bison in some spot where it could be sure of protection and where the animals could subsist without artificial feed. Did Payne think bison would have to be fenced in if they were placed in the Wichita National Game Reserve in Oklahoma?

Both Grant and Hornaday were keen to do something about perpetuating the bison in government herds and they were in the fortunate position of having bison in the park that they could offer, for Grant could speak with assurance about the attitude of the executive committee. Hornaday made a formal proposal to Charles T. Barney as chairman of the executive committee that the Zoological Society try to get the cooperation of the Federal government and the authorities of Oklahoma Territory and that the society offer at least twelve animals (fifteen were actually sent) from its own herd in the park. The executive committee promptly agreed, instructed Grant and Hornaday to take the necessary steps, and on March 25 the animals were offered to the government through the Secretary of Agriculture. The reception in Washington was favorable and in late November of 1905 the society sent its former assistant curator of mammals, J. Alden Loring, to Oklahoma to investigate the Wichita range.

Events were moving swiftly and completely without relation to Baynes, who must have felt he was nursing his dream of an American Bison Society in a vacuum, isolated as he was in a forest clearing in Meriden, New Hampshire. Hornaday told him frankly in June that he did not believe it would be possible for the Zoological Society to help in creating a special bison society.

But Hornaday had no patent on tenacity; Baynes had his share. He knew the Zoological Society was moving to establish a government herd in Oklahoma, but he still wanted to form an American bison society, and in the late fall he wrote a fairly acerbic letter to Hornaday:

It is now more than a year since I first took up the question of the preservation of the Bison with you, and in one way or another I have been working very hard on the subject ever since. I feel that I cannot allow another year to go by before beginning an active campaign, backed by a national society such as I have proposed.

Obviously there could be no more putting him off, so invitations to a meeting in the Lion House on December 8 were sent to some two hundred persons known to be interested in the fate of the bison. Fourteen showed up and with hearty unanimity they organized the American Bison Society with Theodore Roosevelt as honorary president, Hornaday as president, and Baynes as secretary. The promise Hornaday had made to Baynes at that Camp-Fire Club meeting had come back to haunt him. As he wrote to an Ohio conservationist a couple of years later:

I have the misfortune to be President of the American Bison Society, and it makes me a great deal of work. The Society and the position were forced upon me by an individual [Baynes], who would not be satisfied until he got it. Sooner than see the thing go entirely wrong, I consented to take hold and try to steer it right. It is making me a lot of work, for which I have neither time nor strength, and I am constantly annoyed by the necessity of doing it.

With the society organized and the title of secretary to give him official status, Baynes threw himself into publicizing the society and raising money. His was a down-to-earth attitude toward the bison. In a press release he issued the week following the organization meeting, he wrote:

There are good economic reasons why this animal should be saved and allowed to increase in numbers. As he stands on his hoofs, he is the most valuable native animal in the country; kill him, and there is no domestic animal in America, whose carcass will bring as much in dollars and cents. The meat is as good as domestic beef, and some parts of it rather better, while the hide alone will sell for money enough to purchase three or four good cows. A fine head is worth much more, and although the value of heads would probably decrease as buffaloes become more numerous, there would always be a good market for the skins, as for many purposes we have nothing quite so good. I know a man who is wearing a Buffalo ulster which has been in use for twenty winters, and it is not by any means worn out. As a winter carriage robe it is generally conceded that a Buffalo skin has never had an equal, and for this alone, the article would probably command a high price indefinitely.

That dollars-and-cents approach probably had a stronger appeal to popular audiences than the more moral, scientific, and it-is-our-duty pleas of other officers and members of the executive committee of the Bison Society. Baynes's lectures were enthusiastic personal statements of his own experiences with bison in the Corbin herd, and if there was a good deal of amateurishness in all he said and did, it certainly went down well with rural and small-town audiences all over the country. In the summer of 1909 he gave more than 150 lectures from New Hampshire to Nebraska, some sixty of them before Chautauqua gatherings, illustrated with slides from his own photographs of bison calves in harness, of the Corbin herd, and such buffalo by-products as a pair of gloves he had made from bison wool.

As the Salt Lake City *News* reported:

To preserve the species from extinction is the task which Ernest Harold Baynes has set himself, and this is the most interesting, romantic, historical, distinctively American species that ever existed, the American bison.

Mr. Baynes deliberately set himself the task two or three years ago of preventing the American bison from being swept off the face of the earth.

He drives the only team of harness-broken bison in the world. He asked the Corbins to turn over to him four calves to be raised by hand and receive a liberal education.

In December, 1905, Mr. Baynes, who had spent several years rousing public sentiment on the matter, organized the American Bison Society.

Well, so he did—essentially. His was the idea originally, and it is certain that without his tenacity the American Bison Society would not have been formed. Oddly enough, although he gave full credit to himself in newspaper interviews, Baynes did not cite the creation of the American Bison Society in his *Who's Who* sketch; he did not, in fact, mention his bison work and experiences at all.

Nothing ever came of his promotion of bison wool as a hard-wearing substitute for sheep wool; a New England mill was mildly interested but the supply was not sufficiently stable to make bison-wool spinning profitable. As for bison as draft animals, Martin S. Garretson, a later secretary of the American Bison Society, reported in his book *The American Bison* (published by the New York Zoological Society in 1938) that "The general opinion as expressed in the rural community in that [the Blue Mountain] neighborhood was: 'Baynes hitches 'em up, and they take him where they d——— please.' "

It was Baynes's amateurishness and constant harping on his personal experiences, rather than the broad issue of saving a species, that seemed to get on Hornaday's nerves. They had a lively row over the first *Annual Report* of the Bison Society, prepared in the main by Baynes and published in 1908. Hornaday thought it was poorly written and atrocious in typography and insisted either that Baynes come to New York and rewrite it under his tutelage or study other annual reports and make it more professional in style. The report as it finally came out is not as bad as Hornaday's strictures would lead one to expect, although it had one blemish that required every copy to have a name deleted in black ink. Maxfield Parrish, probably the most popular artist of the day, was a neighbor of Baynes's in New Hampshire, and Baynes persuaded him to paint a "seal" for the American Bison Society. It depicted a magnificent bison bull standing on a rocky mound with a typical Maxfield Parrish sky of purple, blue, and yellow behind him. "I regret that he cannot have it go out as his work," Baynes wrote Hornaday, "because in the designing of it he used a figure of a buffalo bull drawn directly from a photograph, and therefore it would not be good form to take credit for the design." The illustration was supposed to appear in the List of Illustrations merely as "American Bison (in colors) . . . *Frontispiece*" but somehow the end of the entry wound up in print as "*Maxfield Parrish: Frontispiece.*" There is some indication that Hornaday had inserted the offending name on galley proof, presumably having forgotten that Baynes warned him it was not to be used.

In retrospect one has the feeling that Baynes was more patronized than appreciated at his true worth by the policy-making, money-raising higher officials of the Bison Society. Baynes did raise some money by his own direct efforts—$670 in the city of Worcester, Massachusetts, alone—but he had to make a living by his writing and lecturing and his unpaid Bison Society work was mostly a spare-time operation, so that annual statements of dues were always woefully behind during his years as secretary, and "prospect lists" were not carefully checked. He wrote and invited C. J. (Buffalo) Jones to become a member of the society, although it would have been more appropriate if he had written to Hornaday suggesting that Jones be made a member of the board of managers. (He was put on the board a few weeks later.) Jones wrote to Hornaday:

Well I just sat down and wrote him if the man who had spent a lifetime and several fortunes in their preservation and who actually rescued 58 out of the 82 from which all our buffalo spring was not entitled to be an honorary member of such a society, I would just keep on with a little society of my own. It is such a joke I think I shall have to give it to the press.

Baynes remained secretary through 1908–1909, then was one of the vice-presidents for two years, and afterward until his death was a more or less inactive member of the board of managers. After a couple of interim secretaries, Martin S. Garretson, an old plainsman and historian of the bison, became secretary and made periodic censuses of pure-bred bison and carried on an enormous correspondence with schoolchildren until he retired in 1940, by which time the American Bison Society had long since ceased to exist as a needed or, except for census taking, even as a functioning entity; when Garretson compiled his twentieth and last census in 1934 there were 21,701 pure-blood bison throughout the world: 4,404 in the United States, 17,043 in Canada, and 305 in other countries. In 1903, the world estimate had been 1,644.

The Zoological Society contributed twenty-nine bison from its own collection to the founding of two herds under federal control; fifteen to the Wichita Game Preserve in 1907 and fourteen to the Wind Cave National Game Preserve in the Black Hills of South Dakota in 1913. These were appropriate gestures, for the society had a deep-rooted interest in the bison. Hornaday, indeed, had been that noble animal's friend and defender since 1889, when he wrote a 180-page sketch of its life history and its progress toward extinction for the *Report* of the U.S. National Museum. The twenty-acre Bison Range in the Zoological Park was one of the earliest and best showplaces of the Zoo. For the first two or three years there had been a struggle to keep the herd at exhibition strength; the bison sickened and died when they grazed on the lush and rolling meadows that, on Hornaday's first glimpse of Bronx Park, he had instantly ticketed for bison and pronghorns. The rank grass gave them "gastro-enteritis" against which the

veterinarians seemed helpless, and they continued to die even after the grass was burned off, the terrain plowed, topsoil removed, and the animals shifted to a grassless pasture. But Hornaday persevered and begged or bought more bison, and in a few more years the herd stabilized and began to increase by annual births.

The nucleus herd for the Wichita Preserve, offered and accepted in 1905 a few months before the founding of the American Bison Society, could not be actually delivered for a full two years because of the necessity of acquiring the land and fencing it. In the fall of 1907 Frank Rush, who was to be in charge of the range, came to New York and staged a remarkably smooth crating operation on the park's Bison Range. The selected animals were driven one by one down a

Crating bison in the Zoological Park for shipment to the Wichita Preserve in 1907. Director Hornaday at the left, Superintendent Frank Rush of the preserve at the end of the crate.

266

fifty-foot chute and into individual crates, and in two days all fifteen had been loaded on "Arms Palace Horse Cars" at Fordham station one mile from the Zoo and were on their way to Oklahoma.

Their arrival was a sensational event to the Indians, cow-punchers, and ranch owners of the region. Fifty years later Frank Rush's widow told the Wildlife Management Biologist then in charge of the range how the Indians flocked to see the buffalo return to their old home, with squaws dressed in their brightest dresses, many carrying babies, and old Indians gathering days in advance on their ponies or the open wagons called Indian hacks. Old men peered into the crates as they arrived and told excited young boys about their own hunting of the buffalo in their youth.

The Wichita herd prospered, and before the end of the year two calves were born, one of which was named Hornaday, the other Oklahoma.

The American Bison Society was directly concerned or influential in achieving most of the nine government-owned herds established by 1919, but its greatest triumph was the creation of the Montana National Bison Range near Ravalli, Montana, in 1909. At the Bison Society's request, and with the strong backing of the Zoological Society, the Boone and Crockett Club, and other organizations, Congress bought and fenced twenty-nine square miles of range. The Bison Society undertook to raise $10,000 to buy the nucleus animals. As the society's president, Dr. Hornaday swung into action with a typical hard-hitting national campaign. Letters pointing out that it was the duty of every American to aid in the project went to the mayors of 150 cities of more than 30,000 population (except New York and Boston), to Chambers of Commerce, to banks, to prominent citizens. The money was raised—$10,560.50 in all—but its sources gave Hornaday the pretext for some moralizing. The West, which should have had the greatest interest in preserving the animal that typified it, was disappointingly uninterested. In fact, Montana itself contributed only $366 and was a poor fifth to New York ($5,213), Massachusetts ($2,320), Minnesota ($1,054), and Pennsylvania ($503).

The women of America were a pleasant surprise to offset the indifference of the West. The first subscription to arrive was five dollars from a woman in Massachusetts, and altogether 112 women gave $1,227. There still exists in the Bison Society's archives a penciled letter on lined paper, in the shaky hand of old age:

> Enclosed I send two dollars for the Montana national bison herd. I have seen great herds with countless thousands of the noble animals in them, and would be sorry to know that a time would come when none were left in the United States.
>
> > Respectfully,
> > Mrs. U. L. Parker
> > Union, Iowa.

Nebraska (total contribution for the state, thirty-two dollars) produced some sharp replies to the Bison Society's appeals. The cashier of a bank at Bristow wrote back:

> What do you take people for? In this country we have all we can do to take care of our hogs, horses and cattle to say nothing of investing through you our hard earned money to raise buffalo. You have a "Buffalo Game" sure. No Sir we do not care for stock in the buffalo business. Wonder what will come next from Wall Street?

Some of Nebraska's thirty-two dollars may have come from a woman who wrote to Hornaday:

> We will be glad to contribute some thing for the preservation of the American Bison but if the object of your society is to protect these animals for the sake of having them to kill as they increase we would rather they would be exterminated now. Theodore Roosevelt [he was then the honorary president of the Bison Society] is setting such a bad example to the world for cruelty, most people are rather suspicious of any humane work that he is connected with. The president of the United States

268

cannot make hunting respectable in the eyes of right thinking people.

But objections to the principle of preserving the bison by establishing the Montana and other herds were rare; it was indifference that the American Bison Society had chiefly to contend with. Newspapers across the country were almost uniformly friendly, enthusiastically so. The only exceptions that came to Hornaday's attention (and he subscribed to a nationwide clipping service) were the Kansas City *Journal* and three or four lesser papers that picked up and reprinted its editorial headed "Wanted—Bison to Protect." Some leaden chunks of it are worth reprinting as examples of the style in which the less urbane newspapers of the day expressed their scorn.

It will be remembered that some years ago the American Bison Society was organized. Its object tentatively expressed was the protection of the common, or garden, buffalo. As such mighty organizations are generally deliberate in getting down to business, it was nearly three years before the American Bison Society finally adopted a constitution and by-laws and a year or so later before William T. Hornaday was formally elected president. After these preliminaries, which were effected with many ponderous reports and a great setting of seals upon formidable documents, the American Bison Society declared itself ready to "protect" the remaining bison of America.

It now appears that the American Bison Society is having considerable difficulty in finding bison to protect.

President Hornaday is now in the position of having a government reserve in which to place bison, but he hasn't any bison. He has appealed to the country to get him bison so that he can protect them, but as yet not a single, solitary beast has been driven up to his front door. He thinks that if he had $10,000 he could buy bison, and then protect them with the money congress has set aside for the purpose; but this is not a cause that appeals strongly to the American people.

Well, it appeared to enough people to raise the needed

269

$10,000 and a little more. In October of 1909, thirty-four bison were bought from the herd owned by Mrs. C. E. Conrad at Kalispell, Montana, at $275 a head, and without incident they were delivered to the range on the Flathead Reservation seventy-five miles away. Six more came as gifts immediately or in the following year, and the nucleus of forty had increased to ninety-seven by the American Bison Society's tenth birthday. By that time the society was confident that it had accomplished its purpose and was beginning to wonder whether it ought to disband. It hung together for another fifteen years and concerned itself with a variety of wildlife projects. But its great days were over.

When the decennial of the Zoological Park rolled around in 1909, the executive committee was able to announce that the first period of the park's development had closed and from then on the society would increasingly work for the attainment of its remaining original objectives: scientific studies and the protection and preservation of our native fauna.

Most elements of the first planned period had indeed fallen into place, but not quite all. In the remainder of the Hornaday period ending with his retirement in 1926, a few other major buildings were still to be constructed: the Administration Building (1910), Zebra House (1912), Eagle and Vulture Aviary (1912), Animal Hospital (1916), and, finally, the Heads and Horns Building to round out the Baird Court complex (1922). But scientific work and what we now broadly call conservation had been going on all the time; now it would be intensified.

Hornaday had fired the first blast in his lifelong campaign against the slaughter of wildlife with "The Destruction of our Birds and Mammals" in the society's second *Annual Report* for 1897. He had solicited and then printed reports from observers all over the country, and their estimates of the decline in numbers of American mammals and birds were significantly high in attributions to "sportsmen and so-called sportsmen," as well as to boys who shot for fun, market hunters and pothunters, plume hunters and hunters for the millinery trade, and to egg collectors, chiefly small boys.

Hornaday's own most violent denunciation in that report was of the "side hunt," an American small-town phenomenon that is a dismaying revelation of early-1900s attitudes toward wildlife. As Hornaday put it:

A side hunt may properly be described as a game of murder, in which a body of particularly brutal (or thoughtless) men, sometimes *more than a hundred* in number, choose sides, arm themselves with guns and an unlimited quantity of ammunition, go forth on a given day, and for a fixed number of days shoot any kinds of wild creatures, "for points." At the close of the slaughter,

15

Battles for Wildlife, the Bronx River Parkway, and the Giant Redwoods

the victims are collected, counted according to the "points" agreed upon for each species, and the side which has accomplished the greatest amount of butchery is declared the winner.

The character of the men who engage in such contests may be gauged by the fact that they are not above killing herons, woodpeckers, crows, jays, red squirrels, chipmunks *and skunks*. We have read much of the doings of savages, and seen a little, but so far as known, the side hunt descends a step lower than any hunting operations accredited to Digger Indians, Dog-Ribs, Apaches, or any other savage tribe.

Apparently side hunts were not uncommon, for Hornaday cited them in Leominster, Massachusetts; Lebanon, New Hampshire; Enosburg Falls, Vermont; and Sedan, Indiana, in 1896 and 1897. At Sedan, fourteen Hoosier boys, "no worse than others—in fact, better than they will average"—bagged fifty English sparrows, eight chipping sparrows, five bluejays, twenty-seven nuthatches, seventeen downy woodpeckers, fourteen hairy woodpeckers, twelve red-bellied woodpeckers, and two flying squirrels on Thanksgiving Day in 1897, besides an unrecorded number of rabbits and squirrels. Most of the "game" was inedible, of course, and was merely carted off to the town dump after the points were tallied. A social lodge in Rome, New York, planned a monster game supper for the contestants of its side hunt on three days in early November, 1902, the losing side to pay for the suppers of the winners. Surely, though, they could not have intended to eat any of the high-scoring victims: fox, 500 points; coon, 500; hawk, 150; mink, 150; owl, 100; crane [heron] 100.

G. O. Shields of *Recreation,* one of the most ardent conservation publications of the day, sent the announcement of Rome's side hunt to Hornaday, who immediately protested to the captain of one of the sides "in the name of the twelve hundred members of the New York Zoological Society." He warned Rome's sportsmen that they were in danger of being "severely condemned in the public prints," and when he received no response from Rome he sent a copy of his protest to the *Tribune*. That newspaper not only printed it but ran an editorial endorsing it: "If any wild creature of any sort remains alive in the vicinity of Rome on November 5th, it will not be the fault of the 'Noble Three Hundred.' "

Whether Rome heeded the protest and its side hunt and game supper were called off does not appear in the records. They were not reported in the Rome *Sentinel* of those November dates, at any rate.

Side hunts did not die out immediately; as late as 1911 a mammoth side hunt was organized in Alaska and the game warden of the territory was reported to have taken part in it. Hornaday of course protested in a letter to Governor Walter E. Clark at Juneau:

I can not understand how any reasoning being,—civilized or savage,—could find it in his heart to go out into the desolate woods in winter and slaughter the few wild mammals and birds that are bravely struggling to survive the cold and the snows. One would naturally expect that the common promptings of humanity would lead every resident of Alaska to succor and protect every harmless bird or mammal that would endeavor to survive the long, dreary winter in that region.

True to its promise to become more active in wildlife protection and preservation, the society issued a special "Wild-Life Preservation Number" of its *Bulletin* in June, 1909. Madison Grant in an article on "The Future of Our Fauna" was not optimistic about Americans and wild animals living harmoniously side by side:

To bring about such a change in public opinion is a gigantic undertaking, and it may be necessary in many places to go through, in our characteristic national way, the process of complete destruction of the animals we have, and the restocking of the country with new and perhaps in many cases with foreign and less attractive forms.

Professor Osborn promised an expansion of the Zoological Society's efforts on all fronts:

273

Our work will be mainly directed to the state and public lands of North America, but we shall also co-operate with the great conservation movement in all parts of the world, through a special committee backed by the sentiment and funds from the Society and our future endowments.

One of the society's earliest campaigns was against pump guns that could get off six shots in six seconds and automatic shotguns that were loaded and cocked by their own recoil. In 1906 the society sent an appeal to all its members for a special fund to wage legislative wars against these "machine guns" in state legislatures, and more than a thousand dollars was quickly raised. G. O. Shields was employed to work with legislators everywhere he could get a hearing.

Shields was in a way a victim of his own enthusiasm for wildlife protection. As the crusading editor of *Recreation,* he spent so much time and money on game protection that he was thrown into bankruptcy and lost his magazine. Subsequently he started another journal, *Shields' Magazine,* with some backing from members of the society's executive committee. His letterhead billed him as "The Pioneer in the Sledge Hammer Method of Game Protection."

There was, of course, enormous resistance on the part of gun manufacturers and hunters to efforts to outlaw automatic guns, and the campaign had little immediate effect, although the Zoological Society, the League of American Sportsmen, and the Audubon Societies vowed to continue the fight. Pennsylvania did outlaw the automatic shotgun and the pump gun in 1907, and New Jersey in 1912.

One of the first major legislative triumphs was the passage of a law to give at least *some* protection to the mammals and birds of Alaska. It came as early as 1902, when Madison Grant acted for both the Zoological Society and the Boone and Crockett Club in working with Representative John F. Lacey of Oskaloosa, Iowa, to draft and gain passage of the federal law. It prohibited commercial killing and shipment of game, established closed seasons, and gave the Department of Agriculture the right to stop for up to five years the killing of species in danger of extermination. Except for commercial exploitation—shipments of wild meat to the game markets—there was little chance of the law's being effectively enforced in the wild and woolly Alaska of the day, but shutting off the wholesale slaughter for money was important.

Causes ripe for indignation, official protest, or legislative action were never in short supply. Hornaday's reputation as a fighter for wildlife protection ensured that he would be sought out by anyone with a cause, whether it was the protection of box tortoises on Long Island* or the suspected illegal serving of out-of-season quail. One urgent correspondent wanted him to dine anonymously (but with a party of friends as witnesses) at Martin's Restaurant at Fifth Avenue and Twenty-sixth Street. He was to order quail and carry away the breastbones of what was served to him, together with the menu. In true spy-thriller style, he was advised to take something to wrap the bones in so his pocket would not become greasy (this was in the days before doggie bags), and to secrete the bones without being observed. Hornaday was in no mood for intrigue and replied simply that he was too busy to go downtown for dinner.

He was not inclined to work for legislation to protect black bears in the Adirondacks, either. He thought they were in no need of protection, and judging from the number of black-bear cubs that were constantly being offered to the Zoo—and refused—he was probably right. The proposer of the scheme was a brash young man named Harry V. Radford, whom Hornaday had known for many years and periodically chastised in letters. One such spanking came when Radford wrote in *Woods and Waters,* a quarterly out-of-doors maga-

---

* Box tortoises were befriended by the society and under its sponsorship legal protection was given to them. The *Annual Report* for 1905 noted that "This legislation was made necessary owing to the fact that Chinamen were developing a taste for the box turtles which bid fair to result in their extermination, especially on Long Island." The threat from Oriental cuisine disappeared, but a new one against which legislation was powerless succeeded it: the automobile. Thousands are killed annually by speeding cars.

zine which he had founded, an introduction to an article by Hornaday on the protection of Alaskan game. The introduction was all right, Hornaday informed him, "but you spoiled it by saying that I had always 'followed the movements which *Woods and Waters* had led!' I will be a good deal older than I am now before I begin to follow the lead of any boy of your age." Radford was then twenty-two. A few years later, against the advice of Hornaday and a number of older men, he undertook an exploration of northern Canada and an investigation of the herds of woods bison deep in the interior. He and a companion were murdered by Eskimos.

The plight of wildlife not only in North America but in Africa, Asia, and the Far East (the latter treated in an essay contributed by C. William Beebe) was set forth by Hornaday in *Our Vanishing Wild Life,* a book of some four hundred pages. It was printed in 1913 and the Zoological Society paid for ten thousand copies for distribution to legislators and influential persons all over the United States.

The book had enormous impact on pending and future legislation, for the protection of birds in particular. It reached legislators in Washington shortly before the McLean-Weeks bill to protect migratory insectivorous and game birds came up for a vote. Senator George P. McLean wrote to the society: "Your book arrived just in the nick of time, and it put a fourteen-inch hole through the hull of the enemy from side to side." Former President Theodore Roosevelt reviewed it in *The Outlook* and observed:

This book should be studied in every legislature. I commend it to women's clubs just as much as to farmers' associations. It should be read by all intelligent, far-sighted and public-spirited men and women throughout the Union. Moreover, when they have read it, let them not be content with impotent indignation, but let them do all they can to act on the advice it contains.

Our Vanishing Wild Life makes impressive, even horrifying, reading even today. It is a solid, factual, statistical report from the wild-game markets and the feather-trading centers,

276

and it listed new game laws needed in each state, with instructions for drafting new laws. All of it was spiced by the hard-hitting conservation prose that was Hornaday's specialty. How he managed to find time to turn out so many thousands of words while still keeping a tight rein on the Zoological Park is a mystery that only his phenomenal energy and belief in wildlife protection can explain. It was all written at home, after park hours and on weekends. Of course, for the most part he was blessed with ruddy good health. Shortly before throwing himself into the wildlife campaign, he had thanked a pharmaceutical house for a box of sample tonic but went on, "candor compels me to admit that I do not notice any results, one way or another." He weighed, he said, 185 pounds and was eating and sleeping well. The only incapacitating setback in his career, in fact, had occurred in the spring of 1906, when he underwent an operation for mastoiditis, and for a week or two was in a touch-and-go condition. (Some newspapers reported that he had contracted actinomycosis, the "lumpy jaw" to which pronghorn antelopes were particularly susceptible. "I think some of the papers would have gladly seen me buried, for the sake of an additional news item," he wrote afterward.)

The McLean-Weeks Law of 1913 put an end to spring shooting of game birds, among other things, and gave much-needed protection to an estimated 610 species of bird, half of them insect eaters; in fact, the chances of the bill's passing might have been much less if the Zoological Society had not publicized nationally the economic importance of the insect eaters to the farmers of America. More than a thousand newspapers published the appeal to stop the "Slaughter of Useful Birds: a Grave Emergency," and letters poured in on congressmen.

Two other conservation measures in which the Zoological Society, mostly spearheaded by Hornaday, was successful were the Bayne Law of 1912 to stop the sale of native wild game in New York State (a law which was copied by Massachusetts and California), and in 1913 a provision in the Underwood Tariff Act which stopped the importation of wild birds' plumage for millinery purposes. Hornaday wrote the prohibitory clause and with T. Gilbert Pearson of the National Audubon Societies led this fight, which had been foreshadowed by a long chapter in *Our Vanishing Wild Life* filled with gruesome photographs and statistics about the trade in stuffed bodies of little birds slaughtered by the hundreds of thousands to decorate women's hats. At a quarterly millinery-feather sale in London in 1912, the Zoological Society had bought 1,600 hummingbird skins at two cents each. The society made effective use of them. Each skin was glued to a card and mailed to legislators and prominent women across America. They got the message, and fashion quickly changed—as, in fact, it had to when the Underwood Tariff put an end to importations of the skin of hummingbirds, birds of paradise, trogons, quetzals, and similar avian beauties.

It would be pointless here—for this is not a history of conservation—to detail the successes and the rare failures of the Zoological Society in its battles to carry out its objectives in "the protection and preservation of our native fauna," a goal soon extended to wildlife all over the world. But as Hornaday wrote in his *Thirty Years War for Wild Life* in 1931, on a page following photographs of Professor Osborn and Madison Grant:

In looking back through the history of the past 33 years of endeavor in the defense of wild life in North America, it is difficult to recall an important cause in wild life protection which has not in one way or another enjoyed either the support or the cordial endorsement of the New York Zoological Society.

As the society's principal officers, Osborn and Grant were often under attack for their support of Hornaday's controversial campaigns, and the director was probably not exaggerating when he wrote that a "Stop Hornaday" movement was started in Washington while he was battling to save fur seals from overexploitation. The executive committee, he said, "received numerous pressing invitations to remove me from my sphere of influence in the wild life protection field, and seal me up with the other wild animals in the Zoological Park."

Hornaday's loyalty to the Zoological Society told him that the no-holds-barred kind of campaigns he intended to wage were not appropriate tactics for the society, and in 1911 he came up with a plan that would give him independent action. This was the idea of a Permanent Wild Life Protection Fund of at least $100,000, to be subscribed privately, with the annual interest to be expended by himself as its "Campaigning Trustee" on any campaign that he wanted to institute or support. The money did not come easily at first. In his *Thirty Years War for Wild Life,* Hornaday wrote:

All was going very well when like a cyclone out of a clear sky there came on the awful whirlwind campaign of October, 1913, for four *million* dollars for the erection of clubhouses for New York's Y.M.C. and Y.W.C. Associations. That effort, which really was a "side-hunt" for millions, was prosecuted with teamwork, committees, luncheons and publicity galore. It sweepingly absorbed all the loose money in sight, and much more; and for a time it completely wrecked the Permanent Fund.

It is a measure of the confidence conservation-minded people felt in him that by the end of 1915 he had raised $104,750. Battle cries and campaign documents began to pour forth under the imprimatur of the PWLPF, and at one time or another Hornaday challenged the motivation and politics of the National Association of Audubon Societies, the 6,414,454 "licensed hunters now [1930] actually outnumbering all the active standing armies of the world," the American Game Protective Association, and, in fact, just about any organization or individual that disagreed with him on bag limits for ducks, closed seasons, automatic guns, the inviolability of waterfowl sanctuaries, and so on. In 1934, three years before his death, he put together the materials for what he intended

279

to be his last book, *The Passing of Migratory Game: 1931–1940.* The final chapter was to be headed "Memoranda for the Nature Historians of the Future" and was in the form of a letter to "Nature Historians of 1960," dated as from Stamford, Connecticut (where he then lived in retirement), December 1, 1940. It began:

In order to shorten your thankless task of writing game-extermination history for people of your day who are too heedless to care for it, I indict [*sic*] these few lines.* Although our industrious knights-of-the-gun have not yet shot to pieces the very last individuals of America's crows and rabbits, on many species we are down to the "specimen" basis. All forehanded museum curators are busily getting theirs before dawns the morn of total extinction.

Did he intend it as a last, perhaps even posthumous, *apologia pro vita sua,* a settling forever of old scores? He named the "enemies" of true conservation (and they include both men and magazines that he once counted on his side) and documented their iniquities.

It is a pity that the readers for *The Oxford English Dictionary* never got to scan the manuscript. They could have

* Of course Hornaday was here employing his favorite device of stating his case in harsh terms for the sake of their shock value. But whatever may have been the attitude of 1940 (and it was not complete heedlessness of wildlife), his admonishments were still remembered in 1973. Roger Caras, a nature writer and a nationally syndicated columnist, wrote in his column "Our Only World" on February 11, 1973: "The other day on a radio talk show interview a gentleman was bemoaning the fact that certain furs were being denied the fur-wearing public. He made the point that this was, after all, a new fad and that a year or two ago no one even thought about 'supposedly' disappearing fur-bearing wildlife. The hostess of the show, surely one of the least well-informed people I have ever heard, agreed with him." Mr. Caras then quoted from Hornaday's article, "The Fur Trade and the Wild Animals" in the March, 1921, issue of the Zoological Society's *Bulletin,* in which he made a hard attack on the fur trade and the wearers of furs. ("The truly fashionable woman is a cruel animal.")

"And so there it is," Mr. Caras went on. "Over half a century ago a highly respected director of a highly respected zoological society was pleading for wildlife although, by his own confession, he didn't expect it to do any good. So to the gentleman and his lady interviewer, our congratulations for knowing nothing about everything, and that perhaps by design. The plain fact is that there is nothing new about the conservation movement."

Director Hornaday would have been pleased with Mr. Caras.

added a new word to the language: "One of the contributing causes to the final blow-up was the array of smoke screens that were sent up by the enemies of wild life to represent 'causes,' and to muggify the atmosphere, and hide the ghastly truth from stupid or indifferent people." Muggify! A good new word.

On the cover of the manuscript Hornaday wrote "Practically ready for publication," but it was never published, and never will be. It is just as well; the day of the rabid, or Hornaday, type of crusade was already passing. Certainly the American conscience needed awakening, and so great was its lethargy that maybe battles and shouting, outcry and vituperation and extreme statements, were the only means by which it could have been aroused. Sweet reason seldom commands an enthusiastic press, and thick scrapbooks of newspaper clippings testify to the coverage Hornaday's campaigns got. He made news all his life; he *was* news.

But by the end of the 1930s it was time for different men to take up the fight, and to fight in a different way. On the broad conservation front, Hornaday and the men and women associated with him—Mrs. Rosalie Edge and her Emergency Conservation Committee, to name one outstanding example —had achieved worthy successes and had won important battles, insofar as any conservation battle ever may be said to have been won. Poaching and overkilling and unsportsmanlike slaughter of wildlife we have always with us, but today they are not so rampant as they were in the early decades of this century. Unhappily, major menaces have come from a different direction: from pesticides and detergents and industrial wastes, from the destruction of habitats in the name of progress, the draining of wetlands, the invasion of wilderness areas by skimobiles, the paving of millions of acres for high-speed automobile traffic.

New causes and new needs for protection continually arise as pressure is applied on wildlife, now here, now there—the traffic in wild-animal skins and crocodilian hides comes to

281

mind as a current instance—but earnest men and large sums of money have always come forward to meet the challenges. Today there is a more receptive and understanding atmosphere for wildlife protection, nationally and internationally. Radio, television, newspapers, and magazines are sympathetic; ecology with its connotation of survival space for wild things has become a household word. Even princes of England and the Netherlands speak out for wildlife through international organizations. Princess Grace of Monaco has joined with women of the British royal family in pledging not to wear the furs of animals threatened with extinction.

After Hornaday's death in 1937 the principal sum of the Permanent Wild Life Protection Fund, then amounting to something more than $130,000, was transferred to the keeping of the New York Zoological Society by its surviving trustees, and the income continues to be applied to conservation projects as Hornaday intended it to be.

But wildlife was not the only cause that enlisted the support of the Zoological Society, nor was Dr. Hornaday its only spokesman. In their own much quieter way, Madison Grant and William White Niles fought battles that were not so spectacular but were nonetheless effective; theirs was more likely to be the approach of combining the interests of like-minded men and working through legislative halls. One of their achievements was the creation of the Bronx River Parkway, that extends fifteen and a half miles north from Bronx Park to the Kensico Reservoir at Valhalla.

When the Zoological Society took possession of the south half of Bronx Park it cleared away the storm and flood débris that had accumulated in its section of the Bronx River; to the north the Botanical Garden had done the same thing with its portion of the river. But beyond the upper boundary of the Botanical Garden the meandering stream—"river" is a courtesy title; in some places an agile man could have jumped across it—was little more than an open sewer and watery garbage dump. It was choked with tree snags, ash heaps, and the junk discards of villages and towns clustered along its banks and the New York Central Railroad, whose tracks roughly paralleled it. Originally the Bronx River valley had been well wooded, but clearings had been made for tar-paper shacks and billboards advertising any product or service that might attract passengers on the trains. Raw sewage poured into the river, and when summer droughts came it was a succession of noisome, mosquito-breeding, swampy pools.

As early as 1895 a commission had been appointed to think about a sewer for the full length of the Bronx River valley, but rural Westchester was not interested and nothing came of the scheme. In the meantime pollution continued to flow downstream into Lake Agassiz and Bronx Lake in the Zoological Park.

There have been several accounts of the origin of the Bronx River Parkway, but one is surely incontrovertible: that of William White Niles, the man who first had the idea. As Assemblyman Niles he had bulldogged through the legislature the bill creating the Zoological Society, and in 1897 he had become a member of its executive committee. It was as a concerned official of the Zoological Society that . . .

But let him tell his own story, as he set it down in 1929 in a long letter to Jay Downer, secretary of the Westchester County Park Commission:

It has occurred to me that it might be well if I were to write a brief statement on the subject [the origin of the parkway] and ask you to file it away in the archives of the Parkway Commission, which being interpreted, means, I suppose, laid away in the safe, where it will be promptly forgotten, but be available in the event anyone in the future should desire authentic information on the subject.

In 1901 [actually, 1902] I went abroad with Dr. Hornaday, the director of the New York Zoological Society.

He had occasion to visit Mr. Carnegie at Skiebo Castle and I accompanied him as far as Inverness, where I remained for three days while he was visiting the Laird of Skiebo.

Having nothing better to do during his absence, I spent most of my time in walking about the vicinity, and on one occasion, coming upon a little park which bordered the River Ness beyond the limits of the City, I followed the river down through the city, and was greatly surprised to find the water as it issued from the limits of the city as clean, so far as appearance went, which was the only test that I applied, as it was when it entered the city. My astonishment was due to the fact that I had rather assumed that a stream could not go through a built up community without being defiled. I was familiar with many streams running through cities in America, but recalled no instance in which the sewerage and much of the refuse of the city was not dumped into the stream and its banks devastated and shorn of all beauty and in most instances, disfigured and rendered offensive by public dumps, dilapidated structures, coal yards and other unattractive activities.

The experience set me thinking as to whether it was possible to arouse any interest in America in protecting its streams where they flowed through urban communities.

When I returned home I happened on one occasion, to be walking through the northerly part of Bronx Park along the Bronx River and continued northward beyond the Park's boundaries still along the River, and was distressed to see the conditions prevailing there, which had never before impressed me so unfavorably.

I discussed the matter with Director Hornaday and with Mr. Grant, and found them both in a receptive mood, but none of us had a very clear idea as to what could be done nor how to go about it.

In 1904, if my memory serves me right, we had a very dry summer and the water in the stream was much reduced in size and the pollution became more and more apparent.

Director Hornaday had his attention called to the matter by a serious disorder that developed among the water fowl, who were permitted to use the river, and on examining into the cause of the disorder, he became convinced it arose from the polluted condition of the river. He then very ardently championed my proposition that we should take steps to remedy the existing conditions, and so impressed Mr. Grant that he finally said that if I would draft a bill to be presented to the Legislature that he would support it and do his best to procure the support of the Zoological Society. During this period I discussed the matter with Dr. [Nathaniel Lord] Britton of the Botanical Society and found him also interested and obtained the assurance of his support.

What form our action was to take I did not know, but I finally concluded that as we had no public backing and could look for little support, that I should avoid any action which would involve any great expense, and I, therefore, prepared a bill for the appointment of a commission merely to inquire into the subject and report. This bill I submitted to Mr. Grant and received his approval, and I procured it to be introduced in the Legislature in the winter of 1905.

So much for the beginning of the idea. Mr. Niles's recollections, now in the archives of the Westchester County Department of Parks, Recreation and Conservation in White Plains, record at length the legislative maneuvering that resulted in passage and signing of the bill in 1906 and the appointment by Governor Frank W. Higgins of an investigative commission composed of Madison Grant of Manhattan, Dave H. Morris of the Bronx, and James G. Cannon of Westchester County. The commissioners met and elected Mr. Grant as president and appointed Mr. Niles as permanent secretary and attorney.

They toured the area, talked with county and town leaders, held discussions with the Bronx River Valley Sewer Commission that had been appointed in 1905 to lay a trunk sewer from White Plains to Woodlawn, and not unexpectedly reported to the governor in January of 1907 that something ought to be done to clean the river and preserve its banks. So another bill was introduced that was intended to go beyond mere investigation. It was an act "To provide for preserving the waters of the Bronx river from pollution; creating a reservation of lands on either side of the river; authorizing the taking of lands for that purpose and providing for the payment thereof, and appointing a commission to carry out the purpose of the act." The bill was passed in both houses and Governor Charles Evans Hughes signed it, then appointed Grant, Niles, and Cannon as commissioners, Morris having dropped out of the enterprise because of the Governor's known opposition to horse-racing tracks, in which the Morris family had interests.

Years of struggle and travail followed, and Commissioner Grant's files are stuffed with letters that reveal the enormous complexity of acquiring nearly fourteen hundred separate parcels of land, getting allocations of money from New York City and from Westchester County, clearing the river, and laying out the parkway. In 1913 Hermann W. Merkel, the Zoological Park's chief forester and constructor, became consulting forester to the Bronx Parkway Commission and began the planting of trees and shrubs that now make the Bronx River Parkway one of the most beautiful approaches to any American city. The next year the Zoological Society contributed twenty thousand tree cuttings from its own stock.

Merkel was also involved in the designing of the parkway and selection of the route it would follow, and he purposely emphasized the curves that were naturally dictated by the wandering course of the stream. He considered it a pleasure drive, not a speedway for Sunday-afternoon motorists. It still curves more constantly and abruptly than any other parkway leading into New York City, but in the early 1970s some of the happiest scenic stretches, particularly immediately above Scarsdale, were eliminated in favor of a straightaway.

Building the parkway in a parklike setting was a long and laborious task, but on November 5, 1925, a party of distinguished guests assembled in their automobiles at the southern terminus of the parkway just north of the Botanical Garden, then drove in a ribbon of cars to the northern terminus at the Kensico Reservoir dam in Valhalla. There was speechmaking, and the Bronx River Parkway was officially declared open. It had cost $16.5 million, and had taken almost exactly twenty years of effort, but millions of motorists since then must agree that it was worth the money and the time.

In 1938 a memorial to William White Niles was erected at 226th Street and Bronx Boulevard, a short stretch of road now paralleling the lower end of the parkway. A bronze plaque on the pedestal of a flagpole reads: "To record the fact that William White Niles was the founder of the Bronx River Parkway this memorial has been erected by his friends." Madison Grant's part in the achievement was not mentioned. For that matter, the tribute to Niles is almost unreadable through the spray-paint graffiti that disfigure the granite base. No flag flies from the flagpole.

Professor Osborn had written that the Zoological Society was going to interest itself in the state and public lands of the United States. Grant created public lands when he undertook to save at least some of the remaining stands of redwood trees in California.

In 1917, Grant, Professor Osborn, and Dr. John C. Merriam of the University of California made a trip through Mendocino, Humboldt, and Del Norte counties of California. They came away dismayed by the rapidity with which the giant redwoods (*Sequoia sempervirens*) were being destroyed—and for no other purpose than the profit that could be made from them for railroad ties, stakes for the vineyards of California, and shingles. Of many once huge groves, nothing remained but stumps and a fire-blackened wilderness where the slash had been burned away. No one cared, and even highway departments drove roads through the finest remaining stands and sold off the rights to "log out" the trees on either side.

Professional foresters figured that the redwoods would be entirely gone within sixty years; Grant gave them a much shorter time, because of the efficiency of logging with power saws and heavy trucks. He wrote to the governor of California urging him to at least preserve the redwoods in Humboldt County, which were threatened by highways. He re-

287

turned to California for another tour in 1918 and was still more disheartened, but the World War was in full fury and officials had no time to agonize over redwood trees.

Grant did. In the winter of 1918–19 he and Dr. Merriam got the attention of a group of well-to-do Californians, and they organized a body called the Save-the-Redwoods League. Its purposes were to buy up redwood groves by private subscription and county bond issues; to get a state bond issue to acquire the finest groves along state highways; to enlist federal aid in protecting timber along the scenic highways being built so rapidly to keep up with increasing automobile traffic; and to encourage reforestation of redwoods.

Grant's concern was that of a natural-born conservationist unwilling that one of the greatest glories of the North American continent should be wantonly sacrificed. In a special "Save the Redwoods" number of the Zoological Society's *Bulletin* (September, 1919), he wrote:

When Humboldt and Del Norte Counties awaken to a full realization of the revolution effected by the automobiles, which will flood the country with tourists as soon as the highways are completed, they will find that a Redwood grove, such as Bull Creek Flat, is an attraction that is worth many times the full net value of the timber contained in it.

He spoke as a prophet and, unlike some prophets, he was honored for his foresight. The Save-the-Redwoods League immediately formed numerous local chapters and inspired legislation, men, and money; the most important groves were saved and are now state or national parks. In September of 1931, the California State Board of Parks dedicated to Mr. Grant, Professor Osborn, and Dr. Merriam what was believed to be the tallest tree in the world—the Founders Tree, a 364-foot redwood in Humboldt Redwoods State Park. Since then it has been damaged by lightning and sóme seventeen feet at the top destroyed. Several other trees were subsequently believed to be taller than the Founders Tree ever was, but it is still a magnificent giant among redwoods.

After Grant's death on March 25, 1937, his brother, De Forest, proposed to the Boone and Crockett Club that a stand of redwoods near Orick in northern Humboldt County be acquired as a memorial to him. It was an ideal site, for it contained meadows and glades that were the haunts of the last herd of Roosevelt, or Olympic, elk surviving in California. The response was immediate and generous from individuals and organizations that had shared Grant's dreams: the Zoological Society, the Boone and Crockett Club, the National Audubon Society, the American Wildlife Foundation, the Save-the-Redwoods League, and the California State Park Commission. Thus the Madison Grant Forest and Elk Refuge of 1,605 acres came into being and was dedicated in July of 1946. Today it is marked by a small, unobtrusive sign alongside the road that winds through silent, green-topped canyons of redwoods—one of the many inconspicuous signs naming specific groves. Perhaps few of the thousands who roll past every summer realize that this is not just another named grove. *This* is a memorial to the man who saved the redwoods for all generations to enjoy.

William Beebe* set the pace for the Zoological Society's third objective: promotion of zoology through research, exploration, and publication. His was not the first scientific paper published by the society; the *Annual Report* for 1898 contained a paper by Andrew J. Stone entitled "Field Notes on the Larger Mammalia of the Stickine, Dease, and Liard Rivers, British Columbia," and in 1900 Dr. Hornaday contributed "Notes on the Mountain Sheep of North America, with a Description of a New Species." Formal scientific papers by Hornaday, Ditmars, Grant, J. Alden Loring, Charles H. Townsend of the New York Aquarium, R. H. Beck (on the giant tortoises of the Galápagos), and various other investigators on or outside the staff appeared in the *Annual Reports* as late as 1912, when Major Hans Schomburgk wrote about the "Distribution and Habits of the Pygmy Hippopotamus." The early *Reports* also embodied papers on pathology observed in the park's animals, such as "Osteomalacia of Primates in Captivity" by Drs. Harlow Brooks and W. Reid Blair. But the research and publication program did not become a recognized, almost obligatory, part of the society's activities until *Zoologica* was established in 1907.

Zoologica, subtitled "Scientific Contributions of the New York Zoological Society," may be said to have been established specifically as an outlet for Beebe's research and writing. Hornaday initiated it.

In May of 1907 he wrote to Professor Osborn that in line with his understanding that the professor wanted more scientific work done in the park, he had encouraged Mr. Beebe to do it, and was in fact allotting him fifty dollars a month to pursue his studies on the development of birds under various conditions. Beebe was now about ready to publish his results, and needed to know whether the society would print his paper or whether he should look to *Auk,* the journal of the American Ornithological Union.

16

William Beebe Charts a New Course

---

* C. William Beebe did not drop the "C." (for Charles) until 1915, but he became so well known under the shortened form of his name that it might as well be adopted here and henceforth.

In Hornaday's opinion, now was the time for the society to start its own scientific journal, perhaps under the title *Zoological Park Records*. Professor Osborn, however, did not think the time was ripe; he had read Beebe's manuscript, entitled "Geographic Variation in Birds, with Special Reference to the Effects of Humidity," and liked it, but we couldn't afford to start a publication of our own just now.

The old cry of "Where's the money coming from?" never impressed Hornaday when he wanted something. By this time he was on fairly stable and friendly terms with Madison Grant, and he knew that the society's secretary was interested in scientific work and would give just the extra pressure to tip Osborn in favor of a society journal immediately. He was right; Grant weighed in in favor of the project, and before the end of May Osborn wrote to Hornaday:

I am as desirous as you are to begin our scientific publications. I talked to Mr. Grant last night and he thinks we should go ahead. How does this impress you?

ZOOLOGIA

Scientific Papers of the New York Zoological Society

In a penciled note, apparently written to himself, the professor added: "Ruled out: Proceedings of the Zoological Society, Transactions, Records, Bulletin. Consider: Researches, Investigations, Contributions, Studies."

He favored *Zoologia,* however, and it was adopted as the official name of the new journal. It was printed thus on the title page of Volume 1, Number 1, and on the left-hand running head of Beebe's forty-two-page paper. When it was too late, for the paper was already off the press with the publication date of September 25, 1907, the professor had second thoughts about the soundness of his Latin and consulted Professor Harry Franklin Peck of the Department of Latin at Columbia University. Peck said it should be *Zoologica,* "regarding the word as being a nominative plural neuter and therefore equivalent to 'Zoological Studies' (studia zoologica) ." The only thing that could be done was to paste an Erratum slip over the title *Zoologia,* changing it to *Zoologica.*

The first volume of *Zoologica* ran to 436 pages, including the index, and contained twenty papers, ten of them by Beebe alone and two more jointly written by Beebe and Lee S. Crandall, the assistant curator of birds. It was a fast pace for one man to set, but Beebe maintained it the rest of his active life.

Outsiders were immediately eager to share in this new outlet for their observations. The standards were high, however, and members of the staff had first preference. Few rejections of manuscripts can have been as abrupt as the one Hornaday sent to a man in Florida who submitted "Observations on a Partially Albino Meadow Vole." It was a good enough paper, but the author confessed that after making his observations, he fed the vole to his cat. "What a ridiculous thing to do!" Hornaday wrote him.

The director could not have known it, but he was about to lose Beebe as an integrated, working member of his staff at the Zoological Park. Not wholly, at first; it was not until 1919 that Beebe cut active ties and became honorary curator of birds. But certainly the handwriting was on the wall and could have been read as early as 1900—less than a year after he joined the staff—when he made a holiday trip to Nova Scotia to study sea birds. Trips followed fast, on his own or the society's time, to Cape Cod and Nova Scotia in 1901; Gardiners Island in Long Island Sound (he brought back an osprey's four-hundred-pound nest and perched it in a cedar tree at the western end of Cope Lake; seven young ospreys were installed in it, but the nest never seemed like home and they all flew away) ; a return trip to Nova Scotia in 1902; the east coast of Florida and Cobb Island, Virginia; Mexico in 1904. . . .

William Beebe was, in a word, restless. The practice of traditional or even innovative aviculture in the care of the park's bird collection did not absorb his energy, nor did captive birds provide the kind of research material he wanted.

There was more than a hint of the way his mind was tending in one paragraph of his first paper in *Zoologica*. He cited examples of melanism and dichromatism, and then:

We should keep them all in mind while endeavoring to interpret the results of future field studies or experimental researches along these lines. The collecting of thousands of skins will be of no service nor will the study of those now in our museums be of any direct use. We must have careful and minute tabulation of the ecological conditions under which the phenomena under discussion appear.

In other words, the research man must get out into the field and find out what happened to his subjects in their natural habitat. In still other words, William Beebe must get out into the field.

His predilection for field work had the official approval of the Zoological Society. The preface to Volume I of *Zoologica*, obviously written by Professor Osborn, gave a blessing to the new ways of study:

Members of the scientific staff of the Park and of the Aquarium did not, however, enter the well trodden field of the lifeless cabinet or museum animal, nor of the older systematic or descriptive zoology, but sought a new and inspiring field which had been relatively little pursued, namely, the observation of the living bird and the living mammal, wherever possible in its own environment. This is a path pursued by the older naturalists and travellers, abandoned for a time in the work of the laboratory, but which is now followed with the new ardor of a larger knowledge of the problems and a deeper insight into the search for causes.

This expression of the society's research policy was not exactly a *carte blanche* for continuous travel and absence from his duties in the park, but in one way or another Beebe got into the field. In 1903 it had been his health; he was having trouble with his throat, and four winter months in Florida and Virginia were indicated. Hornaday, indeed, was doubtful whether Beebe's throat could ever again endure the

New York climate. Off he went in December, and at a bargain salary of seventy-five dollars a month W. Seward Wallace was engaged as acting curator of birds in his absence, an elevation from Wallace's former head keeper's job. The next year Beebe's health dictated the warmth of Mexico for the winter, and out of that jaunt came the first Beebe book, *Two Bird Lovers in Mexico*—the other bird lover being his wife, Mary Blair Beebe.

Expeditions rapidly became an addiction: Trinidad and Venezuela in 1908, British Guiana in 1909. Up to this point, at least, Dr. Hornaday went along with the here-today-and-gone-tomorrow habits of his curator of birds, for he believed wholeheartedly in the duty of the society to pursue scientific goals. Technical papers and books (*The Bird* and *Log of the Sun* had come out in 1906) were flowing from Beebe's ever more facile typewriter. When Beebe took off for British Guiana the first time, Dr. Hornaday begged a letter of introduction for him from the Secretary of State:

Mr. Beebe is a most perfect American citizen,—a thorough naturalist, a valuable investigator, and an absolutely perfect gentleman who knows too much to presume too far on the goodwill of foreign hosts. Mrs. Beebe is a lady of most charming personality, and the pair could be safely trusted to represent this country in any foreign court or country. Mr. Beebe is an author of international representation.

Professor Osborn more than tolerated the Beebe travels; he encouraged them and in 1906 suggested the title of Tropical Research for his extra-zoo scientific activities. The title was not actually used, however, until the department of tropical research was founded in 1916 and "Directing Curator" Beebe and his first staff sailed for Bartica District in British Guiana.

Professor Osborn's benison was an essential fact in Beebe's career, but almost equally decisive was the chance that brought Lee Saunders Crandall to the Zoological Park in the spring of 1908. Crandall was by temperament an aviculturist and a *zoo* man—neither of which Beebe was by inclination—

even though he was a young and inexperienced practitioner in 1908; he was just twenty-one years old to Beebe's mature thirty-one. In time, and in fact surprisingly soon, Crandall equipped himself to run the bird department and Beebe was thereupon freed from most of the day-to-day routine that was so distasteful to him. No doubt Beebe's career in the tropics and on the sea and under it would have developed much as it did whether Crandall had appeared or not, for his determination to have his own way matched Hornaday's. But certainly the Beebe-Hornaday relationship would have been even stormier than it sometimes was had not Crandall been there to keep the bird department running smoothly.

Crandall's part in the history of the Zoological Park is so vital to it—from unpaid student keeper in 1908 he rose to the general curatorship, published his 300,000-word classic, *The Management of Wild Mammals in Captivity,* in 1964, and altogether gave sixty-one years to the service of the society—that its inception should be recorded here. Fortunately he wrote about it himself near the end of his life in *A Zoo Man's Notebook.*

He was the son of a doctor in upstate New York, and in those leisurely horse-and-buggy days he often accompanied his father on visits to country patients outside Utica. He collected the local wildlife while his father was making calls, adding specimens to his private zoo at home.

Medicine had been the family profession for two generations, and it was taken for granted that Lee would become a doctor. In 1907 his family moved to New York City and the boy was enrolled in Cornell Medical School.

I stuck it out for one whole year, but my heart was not in medical studies. What I really wanted was something to do with animals—wild animals. In those days you did not lightly confess to your father that you were not enthusiastic about the career he assumed you would follow, but I had no such reticence with one of my classmates. I confessed to him that I would much rather be working with animals than with sick people, but that there didn't seem to be any way of doing it.

His classmate was more resourceful. He wrote a note of introduction to his uncle, William White Niles, then a member of the Zoological Society's executive committee, and Niles in turn gave young Crandall a note to Hornaday.

Dr. Hornaday listened to my account of the wild and domestic pets I had kept at home in Utica, my disenchantment with medicine, and my desire to work with animals. He was a decisive man. After very few questions, he announced that as soon as medical school was out that spring, I could come to work in the zoological park as a student, rotating duties in the mammal, reptile, and bird departments. He did not say anything about payment, and so I assumed that this glorious opportunity was free—I would not have to pay for the privilege he offered.

Thus it was in June of 1908 that I became a student in the mammal department of the zoological park. My duties were simple: I was to do what I was told to do. This did not vary greatly from building to building: cleaning cages, washing floors and windows, breaking open bales of hay, and carrying buckets of food were the major items.

The climax of that summer was working in the bird house, for I had always wanted to try my hand at keeping wild birds but had no idea how to go about it.

Sam Stacey taught him how to do it. Stacey was an Englishman who had been the Duchess of Wellington's "bird boy" and later a keeper in the Zoological Gardens of London. Hornaday had hired him in 1904 as a bird keeper and he rapidly rose to become head keeper of birds. Crandall's boyhood hobby had been rearing Sebright and Cochin bantams, and with this link between them Stacey—a compulsive talker —poured information into the receptive boy.

I had been working in the zoo most of the summer when one day, as I was cleaning cages in the south end of the zoo, the curator of birds stopped to speak to me. I had seen William Beebe at a distance, of course, but never to speak to; student keepers did not waste the time of curators.

"Mr. Stacey tells me you like it here," was the way the conversation started. I don't remember any more of the exact words,

296

but I still remember my feeling of gratitude to Mr. Stacey for having created this opportunity for me to actually speak with Mr. Beebe.

Mr. Beebe explained that he expected to be away a good deal in the future and would need an assistant. I could have the job if I wanted it. The salary would be $30 a month.

Such happiness comes few times in a lifetime; the human system could not stand repeated shocks like that. In the fall of 1908 I became a *salaried* employee of the New York Zoological Park. I have never regretted it.

Beebe had forecast his own future accurately; he *did* expect to be away a good part of the time, and he did need an assistant both in the field and in the operation of his department in the park. He took Crandall along as field assistant when he made his first expedition to British Guiana in 1909 and found him eager and reliable. When the party returned he reported that young Crandall had gotten himself bitten by a perai, a savage fish, and had come into camp one day with a live bird in each hand and one in his mouth. Crandall himself recalled struggling up the river bank with a 10-foot anaconda he had captured, desperately trying to keep its head and tail apart so it would not squeeze the breath out of him. An old Negro woman was rocking on the porch of a shack as he passed.

"In the midst of life we are in death!" she intoned.

Scientific work, to Beebe, meant field work: observations of living birds in the wild. With the approval of the executive committee he was determined to make a career in tropical research, and in the summer of 1909 the first great opportunity fell into his lap. Colonel Anthony R. Kuser of Bernardsville, New Jersey, a wealthy vice-president of the Public Service Corporation of New Jersey, was a pheasant enthusiast, and he offered Beebe a chance to explore the haunts of pheasants in the Himalayas, Borneo, China, Mongolia, Japan, or wherever else pheasants might be found, and to write a superbly illustrated monograph of the Phasianidae. He would put up $60,000 for the expenses of the expedition and bear the cost of engaging the best bird artists to make paintings, and of printing, binding, and advertising. The book would be published in the name of the Zoological Society.

It was a fair, reasonable, even generous, and public-spirited offer on Colonel Kuser's part. There *was* no definitive work on the pheasants of the world and one was needed. William Beebe had demonstrated his interest in that family by the pheasants he kept in the Zoological Park; he had also demonstrated a scientific attitude and an ability to write accurately and graphically. He was the ideal man to undertake such a commission.

Dr. Hornaday's reaction was hot indignation.

On August 19, 1909, he wrote to Madison Grant:

298

Mr. Kuser is a very wealthy man, amusing himself just now with birds and aviaries.

Finding in Mr. Beebe a congenial and admiring spirit, he decides to annex Mr. Beebe; for it is the way of some wealthy men to reach out and take whatever they specially desire.

Mr. Beebe is so finely caught that I think he is today ready to fling away a great career as an ornithologist,—if he is denied what he now asks,—and all for the privilege of becoming, for a brief season, only, a rich man's plaything, and making a picture book that he never of his own initiative would have dreamed of making.

So completely is Mr. Beebe under the spell of his evil genius, —Mr. Kuser,—that he is now dead to all sense of loyalty to the Park and its Director, and is doing his utmost to influence the Executive Committee to support him in not only ignoring my expressed wishes of his chief, but even in openly defying the decision on Zoological Park policy that I have already rendered.

What, I ask you in all seriousness, will become of the present soldierly discipline of the Zoological Park if Mr. Kuser and Mr. Beebe succeed, *in any measure*, in the effort they are now making?

Shall any man be permitted to inflict serious injury on the Zoological Park by cajoling away from it its best men under the pretext of doing the Zoological Society a "service"? (If Mr. Kuser gets Mr. Beebe away from me, Mr. Kuser must thenceforward be known as the Evil Genius of the Zoological Park; for no man shall injure this force, and at the same time be credited with having done us a "favor.")

The value of the Society's imprint on the proposed pheasant book would not counterbalance to the Park the loss of the poorest keeper on the force. Very few persons will see during the next twenty years the costly book that is proposed.

The most serious question of the present campaign is the fate of Mr. Beebe. If he goes to the orient as proposed, no matter what the *modus vivendi* may be, unquestionably it will end his career as Curator of Birds in the Zoological Park. I never will consent to his going for a longer period than four months; and he never will go for an absence as short as that. If he goes contrary to my views of the needs of the Park, I shall ask that his position at once be declared vacant, and a successor appointed who can assume his duties.

The wreck of Mr. Beebe's legitimate career will hurt me personally far more than would the mortification of having him triumph over my authority.

Mr. Grant and Professor Osborn—indeed, all members of the executive committee—knew their man. They knew how to assess such explosions; they had had plenty of practice. Given time to calm down, Hornaday would realize that the executive committee saw the situation in a different light, that it was united on the desirability of this pheasant expedition, and that there was really very little he could do about it. He was angry and he *had* to lash out, but he could not change the situation. As Grant had said in a letter to Osborn a couple of years before: "The best way is to let Mr. Hornaday speak his mind, and then we can meet privately and decide what we are going to do."

The summer and the situation dragged on. Without anything yet being put into writing, as an undertaking on Colonel Kuser's part, it was understood by everyone that William Beebe was going to make his pheasant expedition and very likely it would take two years instead of four months (and then more realistically, the one year) originally talked about. Dr. Hornaday started lining up a replacement, either temporary or permanent, for his defecting curator of birds.

Professor Joseph Grinnell of the University of California was approached and so were Frank Finn, editor of *Avicultural Magazine* in London, and E. W. Harper, another Englishman. To Grinnell he wrote:

The routine work [in the Bird Department] is well provided for through a very competent force of keepers, aided by a very satisfactory office assistant, Mr. Crandall. My private opinion is that as soon as Mr. Beebe finishes his monograph of the Phasianidae, he will plunge into South America for ornithological investigations there, and that we shall never again have the benefit of his services as a de facto Curator of Birds. I think this is Mr. Beebe's own expectation regarding the future, and naturally, I am looking out for a real working curator of birds, whose interests will lie here in the Zoological Park, and on whom I can depend from day to day, and hour to hour.

Grinnell, Finn, and Harper all turned down the opportunity to become, probably, the permanent curator of birds. Beebe himself minimized the importance of finding a replacement for the two years he thought the job would take; young Crandall could easily keep the department running.

But Dr. Hornaday was not to be deflected and he excoriated Beebe in a letter to Grant.

When I told Mr. Beebe that we mean to have his place filled by some other man than Crandall during his absence and during his work on that pheasant book, I knew full well that he would go to Professor Osborn as quickly as possible, and try to thwart that plan! That is Mr. Beebe's way of being "loyal." He is "loyal" just so long as he gets his own way in absolutely everything; but not one moment longer.

His course is now getting on my nerves; and if he is permitted to interfere in any way with the plan that has been fully approved by the Executive Committee, my friendly relations with him will come to an abrupt end, and for all time to come.

Even if he does return in one year, I don't want a curator who will be absolutely certain to spend the whole of the next year in writing books. The position for him hereafter is "Honorary Curator"; for you know very well that he is looking forward to extensive travels and bird studies in South America, as soon as the pheasant diversion will permit.

Beebe has had his own way in this matter, in every single detail up to the present moment. I was called in at the eleventh hour—to acquiesce, and look pleasant about it. I have done so. Now I shall not yield another inch from what I know to be right, and necessary for this Park. If I am to be ruled by Mr. Beebe, the best time for me to know it is now.

The plan "fully approved by the Executive Committee" was that of hiring a temporary curator during Beebe's absence, but this plan failed because of the unavailability of candidates rather than interference on Beebe's part. When he, Mrs. Beebe and the bird artist R. Bruce Horsfall sailed for London on December 31, 1909, on their way to the Far East, Crandall was left behind as his only surrogate in the bird department. Bowing to the inevitable, Dr. Hornaday named Crandall acting curator of birds. The bitter pill was somewhat sweetened by the fact that Colonel Kuser offered to pay half of Crandall's salary.

Hornaday's quick-springing ire had as usual led him to use hot words, and at the moment he could not forgive Beebe for "triumphing" over him, but he was too practical to nurse a grudge. Moreover, for all but three of the seventeen years that remained of the Hornaday era in the Zoological Park Beebe was in tropical rain forests or on warm seas for the greater part of every year; and even if a little resentment lingered, Hornaday was much too busy with the park and his conservation work to spend much time being annoyed with an ex-curator a thousand miles away. By 1919 Beebe had faded to honorary curator of birds, and Crandall was curator of birds and working industriously for the betterment of the bird collection and the welfare of the Zoological Park, the Hornaday goals.

On the surface, even during the pheasant expedition when Hornaday's feelings were probably still ruffled, relations were outwardly friendly. Beebe sent back voluminous letters to the director, especially after he reached areas where Hornaday himself had collected for Ward's Natural Science Establishment many years before. One from aboard the steamer en route to Calcutta was conciliatory enough:

I am certainly coming across traces of your visit to the East and some of the memories are of considerable help. For example, I wrote to Theodore Bias in Mysore, asking for information about *Gallus* [sp., indecipherable] and they answered my questions courteously and said they knew you personally and were certain I would use specimens for scientific purposes, and hoped I would accept a series of birds with their compliments.

The director's replies were in an equally friendly tone and he was able to report that the bird department under Crandall was giving him no problems. Beebe, on the other hand, was having some minor difficulties. In Singapore, Horsfall "had a sudden transition from Jekyll to Hyde, and from do-

302

ing good work, slumped to nothing." Beebe thereupon sent him home. "I have longed many times for a man like Crandall," he added. "[He] (as you must know by now) has horse sense and keeps his head in a crisis."

Hornaday had certainly been right about one thing; this was no mere one-year expedition. Field work kept Beebe traveling for a year and almost five months—he did not return until May of 1911—and three months of 1912 had to be spent in research in European museums. Then came the writing of four huge volumes, and Dr. Hornaday, by this time reconciled to the Beebe temperament, so far unbent as to offer the reading room in the new Administration Building as a place where the author could spread out his papers and maps. The writing went easily enough and the manuscript was finished, but then World War I intervened. The monograph was to be printed in England, the colored plates in Vienna; and fortunately the plate work had been completed when hostilities broke out. The illustrations were all by masters of bird illustration: Louis Agassiz Fuertes, H. Gronvold, H. Jones, Charles R. Knight, G. E. Lodge, E. Megargee, and A. Thorburn. Volume I was published in 1918, Volume II in 1921, and Volumes III and IV in 1922.

Hornaday's denigrations of the book, of Beebe, and of Colonel Kuser in his first outburst were merely an expression of private pique, and when Volume I came out the director gave it a fulsome review in the society's *Bulletin*. In his beginning paragraph he betrayed, unconsciously, the gap between the old-style naturalist and the new; Hornaday thought first of the sport of pheasant-shooting, Beebe of observations of the living birds. Hornaday began his review:

After everything else has been said about sport in game-bird shooting, the last word is that pheasant-shooting is the finest of the fine. As mountain-sheep hunting is to other sport with the rifle, so is the pursuit of the pheasants of the world in comparison with other bird-shooting.

Of all game birds the pheasants of the world are the most beautiful, and also the most difficult to find and to kill.

He did not need to take back publicly the harsh words he had written about Beebe and Colonel Kuser; they had been seen only by Osborn and Grant. His publicly expressed opinions could not have been handsomer:

To build a Monograph of the Phasianidae that will do the subject even-handed justice is a task for Men. On one side it was Mr. William Beebe whose well trained scientific mind, tireless industry, skill as an explorer, and skill as a writer and book-maker that rendered this monograph possible. On the other hand, it was the profound love of birds and splendid imagination of Col. Anthony R. Kuser, combined with ample resources, that brought about the union of foresight and forces that produced the great result now laid before the bird-lovers of the world.

To Col. Kuser, Mr. Beebe, the various artists represented, and the publisher we say—*well done!*

By the time Volume I came out in 1918, Hornaday and the Zoo had all but lost William Beebe. He had made further expeditions to British Guiana in 1916 and 1917, and was already interested in flying, a skill which was to carry him into the skies over France. He was doing "a little flying for recreation" at Georgetown, British Guiana, in July of 1916 and was in the "Aviation Service" by April 19, 1917, according to a casual note by Hornaday. In May of 1917 the director wrote to H. E. Meeker of New York City:

I am delighted beyond measure by your keen appreciation of Mr. Beebe's efforts to serve our country, and I thank you a thousand times for your generous gift of $100. toward the running expenses of Mr. Beebe's flying machine. It is rather a curious but proper coincidence that our bird man should become an aviator.

So voluble about any natural-history experience, Beebe was reticent about his wartime flying; he wrote one article in the May, 1918, *Bulletin* about "Animal Life at the Front" as he had been able to observe it from the air and from the trenches during the winter of 1917–18, and he told a little more in a letter to Hornaday written from somewhere in France and dated January 22, 1918:

I am writing in a dug-out quarter cellar affair with my feet under me to keep them out of the two inches of water on the floor. The air is heavy with stale perspiration, old dried wine, ancient clothes, and a smell which was new to me until I found that it was Iroquois or Chippeway, for the platoon here consists of full-blooded American Indians from Canada.

Two days ago in Paris Dr. [unreadable] told me of having seen a balloon brought down by a German aeroplane and curiously enough I saw the same thing from 18000 feet over head. I have frozen two fingers but they have almost stopped itching.

We had a terrible trip over, storm after storm, & a Frenchman fell against my wrist and put it back two weeks.

I have been up 21200 feet, well ahead of my Himalayan altitude, but a half hour is quite enough at that height. If we *only* had planes our boys could start in now, but they cannot as yet.

I hope to take the steamer from England about Feb. 15th. Am trying to take care of my wrist but am discouraged about it.

Natural history and the interests of the department of tropical research were on his mind even in a wartime letter: "Tell John [Tee-Van, his assistant at the British Guiana laboratory] I have secured a copy of 'Histoire Naturelle des Araignées' which we have wanted very badly."

Beebe had been serving as an instructor with a French escadrille and with what Hornaday referred to on one occasion as "the American Flying Corps"; his age—he was then forty-one—kept him out of combat flying. Eventually his injured wrist unfitted him for further service and he returned to New York in March of 1918.

He was back from the war, but not to settle down in the park. Thereafter he spent the greater part of each year in preparing for expeditions to the tropics, studies in the field, and sessions at his typewriter as he turned out technical papers and popular books about his work. And thus it was to the end of his life.

When the Heads and Horns Museum was opened on May 25, 1922, "in memory of the vanishing big game of the world," it not only completed the architectural design of Baird Court but also presented an arrangement of big-game trophies that Dr. Hornaday felt "will stand for at least 200 years."

It stood for less than fifty years.

By the beginning of the 1970s the two large halls, where mounted heads of rhinoceros and tapir, giraffe and mountain sheep, gazed at visitors with their glassy eyes, had temporarily ceased to be open to the public. The rooms had been designed so that "60,000 visitors" a day [an impossibly over-enthusiastic figure] could comfortably inspect the heads and the head ornaments of the big game of the world, zoologically arranged in one and geographically grouped in the other. In the 1970s the South Hall had been converted to a gallery for the current work of animal artists and the North Hall to a headquarters for volunteer guides for parties of schoolchildren. The spacious downstairs rooms where it had been intended that sportsmen might sit and spin their yarns had become a lecture hall and the offices of the Zoo's Department of Education. (Plans for revitalizing the museum's concept are mentioned in Chapter 27.)

Dr. Hornaday and Madison Grant, whose dream the museum was, would have been unhappy. But by then it was an obvious fact that public interest in sportsmen's trophies—even magnificent ones and many that were world records—had long since vanished. For many years before living services took over from dead trophies, the number of daily visitors to the museum was but a tiny fraction of the number who streamed through, say, the Monkey House next door. "Just dead animals" was the usual comment as some member of a family peered in and hastily backed out.

Nevertheless, for its era the museum was a logical and valid appendage of a great zoological park. Hunting big game was a recognized sport, at least among men wealthy and hardy enough to penetrate the wildest and most difficult parts

17

Heads, Horns, and the Chimpanzee that Knows Everything

of the world. Books on tracking and hunting abounded—shelf after shelf in the Zoological Society's Library is filled with them—and not all are mere literary trophies recording the exploits of intrepid hunters. Many book-writing sportsmen and explorers were accurate observers of animal habits and habitats, and of the lives and customs of little-known native peoples who served them as guides. Along with the heads and horns and skins they brought back to decorate their homes, they brought a good deal of solid natural-history information. It was valuable as far as it went, but at the beginning of this century the day of the field naturalist trained to observe scientifically and record without killing had not yet dawned.

It could be argued that books by a George B. Schaller (gorillas) or a Jane Goodall (chimpanzees), a Hans Kruuk (spotted hyena) or a David Mech (wolves), contribute more to our intimate knowledge of wildlife than a shelffull of the outpourings of the sportsmen-writers, but it is hardly fair to stress this in the context of a different time and a different world. One museum case hung with the mounted heads, or the simple horns attached to a fragment of skull, of the mountain sheep of the world *did,* undeniably, give a synoptic view of . . . well, of the heads and horns of the mountain sheep of the world. And it was true that some idea of the variety and similarity of a related group of animals could be grasped even by a non-zoologist or non-sportsman interested enough to walk into the museum and stare for half an hour. Such exhibits certainly have something to say, but today their message needs to be expressed in a different way.

Late in 1906, Dr. Hornaday and Mr. Grant created what they called the National Collection of Heads and Horns with the approval of the executive committee. There was some carping by the secretary of the Smithsonian Institution about the name; he thought it should be called the American Collection of Heads and Horns, leaving "National" to be applied to collections under governmental auspices. But sportsmen welcomed the prestige of "National Collection" as a reposi-

tory for their trophies, and gifts wanted and unwanted poured in. It can be suspected that as times and taste and the size of habitations changed, many a head was sent to the museum simply because its owner did not know what else to do with it.

Hornaday contributed his own private collection of 131 trophies, Grant a lesser number. Sportsmen and taxidermists were expected to contribute the rest, and they did, either by gifts from their own trophy rooms or money to buy outstanding heads. Emerson McMillin, always generous, put up $5,000 to acquire the enormous collection of heads, horns, and skins of Alaskan big game formed by an Englishman, A. S. Reed.

Until the Heads and Horns Museum was opened in 1922, the collection was housed in two halls on the second floor of the Administration Building. The two African elephant tusks in the center are the second largest known pair from a living species.

Sometimes bargains came along. A Chicago taxidermist had an interesting pair of Alaskan moose antlers locked together when the bulls charged each other in combat, and he offered them first at $1,000, then $700, and finally a desperate $325. Hornaday was covetous but could not raise even the $325 before they had been sold. Eventually he talked their new owner out of them by paying $500, a premium of $175. It was money well spent, for the moose antlers and three or four other sets of locked antlers formed the "Combat Collection" in the museum that was often the only exhibit casual visitors paid much attention to. Another worthy set piece was the imposing pair of tusks of an African elephant, long believed to be the largest pair known from a living species. (Two longer and heavier tusks were in existence but they were not united as a pair. The British Museum [Natural History] owned one, and the other was in the collection of ivory cutters in England. In 1933 the museum acquired the latter and exhibited them as a matched pair. Each was more than twelve feet in length, and their combined weight was 460 pounds.) The left tusk measured eleven feet five and one half inches on the curve, the other eleven feet, and their combined weight was 293 pounds. They were said to have been presented by King Menelik II of Abyssinia (Ethiopia) to a European political officer, but their history is not really well documented until they showed up on the ivory market in London in 1906, where they were acquired by Rowland Ward, whose *Records of Big Game* is the bible of the trophy sportsman. Ward wanted 500 guineas for the pair, but Hornaday beat him down to £500 and congratulated himself on saving $125 by paying pounds instead of guineas. Charles T. Barney, chairman of the executive committee, put up the money.

A prize big in another sense was the mounted head of a gigantic African elephant shot in British East Africa (Kenya) in 1906 by Richard Tjader and presented to the museum in 1925 by his son, Richard Thorne Tjader. The elephant was said to have stood eleven feet four inches high and it was certainly one of the largest ever shot.

McMillin, inspecting the Reed collection he had bought, told Hornaday he would rather have his name connected with the National Collection than with anything else he knew of. "For a millionaire banker, this is saying much," Hornaday commented. But McMillin was not a stereotyped millionaire. On one occasion he returned a book of member's tickets to the Zoological Park:

> For two reasons: first, I would not carry the book in my pocket for the price of forty books, and, second,—I never use a pass to anything or anywhere. I never travelled a mile on a railroad pass in my life, and always pay fare on street cars run by Companies of which I am President. Its a hobby with me.

If there is any one building in the Zoological Park that is more than another a monument to Dr. Hornaday, it is the Heads and Horns Museum. True, Madison Grant shared and abetted his enthusiasm for it, but Hornaday took the lead in writing and publishing two elaborate prospectuses in 1907 and 1908, appealing to sportsmen all over the world to give their finest trophies to it, and single-handedly he raised the $100,000 that the building was estimated to cost. He solicited $10,000 each from ten donors, and he got it: from Mrs. Frederick Ferris Thompson, Mrs. Russell Sage, John D. Archbold, Jacob H. Schiff, George F. Baker, Mrs. Andrew Carnegie, Andrew Carnegie, Edmund C. Converse, Samuel Thorne (in memoriam) and George D. Pratt.

By the time Hornaday had raised the money, the First World War had come along and construction prices were rising so rapidly that the Executive Committee advised delay. Worse than that, it changed the design that Hornaday had worked out, and for reasons that are not now apparent decided that there should be two entrances to the building, one on the south end and one on the north, instead of a single entrance and exit on the west side facing Baird Court. In a lifetime in which affronts to Hornaday's wisdom were almost

The mounted head of a gigantic African elephant was presented to the Heads and Horns Museum in 1925 by Richard Tjader, whose father had shot it in British East Africa in 1906. The elephant was said to have stood eleven feet four inches high.

310

commonplace (according to his letters of protest), this was the worst. In December of 1916 he wrote to Professor Osborn:

Fancy conducting the President of the United States and the donors of the Heads and Horns building to an entrance *behind* the Monkey House, or *behind* the Administration Building, *fronting on nothing!*

How will you feel?

No explanations, no excuses would suffice.

What will this jibing world say of an Executive Committee that puts the blind side of a long and plain-sided building on the only axis of a great "civic center" that strikes a building,—with no front, and no facade or pediment on that axis!!!

And think of paying $25,000 extra for an extra finished and decorated end, in order to make a record-breaking mistake!!!

But for the time being the Executive Committee stood firm, and it impressed upon the director that in this matter, at least, he was not going to have his own way.

Hornaday felt he could speak his mind freely to Frank K. Sturgis, the second vice-president of the society, and to him he wrote in 1919:

The last time Mr. Grant and I discussed those matters, which was in 1916, he said to me very positively:

"The plans of the Executive Committee are not going to be changed; and if you don't like it you can lump it."

Ever since that time I have endeavored to avoid thinking of the Heads and Horns building, or the treatment I have received from the Executive Committee on account of it. I have regarded the whole matter, both building and collection, with the feelings of a man who looks upon the face of a dead friend. Had my plans not been set aside in 1916, when I finished raising the $100,000. entirely alone, the building would have been erected in 1917 with the money, and dedicated on May 20, 1918.

This was mere bombast, for construction costs had gone out of sight by 1917 and the $100,000 in hand would have been entirely inadequate. As it was, even after the war ended, the society had to wait for prices to come down—which they did, gradually—and raise more money before the building could be erected. Its final cost was $145,646.95.

In the meantime the heads and horns that had been generously bestowed were for the most part on display in the halls and upstairs rooms of the Administration Building or stored in an unused room of the Lion House. And time— and perhaps the attrition of Hornaday's arguments—came to his aid. The executive committee backed off from its insistence on two entrances, Hornaday made some slight concessions about the width of the entrance hallway facing Baird Court, and all was harmony when the building was finally dedicated at four o'clock on the afternoon of May 25, 1922, with speeches by Professor Osborn, the Honorable Joseph P. Hennessy, Commissioner of Parks of the Borough of the Bronx, and Director Hornaday. The only sour note was the refusal of the city to put up $1,500 a year for the salary of an attendant in the building. Hornaday wanted to threaten to close the building but the executive committee decided to provide the money out of society revenues.

The executive committee had one other idea that Hornaday vetoed. In 1921, by subscription among members of the committee, a handsome portrait of the director had been painted by George R. Boynton, and it was felt that the Heads and Horns Museum would be a suitable place to hang it. Hornaday, however, preferred that it be placed in the Administration Building and his wishes prevailed.

With conservation battles raging on half a dozen fronts, the curator of birds skipping off to the Himalayas, paintings and trophies having to be acquired, and money in short supply after the Panic of 1907, the Zoological Park knew few of the somnolent days that were so typical of its middle age a couple of decades later. It took Hornaday a long time to dig his way out of correspondence that accumulated while he was writing *Our Vanishing Wild Life* and clubbing the "game hogs" (an epithet coined by G. O. Shields of *Recreation*) —some letters did not get answered until eight months after they

Lesser pandas.

313

were received. Even the routine business of the Zoo held exciting possibilities. For a time in 1910 it seemed that the Bronx Zoo might actually get a duck-billed platypus—the first live one ever to come out of Australia. Director A. S. Le Souef of the Sydney Zoo could get platypuses and was willing to try sending one in the care of an animal man whom the society had engaged to look after a shipment of sea lions from New Zealand. Then romance wrecked all. The animal courier got married in Cape Town, abandoned the whole animal project, and returned to England with his bride.

The period was notable for the arrival of the Zoo's first "Clarence." In 1909 Bayard Dominick, Jr., made an expedition to Africa and came home with a warthog he had named Clarence, which he presented to the Zoo. All subsequent warthog accessions—and there were many—were called Clarence by their keepers. For all their ferocious appearance (and warthogs have been called the only truly ugly animals that nature ever made), they are usually of amiable disposition and when summoned by name will wake up, waddle over on their knees, and hold still to have their backs scratched. (It may be a long, long time before Zoo visitors can again admire Clarences. Because of the African swine fever, importation of warthogs is prohibited.)

The Zoo's first lesser pandas came in 1911 and got front-page billing in the Society's *Bulletin*, although the adventures of one of the pair were not mentioned. It escaped while being unloaded on the New York docks and for several days frolicked among the piles of freight until a barge captain captured it. The Zoo had posted a reward of twenty-five dollars for its return alive, but the captain had bigger ideas. He fled upriver in his barge and let it be known that he would deliver the rusty red, cream, and white "cat" for a hundred dollars. Police traced him, however, and under threat of a summons for grand larceny he yielded up the panda.

Lord Northcliffe, the British newspaper publisher, came

to New York in 1908 and was entranced by the Zoological Park. Nobody at that time worried about the introduction of exotic species and what they might do to the local fauna, so at Northcliffe's request Hornaday had ten gray squirrels and twenty American robins trapped and shipped to him on the *Lusitania*. They arrived safely—it was not until seven years later that the *Lusitania* was torpedoed by a German submarine—but the introductions were not entirely successful. Although "Bird-Lover" wrote an enthusiastic letter that was published in Northcliffe's *Daily Mail,* saying the robins would "look thoroughly English in a few years," they did not thrive. The gray squirrels had better success, to the regret of present-day Englishmen who consider them pests.

Northcliffe reciprocated by sending wood pigeons which his men trapped in St. James's Park in London. Stories in a Northcliffe paper said they were "of royal stock, sprung from some birds set free from Buckingham Palace." The climate of this democracy did not suit them, however, and they quickly died out.

Snakes were presumably the greatest American curiosities the Bronx Zoo could send the Royal Zoological Society of Ireland, and a gift of a diamondback rattlesnake, a banded rattlesnake, and a copperhead brought a handsome certificate of acknowledgment.

Although there were plenty of active animal dealers on both sides of the Atlantic, it was advantageous to deal with European zoological gardens on an exchange basis, and so in May of 1909 Curator Ditmars sailed for a tour of European zoos with $2,000 in cash for purchases and many boxes of American reptiles for exchange purposes. He came home in July with some four hundred specimens of one hundred and eleven species, by no means all reptiles. The prize acquisition he considered to be a Cape hyrax, whose Syrian race is the "coney" mentioned in Leviticus 11:5 as "unclean" because "it cheweth the cud, but divideth not the hoof." Better naturalists than the writer of Leviticus have since reported that

Clarence the warthog— one of many Clarences before the importation of wild swine was prohibited.

315

it doth not chew the cud, even though its jaws sometimes make motions as if it were chewing, and that its toes have tiny, hooflike nails. It truly divideth the hoof.

One welcome dividend of the Ditmars trip was the falling off of a certain kind of newspaper publicity while he was away. Publicity was most appreciated—by Dr. Hornaday, at least—when it was reasonably accurate, but the kind of newspaper stories Ditmars inspired when he was in residence more often than not took off into realms of imagination where there were no fixed points.

"The writers of foolish stories in the newspapers have given us quite a rest!" the director wrote to Ditmars in London.

It was not that Curator Ditmars himself faked stories for newspaper reporters. For one thing, there was no need; they were quite competent to develop stories on their own. Imagination was the important thing. As everybody knew, animals were *ipso facto* funny, unpredictable, capable of doing all sorts of crazy things. Ditmars was a godsend to the New York press, for he happened to be in charge of the two animal groups of greatest interest—reptiles and mammals—and he had a knack of saying quotable things.

For some years the most celebrated chimpanzee in the collection was an individual named Baldy, trained to walk into a prepared cage, pull on a flowered dressing gown, and sit at a table to eat with a knife and fork and drink from a bottle. On occasion he would also do what were called acrobatic stunts.

"Curator Ditmars declares that he is the chimpanzee that knows everything," one paper announced.

Whether Ditmars did or did not say that—and he probably did—for years he was quoted whenever Baldy got his picture in the papers. Thousands must have come to see "the chimpanzee that knows everything."

In the fall of 1910 the collector and explorer R. L. Garner came back from Africa with a chimpanzee named Susie who was reputed to be able to carry on a conversation with Garner.

This is Baldy and one of
the mammal keepers.

317

At least she could say "feu," the French for "fire," and Garner himself was said (by himself) to be able to speak twenty-five words of "Chimpanzese." Susie soon wound up in the Bronx Zoo—not, as the newspapers told it, in order to hold a *conversazione* and take tea with the Zoo's own chimpanzees and orangutans and to meet "Mr. Baldy Ditmars," but because Garner was not having much success with a lecture tour featuring Susie and wanted a place to deposit her. Anyway, Susie came to tea in the Zoo and got impressive newspaper coverage. She did not seem to have much to say to the other animals.

Sometimes the newspaper stories were outright fakes of varying degrees of humor and whimsy:

Catching sight of his reflection in the bottom of a shiny tin drinking pan, a buffalo calf fell dead in the Bronx Zoo. The monkey is the only animal capable of seeing himself as he really is, in a mirror, and surviving. That's why he's called the missing link.

The Brooklyn *Daily Eagle* reported that there was a mandrill in the Bronx Zoo called Nightmare because his face was blue and his nose red:

It is said that the varying shades of his visage foretell the coming weather conditions, rain, snow or wind. Yesterday morning Curator Ditmars was horrified to see his face bright green. He summoned others to make sure of his discovery and they all prepared for a cyclone.

The payoff was in the last line: the mandrill had rubbed against a freshly painted door.

"Curator Ditmars" was for a time in the news more consistently than Dr. Hornaday—Zoo news, at any rate—but at that time there seems to have been no inner-circle jealousy, perhaps because Dr. Hornaday was intent on the much more serious business of publicizing his own and the society's wild-life protection programs and had little time to meet with reporters on purely Zoological Park stories. Anyway, Ditmars had a genius for news; he never lacked a peg for a good story.

In 1910 he was preparing to open an insect exhibit in the porch between the Ostrich and Small Mammal houses, and as a July 4 feature he announced what the papers called a "bug concert." The exhibit contained insects from several countries, and it was said that Curator Ditmars, by stimulating in turn insects capable of making a variety of sounds, would harmonize them in playing "The Star-Spangled Banner." The proclaimed purpose of the concert was to introduce the new exhibit and educate the public in good (beneficial) and bad (harmful) insects. The press covered the event and had great fun with it, while admitting that no patriotic strains were distinguishable.

Even a random dip into the crumbling albums of press clippings of 1910 and 1911 leaves one with a small suspicion that perhaps Curator Ditmars had a certain amount of wiliness and calculation in his disposition. After all, he had been a *Times* reporter before he became a Zoo curator. . . . For example, the city had for some years provided funds for summer-afternoon band concerts on Baird Court, but times grew hard and the money was cut off. Then a small sum was raised and the concerts could be resumed. As news, it was perhaps worth a very short paragraph that would attract few if any visitors to the Zoo. So it was built up.

The animals were reported to have grown so accustomed to music with their meals that they stopped eating when the band concerts ended. Curator Ditmars ordered "20-pound morsels" of meat thrown to the big cats in the Lion House, but they could not be tempted. Then the concerts resumed "and there was an uproar in the cages of the lions and tigers, they straightaway cleaned up five days' accumulation of food, and clamored for more."

If any day without an animal crisis or excitement ever did come along, the morning mail usually brought an antidote to ennui. It might be a spate of letters protesting an experiment to learn whether chimpanzees really are frightened by snakes, in which Ditmars hid a garter snake in a suitcase and let Baldy and Susie open it (they were frightened, all right), or indignation because a small dog was allowed to run snapping at the heels of the elephant Gunda (an experiment to see if Gunda could be cured of his cussedness by frightening him into taking more exercise; he wasn't cured), or an enclosure from the mayor of a letter from an irate German-American citizen because the Zoo (according to the *Journal*) had bestowed the name of Kaiser Wilhelm on the offspring of a pair of baboons. (There was not the slightest truth in the story, Hornaday wrote back.)

The phenomenon of the public loudly proclaiming its rights is not peculiar to the present day. Anyone aggrieved by the attitude of a Zoo attendant—or the alleged paucity of drinking fountains in the Zoo—or the shortcomings of directional signs—or the rules against walking or sitting on the grass—or the prohibition against bringing unshelled peanuts into the Zoo—was quick to write a letter to the mayor or the park commissioner or the newspapers. Answering them was one chore the director never put off. It almost seems as if he enjoyed the chance to hit someone over the head with incontrovertible facts. More often than not his replies were savage counterattacks, but sometimes he was moderate and almost paternal, as when he replied to a man who had tried to enter the park at Fordham Gate just after the gate had closed for the day. The gateman did open up to let him in, but his tone was surly and the would-be visitor stalked away in a huff— and of course wrote to the park commissioner. Hornaday replied direct to the complainant.

It seems to me you are rather too sensitive. The hour for closing had arrived and the gatekeeper was in a hurry to get to the Chief Clerk's office and give an accounting of the day's business. It may be quite true that his tone was not quite as suave and gentle as it might have been; but it is a fact that in the hurry and busyness in New York City, one cannot always expect, or receive, Chesterfieldian courtliness. It is the misfortune of life in crowded and hurried New York that the rule of the day is to "step lively." Had I been in your place, I am very sure I would have said "Thank you," and entered as quickly as I could, and forgotten the gate-keeper in less than two minutes after.

The director was in his most diplomatic mood when he wrote to William White Niles:

I think it would be well for you to intimate to your nephew [the son of Robert L. Niles, one of the original incorporators] that it is dangerous to run an automobile to the Antelope House, and twice around it, tooting the horn, especially when the animals are out in the yards, and some of them are liable to injure themselves from fright.

Mr. Niles passed the mild rebuke on to his brother Robert, who wrote to apologize for his son's thoughtlessness.

Some time, last summer, I know we gained the impression that Steam Automobiles, being free from all noise, smoke and odor, were to be permitted to enter the park, and I remember that it was a matter of comment and consolation to us that whereas Autos were shut out from many places, there was one, at least, where certain of them were to be admitted, where horses would be barred. A privilege, however, applied only to the steam machines, of which type we have ever been firm upholders.

Mr. Niles promised that his son would not endanger the animals again and Hornaday closed the correspondence with a benign "Boys will be boys."

The daily post was not always the kind that provoked the director to wrath or rebuke. At least one letter (never answered) must have been puzzling:

I am a buyer of snake faeces for a special work. If you are seller of same, I would be happy to have an appointment with you or your agent. If you agree I may probably reserve all the future production of the Garden.

There were light moments, too, even in the business letters that flowed in an almost daily stream between Hornaday and

Dr. Cecil French, the animal dealer in Washington. French wrote to Hornaday:

I sold one of my cubs to Anna Held the other day. If you go to the Broadway Theatre look closely with your opera glasses and see if it has taken a piece out of her beautiful dairy by this time. She wanted to use it in her song "Won't you come and be my Teddy Bear?"

Hornaday did not promise to check up on Miss Held's "beautiful dairy," but he did have enough experience with theatrical people to have an opinion:

Anna Held's bear was undoubtedly purchased for the use of the press agent, and from this time forth we may all look forward to blood-curdling stories of what the bear has done to Anna Held, which should be good for at least a column a week for four months, in sixteen newspapers. I think, on the whole, she has made a very good investment.

The Zoo had always been proud of its anthropoid apes. Except briefly in 1902 when an infestation of *Balantidium coli* wiped out all but one orang, there was a good collection of chimpanzees and orangutans in the Monkey House and their antics were a source of great enjoyment and publicity. Thus it was a major tragedy when tuberculosis struck the anthropoids in midwinter of 1913–14; in a few weeks all nine chimpanzees and orangutans died.

Dr. W. Reid Blair, the Zoo's veterinarian, made a written report to the director:

> The epidemic demonstrates the great necessity for providing a suitable place for the isolation of these animals when suffering from infectious diseases, and where the keeper caring for sick animals would not have to take care also for those that were in good health at the same time, as is the case at present.
>
> We have been comparatively free from tuberculosis for six or seven years.
>
> It is impossible to trace definitely the source of infection of tuberculosis in these particular cases. It is, however, important to remember that the animals are always exposed to infection from tubercular visitors while on exhibition as at present.

The veterinarian then cited some startling statistics. The London Zoo had reported that the *average* longevity of twenty chimpanzees in its collection was eight months, and only one animal had lived as long as three years and nine months. Of twenty orangs, the average life was five and a half months and the best record was twenty-one months. The Bronx Zoo, on the other hand, could point to a still living chimpanzee of five years six months, and an orang, also still living, of six years nine months. (A week or so later tuberculosis claimed them, too.)

The veterinarian had rather pointedly indicated a source of infection—contamination from tubercular visitors—but Dr. Hornaday did not accept that theory in his own report to Mr. Grant:

> Thus far we have not the faintest clue regarding the manner in

18

Keeping the Animals Well

which it [lymphatic tuberculosis] was conveyed to our apes,—unless it was through the rats of the Primate House, which cannot by any possibility be exterminated, and kept exterminated, or kept out of the cages.

Two days after receiving the director's report, Grant came back with an idea that was (as far as execution in the Bronx Zoo was concerned) thirty-six years in advance of its time and which he did not live to see carried out. To Hornaday he wrote:

I am more than ever satisfied, as I have been for many years, that the north end of our Primate House is not suited for valuable animals like apes. I trust you will assist me cordially in seeing that the next building constructed in the Park, after the completion of the Hospital, will be an Ape House. It is a building that I propose to largely design myself. My mind is absolutely made up on the necessity of a separate building for our anthropoids in which the public is absolutely screened off from the apes, and each side provided with separate ventilation and heating. There should also be on the roof something in the nature of a green house or roof garden, which will serve as a play ground, together with absolutely isolated wards.

In this connection, I wish you would do what you can to push the experiments already made in the direction of a more open air life for our animals, and of a lower temperature. There is no enemy to tuberculosis like sun-light in abundance, and our Ape House, with its easterly exposure, I do not think is an ideal structure by any means.

Grant was an astute man, but he was less diplomatic than usual when he wrote that last sentence. Hornaday had himself designed the Monkey House, and what he designed he defended. He replied:

Of course I will cheerfully cooperate with you in your intention to design an Ape House yourself. At this juncture, I wish to go on record with a statement that according to my view, our present Ape and Monkey accommodations are not only the best to be found in any Primate House in the world; but also that it will be exceedingly difficult to improve upon them. Our success in main-

taining apes in their present quarters has been so great that in this line of work no other Zoological Park or Garden in the world is even a good second to us.

Your remark about making experiments in the direction of more open-air life for our animals is pertinent. I attribute the health, activity and extreme longevity of our apes to the fact that they have had the greatest abundance of fresh air that apes in confinement in zoological gardens are anywhere permitted to have. I believe that to pen up apes or monkeys behind a wall of glass, produces conditions which render it impossible for the apes to live as long as they should in captivity. The wall of glass that was erected by your direction, and without my approval, in our Ape Hall, has the effect of greatly reducing the amount of fresh air which formerly reached the apes, and which I once regarded as so necessary to their health. Formerly, the excess of cool, fresh air which came to them, often gave them colds in their heads, and sometimes Bronchitis; but it promoted their health and vigor, and I think that the end more than justified the means. We had reduced Tuberculosis among our apes to so low a point that it was no longer to be regarded as an ever-present scourge. The present outbreak is on the same basis as an outbreak of Bubonic Plague, Smallpox, or any other virulent disease. I regard it as absolutely

325

certain that this attack of Lymphatic Tuberculosis did not come from any human being, and I believe that Mr. Ditmars' theory that it was introduced into the cages by rats or mice, is correct.

Before entirely closing this subject, I ought to remark that the public is becoming much dissatisfied with the glass now in front of the three large ape cages, because of the reflections.

The glass shields between apes and public that Grant had insisted on having installed as soon as he heard of the illness of the animals had come too late; the damage was already done.

Hornaday was not shaken by what now seems the scientific justification and common sense of Grant's proposal, or by the report of the society's prosector on the dead anthropoids that "the results are conclusive that these animals were attacked by a human type of tuberculosis, conveyed by spectators." Two months later he was advancing another theory of Assistant Curator of Mammals Ditmars that the tuberculosis was being spread by cockroaches that swarmed through the cages at night.

Rats, mice, and cockroaches could, of course, have acted as mechanical vectors of the disease, but their role—if it existed —was certainly minimal. Undoubtedly tubercular spectators were the source of infection, for the disease was much more prevalent in those days than it is now and it was a favorite sport of Sunday crowds to spit at the "monkeys" in order to "stir them up," and to throw bits of food at them. The mystery is not that the anthropoids contracted tuberculosis but that any of them survived as long as they did, and that their replacements survived—for it was not until some years after Hornaday's retirement that all compartments in the Monkey House were shut off from the public behind glass. Even so, there was another small outbreak of tuberculosis in 1941 that was especially frustrating to the veterinarian of the time, Dr. Leonard J. Goss, for it appeared in hit-or-miss fashion all over the building. One primate might be infected, yet the occupants of cages on either side were free of the disease.

Dr. Hornaday's promise of "cheerful cooperation" with Mr. Grant in campaigning for a new building devoted solely to the Great Apes was, it is to be feared, merely a paper promise. It had been made in the beginning of 1914 when Dr. Hornaday was working up a head of steam to force his dream of the Heads and Horns Museum through the executive committee, and he was also thinking that someday the park ought to have a special building to exhibit the great collection of wild-animal paintings he had sponsored. He had no time to spend on what he considered Grant's impractical and unnecessary visions. But Grant had not forgotten Hornaday's promise, and in the spring of 1915 he made an uncharacteristically plaintive appeal to the director:

I hope you will remember that you promised me sometime ago that I could be assured of your cordial cooperation in securing the Anthropoid Apes House. Aside from any official question, I think you should be in sympathy with this, as I have frequently backed you in undertakings which did not have my full approval or sympathy, but deferred to your wishes in the matter. You will find that President Osborn is entirely in sympathy with this matter, and I am quite clear on it myself. The tragedy of the loss of our grand collection of apes last year could have been averted if we had had proper accommodations. I am relying on your good faith to put yourself squarely behind this. The time for the Museum, either of Pictures or Heads and Horns, has not yet arrived, but when it does come you will find me cordially in sympathy with it.

The time for a Great Apes House had not arrived either. Its time came on October 12, 1950, when the present structure was opened with a ceremony in which President Fairfield Osborn held Andy, a baby orangutan, within reach of a bunch of grapes that joined two ends of a ribbon across the door. Andy gravely plucked a grape, the ribbons parted, and members of the Zoological Society entered the first major animal building opened in the zoo since the Zebra House in 1914. It is unlikely that any of the two thousand guests gave a thought to Madison Grant at that moment, but the $386,000 building was a triumphant testimonial to the principles he had laid before Hornaday in 1914. There was no "green house" on the roof—but there were five large moated "play yards" outside the south, east, and west sides of the building where gorillas, orangutans, and chimpanzees could play in open air and sunshine in all the warmer months. And inside, their big compartments were sealed off from the public by a continuous wall of glass. It is a pleasure thus to link Grant's memory with a building that he was the first to advocate.

For a lawyer, a man not trained in the veterinary or medical sciences, Madison Grant was sensitive to the needs of wild animals to an unusual degree. He did not make many suggestions as to practical daily care, but when he did they were often likely to be correct ones—as present-day veterinarians and practitioners of animal husbandry see them. As early as January of 1902 he had made certain proposals to Dr. Hornaday—and as usual the director found little of value in them. As Hornaday wrote to Professor Osborn:

Mr. Grant has asked me to write you in regard to two propositions,—isolating all primates that come to us, for an unknown period;—and also, attempting to create a specially moist atmosphere in the Monkey House.

Regarding the isolation of monkeys,—I thought, when the matter was talked over with Dr. Miller, some months ago, that the idea was a good one; but, on careful reflection, I have changed my mind. In the first place, it is our invariable rule never to buy, nor accept as a gift, a primate of any kind which shows symptoms of disease. Monkeys are not so expensive to buy, nor so subject to epidemics, as to justify the amount of extra labor and management that would be required to isolate all arrivals long enough to make sure that they were free from contagious diseases. In other words,—I do not believe in taking more trouble with monkeys than they are worth!

When monkeys reach us, in what appears to be a sound, healthy condition, it is much more important for them to be set free at once in a large cage and made comfortable, than for their captivity in small quarters to be continued, even for one week. Thus

328

far, it has been our policy to give all new arrivals a bath, and at once place them under the best possible conditions. In order to keep monkeys in quarantine long enough to make such a measure effective, it would have to be continued about two months.

In regard to creating an artificially damp atmosphere,—I am contemplating exactly the reverse, namely,—taking special pains to acclimatize our primates in the atmosphere of the Zoological Park, and live out doors as much as possible. While it is entirely true that the atmosphere of every animal building needs a certain amount of moisture, (and which, in most cases, we look upon the plant life to give) I do not think it would be at all advisable to endeavor to create the hot-house atmosphere of the tropics. In my belief, it will be possible to accustom our monkeys to quite a cool atmosphere, providing it is dry; but this can never be done if the atmosphere is moist and cold. I am looking forward to making some very interesting experiments next fall and winter with certain species of our primates. In fact, I expect to be able to succeed in acclimatizing at least a number of specimens to such an extent that they can live out doors all next winter!

Just why Dr. Hornaday was so opposed to the quarantine of newly arrived animals is hard to say. It can only be conjectured that he was convinced that experience had given him more knowledge of animal management than his associates could possibly possess—even veterinarians. In fact, he seems to have distrusted veterinarians particularly. Yet the Zoological Park had pioneered in professional veterinary care of its animals. Dr. H. Amling, Jr., veterinarian of Bostock's Circus, had been employed on a part-time basis in December, 1900, and it was with great satisfaction that the executive committee announced in the *Annual Report* for 1901 that Dr. Frank H. Miller had been engaged as veterinarian and Dr. Harlow Brooks as pathologist. They constituted the park's "Medical Department," and "So far as we know this is a new feature in zoological park administration." Dr. Miller was a successful veterinary practitioner with offices on East Forty-second Street and Dr. Brooks, an M.D., was one of the outstanding pathologists and internists of the country; he was

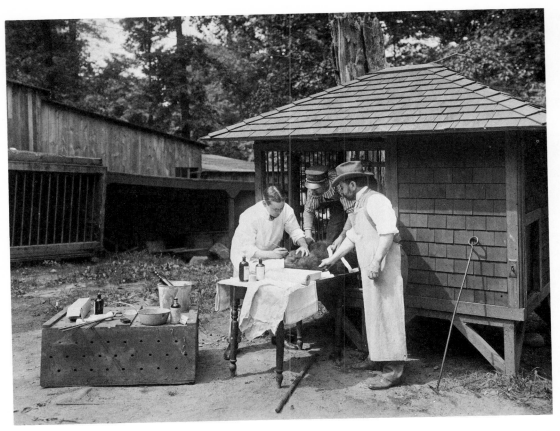

sometimes called "The Doctor's Doctor." By 1902 Dr. W. Reid Blair, a veterinarian trained at McGill University, had been added to the staff as an assistant to Dr. Miller. They were all good men, well trained and thoroughly competent—and yet as late as 1903, Professor Osborn was writing to Hornaday:

Before the Animal Hospital was built in 1916, the veterinarian's operations usually were open-air affairs. Here Dr. W. Reid Blair operates on a bear, assisted by Director Hornaday.

I have sent you by Mr. Mitchell the Pathological and Medical reports, which I find extremely interesting and valuable. I fear you are still not in full sympathy with this work. I wish you would take my judgment for it, as in matters of this kind I am perhaps better qualified to judge than you are; whereas, in matters of *many other kinds,* I take off my hat to you as a qualified expert who knows far more about the subject than I do! Unless you are in sympathy with this work, and believe in it, and encourage and support it, and show your enthusiasm, it will be difficult to carry it on successfully.

Hornaday may not have been enthusiastic about the veterinary work but he did not oppose it; for the first few years he extended at least benevolent neglect and Drs. Miller and Brooks found Professor Osborn their most sympathetic audience when they had problems. There were plenty of those— one of the earliest being the lack of facilities, instruments, books, journals, and laboratory equipment. Dr. Brooks had been engaged at an honorarium of $150 a year "to examine into the hygienic conditions of the animals, to recommend such treatment and to make such autopsies and microscopic studies as will tend to advance our knowledge of the prevention and treatment of diseases peculiar to animals in captivity." It was not to be a full-time job, for he was active on the staffs of Bellevue, Harlem, and Montefiore hospitals, but he was expected to make regular visits to the park and he did so; he saw the work as an unusual opportunity to study comparative pathology. In 1902 Dr. Hornaday released a small sum to buy autopsy instruments but the veterinary department still had no microscope of its own; it was using one that belonged to William Beebe, and Beebe wanted it back. Brooks informed Professor Osborn that he could borrow a microtome, but that a microscope really was essential, and he offered his honorarium as the nucleus of a laboratory fund. "It would go a good way toward the purchase of a few books and the subscription to one or two good journals." The executive committee generously provided a microscope and a microtome out of society funds.

Given such handicaps as the minimum of equipment and facilities—the "autopsy room" was a shed in the service yard behind the Service Building—it is remarkable that so much good work came out of the veterinary department. In the 1902 *Annual Report* the reports of the veterinarian and the pathologist were merely descriptive of the various diseases and pathological conditions found in the collection, but by 1903 they began to be serious studies of "cage paralysis" and internal parasites in wild animals. By 1904 Brooks and Blair had studied cage paralysis, or "cripples," so deeply that they could report: "The recognition of 'cage paralysis,' familiar to all animal men under that name, as osteomalacia, we believe to be now stated for the first time." They were still uncertain as to the essential causes of the disease, but they were on the right track when they supplied bone dust and limewater to the victims and noted that "sunlight, dry and well-ventilated quarters are absolutely essential." They found it interesting that there had never been a case of osteomalacia in the large lemur cage in the Monkey House—a cage which received abundant sunlight for a large part of each day.

We now know a good deal more about the crippling diseases that were so prevalent at the beginning of the century. Osteomalacia is a softening of the bones because of calcium-phosphorus or vitamin D deficiency; rickets is caused by a vitamin D deficiency producing demineralization of the bones; cage paralysis is a symptom of poor nutrition leading to rickets or osteomalacia and eventually to irreversible paralysis. But the science of animal nutrition was in its infancy around 1900 and the role of dietary deficiencies was only beginning to be recognized; Brooks and Blair pointed the way to understanding and improvement.

For years a recurrent problem was gastroenteritis among wild sheep and goats kept on grassy ranges and enclosures. This inflammation of the stomach and intestinal tract was a symptom rather than a disease entity, and it was not caused by the "poisonous nature" of the grasses in the park, as Dr. Hornaday believed, but was largely a matter of diet and parasites. Dr. Brooks pinned it firmly on faulty hygienic conditions prevailing on the buffalo range when an "epidemic" of gastroenteritis attacked the herd in 1902. He suggested the elimination of dirty pools of stagnant water and relocation of the herds of buffalo, caribou, moose and native deer:

They must be placed where the food and water supply is absolutely under the control of the keepers. We could not expect domestic cattle to thrive under the conditions which we are able to provide in the way of pasturage.

He was right; when his recommendations were put into effect, gastroenteritis declined.

Dr. Miller returned to more lucrative private practice in 1903, although remaining as consulting veterinary surgeon, and Dr. Blair became the official veterinarian at a modest $90 a month, only twice what the janitor of the Reptile House was paid. It was not an easy job, for he was frequently under conflicting orders from Dr. Brooks and Hornaday. There was the perennial problem, too, of whose interests came first: the veterinarian's, to make a complete autopsy of animals that died in the collection, or those of the American Museum of Natural History, which wanted more or less intact specimens for mounting, skeletonizing, or some other scientific purpose. From the beginning it had been understood that the museum should have first call (subject to the requirements of the veterinarian), but Dr. Hornaday had extended the offerings to various other museums, notably the Museum of the Brooklyn Institute of Arts and Sciences, which, as a less well-endowed institution, he felt needed them more. He did try to give first choice to the American Museum, but when he was positive it had many duplicates he did not hesitate to give specimens to Brooklyn, to the Carnegie Museum in Pittsburgh, or even to a museum in Iowa. Dr. Joel Asaph Allen, the American Museum's curator of birds and mammals, complained to Professor Osborn that he was not getting all he should get, was not notified promptly of a death, and that the veterinarian was so slow in making his examinations that the specimen was often useless.

Dr. Hornaday wasted no time in punching back:

I am both surprised and pained at finding that Dr. Allen thinks I am not to be trusted with discretionary power in one of the most thankless and disagreeable functions I have to perform.

333

I have indeed exercised my discretion in the disposition of the remains of our dead animals. If I do not do so, who else can? Our medical staff has now, and always should have, *the first call* on everything for whatever examinations they may wish to make. If in the course of their investigations a specimen is necessarily used up, completely, it is because our own interests demand it. I can not undertake to serve two masters. If the Museum is to be allowed to dictate in any way to me, or to Drs. Miller and Brooks, then the pathological work of the latter may as well be dispensed with at once. If I am not to be trusted to do what is right in these matters, then discretionary powers should be vested in some one else, and I should be wholly relieved of the disposition of our dead animals.

This is the Zoological Park of *Greater New York*. The Brooklyn Park Department has treated us handsomely in the matter of live animals and plants, and requested our help for the Museum of the Brooklyn Institute,—which now has practically nothing, and needs everything! Should the disposition of our surplus of specimens be regulated by the Curator of Birds and Mammals of the American Museum?

There was more than a question of sovereignty here; Hornaday had asked Dr. Allen for a copy of his manuscript list of North American mammals some time before, and Allen had refused. "Thus far," Hornaday went on, "it seems that the cooperation between the Museum and the Park has been wholly on one side."

Hornaday's jealousy of the American Museum of Natural History was an old story to Professor Osborn, and he declined to get into the fight between Hornaday and Allen. Over the next few years they reached a more or less amicable equilibrium. Quarrels over the bits and pieces of dead animals continued for years, however, on a different front; in 1913 the executive committee appointed Dr. George S. Huntington of the College of Physicians and Surgeons as prosector "for the scientific utilization of the soft parts of animals." Blair's, Huntington's, and the museum's requirements were so often and so strongly in conflict that Hornaday was inclined to dump the whole matter in the lap of the museum. He would send the museum everything it wanted and everything he and Dr. Blair thought it might want—and the museum could thereafter fight it out with Dr. Huntington. It was another of his all-or-nothing attitudes, but as usual he simmered down quickly and everybody learned to work more or less in harmony.

Perhaps the only time when everybody was satisfied was after the 1913–14 outbreak of tuberculosis among the anthropoids; with nine cadavers available in the course of a few weeks, they could be dispensed lavishly. The body of the last orangutan that died was sent to the Sprague Memorial Institute of the University of Chicago and Dr. Hornaday informed Mr. Grant that it had been shared among six investigators. "I am quite certain that no specimen that ever died here has been made to cover so much ground as that one did."

The veterinary department was involved in one unpleasant incident in 1907. The year before, a young male Indian rhinoceros had been captured in Assam and Hagenbeck sold it to the Zoological Park for $6,000. Its right eye was injured during capture, but otherwise it was a perfect specimen and the society accepted it. After it had been exhibited a few months it was noticed that the left eye was beginning to be affected, and Dr. George G. Van Mater, a Brooklyn eye specialist, was called in. He diagnosed cataracts and recommended "needling" of both eyes. At the end of May, Mogul, as the rhino had been named, was immobilized on the floor of his compartment in the Elephant House, by means of side lines and hobbles, and an anesthetist began administering a mixture of chloroform and ether. It took a pound and a half of the former and three-quarters of a pound of the latter before the rhino succumbed, and by that time Dr. Blair, two other assistant medicos, and a number of keepers were almost as exhausted as Mogul. A local anesthetic was then applied around the eyes and Dr. Van Mater went to work. The entire affair took three hours. Less than forty

minutes later, Mogul was on his feet and apparently seeing clearly, at least with his left eye.

Editor Elwin R. Sanborn wrote a short account of the operation in the *Bulletin*. His final paragraph was: "The services of the operating surgeons, Drs. Van Mater and Gwathmey and their assistants, Drs. Ryder and Ellis, were gratuitous."

For the moment they were. Dr. Van Mater made subsequent house calls on his patient and in January of 1909 advised a second operation, which he performed. He followed it with a bill for $1,000.

Dr. Hornaday was outraged and wrote to the surgeon:

In 1907 and again in 1909 a young Indian rhinoceros named Mogul underwent eye operations.

336

I greatly regret that you have seen fit to send to the Zoological Society a bill for $1,000. for the operation on the rhinoceros. As you are very well aware, the operation on the rhinoceros was undertaken by you at your own request, and the service was to be gratuitous. At the beginning, I had very little faith in its success, and have still less now. I regarded the whole undertaking as an experiment on your part, and it has been so very slightly successful that the difference to the vision of the animal is only barely perceptible.

In the most offhand way in the world, and without for one moment thinking that I would be taken seriously, I waved my hand to you in good-bye, and said, "send in your bill." I see that you have taken me seriously, and have sent in your bill.

I now return it herewith, with the assurance that it never will be paid. We propose to stand on your proposition to operate on the rhinoceros gratuitously.

Both sides stood firm, however, and Dr. Van Mater filed suit to collect his bill. Dr. Hornaday sent a detailed chronology of the matter to William White Niles, the society's attorney, emphasizing the fact that the park had provided the surgeon with a large number of enlarged photographs of the operation, and that he had obtained much advertising from news stories about it. The case dragged on and was finally set for trial on February 20, 1911. A week later Madison Grant wrote to Hornaday: "The suit of Van Mater against the New York Zoological Society was discontinued last week without costs."

Mogul's sight was not referred to again in the society's records, so presumably the second operation improved his vision. He was the greatest prize in the park's mammal collection until the night of August 27, 1918, when a watchman found him dead in his stall.

Even before he became the park's veterinarian in 1903, Dr. Blair had demonstrated the quiet competence and diplomacy that were to carry him to the directorship as successor to Dr. Hornaday. He was so reliable and hard-working, so obviously able to deal with the problems of disease and injury in the

337

collection, that after 1908 Dr. Harlow Brooks discontinued his part-time work in pathology at the zoo.

Research that did not conflict with the primacy of exhibition was always welcome. In 1900 a research man was given permission to test the color vision of primates in the collection and to compare their order of preference with that of children, and a few years later Dr. Robert M. Yerkes of the Psychological Laboratory at Harvard arranged for a student to work for several months on imitation in monkeys. More elaborate work was done in 1915 when Dr. Francis G. Benedict, director of the Nutrition Laboratory of the Carnegie Institution in Washington, began a five-year study of the metabolism of mammals and reptiles in the Zoological Park. One result was the publication in 1936 of a monograph on "The Physiology of the Elephant," much of it based on work with the park's elephants.

From the veterinarian's point of view there was one supreme event in 1916: the Animal Hospital was built and turned over to Dr. Blair. It cost just under $18,000, which was probably why it could be constructed at a time when Dr. Hornaday was moaning about his unsuccessful efforts to get started on building the vastly more expensive Heads and Horns Museum. But the director was magnanimous. In the *Annual Report* he wrote: "It is a great satisfaction to feel that henceforth Dr. Blair will have a fair show in the treatment of diseases and accidents among the Park's animals."

On January 10, 1918, the *Bronx Home News* published a long list of charges against the Zoological Society's management of the Zoological Park. They occupied half a page under the headline "Commissioner of Accounts Should Investigate Bronx Zoo."

It was not the first time the newspaper had attacked the park. Four years before it had campaigned for an investigation of the park's "concessions," on the grounds that the society kept all the income from restaurants, animal rides, photographs, and the like, whereas concessions in other parks were let to the highest bidder and paid a return to the city. The society's reply was that these privileges were specifically reserved to the society by the Commissioners of the Sinking Fund in the grant of southern Bronx Park in 1897, the income to be used for the increase of the collections. It was an unassailable position and reform Mayor John Purroy Mitchel took no action. But now Tammany Major John F. Hylan was in office and his Commissioner of Accounts was David Hirshfield, who was always ready to investigate anything or anybody. The *World* reported in 1920 that he had made 1,100 investigations that year, more than double his record for 1919, but that only three of them resulted in reports to the Board of Aldermen. "His published reports have found little complaints against anything under Hylan's control," the *World* went on.

Thanks again to the Commissioners of the Sinking Fund, the Zoological Park was *not* under the control of Mayor Hylan or any other mayor; the society had the sole right to appoint and remove its employees. There was thus no patronage, and when Hirshfield's report finally came out after eleven months of investigation at a cost of $9,926.06, it was obvious that one, if not the only, purpose of the investigation was to take the management of the park away from the Zoological Society and turn it over to the city. In other words, to Tammany.

The charges made by Editor James O'Flaherty of the *Bronx*

19

The Zoological Park Is Investigated

Home News were the excuse for the investigation. O'Flaherty's complaints were easily rebutted, and another Bronx newspaper, the *North Side News,* gave Dr. Hornaday three columns of space for reply. Some samples:

Charge: "For upward of twenty years the most valuable portion of Bronx Park has been held practically as the private estate of a private society."

Answer: During that period the Zoological Park has received, made comfortable and safe, and entertained and instructed 24,934,499 visitors.

Charge: "It [the society] has conducted itself as an absolute autocracy."

Answer: This is true only in the sense that every department and bureau of the City government is an autocracy, in the making of rules for the conduct of its business with the public.

Insinuation: "For many years prior to the establishing of the private monopoly, the Bronx River was open to skaters in season, and thousands of people enjoyed its use."

Answer: This is intended to lead the public to believe that the Bronx River is no longer open to skaters. The Bronx River NEVER has been closed to skaters save when the ice was dangerous.

Eight days after O'Flaherty's blast the Commissioner of Accounts wrote to Professor Osborn that "Complaints have been made to the Mayor by citizens, concerning the management of the New York Zoological Park," and that the mayor had asked him to investigate and report. An accountant had been assigned to the case, and it was requested that he be given credentials to any person having jurisdiction over the financial records of money appropriated by the city of New York. This was done; and a crew of accountants began scanning the records and taking depositions from past and present employees. Neither Dr. Hornaday nor Chief Clerk H. R. Mitchell was questioned or given a chance to testify.

By early summer it was clear that the Commissioner of Accounts was not interested in hearing any defense the society might be able to offer, but the executive committee made a formal request to the commissioner that Dr. Hornaday be permitted to testify, and that the society be furnished with a copy of the report before it was made public. It was no use; the commissioner replied that "the regular procedure" would be followed and that if his office wanted to talk to Hornaday, he would be called. As for furnishing a copy of the report, "provisions of the charter require that official reports of this office be made to the Mayor and to the Board of Aldermen."

It was not until March of 1920 that the Hirshfield Report was released. It went to the newspapers as well as the mayor and the aldermen—but not to the Zoological Society. But Hornaday had a friend on the staff of the *Morning Telegraph* and he passed on the copy that came to his paper.

It was a remarkable document of eleven legal-length pages packed with insinuations, opinions, misinterpretations of innocent facts, and trivialities. Hornaday and the two Mitchells (William Mitchell was cashier) were the principal targets. Among other things it charged:

That Director Hornaday rules the Zoo and the City's park lands like an autocrat—a monarch in his own principality—and looks down with disgust upon the common people whom, in his report of the year 1912, he described as "dirty and lowered."

That H. R. Mitchell obtained fresh laid eggs from the nursery in the Zoo and gave storage eggs in return, the records showing that the quantity returned by Mr. Mitchell in 1917 was far less than the quantity received.

It was not the first time Hornaday had been called an autocrat, but having strong opinions about how to operate a great zoological park is hardly an indictable offense. As the executive committee said in a pamphlet which it issued immediately for the information of the society's members:

The fact is that the Director is one of the most democratic and approachable men in the world, has devoted his life to the service of the public and the furtherance of public interests in the protection of wild life, and in making the Park an agreeable and delightful place of resort for all the people. He never used the language attributed to him in the report, and such language as he has used in reference to any part of the visitors to the Park has been limited solely to that small disorderly element which takes pleasure in despoiling and defiling public property.

The charge that H. R. Mitchell stole eggs seems a little incongruous in such a ponderous document, but the fact was that he did take fresh eggs from the nursery at a period when Mrs. Mitchell was in poor health. As the executive committee's commentary pointed out, further research would have shown that he replaced them egg for egg, and that since the storage eggs were fed to reptiles "which are probably not connoisseurs in eggs," it was hardly a serious matter. Other employees had been permitted to do the same thing when there was sickness in their families.

The formal statement by the executive committee refuted the Hirshfield charges item by item, down to his final one that "In order to save for its own Privilege Department purposes the beauty and purity of that portion of the Bronx River flowing through its park domain, the Zoological Society, through its influential members, initiated the project and was responsible for the passage of Chapter 594, Laws of 1907, providing for construction of the Bronx Parkway." The Society answered:

The inference suggested is that the City has paid, or become obligated to pay, an enormous sum for an improvement which is wholly for the benefit of the Privilege Department of the Zoological Society. This is both untrue and ludicrous. The Zoological Park will undoubtedly be the gainer if the Bronx River is cleaned and improved, but the New York Zoological Society is not the only gainer by this improvement. The entire population in the Bronx Valley south of White Plains have been immeasurably benefitted as well as the 2,000,000 citizens of the City of New York who annually visit the Park.

The statement ended on a sorrowing note:

The Society feels aggrieved that for the splendid record it has made there is not one word of appreciation or approval; that the liberality of the Society in donating more than $700,000 through the Park to the public has not been referred to; that the care and attention given to its affairs by its Board of Governors which has resulted in the monies donated by the City being expended with such care and honesty that the very careful scrutiny of its affairs made by the Commissioner of Accounts has not resulted in unearthing one single instance of embezzlement or misappropriation during the twenty-five years that the Society has been operating the Zoological Park has not been mentioned.

The newspapers of New York City—with the exception of the *Bronx Home News*—were unanimously on the side of Hornaday and the Zoological Society, and news stories and editorials denouncing Hirshfield's tactics blossomed for weeks. Calling Hirshfield "Mayor Hylan's Heaviest Liability," the Citizens Union called for his removal from office, and a resolution to remove him because of "secretiveness, bias, prejudice, partiality, pettiness and general unfitness for public office" was introduced by a Republican member of the Board of Aldermen. It was defeated by a vote of 37 to 25 along strict party lines. The Democrats all supported the Commissioner of Accounts.

Hirshfield's report had closed with recommendations that the city take over the operation of the Zoological Park:

Public parks and institutions paid for and maintained with public funds are intended for the instruction, enjoyment and recreation of the people under the supervision of their duly elected governmental officials without hindrance or interference by self-constituted uplifters or even well-meaning benefactors.

I am submitting the following recommendations:

That your Honor appoint a committee, consisting of representatives of the New York Zoological Society, the Department of Parks, The Bronx, Department of Finance, the Law Department and the Commissioner of Accounts, for the purpose of studying the advisability of terminating the agreement between The City of New York and the Zoological Society, the City regaining its park land and taking over the entire activities in connection with the operation of the Zoological Garden, and thus secure more

343

effective service to the people with a substantial decrease in the cost to the tax and rent payer.

That the Rules and Regulations of the Municipal Civil Service Commission . . . be extended to control the appointment, removal, grades, etc. of all employees engaged or employed in the operation of the Zoological Garden.

Editorials were scornful of Hirshfield's obvious patronage grab, under such headlines as "Shall We Hylanize the Zoo?," and the Zoological Society flatly refused to participate in any committee to discuss abrogating its right to operate the Zoological Park. For one thing, the committee would be loaded against the society, and for another the original establishment of the society came from the state legislature—and the executive committee felt very certain the legislature would not withdraw the charter and give the park's operation to the city. So the recommendations of the Commissioner of Accounts were quietly shelved and in due course forgotten.

But not before one final blast in the newspapers from Hirshfield. He released some of the testimony he had taken during those eleven months. It came from a Manhattan dentist, Dr. Anton Joseph Hecker, a member of the Zoological Society who for years, despite multiple infirmities, had been in the habit of visiting the Zoological Park once a week.

He had testified under subpoena and the Commissioner of Accounts gave a transcript of his testimony to the papers at the height of their attacks on his conduct of the investigation.

Dr. Hecker said that the 1,600 members of the Zoological Society had no voice in the management of the park and he was convinced that the Zoo should be under the absolute control of the city. He was quoted as saying:

I go to the Zoological Garden to find recreation. I became acquainted with every employee, from the lowest garden digger up to the Director and became friends with them all. My friendship with Dr. Hornaday is such that he dedicated to me his work about wild animals, "to my esteemed friend Dr. Anton Joseph Hecker," and sent it to me.

344

Asked who Madison Grant was, he said:

He is Secretary of the Society and gets $5,000 outside of office expenses and an assistant secretary. Nobody does anything. They all draw high salaries. If I ran that business I would discharge more than half the employees and cut expenses to half and give better service.

Despite the friendship he claimed to have with Hornaday, the dentist apparently could find little good to say about him:

Q. [The employees] don't want to be at the mercy of one man, like Dr. Hornaday?

A. Everybody trembles when they see him.

Q. What about those two nephews, the Mitchells?

A. Well, I know one, H. R. Mitchell, the chief clerk and purchaser, was a railroad ticket seller somewhere West, and the other, his brother, was a railroad conductor.

Q. Do you think that their education and previous experience fit them to run a zoological garden research station?

A. No. The older, I think, is a shrewd fellow, but the other one is a damned fool. If I were director I would not even employ him as a porter.

The Hornaday-Hecker friendship terminated with the publication of Hecker's testimony. Hornaday wrote to him:

For more than ten years your infirmities have caused you to receive the most considerate sympathy from all officers and keepers of the Zoological Park. You have been permitted privileges that no visitor should have received. Now, as if you had been watching for your chance to do the greatest possible harm, you traitorously traduce the administrative officers of the Park, denounce their management, and blackguard at least one of them. We now know that you are the bitterest enemy, and the Judas Iscariot, of the Zoological Society.

It was a protracted, painful, often exasperating incident in the history of the Zoological Society, but because of the absurdity of the charges, not an important one. Actually, the Zoological Park and the society that sponsored it emerged stronger than ever in the allegiance of New Yorkers.

"Undoubtedly the highest desire of every zoological garden and park, and of every showman, is to own and exhibit a real, live gorilla of a size sufficiently large to compel both admiration and awe."

Thus Dr. Hornaday began his discussion of "Gorillas, Past and Present," in the January, 1915, number of the society's *Bulletin*. It was a fair statement for the times. A "real, live gorilla" was the crowning exhibit of any collection of primates then—except that very, very few had ever possessed such a treasure—and it still is today. But the prestige thing today, of course, is not mere possession of gorillas but whether you have managed to breed them. Such an accomplishment was unthought-of in the early years of this century.

The New York Zoological Park wanted a gorilla more insistently than it had ever wanted any other animal, and Dr. Hornaday spent an inordinate amount of time casting around for a way to bring one out of Africa. This despite the fact that gorillas seemed especially designed by nature to try his patience. Repeatedly in letters and articles in the society's magazine, he described them as "sullen, morose, intractable." His two most celebrated pronunciamentos were made in that 1915 survey of gorillas past and present:

It is not an animal of philosophic mind, nor is it given to reasoning from cause to effect. What can we do with a wild animal that is not amenable to the pangs of hunger, and would rather die than yield?

There is not the slightest reason to hope that an adult gorilla, either male or female, ever will be seen living in a zoological park or garden.

The society's quest for a gorilla began in 1905 when Dr. Hornaday received a letter from Miss Jean W. Simpson, the little daughter of a member of the Zoological Society:

My father says I may give a gorilla. Please place an order for him. I would like to name him "Cheese."

Love from, Jean

20

Gorillas and Other Great Rarities

As it happened, there was a gorilla to be had in Europe through the Washington animal dealer Dr. Cecil French, and an order was placed. A note about the imminent arrival of this "most interesting of all apes" was written for the October issue of the *Bulletin* but it was cut off short by a paragraph in italics: "Later: *At the moment of going to press, the editor regrets to announce that the Gorilla died aboard ship.*"

At the end of 1906 Dr. Hornaday tried again. A rather fast-talking animal collector named Gustave Sebille offered to go to West Africa to try for a gorilla, and he accepted the society's terms: a salary of $66.66 a month for six months, travel and living expenses, and a bonus of $200 if he brought back a gorilla that lived until it reached the Primate House. Sebille did manage to capture a baby gorilla but it died in his camp.

Success, of a kind, came in 1911. R. L. Garner was an experienced African traveler and collector, and the society commissioned him to go to the French Congo and collect gorillas and chimpanzees. So sure was he of success that he worked out an elaborate cable code to send back news:

Abasement. "I have secured 1 gorilla."

Ablative. "I have secured 2 gorillas."

Abrogate. "I have secured 3 gorillas."

(And so on up to six gorillas.)

There was a similar code to signal the capture of chimpanzees and common species of monkey, and on September 11 he cabled CABINET SUPERB LINOLEUM, meaning "I have one superb gorilla, one chimpanzee, and three common species of monkey."

Unhappily, he missed connections with a direct steamship to New York and had to transship in France. By the time he arrived in New York on September 23, the gorilla was emaciated and sickly. Its food preferences, Dr. Hornaday wrote in the *Bulletin,* "were at once the rage and despair of its keepers."

Of the score of good things offered that gorilla, and of which it should have eaten, it partook of not one. It refused the finest bananas, but it did attempt to eat microscopic portions of the inner lining of banana skins. It desired either plantains, or the succulent centers of banana plants; these, and nothing more. The New York Botanical Gardens loyally sacrificed to science, as represented by the emaciated body of a food-sick gorilla, two perfectly good banana plants, and their hearts were duly consumed. By the time we had secured a small lot of spoiled plantains from New Orleans, and two dozen good ones from Cuba, the gorilla was dead; which, as a purely logical proposition, it deserved to be, for its obstinacy.

This first gorilla had lived only two weeks, but the unexpectedly protracted sea voyage was probably a factor; Garner was obviously competent, and so late in 1912 the executive committee authorized another expedition. This time he would keep his gorillas in a base camp for several months, or maybe even a year or two, and get them settled on acceptable and readily available food before sailing for New York.

Within a few months he had captured two young gorillas and reported jubilantly that they were in good condition, lively and playful. Back went a letter from Hornaday warning him to expect a visit from Buffalo Jones, who had big ideas about lassoing gorillas and giraffes in front of a motion-picture camera:

I have warned the Colonel of the drawbacks and obstacles that he will have to meet and surmount; but nothing daunts his indomitable spirit. He will not be happy until he gets his rope on some of those gorillas, and at least makes a bluff at bringing them under his control. Treat the Colonel very kindly, for my sake, and put him in the way of getting all the gorillas he wants, in the shortest possible time. If he should be stricken with blackwater fever, or any of the other infernal diseases of Equatorial West Africa, spend your last dollar, if necessary, in getting him out, keeping him alive, and sending him back to his own country.

Jones did get some footage of himself playing with Garner's baby gorillas, but the attempt to throw a lasso around an adult gorilla resulted as Hornaday had expected—in failure.

Gorillas were a sore trial to Director Hornaday; they refused to eat what he thought was good for them, and they persisted in dying. This is Dinah, the Zoo's second gorilla. She came in 1914 and survived about eleven months.

348

The smaller of Garner's two gorillas died in January of 1914 "of general lack of stamina," but Garner reached New York on August 24, 1914, with a "cheerful, lively and affectionate" three-year-old animal named Dinah. She was the last wild animal to be shipped out of Africa before a total embargo caused by the war.

Dinah was playful and took plenty of exercise, and she ate well. The evil spell that hung over gorillas seemed to have been broken. To mark the happy event, Watson B. Dickerman, a member of the Board of Managers, commissioned Eli Harvey to make a life-sized bronze figure of her at a cost of $880.25. Rejoicing was premature. Dinah began to lose interest in food by mid-November and her muscular movements were impaired. By July 31, 1915, she was dead, having survived just a little more than eleven months. Thereupon Dr. Hornaday threw up his hands and announced that an adult gorilla would never be seen alive in a zoological park.

He had been retired for a year when the next gorilla came to an American zoological garden. It was an infant named Bamboo that came to the Philadelphia Zoological Garden in 1927 and it lived to the remarkable age of thirty-three years, five months, and sixteen days. Even his own zoo soon disproved the Hornaday prediction; Janet Penserosa came to the Bronx Zoo on October 31, 1928, and lived in the collection for eleven years, eight months, and twenty-nine days, after which she was turned over to the Yale School of Medicine because she had a partial paralysis of her legs. Since then there has been a steady flow of viable gorillas to many American zoos—the Bronx Zoo has had seventeen—and the first captivity-bred baby was born in the Columbus, Ohio, Zoo on December 22, 1956. The Bronx Zoo's first baby was born on October 2, 1972.

Lee S. Crandall, in his *The Management of Wild Mammals in Captivity*, remarked on the reasons why Dr. Hornaday's discouragement was not justified. Among them were a gradually evolving understanding of the needs of gorillas in captivity and, in recent years, the great advantage of swift airplane transportation. Not for nothing are they called the "manlike apes"; baby gorillas have essentially the same physical requirements as human babies. We know now that wild-caught gorillas must be taken at an early age and quickly attached to someone who will give them the care and feeling of security they would get from their own mothers. It is the foster mother's role to introduce them to suitable foods, and they will then usually transfer their affections readily enough to another person—their regular zoo keeper, for instance. When these conditions are met, as they were in the Bronx Zoo during the years when Mrs. Helen Martini was in charge of the Zoo's "Animal Nursery" in the Lion House, baby

Mrs. Helen Martini and one of her "babies"—a black leopard cub.

351

gorillas may be expected to thrive about as human babies would under similar conditions of affectionate supervision and care. Other foster mothers have followed that prescription since Mrs. Martini's retirement and found that it works.

But gorillas were not the only prizes the Zoological Society sought in the great African storehouse of animal rarities, and the okapi of the dark Ituri forests in what was then the Belgian Congo was first among them. It had the distinction of being the first major animal discovered in Africa since the turn of the century. The members of the society learned of it quickly, for its discovery was reported in the *News Bulletin* in July of 1901, only a few months after it was announced in the *Proceedings of the Zoological Society of London*. The haunts of the "very remarkable new horse," which the okapi was at first supposed to be, were in such a remote and forbidding region that there seemed to be no chance of getting one, until the American Museum of Natural History sent a collecting expedition to the Congo in 1909. It was to be led by Herbert Lang of the museum's staff, with James P. Chapin as his only companion, and before setting out Lang consulted Dr. Hornaday about desiderata. An okapi and a white rhinoceros were at the top of the list. Lang told about his near success in the May, 1918, issue of the *Zoological Society Bulletin*. The Lang-Chapin Expedition worked for more than six years in okapi country, "in the Belgian Congo, west of the Ruwenzori, across a portion of the Ituri and Uele districts to the Ubangi River."

Lang and Chapin came out of the Congo with fifty-four tons of museum material and without having a single accident or a day's illness. They were more fortunate than many of their predecessors who had explored the region:

Whoever penetrated here was, so to speak, "on the wing," and wings beat doubly fast across these inhospitable regions. The numerous sportsmen who have visited nearly all parts of Africa found no attraction in these forests. Indeed the many pale, haggard faces that emerged from the western half of equatorial Africa were no incentive to pleasure-seeking people. The immensity of the wilderness is appalling; for over eighteen hundred miles without a break it stretches more than half way across the continent, from the coast of Guinea to the Ruwenzori. In spite of tropical luxuriance, it is one of the most dismal spots on the face of the globe, for the torrid sun burns above miles of leafy expanse, and the unflagging heat of about one hundred degrees day and night, renders the moist atmosphere unbearable. Over the whole area storms of tropical violence thunder and rage almost daily. Here natives have become cannibals, and the graves of thousands of white men are merely a remembrance of where youthful energy and adventures came to a sudden end.

Near the end of the Lang-Chapin Expedition, friendly Pygmies found a newborn okapi calf and brought it into camp. Accustomed to stalking and killing adult okapis for food, the Pygmies were wary of the calf and hastened to bind it tightly with lianas, but "the terrible beast had no other desire than to lick the face of its captor and to suck the fingers held out to him."

Momentarily it appeared that the New York Zoological Park was to have the honor of exhibiting the first living okapi. But it was not to be. Lang wrote:

Within four days my store of eight cans of condensed milk had given out, and it was a severe shock when my messengers returned from Poko and Medje, six and seven days distant, without a new supply. I tried a mixture of rice flour and water, but the calf became so weak that ten days later I lost all hope of saving him. It was a sad disappointment, yet more than ever I was convinced that under proper conditions okapi could be brought to civilized countries.

His predictions came true even while the expedition was on its way home. An okapi only a few days old was brought into the mission station at Buta and the wife of the district commissioner reared it on a bottle. It became so tame that it wandered at will around the mission, browsing for itself after it outgrew the milk stage, and at the end of World War I it was shipped to the Antwerp Zoological Garden, which thus

The okapi of the Ituri forests of the (then) Belgian Congo was the first major animal to be discovered in Africa after the turn of the century. Since 1937 several have been received by the Bronx Zoo and have bred there and elsewhere.

353

became the first to exhibit a live okapi. Several others went to Europe from the Buta mission in the next few years, and Dr. Hornaday tried hard to acquire one from that source, offering $2,500 plus $500 for transport, but without Belgian governmental services to ship and care for the animal en route there was no way to do it. It was not until 1937 that Dr. Blair, who had succeeded Dr. Hornaday as director, was able to buy one of three young specimens shipped to Antwerp from Buta. It arrived in New York on August 2, 1937, was promptly named Congo, and lived until September 5, 1952. Several others have been received since then and they have bred in the Bronx Zoo as well as in other zoos here and abroad.

Doreen, a bongo from the Aberdare Mountains of Kenya, came to the Bronx Zoo in 1932. She was the first bongo exhibited alive anywhere.

Dr. Hornaday seems to have made no attempt to get another great African rarity, the bongo, although he was proud of a mounted bongo head in the Heads and Horns Museum. It was left to Dr. Blair to secure that prize. He began negotiations as soon as he learned that Colonel E. Percy-Smith, a British big-game hunter and collector, was planning an expedition to the Aberdare Mountains of Kenya. Percy-Smith managed to snare a half-grown female bongo, and without difficulty she was shipped to England and then to New York, where she arrived on June 6, 1932—the first bongo exhibited alive anywhere. Doreen settled down calmly in the Antelope House and fully justified the bongo reputation of being the most beautiful antelope in the world. To the day of her death in 1951, she was quiet, gentle, and friendly toward her keepers and admiring visitors. Bongos are still among the rarest of all antelopes in zoological collections (although they have bred in several zoos in the United States and in Europe), and the Bronx Zoo has had only Doreen. It came close to getting another one in 1949. At that time Charles Cordier was working in the Congo as a collector for the Zoological Society and captured an adult male which, in typical bongo fashion, became tame enough to approach anyone who offered food. But while Cordier's collection of birds and mammals was being moved from one camp to another during his absence, his native helpers so manhandled the animal that it did not survive.

From a purely zoological point of view, the greatest triumph of the Hornaday era was the exhibition for forty-seven days of the duck-billed platypus of Australia—the first example of this egg-laying mammal ever seen alive outside that continent. The other egg-laying mammal, the echidna or spiny anteater, had long been well known in the Zoo's collection, but efforts to match it with a platypus were always unavailing because nobody knew how to transport it safely over long distances. Fishes of course have to be transported in their native habitat—water—but no other animal is so exigent as to require a replica of its home while traveling. And the platypus's home and its life style are extremely complex.

"The spell of ten thousand years has been broken," is the way Dr. Hornaday began his article on "New York's Duck-billed Platypus" in the *Bulletin* of September, 1922:

The most wonderful of all living mammals has been carried alive from the insular confines of its far-too-distant native land, and introduced abroad. No matter what evil fate may hereafter overtake the platypus species, nothing can rob us of the fact that New York has looked upon a living *Ornithorhynchus paradoxus* [= *anatinus*] and found it mighty interesting. It cost us $1,400, but it was worth it.

Actually, an Australian naturalist named Harry Burrell had begun in 1910 to break the spell that had confined the primitive egg-laying mammal to eastern Australia and Tasmania. He managed to keep a platypus in captivity for sixty-eight days before it escaped, and in the course of that and subsequent experiments he invented what he called a platypusary, a tank of water from which the animal could follow a labyrinth of tunnels to its dry sleeping quarters. On the way, it had to pass through a number of rubber gaskets that squeezed the water from its fur, so that it arrived "home" fairly dry.

Burrell's contraption was portable only to moderate degree,

and it remained for the Australia-based animal dealer Ellis S. Joseph to work out with him the details of a truly portable, sectional platypusary that could be managed aboard ship. Joseph, a grotesquely large and abundantly energetic man, had gotten into the international animal business in 1916 and 1917 when he reached New York with great collections of Australian birds and mammals, and he was determined to find a way to get platypuses to the New York Zoological Park. He had a platypusary constructed more or less along Burrell's lines, and in May of 1922 he started for the New World with a large cargo of kangaroos, birds, lizards and snakes, five platypuses, and what he hoped was a sufficient supply of platypus food, mostly earthworms. Despite Burrell's experiences which showed that a platypus weighing between two and three pounds could and would eat almost its own weight of earthworms and freshwater crayfish in one night, Joseph started out with quite inadequate supplies and was lucky to reach San Francisco with one platypus still alive. He rested his animals—and himself—and gathered more earthworms, and reached New York by train on July 14.

Specifications for a permanent platypusary had been sent ahead, and it was already set up in the yard off the east end of the Reptile House. Visitors were permitted to file past for an hour each afternoon, between three and four o'clock; when VIP visitors came along, Head Keeper John Toomey would scoop the wriggling, protesting little creature out of the water and hold it up to be admired.

Proud as he was of it, Dr. Hornaday was shocked by the voracious appetite of the platypus. It was costing four to five dollars a day for earthworms, small shrimps, and wood grubs (the latter then cost ten cents apiece). "We looked forward with apprehension to the horrors of winter." His apprehension was needless; the platypus died on August 30. We now know that it was not getting nearly enough to eat, for its daily ration—half a pound of earthworms, forty shrimps, and forty grubs—met only about a third of the animal's needs.

It was twenty-five years later, in 1947, when the platypus again came to the Bronx Zoo. This time there were three of them: Cecil, Penelope, and Betty Hutton. David Fleay, the director of the Sir Colin Mackenzie Sanctuary for Native Fauna in Healesville, Victoria, was the entrepreneur this time, and the science of keeping and transporting platypuses had advanced a great deal since 1922; in fact, Fleay had kept them so well that his pair named Jack and Jill bred in 1943 and produced the first—and to date the only—viable captivity-bred baby, named Corrie. (Fleay's Big Bill and Penny bred in 1972, but the single young was found dead sixty days after egg-laying. Suspicion points to the DDT contained in most of the freshwater crayfish fed to the parents.)

Fleay was experienced enough to have no illusions about the amount of food that would be needed on a voyage from

In 1922, "the spell of ten thousand years" was broken when the Zoo received its first duck-billed platypus from Australia. It was exhibited for an hour every afternoon and Head Keeper John Toomey usually picked it up to show to especially interested visitors—probably one of the reasons why it lived for only forty-seven days.

Australia to New York (he had ruled out air transport because of the difficulty of managing a traveling platypusary aboard an airplane, and also because a short experimental flight had convinced him that it seriously disturbed the platypus). He collected an enormous quantity of earthworms and "yabbies," a kind of freshwater crayfish to which the platypuses were partial, and as a reserve he counted on a kind of egg custard which they would eat as a supplement to live food. Nevertheless, supplies ran low as he crossed the Pacific and he had to radio ahead to Pitcairn Island to have more earthworms waiting. They were—but they were spoiled by being dunked in sea water in the rough surf. He then sent an emergency message to the Zoological Park asking that earthworms be flown to meet the S.S. *Pioneer Glen* at Panama. Fortunately, the park had had the foresight to establish a gigantic earthworm nursery in the basement of the Lion House, and ten thousand earthworms were hastily packed and conveyed to Panama by air. They saved the day, although there was a final hitch at the end when it was found that the *Pioneer Glen* had to dock in Boston instead of New York. A small party from the Zoo flew to Boston, hired a capacious limousine, and rushed Mr. and Mrs. Fleay and the precious platypuses (in an ordinary animal traveling case, for there was no room in the limousine for the shipboard platypusary) to the Zoo. The platypuses arrived late at night and spent the rest of it frantically swimming and rolling over and over—a sign of acute disturbance—in the bathtub in the Zoo apartment of George Scott, the head keeper of birds. They went on exhibition three days later on April 28, 1947, in the huge permanent Platypusary that the Zoo had built to Fleay's blueprints, among the trees just north of what is now the Zoo's Safari Shop.

It would be too much to imply that the Zoo regretted its second venture into platypus exhibition, for it made a third one eleven years later, in 1958. But there were moments, even days, when . . .

It *is* safe to say that no animals in the history of the New York Zoological Park called forth so much work, worry, and nervous energy as Cecil, Penelope, and Betty Hutton. In line with its ancient principle of giving its animals plenty of room, the Zoo had built its Platypusary six inches wider than Fleay had specified. The platypuses didn't like it, so false sides were built into their swimming pool. They didn't like the color of the false sides, so they were repainted. Neither did they like any noise above a low murmur, or women in bright dresses, or black umbrellas, or sudden movements by visitors on the walks overlooking their tank. . . .

They were a great success with the public; no doubt about that. Every afternoon double lines of visitors sometimes hundreds of feet long formed in front of the entrance to the canopied Platypusary, and 200,000 saw them that first summer. In late fall they were put in winter quarters in a modified platypusary in the basement of the Large Bird House, a routine followed as long as they lived in the Zoo. Betty died in the fall of 1948. She was the smallest of the trio and it was subsequently surmised that her girth was not great enough for the rubber squeegees in the labyrinth of tunnels to remove the water from her fur, so that she went to bed wet and got pneumonia. Cecil and Penelope continued to thrive and summer after summer were returned to exhibition.

Penelope's finest hour came in the summer of 1953 when she showed every sign of pregnancy. In May she and Cecil had been observed going through the platypus courtship ritual, in which Cecil seized Penelope's tail in his bill and floated behind her while she towed him around the pool in slow, dreamy circles. Then she began to follow, step by step, the timetable of platypus pregnancy that Fleay had observed and chronicled when Jack and Jill bred in Healesville—such things as plugging the entrance to her earthen tunnel, staying inside for longer periods, emerging to eat ravenously, carrying eucalyptus leaves underground. Keeper John Blair, who had been assigned exclusively to the platypuses since their arrival, kept his own timetable of Penelope's behavior. By the end of the summer the Zoo's staff compared the Healesville–Bronx Zoo figures and in a solemn staff meeting decided that Penelope was certainly pregnant.

Everything corresponded so neatly that the day on which the egg must have hatched could be pinpointed: July 16. Fleay's baby Corrie had emerged from the underground nest just seventeen weeks after hatching. It was anxiously debated whether to wait out the full seventeen weeks or take a chance and open the burrow at sixteen weeks, for it would then be November and the weather was uncertain. A deadline of November 5 was set, abruptly decided by a forecast of heavy snow the following day.

It would be a kindness to the sensibilities of the staff members and keepers of that day who are still around if the events of November 5 were not recalled here. In short, under the eyes of virtually everyone in the Bronx Zoo from President Fairfield Osborn down, and of two-score newspaper and newsreel photographers (for whom a special viewing platform had been built) , the 280 cubic feet of packed earth in Penelope's section of the burrow was shoveled out, slowly and carefully, without the slightest sign of nest, baby, or even of Penelope until the last two cubic feet in the furthest corner were disturbed. There was Penelope, fat, surprised, and seemingly not at all repentant at having given promises she had no intention of redeeming.

The staff and the press departed. What could anyone say except that Penelope had been riding the gravy train for months, sleeping late and gorging on the choicest earthworms —and that *maybe* her behavior was an example of false pregnancy.

Robert M. McClung, the acting curator of mammals, reported the debacle in the society's magazine, now named *Animal Kingdom,* and speculated about why no trace was found of the mound of eucalyptus leaves which had been provided for Penelope's nest and which she had assiduously dragged into her burrow; he could only suppose she had scattered them haphazardly through the tunnels and that they had disintegrated. But:

Lastly—why, oh why, did Penelope act out Platypus breeding behavior so closely, all to no avail? Several theories might account for it. Penelope may actually have laid eggs and even hatched baby Platypuses. [McClung was one of the first to be convinced there were *babies*—not just a baby—on the way.] Something perhaps happened to destroy the eggs or tiny babies at an early stage. Again, it is possible that Penelope was ready for mating in June, but that the moment when mating and fertilization of her ova should have occurred had already passed when she and Cecil were given the opportunity for mating. Her aroused maternal instinct might still function and cause her to go through all the phases of maternal behavior without actually laying eggs.

An optimist to the last, McClung concluded his article with: "In spite of our disappointment, we still have hopes for the future. There's always next year."

There wasn't, though; Penelope had had her fun and there were no repetitions of the great maternity act. On August 1, 1957, she was found to have escaped from the Platypusary, and although keepers searched the Zoo's ponds and the Bronx River for several weeks, no trace of her was ever found. (Letters and telephone calls reported sighting her from distances as much as 150 miles from the Bronx.) She simply disappeared, and on September 18 Cecil was found dead in one of his hay-filled tunnels. He had lived in the Zoo for ten years, four months, and twenty-four days, and Penelope just forty-nine days less. Only David Fleay had done better; except for five or six weeks when Jack escaped and was at liberty at Healesville, Fleay had kept the platypus for fourteen years.

The Fleays brought three more platypuses—Paul, Pamela, and Patty—in June of 1958, but somehow conditions were not right and by next March 25 all three had died. Since then there has been no noticeable eagerness on the part of the Zoo staff to try for platypuses a fourth time. It would be a vain hope, anyway; in 1970 Australia placed an absolute embargo on the export of both platypuses and koalas.

The outbreak of World War I on August 1, 1914, did not immediately affect the Zoological Park. It had entered that fateful year with its collections at a peak of 4,729 specimens of 1,290 species so that there were no immediate worries about animals, although it was an ominous sign when Dr. Hornaday noted that the gorilla Dinah was the last animal to come out of Africa before a total embargo was placed on such nonessential shipments.

The society's—or at least Hornaday's—attitude toward the war was one of regret for friends on both sides, and an implied promise to help restore the inevitably shattered European zoological gardens at the end of the conflict. In an editorial in the *Bulletin* a month after war was declared, the director wrote:

> The closeness of our relations with the defenders of wild life and the zoological gardens of England, France, Germany, Belgium and Holland bring the horrors of war closely home to us. Whichever side wins, we will be sorry for those who have lost. When the awful conflict is over, it will be our duty to see what we can do to help heal the wounds of the zoological gardens that have suffered most by the world-wide calamity.

In the meantime it was business as usual. Even before the war, the park was beginning to tap the animal resources of Latin America, and in March of 1914 it sent Crandall and young T. Donald Carter to Costa Rica for birds, mammals, and reptiles—anything they could collect on a six weeks' expedition. They came back with more than three hundred specimens, even including batrachians, fishes, and insects, many of which the park had never before exhibited.

If the war in Europe seemed far away, there was an equally bitter one at home: the Rubbish War (Hornaday's own name for it) in the Zoological Park. Rubbish-throwing and vandalism began to get out of hand, and Hornaday bombarded the courts, the mayor, and the newspapers with protests. For several summers he hired a crew of Burns Detective Agency operatives to patrol the park on weekends and arrest anyone

21

Dr. Hornaday Adopts a World War

caught littering. He had the press behind him, and the "decent" public as well; a woman in London advised him to set up a public whipping post. Lashing "just one dozen of those malevolent cowardly ruffians would stop it."

He actually made progress. The city's Chief Magistrate became interested, held Sunday sessions in West Farms Court, and on one May Sunday heard 126 cases and passed out stiff fines to all but two or three miscreants. Hornaday was gratified:

Today the cleanliness of our walks and walk borders is a constant joy. One can walk through our grounds without feelings of rage and mortification. The only way to keep the lawless element down is to deal with it diligently, persistently and severely. Remonstrances addressed to swine with human bodies are of no avail.

The public did not have to litter to get into trouble. In midsummer Hornaday had to deal with a visitor who asserted that he had been attacked by one of the park's groundsmen. He had, he said, been looking for a public toilet and finally asked the uniformed groundsman where it was. The man civilly pointed it out, whereupon the visitor exclaimed, "Gee, I am looking for that half an hour already." Instantly the groundsman rushed him, struck him, and ordered him to leave the park.

Hornaday's rule was to stand up for his own men and he never accepted a complaint on face value. He called in the groundsman and got his story—which was identical up to the crucial point. According to the employee, the visitor exclaimed "Jesus Christ!" when the toilet was pointed out. And the employee (whose name was Fitzgerald) said that he "was much incensed by the use of the name of the Son of God at the end of a conversation concerning a toilet building, and that it was on this that the subsequent altercation was based."

America was officially, and in the main unofficially, neutral in the first year of the war, but Hornaday was soon to take sides. In December of 1914 he wrote to Dr. P. Chalmers

363

Mitchell, secretary of the Zoological Society of London, urging him to think seriously about Britain's setting up a depot for wild-animal collections, for he felt sure the previously pre-eminent German animal market would not recover for a long time. In a paragraph marked "Confidential" he went on:

There is a great deal of talk about the neutrality of America, but I can assure you that there is mighty little "neutrality" among individual Americans! I am no longer neutral; and I do not care who knows that. I feel so enraged at Germany and the Germans that it would not grieve me if we never again have anything to do with the people of that nation.

Mitchell did make some inquiries of his government about laying the groundwork for capturing the animal market, but Britain was too hard pressed to look that far ahead and turned him down. Hornaday persisted with other individuals in Britain and at the end of the war a British group did make an attempt, but it was poorly organized and financed and nothing much came of it.

Gradually the United States took on a more warlike posture and inevitably the Zoological Park was affected. Here and there a man slipped away to join the armed services, and in the summer of 1915 Madison Grant passed word from the executive committee that men in the services would be granted leave of absence with full pay. The cost of living was going up, and to help the employees—for there was no chance of getting money from the city for an increase of salaries—the park established a cooperative store with $700 worth of staple stock.

Still, throughout 1916 the Zoological Park was essentially on a peacetime footing, and the society could look ahead confidently to expanding its scientific work. William Beebe's *Monograph of the Pheasants* was finished, if not yet published because of the war, and in 1915 he had spent seven weeks in Pará (Belém), Brazil, and had brought back sixty-two Brazilian birds, a fourth of them new to the collection. He was eager to get back to the tropics, and this seemed a

364

good time to establish a permanent Tropical Research Station in British Guiana, with the double object of making "studies of the evolution and life histories of birds, and various problems of avian development that can be studied successfully only with the aid of living material fresh from the jungle," and of collecting mammals, birds, reptiles, amphibians, and insects for the Zoological Park. It was made explicit in the announcement in the *Bulletin* that Beebe was not going to catalogue the birds of the Guianas or make a collection of skins; those chores could be left to museums and old-style naturalists. Field studies were the only thing that interested Beebe when he sailed for British Guiana in mid-January of 1916. With him went T. Donald Carter from the Bird Department of the Park as official collector; G. Inness Hartley as research associate; Paul G. Howes as research assistant specializing in microphotography and invertebrates; and the first of a long series of artists, Hartley's sister Rachel and Miss Anna H. Taylor.

Beebe expressed gleeful justification for his field approach in a letter he sent to Hornaday from his laboratory at Kalacoon, two-hundred feet above the Mazaruni River in Bartica District:

I have worked out a new plan to put a crimp on the characters which taxonomists are using and think I shall get some good things. The item about the tinamou is one. These differences are taken for granted and their relative importance or significance are lost by the fact that they are discovered by museum workers. All the members of the Tinamus have exceedingly rough corrugated hind tarsi, while those of Crypturus are perfectly smooth. Why? Chapman [Dr. Frank M. Chapman, curator of birds at the American Museum of Natural History] would say in order to make it easy to differentiate between genera! I noticed in freshly killed specimens that the rough tarsi were much soiled and coated with mold and fibres. I made some cultures from this soil and have reared some sprouting airplants! Then I studied the live birds and independently three Indians have confirmed the fact that all the birds of this group roost in trees, well up while Crypturus

365

roost on the ground. As the hind toes are too weak to support them, they crouch on the pineapple-like corrugations of the entire tarsus and sleep safely! q.e.d. That is the only way that I can find any pleasure in pure taxonomy.

Teleology might not have led Dr. Chapman to the opinion Beebe ascribed to him, but certainly he could not from a thousand museum skins deduce the real usefulness of the tinamou's corrugated hind tarsi; that took field work on living birds. And the Beebe kind of mind.

If there was any doubt that Beebe was dedicated to field studies, his next letter to Hornaday would have dispelled it. (Incidentally, it revealed that now, six years after Hornaday's storm over Beebe's desertion of the park for his pheasant expedition, their relations were entirely friendly) :

You are so refreshingly sane, & believe things when I tell you and dont always suspect that I am concealing some remarkable plot or thing up my sleeve. I am getting exceedingly tired of many members of my race, but I like you immensely, and shall do all I can to make our work go smoothly and efficiently. But the thing I am most amazed at is our tremendous scientific ignorance, and the absolute purility [sic] and uselessness of spending a life at naming things. After 38 years of work (more or less) I am willing at any time to confess that I have only learned some of the things *not* to do in this world.

"The item about the tinamou" Beebe had referred to in his letter to Hornaday concerned the chapter on "The Ways of Tinamou" he had written for a book, *Tropical Wild Life in British Guiana,* published by the society in January of 1917. Beebe, Hartley, and Howes each contributed sections based on their 1916 studies at Kalacoon, and the profusely illustrated 504-page volume is a remarkable testimonial to six months' hard work. But Beebe was always a slave driver in the field. As he wrote to Hornaday soon after settling in at Kalacoon, in reply to a letter saying several research men were interested in spending a little time at the station:

We don't want broken-down zoologists and if such come we will kill them with work. If they can stand the pace we are setting they will have to be sound of wind to start with. The first rush being over, I am making the fellows slow up a bit, and we take a half hour's rest at midday now.

Former President and Mrs. Theodore Roosevelt visited Kalacoon three days after the staff moved in, and T.R. was so entranced by the station that he wrote a long article about it in the January, 1917, issue of *Scribner's*. The staff, he said, "were enjoying the rare combination of working hard at a task in which their souls delighted, and of also taking part in a thrilling kind of picnic."

After the productive research year of 1916, the station operated for a brief two months in 1917, but then the society decided that maritime travel was too risky and uncertain, and so it was closed, not to reopen until 1919.

A great plumage seizure was one of the important events of 1916. Ever since 1913, when Hornaday had written the clause in the Underwood Tariff Act that prohibited the importation of wild-bird plumage for millinery, he had been in constant correspondence with customs officials, feather importers, and individual wearers of feather-adorned hats whose plumes might or might not come under the provisions of the act; there were countless debatable areas or loopholes, such as the classification of certain pheasant feathers. The Chinese asserted they were breeding rare pheasants on "farms," and the plumes should be considered those of domestic fowl. Hornaday got authoritative opinions from consuls and travelers in China that there were no such farms, and soon stopped that source. By 1915 most of the gray areas had been illuminated and smuggling was at a minimum. Then, in January of 1916, a feather smuggler was caught at Laredo, Texas, with a trunk containing 527 skins of the greater bird of paradise, valued at $52,700. Plume importations had been banned, but plumes already in the country and in the hands of feather dealers could still be sold, and it was the usual practice of successful smugglers to turn their

An important event of 1916 was the seizure by customs officers at Laredo, Texas, of a trunk containing 527 skins of birds of paradise. Importation had been prohibited by a clause in the Tariff Act of 1913 written by Dr. Hornaday. The skins were released to the Zoological Society, which doled out some of them to museums for exhibition.

367

cargo over to unprincipled dealers who sold them as long-held stock. The Laredo catch was the most important one the government had made, and the society publicized it widely. At Hornaday's request the customs people turned the shipment over to the Zoological Society so the plumes could be used for educational purposes, and for years the skins were doled out to museums over the country as examples of beautiful birds slaughtered for mere decoration. Reeking of mothballs, several hundred of them still reposed in their original trunk in a storeroom in the Zoological Park's Administration Building until 1940, when they were given as a lot to the American Museum of Natural History.

The United States went to war on April 6, 1917, and the Zoo went with it—all except the animals. Unpatriotically they declined to do their bit by eating less. Dr. Hornaday reported their disloyalty in the *Annual Report* for 1917:

> During the early summer of 1917, in order to make a test of the rationing system of the large Mammals, the Director ordered a horizontal reduction of the daily rations of elephants, rhinoceroses, bears, lions, tigers and leopards. The reduction varied from 10 to 30 per cent. The result was a complete failure.

The animals lost weight and went out of condition; it took three months of heavy feeding to bring them back into shape.

Animals might not cooperate with wartime rationing but there was no reason why people shouldn't. Hornaday was rapidly adopting the war as his own, and in numerous letters he urged correspondents to use and publicize corn products as a way of saving precious wheat. *He* had gone over to corn at home, and found it satisfying.

Alas! Americans were just as obstinate as zoo animals. He had to report failure on that front, too. To a friend in Louisiana he wrote:

> I have been very much disturbed in mind by the inability of the nation to appreciate corn bread and corn meal mush. At one time I was on the point of starting a newspaper crusade to arouse the people regarding this valuable food. But in thinking it over

I said to myself: "What's the use? I am already devoting all my spare time and much more to trying to save wild life; and if people will play the fool about corn products, let them do so."

A week before war was declared, the Zoological Park had already "made a beginning in taking up the general burden of civilization." Two fifty-five-foot flagpoles were erected at the north end of Baird Court and a forty-five-foot pole on Rocking Stone Hill, and at four o'clock on March 31, a fine, clear afternoon, the flags were raised with appropriate martial ceremonies. Nine hundred Boy Scouts from the Bronx were mobilized on six hours' notice and stood at attention, the band of the Catholic Protectory at Van Nest Avenue played patriotic airs "very acceptably," and the Borough President and Director Hornaday made speeches.

With the approval of the executive committee, the north half of the Lion House was turned over to the Bronx Branch of the American Red Cross, and by the day of the flag raising an elevated platform ninety feet long and twelve feet wide had been installed in the hall, opposite the cages, and sixteen sewing machines had been set up on work tables.

Those were more or less passive wartime measures; more actively, Company A of the Zoological Park Guards was formed, armed, uniformed, and drilled at the expense of the Zoological Society. Curator Ditmars was captain, Cashier William Mitchell was first lieutenant, and Dr. Blair, the veterinarian, was second lieutenant. There were many vague fears of civil disorders, and the first duty of the guards was to protect the Zoological Park; armed patrols were assigned to tours of the park from sunset to sunrise, and fifty printed notices warned visitors to leave before sundown in order to avoid danger.

No uprisings of the populace occurred and no guns were fired in anger in the park, but the attrition of war did become noticeable. Seven employees joined the colors, Dr. Blair as a major in the Veterinary Corps. The employees subscribed to $7,000 in Liberty Bonds, the Elk Range was

plowed for crops to feed the animals. On Members' Day, May 17, the khaki-clad guards presented arms "in perfect alignment" on Baird Court in front of the Lion House and received a flag from President Osborn. Director Hornaday declared the guards fit for duty:

All the members of this Society subscribe to the admirable motto of the Boy Scouts of America,—"Be Prepared." In war as well as in zoology we try to be ready to meet every emergency as it arises. These men, Mr. President, are armed with real guns, and it is a rather saddening fact that of all the Home Defense companies of this City, ours is the only one actually armed.

By the beginning of 1918 Hornaday had inserted corn bread into the animal menu, and he asserted that "Some of the animals prefer it to any other food—and this is particularly marked among the bears." What with home-grown fruits and vegetables from the Nursery in the northeast corner of the park the animal-food situation was not too serious, but America's entry into the war had produced a War Trade Board that did not recognize wild animals as essential shipping cargo and the park was feeling the pinch. Before the Tropical Research Station closed in 1917, it had made contacts with officials who could supply mammals and birds from British Guiana, and in the summer of 1918 a nice collection of capybaras, agoutis, monkeys, porcupines, macaws, and the like was waiting for a New York-bound ship. The War Trade Board admitted that "the purpose of this importation is highly important. But importance is a relative term, and in a world crisis such as this things ordinarily important become minor. There is room only for essentials." Hornaday reproduced the board's letter in the *Bulletin* and closed his more-in-sorrow-than-in-anger editorial thus:

Ever since the British government stopped all importations of wild birds into England because birds consume seeds and other foods, we have believed that there is such a thing as taking even a war too seriously, and carrying the rigors of war to unnecessary extremes.

Dr. Hornaday did not single-handedly win the war, but he tried. At one point in 1917 he was involved in seven preparedness and defense movements simultaneously, not counting such a minor gesture as preparing a new edition of the park's guidebook and calling it the "American Eagle Edition."

His most concentrated campaign for preparedness was through the Junior Naval Reserve, whose young members were supposed to be trained in summer camps for eventual service in the Navy or the merchant marine. In the summer of 1916 it was $2,000 in debt and about to die for lack of support when its executive officers, Major Victor H. Stockell and Lieutenant Willis J. Physioc, appealed to Hornaday to accept the presidency of the JNR and get it back on its financial feet. As he was to write to various correspondents later, "If the Reserve had been in a flourishing condition, nothing would have induced me to have considered the proposal seriously; but the fact that the Reserve was in danger of going down and out seemed to put upon me a burden of duty which I could not shake off or avoid."

He could not have known it in the beginning, but he was trying (in one of his favorite expressions) "to make a long shot with a limb in the way." Stockell seems to have had no money sense, and despite a written agreement to keep Hornaday informed of income and outgo, he did neither. By pamphlet appeals and begging letters, Dr. Hornaday raised enough money to open Camp John Paul Jones in Corpus Christi, Texas, and Camp Dewey in New London, Connecticut. On his own, Stockell printed "Camp Dewey" and "Camp John Paul Jones" decorative stamps and their sale brought in considerable revenue—until the Post Office Department ordered them withdrawn. Details of the Post Office complaint are lacking—the original cease-and-desist letter was never shown to Hornaday—but it is probable that some purchasers considered them official stamps and tried to use them for postage.

While the stamp money was still pouring in, Stockell took a three-year lease at $5,000 a year on a building at 231 West Fifty-eighth Street as Junior Naval Reserve headquarters, again without consulting the president of the JNR and without considering that the money was desperately needed to keep the two camps going. He also ordered five thousand miniature metal savings banks whose sale was supposed to bring revenues, but instead brought lawsuits from the manufacturer when there was no money to pay for them.

Then someone offered the Junior Naval Reserve a huge quantity of artificially colored and "artistically" arranged feathers of ducks, geese, pigeons, chickens, and English ring-necked pheasants, which the Reserve sold as "war wings." The Massachusetts Audubon Society rose up in arms on the grounds that selling feathers, even from domestic birds, would incite boys to start shooting American wild birds for millinery purposes. It was not a very sound argument and Hornaday, as the author of the 1913 Tariff Act clause, felt that he was in a better position than the secretary of the Audubon Society to decide what was right and what wasn't.

When Massachusetts complained to New York's Governor Charles S. Whitman and urged him to stop the sale, Hornaday wrote to the Commissioner of Conservation: "Any American boy or man in his senses would no more think of going out to shoot birds for millinery purposes than he would think of shooting babies for food."

Hornaday wrote a hot letter to E. H. Forbush, the president of the Massachusetts Audubon Society, and was assured that Forbush had not sanctioned the complaint. The matter was finally dropped.

Trouble also came from another unexpected quarter. In the spring of 1917 when war fever was at its peak, the Junior Naval Reserve accepted an offer from a motion-picture theater owner in Tarrytown, New York, to show "war pictures" on a Sunday evening, preceded by a patriotic address by Hornaday. A committee of ministers protested strongly against this "opening wedge" that would lead to picture shows on Sunday. The show was held anyway, and some wealthy backers of the JNR were distressed.

By the summer of 1917 the Junior Naval Reserve was $25,000 in debt, thanks to Stockell's overoptimism, and Hornaday began the first of a series of withdrawals and resignations that finally took effect on June 15, 1918. The management of Camp Dewey was atrocious; tents were not waterproof and had no floorboards, boys became sick and returned home, Lieutenant Physioc could not keep discipline in the unheated mess hall and at mealtimes the cadets broke ranks and scrambled for any food they could grab. Hornaday felt he was well out of it, even though there had been a reorganization and Stockell was removed. For a few more months he had the chore of answering complaining letters by saying that he no longer had anything to do with the Junior Naval Reserve and forwarding to the new officers the summonses and legal papers that were served on him by unpaid creditors. His name as a stalwart champion of preparedness still cropped up in JNR promotions, however, despite his efforts to dissociate himself from the unhappy venture. One correspondent in January of 1919 sent him a newspaper advertisement in which his name appeared, and he tried unsuccessfully to find out the name of the paper so he could protest. He wrote back:

I am surprised by your unwillingness to tell me where you saw that advertisement. You should have more moral courage than your letter shows. It cannot be possible that you are willing to shield people who have been misusing my name, and deceiving you!

You are in your boyhood. I am an old man. Now I wish to give you in this connection one piece of friendly advice. Never be afraid to do your duty; and let rogues look out for themselves!

Coincidentally with his Junior Naval Reserve activities, Dr. Hornaday was agitating to have Congress set up a commission to establish honor medals for soldiers, sailors, and Red Cross men and women, and he had long since turned out the first of many pamphlets designed to awaken America to the German menace and disloyalty at home. There was no doubt in his mind that the Allies would win; even in 1917 when his pamphlet called "A Searchlight on Germany" came out in an edition of 50,000 copies, he proclaimed its object as "to discourage an inconclusive peace, and a peace that will leave the road open to another war with Germany in the near future." He was one of the most fiery members of a group of patriots called the American Defense Society, which distributed his writings and got the "Searchlight" pamphlet reprinted in thirteen newspapers.

Food and fuel shortages plagued the Zoological Park severely. In January of 1918 Hornaday closed his office in the Administration Building and moved into the warm comfort of the Bird House to share a small room with Curator Crandall. He was somehow keeping up with routine park business but at the same time "helping to fight the disloyal teachers in the public schools, and . . . making speeches in Hoover's

food campaign as a member of his stock company of performers."

As Food Administrator, Herbert Hoover got more than speeches from Dr. Hornaday. To a Zoo employee who had sent him a postcard from an Army training camp, the director wrote:

On the 5th of November I began to write letters to Mr. Hoover, telling him how people of New York and elsewhere are not obeying his food conservation appeals, and how about 60 per cent of

During World War I, the north end of the Lion House was turned over to the Bronx branch of the American Red Cross.

375

the people are going on gormandizing just as usual. I told him that his policy was not sufficiently drastic to get results with people as devilishly independent and obstinate as a very great many Americans are. I advised him to put on the screws by ordering people, especially in hotels and restaurants, to go on bread rations forthwith. After waiting three weeks without any response from Mr. Hoover, I wrote him again, sending proof that his work up to that date was not getting the results it should. Of that letter his office took some notice. Then I stirred up the American Defense Society and we prepared a memorial to Congress. At last we have results. Mr. Hoover has come out with a drastic order, putting the people of the United States on bread rations and laying down the law to all hotels, restaurants, clubs, dining cars, etc.

Early in 1918 Dr. Hornaday offered his assistance to the chairman of the United States Shipping Board:

I conceive it to be my duty to do something toward furnishing workers for the building of ships in order that our shipyards may run for twenty-four hours per day instead of eight hours only. I have an idea which I am disposed to carry into effect just as soon as I can be sure that the men whom it produces will find work in shipyards and barracks in which to live. I do not feel disposed to try to provide men who cannot have places in which to live when not at work; but if housing is there, I am prepared to take considerable trouble in the gathering of carefully selected men.

The Shipping Board does not seem to have taken advantage of this offer and the society's archives do not reveal details of the director's plan. No matter; he had made the offer, and he had plenty of other outlets for his energy. One was the writing of pamphlets, such as "Awake! America," intended to "awaken Sleepy America to the German menace." Another was feverish activity in the American Guardian Society, which made a nationwide distribution of cards whose signers pledged themselves not to buy any products of Germany for twenty-five years.

By early fall of 1918 it was obvious that the Allies were going to win. They would need guidance in drawing up the terms of the peace. To Major Blair, at that time somewhere in France, Dr. Hornaday wrote:

I am trying hard to induce the American Defense Society to formulate and publish its peace terms to Germany, but there is a little hesitation as to details. The peace terms that I have drafted and submitted to our Society [the American Defense Society] would make any German officer's hair curl if he could read them.

The shooting war ended on November 11, 1918, but Dr. Hornaday kept on fighting. To a correspondent he wrote that he was sending

my pamphlet entitled "A Democracy of Crocodiles," which is intended to warn the peace conference at Paris against being decided by any fake democracy that the German militarists may set up to fool the world and secure a softening of the peace terms.

Until the beginning of the war, Dr. Hornaday had had a great admiration for the German people and the most cordial relations with Carl Hagenbeck. In 1912, two years after moving into the new Administration Building, he had written to the German animal dealer:

When next you come to New York, and come to my office, you will see that I have made of it a private Hall of Fame. For a frieze around the room, next to the ceiling, I have painted the names of the greatest museum builder in the world, the greatest zoological garden builder in the world, eleven great zoologists, three great game protectors, and three great sportsmen-naturalists. Between the names of Roosevelt,—the greatest sportsman-naturalist of the world,—and Henry A. Ward,—the greatest museum builder in the world,—stands the name "HAGENBECK."

Now he was completely disenchanted and wrote to zoological park friends all over the country urging them to buy no more animals from German dealers "until the people of Germany have brought forth fruits meet for repentance and have experienced a complete change of heart." He even asked Madison Grant to "order some of us" to write to Stechert & Co., the sellers of imported books and periodicals, "and say that we do not want any more German periodicals and will subscribe to none hereafter." Grant appears to have felt that the sins of the German people should not be visited on German zoology, and refused to cancel subscriptions.

Peace had its perils, and Dr. Hornaday was ready with counsel. Long letters about the employment situation went to Grover A. Whalen, secretary of the Mayor's Committee of Welcome to Home-Coming Troops, to the Secretary of War, and to the director general of the Information and Education Services of the Department of Labor. To Whalen he wrote:

I hear that a great many of our soldier boys are making the mistake of feeling indifferent to their old jobs, and are looking for something that will give them an outdoor life, and more interesting employment. That is a very bad frame of mind and it should be discouraged in every possible way. Our soldiers need to be not only encouraged but most strongly urged to apply for their old jobs.

To the Department of Labor he was more specific:

I have in mind the cooks, laundresses, scrubwomen, cleaners, waitresses and other working women who ordinarily do various forms of housework but are now filling absent soldiers' positions as ticket choppers, ticket sellers, and conductorettes on the transportation lines of New York City, and who are running elevators in the various buildings of New York. Presumably these women are receiving much higher wages than they ever received before. In fact, they are getting *men's pay,* and naturally they wish to continue to do so indefinitely!

The housewives of New York are at this moment suffering great hardships because of the deprivation of the services of those very women. I know a great many gray-haired gentlewomen, some of them wives of professional men, who during the past year have been forced either to do the cooking for their respective families or see their families go unfed. The domestic help situation is absolutely intolerable, and all on account of the flocking of cooks and houseworkers into men's employment for the big pay and short hours that those positions afford. I hope your Department will take strong action in the matter without delay.

Willfully and obstinately, women went right on working for short hours and high pay. In the spring of 1919 Dr. Hornaday bought a house in Stamford, Connecticut, and moved himself and his wife and daughter there, "having been crowded out of New York by housing and help conditions."

The first postwar year was not a good one for the Zoological Park. Attendance shot up to an unprecedented 2,035,859, but the city cut back appropriations, employees were woefully underpaid and some left to take better jobs, and two old friends of the society had died: Andrew Carnegie in August of 1919 and Mrs. Russell Sage (who had given more than $600,000 to the Society's Endowment Fund) in November of the previous year. Dr. Hornaday remarked in the *Annual Report* that "the Director sincerely hopes that he never will have to pass through another year such as 1919."

But there were bright spots. Major Blair returned from the war in May and resumed his job as veterinarian. The King and Queen of the Belgians visited the park and the Aquarium in the fall, and the society presented His Majesty with Volume I of Beebe's *Monograph of the Pheasants.* (The King's staff somehow misplaced it and there was a considerable brouhaha about it in the next three years. Finally Professor Osborn wrote another presentation inscription in a duplicate copy and sent it to the King. The missing volume finally turned up in the Palace in Brussels and the duplicate was returned.) The brightest spot of the year was the shipment by the Zoological Society of 329 mammals, birds, reptiles, and amphibians to the Antwerp Zoo to help restore it after the depredations of war. With the animals went a huge quantity of animal foodstuffs. Dr. Hornaday had more or less promised such a gift as a "duty" in his 1914 editorial in the *Bulletin,* and the Zoological Society gladly made good his promise.

By midsummer of 1920 the animal tide had turned and once more rarities as well as replacements of formerly commonplace animals were flowing toward America. Thanks to its thriving Animal Fund, swollen because there had been so little to buy in 1919, the Bronx Zoo was able to take its pick and fill some of its collections to the point of overflow; by the end of the year all the gaps created by postwar gifts to the zoos of Antwerp, London, Pretoria, and Johannesburg had been abundantly filled. Scarlet labels saying "Recent Accession" were being flaunted all over the Zoo.

Curator Crandall came back from England and the Continent in July with five hundred birds, mammals, and reptiles. No sooner had they been settled in their new homes than A. K. Haagner, director of the National Zoological Gardens of South Africa at Pretoria, arrived on the *Chinese Prince* with ninety-six cages and crates of African antelopes, small mammals, and birds which he had been gathering for the past three years. Fortunately the Haagner argosy was a joint venture of the Bronx and Philadelphia zoos, so that this huge influx could be assimilated. Then at the end of October, Ellis S. Joseph sailed into New York on the *Belle Buckle* with what Dr. Hornaday called "certainly the greatest and most valuable" collection of wild animals ever to leave Australia. The Zoological Society had assured itself of first choice by cabling $3,000 to Joseph just before he left Sydney, making it clear that it had a "first lien" on the collection at least to that extent. Actually it spent $14,080.50 on the Australian shipment and acquired such treasures as a koala, a kea, four species of birds of paradise, a feather-tailed opossum (about the size of a house mouse, but considered by Joseph to be the prize mammal of his collection), a turquoisine parakeet (at the time supposed to be almost extinct; in 1972 the Bronx Zoo had a young pair that may be expected to breed, and an adult female on loan to an aviculturist who had already successfully bred the species), an "actual living specimen of the famous Australian lungfish,

22

Postwar Years and the Great Cobra Mystery

Ceratodus fosteri [*Neoceratodus forsteri*]," and some seventy-five other eye-catching odds and ends. They were a mere fraction of the cargo but Joseph had plenty of other buyers clamoring for a choice; he easily disposed of the remainder to the zoos of Philadelphia, Washington, Boston, Chicago, Cincinnati, Cleveland, Minneapolis, and a few other cities. They too had felt the wartime pinch.

The Bronx Zoo's most expensive purchase was the koala, which cost $1,250 and was, apart from prestige, not a very good investment. It survived only five days after reaching the Zoo. Koalas feed only on the leaves of certain Australian eucalyptus or gum trees, and although Joseph had started out with plenty of fresh and refrigerated leaves, his supply ran out before he reached New York. No eucalyptus leaves were available here and although the appealing little "Teddy bear" was offered a great variety of other foliage, its feeding habits were too specialized and it refused substitutes.

Ellis Joseph and his huge shipments of animals from all over the world are still legendary among the surviving zoo men of his era. Calling him "A Great Zoological Collector," Dr. Hornaday wrote of him in the society's *Bulletin:*

Mr. Joseph is 48 years of age, he stands 6 feet in height and he weighs 275 pounds. He handles all kinds of wild beasts and great snakes, and he is as proud of a feather-tailed marsupial opossum as some collectors are of elephants. To see him reach into a crate, seize a big kangaroo by the tail, drag it forth struggling and kicking and hold it up in midair for your admiration, is a daily incident possible only to him.

(Sometimes he was a little too intrepid. After he returned to Sydney in 1921, Hornaday wrote to another zoo man: "When he went to kiss the large male chimpanzee that he had left behind in Sydney, which seemed to be overjoyed to see him, the animal bit him on the face and on the back." He continued making large collections for another ten years and then his health failed and he was virtually in retirement in New York until his death in 1938.)

The arrival of rarities was not the only good news from the Bronx Zoo in 1920; there were two interesting births. In 1912 Hans Schomburgk had gone to Liberia for the Hagenbeck firm and captured five pygmy hippopotamuses, the first seen alive outside Africa (except for a short-lived specimen in the Dublin Zoological Garden many years before). In 1912, according to Dr. Hornaday in the *Bulletin* in 1920, "the zoological garden directors of all Germany were industriously engaged in boycotting Mr. Hagenbeck . . . because Mr. Hagenbeck had had the temerity to build at Hamburg

382

a private zoological garden so spectacular and attractive that it made the old Hamburg Zoo look obsolete and uninteresting." Lacking a ready European market for his pygmy hippopotamuses, Hagenbeck sold an adult male and a young pair to the Bronx Zoo for $15,000. None of them was the "dear sensible little beast" that Schomburgk had called them, but the trio thrived in the tanks and stalls built for them in the Elephant House, and finally, two days before Christmas in 1919, the young pair produced a baby—the first pygmy hippopotamus bred and born in captivity. It was a complete surprise, for, as Dr. Hornaday wrote, "the fat and always rotund condition of the female was so pronounced that the usual signs of maternity were negligible."

From the detailed published account of the event, Veterinarian Blair and the keepers seemed to have handled the postnatal care of the male infant with skill and dispatch, but its hindquarters were weak and it was unable to nurse. As Dr. Hornaday described it. "The problem was like a big sack of wheat endeavoring to suckle a sack of salt." (Mr. Grant thought this was an undignified simile.) The baby died thirty-two hours after birth, despite heroic efforts to get it to take milk from a lactating goat and from a bottle. Dr. Hornaday blamed the mother: "The female pygmy's maternal factor of safety is entirely too small."

However that may be, the same female tried again and between 1921 and 1929 produced four more calves, three of which were reared without difficulty. The pygmy hippopotamuses had been expensive, but they paid for themselves in longevity; the male of the breeding pair lived for thirty-nine years, the female for thirty-eight.

The second notable birth was that of a chimpanzee. Only once before had a chimpanzee been born in captivity, in the famous Señora Rosalie Abreu's collection in Havana. Then the Bronx Zoo's Suzette produced a baby on the morning of July 14, 1920—several weeks before the staff expected it.

It seemed to be a perfectly normal baby and there should

A pygmy hippopotamus and its offspring. When a baby was born in 1919 (the first bred and born in captivity), its hindquarters were weak and it was unable to nurse.

have been no trouble, except that Suzette obviously had no idea of what to do with the little stranger. It was a new kind of toy, something to carry around, but she never held it so that it could nurse. It died eight days later and it was only by adroitly distracting Suzette's attention with tempting food that the keepers managed to take the emaciated little body away from her.

She had two more babies in successive years and the result was always the same; she never did learn. Suzette's incompetence as a mother attracted nationwide attention and letters poured in advising Dr. Hornaday how to handle the problem. The most common suggestion was that the Zoo find a nursing human mother and have her sit outside Suzette's cage and give her an ocular demonstration of what you do when you have a hungry baby. The Chicago *American* printed an editorial about the shortcomings of modern mothers and informed the Bronx Zoo that what it should have done was to chloroform Suzette and snatch her baby for rearing by hand before it was too late. The Trenton, New Jersey, *Times* ran a long story about Suzette under the headline

MONKEY MOTHER, MODERNIZED,
LETS HER BABY DIE WHILE SHE
SMOKES CIGARETTES AND KNITS

If that headline had appeared in one of the New York City newspapers, Dr. Hornaday would probably have fired off an angry letter denying that any animal in the New York Zoological Park was permitted to smoke. As it was, he ignored it, and it is doubtful whether he authorized a trick which the *Evening World* said the Zoo tried to play on Suzette in order to get the dead baby away from her. Suzette was said to have approached a woman in the crowd outside her cage, holding up the dead baby with a pitiful expression; whereupon Keeper Fred Taggart was dressed in women's garments and stationed inside the guardrail of the cage, prepared to grab the baby if Suzette approached. The newspaper reported that Taggart "flounced" most realistically, but Suzette ignored him.

At the beginning of the 1920s, age began to catch up with the men who had guided the Zoological Society through its early years. Madison Grant was being progressively crippled by arthritis, and long courses of treatment at Dr. John Harvey Kellogg's sanitarium in Battle Creek, Michigan, and in various resorts in California and Florida gave him only temporary relief. Professor Osborn, whose energies were totally absorbed by his paleontological studies and writing and his responsibilities at the American Museum of Natural History, had long since ceased to keep a sharp eye on routine affairs at the Zoological Park, and in 1925 he resigned as president of the board of managers. Grant succeeded him and continued in the tolerant, friendly relationship with Dr. Hornaday that they had gradually achieved.

Dr. Hornaday's disabilities were intermittently more acute. His eyes were giving him trouble, and in 1920 and again in 1923 he entered the Manhattan Eye and Ear Hospital for corrective operations which were successful but left him temporarily dim-visioned and shaken by his inability to keep up with his correspondence for weeks at a time. Routine letters were written and signed by his secretary, Miss Edith H. Franz, and the curators were encouraged to take care of their own normal departmental mail. Even so, there was an enormous amount of correspondence that only the director's office could handle, and the executive committee agreed with him that he needed an assistant. Dr. W. Reid Blair had been on the staff for twenty years, first as medical assistant and then as veterinarian, and the choice fell on him. In the fall of 1922 Dr. Hornaday wrote to Grant that he had talked with Blair and had offered him the job at $4,000 a year, at the same time warning him that he would be expected to take up the society's work in wildlife protection and carry it on. Blair was weak in that department. Hornaday alluded to this deficiency:

Incidentally, in order to give him standing among sportsmen and practical naturalists, it is desirable that he should make two or three trips into the haunts of wild game, notably to British Columbia, New Brunswick and the Province of Quebec. All this is really necessary as a part of his zoological education.

Quiet and conservative, Dr. Blair was the antithesis of Hornaday, and the contrast showed up immediately and plainly in the style of his letters when he began taking over part of Hornaday's correspondence. Where Hornaday was direct, forceful, often picturesque, Dr. Blair was formal and stilted. A typical letter might begin: "Replying to your inquiry relative to opossums, beg to say that . . ."

And nothing could have been less like the Hornaday approach than the letter he sent to a man in Pittsburgh who had written an abusive letter to Photographer Sanborn, threatening to report him to the executive committee if he did not fill an order for photographs immediately:

I regret that you feel it necessary to write such a letter in making requests for photographs; but in spite of this your order will take the normal course and as soon as the material is available, it will be sent you.

Mr. Sanborn is a very busy man and it is not always possible for him to stop work in progress to fill an order such as yours on short notice. I would suggest that when you are in need of photographs at a definite date, that you make your request as early as possible in order to avoid any delay in filling it.

Dr. Hornaday had turned sixty-five in 1919, but there was no mandatory retirement rule at that age in the Zoological Society and he was still several years away from thinking of withdrawing in favor of a younger and more active man. As his sight improved and Dr. Blair and Miss Franz between them enabled him to get on top of his daily mountain of mail, once more opinions, advice, remonstrances, letters to the newspapers, and magazine articles flowed from him in an only slightly diminished torrent.

The city was being niggardly about maintenance funds and

wage increases for the park, and Professor Osborn had thought it would be a useful diplomatic gesture if the executive committee passed a resolution commending Mayor Hylan's administration. Dr. Hornaday objected strenuously in a letter to President Osborn:

This may be with other institutions the "golden age" of municipal support, but it is very far from being so with the Zoological Society. With us it is the "brass age."

Can it be possible that you have never thought that the Society's resolution of thanks and appreciation will be used conspicuously in the next political campaign, as a high official endorsement of the whole Hylan Administration? I think it will plague the Society for many a day; for you can never recall it!

For many years every new major zoological park in the United States and many abroad had turned to Dr. Hornaday for advice, which he gave freely and at length. He did refuse to go to Cleveland and give a pep talk when expansion of the little Cleveland Zoo was being discussed; if the people of Cleveland were so benighted that they had to be convinced a zoological park was a good thing, he wanted no truck with them. He was not inclined to go along with modern fads in zoological park design, however. The director of the St. Louis Zoo asked his opinion about the moated and barless bear dens it was planning. He had a strong one:

Before we began the construction of our bear dens, in 1899, Mr. Carl Hagenbeck laid before me the idea, original with him, of the so-called "barless bear dens." He strongly urged that we should adopt that idea.

I pointed out to Mr. Hagenbeck the fact that we intended to develop along scientific lines an educational institution in which millions of New York people might study to the best advantage the most important wild animal species of the world. I pointed out the great disadvantage that would be entailed by having our bears separated from our visitors by a distance of sixty or seventy feet. We deliberately decided against the Hagenbeck idea, and the success of our bear collection from that day to this has been so

387

pronounced that we never have regretted that decision.

I think that the St. Louis Zoological Society is making a great mistake in putting all its money into costly piles of rock and concrete to shelter far distant animals.

Fortunately, St. Louis did not allow itself to be persuaded and in 1919 went ahead with its barless dens of realistic concrete rockwork, poured into molds taken on the rocky bluffs of the Mississippi River. They were the first extensive dens of their kind in this country, and are still striking. (The original molds were used for a single den in the Denver Zoo in 1918.)

And speaking of bears, Dr. Hornaday's passing comment on bear cubs deserves to be recorded for posterity. Writing to a man who was thinking of buying a black-bear cub as a pet, he said: "Never buy a black bear cub in the belief that it can be kept for amusement and then be resold at a profit; but if thine enemy offend thee, present him with a black bear cub."

David Garnett's novel *A Man in the Zoo* came out in 1924 and not surprisingly inspired an offer by a man to put himself on exhibition in the Bronx Zoo, "between an Orang and a Chimpanzee, as an educational exhibit." His name was John Cromartie and he described himself as "Race: Scottish; Height: 5 ft. 11 in.; Weight: 11 stone; Hair: Dark; Eyes: Blue; Nose: Aquiline; Age: 27 years."

But Dr. Hornaday had had his own Man in the Zoo long before Garnett's fantasy. To Cromartie he wrote:

Your application for a position in the Zoological Park as an exhibit of the genus Homo has caused me to turn Ruminant, and chew the cud of Bitter Reflection. Your perfectly legitimate aspiration recalls the ghost of vanished Ota Benga, pygmy negro of the Congo, who was our first offense in the display of Man as a Primate.

He sketched the Ota Benga episode and concluded by saying that once was enough and he did not dare try an exhibit of Man again.

In 1918 Lee S. Crandall had officially become curator of

birds, while William Beebe, although holding a tenuous connection with the department as honorary curator of birds, actually was working full time at being director of the Tropical Research Station in British Guiana. He had gone back there for almost eight months in 1919, seven months in 1920, three months in 1921, and almost ten months (including some studies in Venezuela) in 1922, each time with a gradually enlarging staff of collectors, assistants, and artists, each year opening the station to research zoologists who paid a proportionate part of the expenses. Theoretically the basic costs of the station were met by contributions of a few wealthy men whom Beebe had interested in his research, but Dr. Casey A. Wood of Stanford University, an ophthalmologist who worked one season at the station after it was moved to its "permanent" home at Kartabo, wrote to Dr. Hornaday that the financing seemed to him casual and haphazard. The work being done by Beebe and his coworkers was remarkable, considering the cramped quarters and defective laboratory and other facilities, but Beebe had told him that he was obliged to turn over his own salary and the proceeds of his literary work to keep the station operating. Something ought to be done about it. Dr. Hornaday was not sympathetic:

I think that if Mr. Beebe had $20,000 a year [his official budget was about $10,000] to spend on that Station, he would spend it all and still expend his salary and literary earnings. I do not believe that the Society will ever be able to catch up with him, much less to keep up. If I had conducted the Park during the last twenty years as Mr. Beebe has conducted the Station, financially, we would have gone into the financial discard long ago; but fortunately for me and fortunately for the Park, I have been brought up not to spend more money than I have expendable.

I have nothing to do with the management of the Station or with raising funds for it. I am simply an interested and well-wishing bystander.

Dr. Hornaday's attitude toward Beebe inevitably brings to mind the analogy of a parent whose brilliant son has willfully

broken away from the family and insisted on leading his own life. Dr. Hornaday had gladly and even proudly encouraged Beebe's research as long as it was a sideline of his duties as curator of birds, but when he lost control of his curator at the time of the pheasant expedition he flared into anger and then subsided into smoldering indifference. Loyalty to the society and to the executive committee—which was quite happy about Beebe's rocketing rise as a scientist and his literary exploitation of his research—kept him from publicly expressing his resentment of the "son" who had broken away.

Indeed, he could defend him when necessary. When Beebe came back from the Galápagos Archipelago in 1923 after a highly publicized expedition aboard the 250-foot steam yacht *Noma* chartered by Harrison Williams and brought with him some living specimens of the flightless cormorant, a seriously endangered species, Hornaday rebutted a critic. It was simply a matter of opinion and viewpoint, he wrote; should Mr. Beebe have left the birds to be wiped out by vandals? As a scientific ornithologist he had obtained motion pictures, still photographs, watercolor paintings, a nest, and an egg of the birds, and the material had already been used in five magazine articles and would be treated more extensively in Beebe's forthcoming book, *Galápagos: World's End.*

Although he never complained about it—publicly—Dr. Hornaday may well have had another cause for irritation with William Beebe: he had stolen away John Tee-Van, a quiet, serious, hard-working junior in the park's bird department. Young Tee-Van had been hired by Dr. Hornaday in 1911 when he was only fourteen years old, three or four years younger than the usual age of new employees. However, his father, who had recently died, had been an employee of the park and the boy was earnest and eager to do "any kind of work with animals." Assigned to the bird department to do the routine tasks of cleaning and feeding, he began to teach himself by making a card index of waterfowl and pheasants in the collection and taking night-school courses in architectural drawing. By 1916 Beebe was on the point of establishing what was to become his own department of tropical research, and when he learned that John Tee-Van could make accurate drawings—he tested him by asking for a drawing of a bird bone—he drafted the youngster for the new department. The next year Tee-Van accompanied him to British Guiana as a general assistant and from there on Tee-Van, like Beebe, was lost to the Zoological Park—until he came back to it as executive secretary in 1941. He was to become general director of the Zoological Park and the Aquarium in 1956.

391

John Tee-Van rose rapidly in the restricted hierarchy of the Beebe staff. He was one of those rare individuals who could do anything that hard work, ingenuity, and a systematic mind could attack—the perfect lieutenant for the captain of science that Beebe was. If his self-effacing loyalty to "the Director"—Beebe, not Hornaday—sometimes obscured his own great abilities, they were abundantly recognized by others when the park and the Aquarium needed direction in the mid-1950s.

Artists who could make accurate color drawings of mammals, birds, insects, or whatever parts of their anatomy were under study in the field station were an important part of the department's staff, and there was an ever-changing succession of them. Helen Damrosch, who was to marry John Tee-Van in 1923, was signed on as an artist for the 1922 expedition. Fifty years later she was still puzzled to know why she was chosen. Her art work was more than competent, but it was not in question.

"I met Will for the first time at a meeting of the society's Ladies' Auxiliary at the Vanderbilt house," she recalled. "He had been told I was an artist, and he drew me into a corner for a brief talk. At the end he said, 'Would you like to go down to British Guiana with us next season? You've met the acid test, you know.'"

What Beebe's "acid test" was, and what she had said or done to pass it, Mrs. Tee-Van was never to know. "Will applied the 'acid test' to everyone he hired for his expeditions, and I must say some very queer people passed it, but we never knew what it was or why they passed."

(Beebe had an "acid test" for books, too. In the March, 1922, number of the society's *Bulletin* he included a paragraph on that subject to fill out the page allotted to him for notes from the Tropical Research Station. "To read a book in the presence of its subject is the crucial test. On the present steamer trip [to British Guiana] we ran into a three days' storm off Hatteras with waves twenty to twenty-five feet high.

When it was over I took H. M. Tomlinson's 'The Sea and the Jungle' and read the account of the storm from page 22 on, and I found it, as I have always considered it, the finest in the English language. It survived the acid test of direct comparison." But what was the direct comparison Helen Damrosch survived?)

There is no point in recounting here the achievements, scientific or literary, of William Beebe's annual expeditions; his own books and the hundreds of "Contributions" of his department celebrate his work and illuminate every corner of it. By the time he became director emeritus of the department of tropical research on July 29, 1952, at the age of seventy-five, the publications from or about the department numbered 931. True, many of them were no more significant than "Investigaciones del Doctor Beebe en la Fauna Venezolana" published in the newspaper *El Nacional* in Caracas in 1947, but they also included the very large number of technical papers by the director, his staff, or research associates published in proper scientific journals.

Tropical jungles began to lose their fascination for Beebe after he came back from the Harrison Williams Galápagos expedition on the *Noma* in 1923. He mentioned in the *Annual Report* that "Less than six thousand minutes were actually spent on the islands themselves," but he was aboard the *Noma* for twenty-one days and the cruise opened up to him a new field of research: the sea. How rich it was he realized even while the vessel was still in United States waters:

By the time we were off the Florida coast the sea permitted me to occupy my usual perch in a boatswain's seat, over the bow, close to the water, where, with a long-handled net, I secured sufficient fish and sea-weed fauna for days of study.

The expedition sailed from New York on March 1 and returned on May 16—just in time to deliver living specimens of mammals, birds and reptiles to the Zoological Park and to frame and hang for exhibition in the Administration

Building more than a hundred oil and watercolor paintings made on the trip, to astonish the society's membership at its annual garden party on May 17. There are some slight hints that Dr. Hornaday was not happy about having the garden party turned into a Welcome Home celebration for William Beebe, but the expedition had been avidly reported, and after all the park had had its turn the year before when the opening of the Heads and Horns Museum was the big spring gala.

William Beebe in the tropics—land or sea—impinged but little on the serenity of the Zoological Park, but William Beebe back in New York was something else again. From every expedition he returned with a vast amount of gear, specimens in preservative fluid, paintings, photographs, maps, and miscellaneous papers. As early as 1914 an extension had been built on the winter storage house for Raptores, behind the Eagles' and Vultures' Aviary, and this was supposed to be the Beebe research laboratory. He quickly outgrew it and now he appealed to Professor Osborn for room in the Administration Building. His point was a good one: he needed an adequate space to work and to spread out the scientific exhibits he was bringing back from each trip, and especially a setting of some consequence that would impress the potential supporters of his further expeditions. Hornaday protested and there was a vivid stream of letters between him and Osborn, but by August Hornaday had capitulated. He wrote to Osborn:

There is a saying here in the Park that "Whatever Mr. Beebe wants, Mr. Beebe gets." This is literally true. In craft and finesse, and also unparalleled independence; in going around opposition, in persuading other people to do exactly as he wishes them to do, and in having his own way at all times, Mr. Beebe is an accomplished artist. He always was uncontrollable, even by the highest officers of the Zoological Society. Mr. Beebe will pervade this building, and our unfortunate library, setting all our rules in defiance, but we hope that he will not crowd any of us into the

William Beebe bird-watching under a giant saman tree at his laboratory in Trinidad.

street. Please send word to Mr. Beebe that he can take possession of that room and its contents whenever he chooses to do so.

Beebe vs. the Zoological Society's library was a sore spot in Dr. Hornaday's mind. In 1919 he had talked the executive committee into putting up money to hire a professional librarian to organize the books and journals that had been accumulating for many years. As he wrote to Grant, "Now that Mr. Beebe has gone [he was in British Guiana] I think it will be worth while to get the library in order, but while he is here it is very difficult to maintain its arrangement. He is the most lawless man in the drawing of books that any of us ever saw."

The library did get put in order while Beebe was away, but then he came back and before he took off again it all had to be organized anew. Worst of all, the librarian found that while many books had been removed by Beebe and a removal slip left, many others had simply been silently carried off by him to the studio in West Sixty-seventh Street where he did his writing, and some that eventually straggled back even had the Beebe bookplate pasted in them. Dr. Hornaday was still nagging at Beebe to clear up the book tangle two years later. (As late as 1959, Beebe's depredations were still under suspicion. William G. Conway was planning a visit to the Beebe laboratory in Trinidad and Lee S. Crandall, then general curator emeritus, urged him to see if he could find Volume 3 of *Aviculture,* which had been missing for years. Conway made a thorough [but surreptitious] search but could not find it.)

Beebe and his staff returned to British Guiana for about five months in 1924, and upon their departure a group of University of Pittsburgh graduate students took over. Except for a brief return visit in 1926, Beebe was not to be again based in British Guiana for a good many years. He had answered the call of the sea. In 1925 he was off to the Sargasso Sea and a return to the Galápagos Islands, this time on the *Arcturus* lent by Henry D. Whiton, a member of the society's executive committee, with Harrison Williams putting up most of the money for the considerable expenses. From that expedition came the usual torrent of scientific papers and a book, *The "Arcturus" Adventure*.

Dr. Hornaday took one last fling at his wayward ex-curator of birds before retiring in 1926. Wynant D. Hubbard, a writer and explorer well known to the director, appealed to him to intercede with Harrison Williams to back a proposed Hubbard expedition. Hornaday replied:

In regard to Mr. Williams, the ethics of the existing situation quite prevents me from either approaching Mr. Williams myself about anything involving money, or sending to him any one else who might wish to interest him in something involving money. Mr. Beebe regards Mr. Williams as *his* discovery,—which Mr. Williams decidedly is,—and therefore Mr. Beebe would take great umbrage at me, or at any one else in the Zoological Society, who would in any manner invade his Williams preserve. Unfortunately, Mr. Beebe corrals all the money that his patrons are willing to put up, and spends it himself in his own ways; and that is the end of Mr. Beebe's influence, so far as the finances of the Zoological Society are concerned.

As the 1920s progressed, the Zoological Society prospered. In 1923 John D. Rockefeller, Jr., gave $500,000 toward the General Endowment Fund the society felt it had to have, and promised another $500,000 when a matching $1,000,000 was raised. In the same year Edward S. Harkness pledged $100,-000, Mrs. Frederick Ferris Thompson gave $50,000 unconditionally with a share of her residuary estate still to come, and Watson B. Dickerman gave $20,000. Other large bequests trickled in, and in 1926 Anna M. Harkness gave the society $1,000,000 to be paid within three years of her death in that year. The city, too, loosened its purse strings and was more generous with maintenance funds. Attendance boomed at the Zoological Park and soared to 2,572,050 in 1924. Even the weather was good that year and, *mirabile dictu,* Dr. Hornaday found something nice to say about newspaper reporters. He was gratified that the park's educational purposes were being so well served by illustrated animal lectures, books, magazine articles, and "a countless number of newspaper 'feature stories,' great and small." As he said in the *Annual Report:*

For much of this we owe much to the periodical and newspaper press. The high quality of the "wild-animal stories" now put into print annually by the magazines and newspapers of the United States is profoundly gratifying. Twenty-five years ago we labored to convince newspaper reporters and editors that in dealing with wild animals *truth is stranger than fiction,* and the *truth is what the people want.* It is no longer necessary to insist upon the soundness of those two propositions.

He was right; a subtle change *had* come over the attitude of the New York press toward animal stories from the Zoo. Straightforward news about the arrival of animal rarities, descriptions of them, and notes on the interesting things they did were much commoner than they had been ten or twenty years before. They seldom reported "in depth" and sometimes missed the interesting point entirely, but animals were no longer mere pegs to hang the reporter's imagination on. The blue birds of paradise that Ellis Joseph brought from Australia went through a period of spectacular courtship display and the papers described it, but concluded that this was their "way of showing off their beautiful plumage to admiring crowds," without mentioning the real purpose of the display. At any rate they did not announce that some new birds at the Bronx Zoo hung upside down and had "fits," as they might have done twenty years before.

In fact, there was a time in the 1920s when the Zoo enjoyed a golden age of newspaper publicity, for which Curator Ditmars was largely responsible. Ditmars worked easily with reporters and photographers and he knew a good story when it came along—or knew how to make it come along. More or less overtly, Dr. Hornaday turned over to him the chore of dealing with the press, and without issuing formal press releases the curator began to flood the papers with lively and newsy stories. He was, unfortunately, not always careful to insist on credit being given to the Zoological Society or the director. Dr. Hornaday quietly called a halt. To the city editor of the *World* he sent a letter marked "Confidential":

I am very fond of Curator Raymond L. Ditmars, I do everything I can to advance his interests, and about 99 percent of the time I am glad to see him well advertised by the reporters of the World, and other New York newspapers. At the same time I do not want to be killed by an overdose of Curator Ditmars, and as a measure of conservation of directors, I would be glad if you would suggest to the reporters, on your staff, that up in the Zoological Park there are other men beside Curator Ditmars who are endeavoring, in their own feeble ways, to serve the public and that Mr. Ditmars is not really the WHOLE THING!

I am not hungry for notoriety, I am not thirsty to see my name in print, and I am a bit indifferent to public credit for the things that are done by me. But, when I have slaved to secure from abroad and import successfully a particularly valuable animal, it makes me sore to see Mr. Ditmars, or anyone else, put forward as the sole initiator and the only moving cause. Mr. Ditmars does not purchase kudus from abroad, and he does not send expeditions to Africa, but he is great on King Cobras, as stated in your columns.

Tell your men to soft-pedal on Mr. Ditmars for a little while and give us, up here, a much needed rest.

The *World* did soft-pedal and credits got spread around a little more evenly, with no great impairment of the flood of publicity.

As Dr. Hornaday said, Curator Ditmars was "great on King Cobras," and thus he was the legitimate fountainhead of news in the fall of 1923 when a real-life mystery story came along. Ditmars arrived at his office in the Reptile House one morning to find that during the night someone had attempted to steal the cobras.

There were four of them in a glass-fronted cage to which access could be gained by a steel door opening from a rear service alley. On the alley pavement behind the cobras' cage that morning were a carpenter's brace and bit, a pair of pliers, a metal-cutting chisel, a hammer, a long staff with a noose for picking up a snake—and a violin case.

Chisel marks showed that an attempt had been made to spring the steel door off its hinges, but then the intruder abandoned everything and fled, presumably when the night watchman made his rounds to check the furnace.

This was a good story indeed and the press made the most of it, with endless speculation about what might be behind it. Gang warfare? The movies had not yet made everyone aware that when a sinister figure carrying a violin case came into sight, someone was going to be given "a singing lesson," but the potentialities of a deadly cobra in an innocent violin case were deliciously obvious. Dr. Hornaday expressed the Zoological Park's own speculation in a letter to a concerned correspondent:

Mr. Ditmars is of the opinion that the attack on the cobra cage was in some way connected with a strange Hindu who comes here about once a week and actually worships the cobras. The worship is no joke, it is a fact! The man stands like a statue for as much as five minutes at a time grasping the rail in front of the cage containing the four cobras now made famous by the attack. When he reaches the cage of the King Cobra, he makes a profound and prolonged bow to the serpent, which sometimes attracts considerable attention from visitors, but he is perfectly oblivious to his surroundings. The method of attack was so ill-judged and clumsy that it might well have been done by a Hindu who knows mighty little about the movement of snakes. However, the attempt was studied out long in advance and the preparations for it were carefully made.

We have not found the party and I have no idea that we ever will, but we have as souvenirs of this visit, the mutilated violin case, a first class extension bit and brace, and a second-hand pair of side cutting pliers of large size.

Ditmars had a lifelong interest in the production of serum against snakebite. As a young man he had followed the work of Dr. Albert Calmette of the Pasteur Institute in France in developing a serum against cobra venom, and he knew about Dr. Vito Brazil's production of serum against rattlesnake venom at the Institute of Serum Therapy in São Paulo, so that when American troops were involved in punitive action against General Francisco Villa in Mexico and others were stationed on the Mexican border in the summer of 1916, he induced the Zoological Society to order a supply of serum from Dr. Brazil. Of the 250 tubes the society received, 150 were turned over to the Army and the rest kept in the Zoological Park for local emergencies. In payment, the society sent a large number of Texas diamondback rattlesnakes to Dr. Brazil, who extracted their venom, immunized horses, and produced more serum.

This awareness of Dr. Brazil's work paid off dramatically in January of 1916 when Head Keeper John Toomey was bitten on the right thumb by a Texas rattler. The Brazil serum had not yet been ordered, but Calmette serum had been kept in the Reptile House for several years. Although it was not specific for the venom of rattlesnakes, Dr. Gilbert Van der Smissen (who had been the park's official physician since about 1900) administered it and did what he could. Then someone remembered hearing that Dr. Brazil was in New York to attend a conference, and through the medical grapevine Dr. Van der Smissen located him. He happened to have some tubes of rattlesnake-specific serum and he hastened to the German Hospital [now Lenox Hill Hospital] where Toomey was "in the last stages of collapse." The serum was injected and within two hours there was what was called a miraculous reaction for the better. Toomey recovered completely.

Both Ditmars and (naturally) Toomey were so enthusiastic

about antivenomous serum that in 1925 the two of them "milked" a huge number of rattlesnakes of their venom and dried it to crystalline form; then in the late summer Ditmars and his family made a trip to São Paulo to deliver their lethal package in person. "It represented," Dr. Hornaday wrote to Madison Grant, "the same as a fluid gallon of the venom and Dr. Brazil said that the supply would be sufficient for his purposes for thirty years to come."

There was no Zoological Society pressure for the curators to write books (although they were expected to turn out most of the articles for the society's *Bulletin*), but there was certainly an economic compulsion, salaries being what they were. Ditmars was second only to Beebe in literary output, starting with his *The Reptile Book* in 1907 and *Reptiles of the World* in 1910. Most of his eventual twenty volumes were the product of later and more leisurely years, however; around the beginning of the 1920s he was deeply involved in producing his own motion pictures.

Dr. Hornaday had long since learned to live with the motion-picture industry—and it with him. He never ceased to insist that the society be paid for the trouble of setting up animal scenes, and producers of newsreel subjects agreed to the fees of ten to twenty-five dollars. Ditmars was made chairman of a publicity committee to act as liaison man. As time went on, the director not merely tolerated but embraced the motion-picture concept, and he suggested that Staff Photographer Sanborn try his hand at it. Sanborn tried, but his time was so taken up with routine still photography and with editorial chores that the results were not very useful. Then Ditmars offered to operate the movie camera and the society encouraged him. He started by taking movies of reptiles stirring about at night, the pulsating throats of tree toads calling, snake eggs hatching, and the like. Ever meticulous (a favorite word), he realized that he needed a studio where he could set up realistic backgrounds and control the lighting. The park was not prepared to give him these facilities, so he built a studio at his home in Scarsdale. With the enthusiastic cooperation of his wife and two daughters (who soon learned how to stage-manage any small animal) he embarked on a career as a professional moviemaker, yet without neglecting his park work. As Dr. Hornaday wrote to someone, he

. . . has been in the habit of working every night until 11 o'clock, and yet reporting at 9 o'clock in the Zoological Park ready for duty. I have for sometime been afraid that he would actually kill himself by this strenuous work, but he seems to have wonderful vitality. His whole life has been given over to his work in the Park in the first place, and his work at home in the second place in developing motion pictures of zoological subjects.

Ditmars soon graduated to motion pictures of large animals in the Zoo itself with the hearty approval of the Zoological Society, for he was generous in showing his films at the society's annual members' meetings and giving illustrated lectures in the homes of members of the board of managers. "Nature films" actually intended to tell the viewers something about the lives and habits of animals were a novelty, and by the time Ditmars had built up his film collection to forty-three reels called the "Living Natural History" series, they were being shown in theaters and schools all over the country. The Strand on Broadway ran the series consecutively for thirty-seven weeks, and in 1925 the Zoological Society bought one complete set for $3,500 for showing to its membership and in schools above the Harlem River.

The society got good value for its encouragement of Ditmars in his film project. To the Pratt Institute, which had inquired about the mechanics of setting up a film program, Dr. Hornaday wrote:

I attribute Mr. Grant's success in obtaining $100,000 from Mr. Carnegie as a pension fund to the tremendous interest which a show of Ditmars' pictures at Mr. Carnegie's house excited in the mind of Mr. Carnegie. He was completely carried away with the show, and took no pains to conceal his surprise, his interest and his delight. It was only a short time after that when Mr. Grant fortunately called upon Mr. Carnegie for a large donation to the Endowment Fund, and immediately received $100,000.

Motion pictures had forced Dr. Hornaday into acceptance of modern times, and it was only a small step to acceptance of radio. In 1925 he wrote to Grant that radio people had been urging him to allow the staff to "be drawn into a rather extensive line of radio speaking." Up to now, he said, he had been opposed to it; radio speaking entailed a great deal of preparation and the radio people paid nothing. Still, the staff felt that the society should get into it as a means of educating the public and promoting the Zoological Park. He now agreed, and suggested that the executive committee authorize him to pay the men twenty dollars for each talk.

The proposal was approved, and for the next year all the curators at the Zoo, as well as the staff of the Aquarium, took turns appearing weekly for fifteen minutes on Station WJZ of the Radio Corporation of America. Dr. Hornaday himself led off the series on May 15 with a talk on "Bad Elephants" —a subject on which he might rightly consider himself an expert. Veterinarian Blair spoke on successive weeks on "Medical Treatment" and "Surgical Treatment" of Zoological Park animals. Most of the talks were a good deal more informal and chatty, however, and they were well received; at least WJZ was still eager to continue them when Dr. Hornaday decided enough was enough and canceled the series after one year.

With his natural instinct for showmanship, Curator Ditmars produced a hit broadcast, although it was on Station WOR and not on the WJZ series. It was a broadcast of the warning rattle of a rattlesnake. The reptile department was always getting letters from curious people who wanted to know exactly what kind of sound a rattlesnake makes, he

404

wrote in the *Annual Report,* so . . .

The Curator decided that the broadest and most satisfactory answer would be by utilization of the snake itself by radio. The Curator of Reptiles spoke briefly about the habits and structure of the rattlesnake, then had a vigorously buzzing specimen (in a mesh-fronted box) brought into the studio from an adjoining room, and placed before the microphone. We were rather appalled by the interest created. More than 400 letters were received within a week's time. The rattling of the snake was clearly picked up by receivers as far west as western Iowa, in Canada, Nova Scotia, by ships at sea (one of these 1,200 miles from shore), while southern acknowledgments came from Texas, Florida, Georgia, South Carolina and Tennessee. We have posted a wireless map in the lobby of the Reptile House, with red pins indicating the territory through which the demonstration carried.

Beebe and Ditmars were constantly in the news in the 1920s (and for the rest of their lives), but so little was heard from or about their associate in the bird department that it might seem that Curator Crandall was a colorless nonentity. He was anything but that; it was just that he was supremely happy in his own department, content in a job through which he was to become known as the best birdman in America and perhaps in the world. Beebe's flamboyance gained him backing for his expeditions; Ditmars's writing, showmanship, and instinct for a good story brought him national fame as an author and lecturer about reptiles. (In an obituary of Ditmars in *Copeia,* Clifford H. Pope said of him: "*The Reptile Book* (1907) and *Reptiles of the World* (1910) long remained almost the sole popular works of their kind readily available to the public; librarians throughout the land unhesitatingly recommended them as the last word. Thus he became *the* educator in his field, and was without rival, even 'the man in the street' equating his name with 'snake.'") But Crandall was interested neither in going on expeditions (except the one he made to New Guinea for

405

birds of paradise in 1928–29) nor in publicity, lecturing, or writing. Management of the bird collection, and later of the mammals as well, fulfilled him, and it is significant that the book he wrote after his retirement in 1952, the 300,000-word *The Management of Wild Mammals in Captivity,* was immediately acclaimed as "the zoo man's bible."

As the Zoological Park approached its twenty-fifth anniversary in November of 1924 (the employees gave a dinner in the Boat House Restaurant and presented Mr. Grant with a loving cup, Dr. Hornaday with a gold watch), a feeling of impending change from the old patterns was in the air. Paternalism was all very well (a Zoological Park Relief Association for the aiding of distressed employees had been formed as early as 1901 and Dr. Hornaday had a "Secret Fund" of $200 for emergency help), but the cost of living was going up and the working force wanted more money and fewer hours. Carpenters, machine-shop employees, and painters in the spring of 1923 petitioned Dr. Hornaday for a half day off on Saturdays, but he regretfully denied it on the grounds that the city was not giving the society nearly enough money for maintenance and that half a day's holiday would amount to 8.5 percent of the men's services—and all the other employees would want the same. His cold-comfort advice was to hang on, and if times improved the society would try to pry more money out of the city. The men didn't like it, but they hung on.

New names and new faces began to appear in the tight little circle of the staff and the society's administration. Henry Fairfield Osborn, Jr., Professor Osborn's son, thirty-five years old in 1923, began to interest himself in the well-being of the society and took on the job of building up membership. To Dr. Hornaday he submitted the text of a membership promotional pamphlet he had written, and the director praised it and urged him not to let *anybody* change a word. The main thing was to get a good mailing list, and he offered the membership rolls of the Camp-Fire Club, an organization of sportsmen and out-of-doorsmen he had founded in the winter of 1897.

On May 1, 1924, Martin S. Garretson, the onetime cowboy who had long been secretary of the American Bison Society, was engaged as full-time attendant at the Heads and Horns Museum, and the next year Hermann W. Merkel left to join the Westchester County Park Commission and Charles J. Renner replaced him as chief constructor and engineer. Dr. Hornaday's own retirement was finally coming up, and it was understood that Dr. Blair would succeed him, which meant that a new veterinarian had to be found. Dr. Charles V. Noback was hired away from the Department of Health in Albany at $3,000 a year. He took over on June 1, 1926, the day of Dr. Blair's elevation to the directorship.

Dr. Hornaday did not abdicate in advance of his retirement. Commuting from Stamford to 125th Street and then to the park by subway was getting to be a wearisome chore, but once at his desk he was in full command. He did complain to Professor Osborn about being forced to write his autobiography: "I have made a bold beginning, but for the life of me I cannot convince myself that anyone will care to read it. It is done solely and only because you and Mr. Grant have recommended it." He informed a correspondent that he was "fully convinced that Francis Bacon wrote the works that are attributed to William Shakespeare." He chided Herbert Friedmann, who was later to become one of the country's leading ornithologists, for wasting his time on impractical studies:

I would like to enquire how it is possible to spend so much time as two years in studying the parasitic habits of the cowbird, and why any practical end is served in that very prolonged investigation. To be perfectly frank I am of a very practical turn of mind, and I like to see practical results accrued or to accrue from the work of an educated man. To be still more frank, I do not see how it is possible to justify devoting any great length of time to the study of parasitism in birds.

Martin S. Garretson, a cowboy on the Western plains in his youth and for many years secretary of the American Bison Society, became attendant at the Heads and Horns Museum in 1924. His office was filled with trophies of his past.

He advised the Tribune Syndicate that while he knew of no experiments on training chimpanzees to do housework, he believed it could be done. "It is my belief that a chimpanzee could be taught to obey from 50 to 100 different commands and could learn the names of from 50 to 100 different objects of household use." He did admit, however, that chimpanzees become erratic as they grow older and might become unruly just at the time they were old enough and strong enough to be most useful.

He had to watch his health more carefully and got permission from the executive committee to take two months' vacation in California in 1923. He returned with greatly renewed vigor, some of which he attributed to "one glass per day of real Dublin stout." This was a tip he passed on to Dr. C. B. Penrose of the Philadelphia Zoological Society, who was also feeling rather down and out on occasion. "Of course it is the richness of the malt and hops joined with the small modicum of alcohol that does it. Occasionally there are bootleggers of high standing and with good reference who are able to produce the goods, but it is not all of them who could do it."

In the last year of his directorship it had come to be understood that he would retire in the spring of 1926, when he would be seventy-two. On May 4, 1926, he dictated his letter of resignation, addressing it to Madison Grant, who had succeeded Professor Osborn as the society's president in the previous year:

I have long maintained the belief that an officer in a responsible position should not seek to retain his position too long, nor to the detriment of the interests to be served by him.

I am now convinced that this age I have now attained, and the physical handicaps which now impair my usefulness, demand that for the best interests of the Zoological Park a younger and more vigorous man should take my place as Director. The daily duties to be performed call for a thoroughly vigorous successor.

For the reasons stated above, I now respectfully request to be retired on a pension, on or about June 1, which will represent a little more than thirty years in your service.

In making this application, I desire to record with it an expression of my profound gratitude for the opportunity that I have enjoyed of this long period of active and interesting service with the Zoological Society, and the honor and satisfaction that I have derived through that service.

The patient and never-failing courtesy and consideration that I have received from the Executive Committee and the Board of Managers of the Society during my entire term of service fills me with gratitude beyond my power to express in words. I feel that

I have been absolutely the most fortunate and most favored of men.

In profound appreciation and gratitude,

Respectfully submitted,

WILLIAM T. HORNADAY
Director

Acceptance of his resignation was of course automatic, and the executive committee passed a resolution of *its* gratitude to the retiring director:

As Administrative Director of the New York Zoological Park for thirty years, Dr. Hornaday imparted, by his own example, continued intelligence, energy, and enthusiasm, and inspired his increasing staff with loyalty and devotion to the spirit of Public Service, thus creating the largest and most beautiful, the most popular and the most widely known zoological park in the world.

Dr. Hornaday retired on a pension of $5,000 a year and the executive committee supplemented this with an additional $2,500 a year. The added sum made all the difference between a bare sufficiency and modest affluence. To Grant he wrote: "It will enable me to live out my allotment of life with a degree of comfort and peace of mind that otherwise would hardly be possible."

His last official letter was written to Park Commissioner Joseph P. Hennessy of the Bronx on June 1, the day of his retirement, and expressed his pleasure that Hennessy had been re-elected for another four years. It was a cause for congratulation by the borough and by the Zoological Park, he said.

He closed his rolltop desk and took the train for Stamford, to begin immediately on the rewriting of the park's guide-book and to throw himself into conservation battles that were to continue for the next eleven years.

There were no abrupt changes in the operation of the Zoological Park when Dr. Blair inherited the rolltop desk, the revolving bookstand, and the tall-backed, leather-padded chair in the director's office; indeed, there were no immediately discernible changes of any kind. Director Blair was not lacking in ideas, but he was a naturally conservative man responsible to an executive committee that itself was not as innovative as it had been when its members were a quarter of a century younger. The committee knew it could count on Dr. Blair's moderation when, as soon as he assumed office, it asked him to draw up a list of things to be done, promising that "as soon as funds are available, the suggestions, or at least some of them, will be carried into effect."

He published his list in the *Annual Report* for 1926. There were seven suggestions:

A more representative collection of the wild cattle of the world.

An experiment with the Hagenbeck idea of barless enclosures for animals, substituting moats for bars. (He pointed out that this idea was catching on among the newer zoological parks—St. Louis and Chicago had adopted it—and "we might experiment along these lines in a modest way.")

A separate building, or an addition to the old Primate House, especially for anthropoid apes. (Mr. Grant had urged this several years before.)

An isolated building to promote the breeding of the big cats, small mammals, and monkeys.

A separate exhibition house for parrots and psittacine birds generally, since we now had 90 species and they were filling the entire south hall of the Bird House.

An auditorium for lectures and meetings of members.

A cooperative research program with local universities to make better use of the park's animals both alive and dead.

He did get a cooperative research program going eventually —although not with society-funded grants he had hoped for—

23

New Faces, New Ways at the Zoo

and that was all. Money was not available and it was to be in even shorter supply in the next few years after the stock-market crash in 1929.

Temperamentally Dr. Blair was not a man to be impatient for quick action on his "suggestions," and he was happy enough that the board of managers subscribed a special fund so he could experiment with Vita glass in the Lion House studio; it passed the beneficial ultraviolet rays of sunshine and he was sure it would improve the health of the animals. Mr. Grant was no longer willing to put up a fight for an anthropoid house, but he did urge Dr. Blair to "go as far as possible in keeping our animals outdoors, which is the modern method. Dr. Hornaday was always very old-fashioned and stubborn about this."

Blair's proposal to experiment "in a modest way" with bar-less enclosures had struck an immediate spark from Dr. Hornaday. Grant had "a long and intense letter about barless dens" from him. "I replied," Grant wrote Blair, "that we had no serious intention at the present time of building new dens."

Hornaday simply could not let go. He was waging a series of wildlife protection wars from his little office in Stamford, but he had time to make sure the Zoological Park stayed on the rails. He forwarded to Grant a letter he had received from Director C. Emerson Brown of the Philadelphia Zoological Garden, urging him to fight Hagenbeckization of American zoological parks. Brown was convinced that the Hagenbecks—who had been the European pioneers in barless enclosures—were mostly interested in getting American zoological parks to buy their models and hire their men to do the artificial rockwork. On Brown's letter Hornaday penciled a note: "I think that you and I quite agree with Mr. Brown. The Hagenbeck fad has inoculated some half-baked western zoo-makers by German 'boring from within.' "

Grant passed the letter on to Blair with the comment that "There are some Managers who occasionally come to me and urge the ditch rock pile scheme for the Zoo. As you know, I

Dr. W. Reid Blair succeeded Dr. Hornaday in 1926 as director of the Zoological Park.

do not approve of artificial rock work and I have always opposed such ideas."

Dr. Blair had a mind of his own, however, and ventured a mild protest to Grant:

I think both [Brown and Hornaday] are unduly alarmed about Hagenbeck's scheme to modernize American zoos and in this way undermine American institutions. If we do not use up all our energy in trying to maintain that we have spoken the last word in zoological building and exhibition we may be able to pick up a few ideas worth considering from time to time.

That was the first faint flickering of a disposition to change the old ways and to recognize the fact—now so obvious—that the great Bronx Zoo *was* being outmoded by the "half-baked western zoo-makers" who were taking advantage of the new technology that had developed in the generation and a half since Hornaday crystallized his Final Plan. The flicker did not survive the rough wind of the Depression, and anyway the declining energies of the men on the executive committee, who had fought so many good fights during the Hornaday years, did not suffice to keep it alive. The Blair era, from 1926 to 1940, was destined to be a holding period; it conserved, but it did not innovate. The only physical changes of any consequence in those fourteen years were the addition of a restaurant near the Boston Road Gate (1928), the Buffalo Parking Field in the same area (1928), a Reptile Island (small, but moated and barless!) in front of the Reptile House (1932), and the Rainey Memorial Gate at the Pelham Parkway–Concourse entrance (1934).

A different man might have given the park's fourth decade some feeling of the vigor that characterized its first two. But Dr. Blair was self-limited. He had come to the park in 1902 when Hornaday had just begun to work out his concept of what a great zoological park should be, and he inherited it as a mature institution: complete in the terms of Hornaday's and the founders' dreams, successful in its operation, envied and looked up to by newer zoos even though they looked elsewhere for models to adapt to their own needs. Blair had come to maturity as the park matured, and he could not have been expected to become an apostle of radical change. Nor was it expected of him; the executive committee was satisfied with things as they were. It was enough that from time to time he put forth tentative ideas for improvements—as long as he didn't get excited about them.

Certainly his philosophy of zoo-keeping differed from that of his predecessor; his interest in encouraging breeding is an example. In 1920 Hornaday had written in the *Annual Report*:

The first, the last and the greatest business of every zoological park is to collect and exhibit fine and rare animals. Next comes the duty of enabling the greatest possible number of people to see them with comfort and satisfaction.

In comparison with these objects, all others are of secondary or tertiary or quaternary importance. The breeding of wild animals is extremely interesting, and the systematic study of them is fascinating, but both these ends must be subordinated to the main objects.

Times change. Today the Zoological Park sees no reason why breeding of rare and vanishing animals, systematic study, and more exciting exhibition than Dr. Hornaday ever dreamed of cannot be carried on simultaneously.

It should not be imagined that Director Blair sat quietly behind Dr. Hornaday's desk and waited for his retirement and pension. He was in fact a very busy man and enough of an executive to turn over what correspondence he could to his secretary, Miss Edith H. Franz, who had been Hornaday's secretary for the last fourteen years of his directorship. The society sent him to Europe in 1927 to see what new ideas were coming to the fore over there (he was not impressed by the London Zoo, where he was told that the reason no information was put on cage labels beside the name and habitat of the animal was that visitors wouldn't buy the guidebook if they could get the information free), and he was trying his

Before the Rainey Memorial Gateway was erected in 1934, the Zoo's main entrance on Pelham Parkway was functional but not particularly ornamental.

414

hand at getting publicity for the Zoological Park and beginning to be concerned about its educational activities.

One New York newspaperman sought a job as a sort of public-relations aide, but the executive committee didn't think one was necessary. Dr. Blair did, and periodically sent out staid and not very enticing press releases about the first living hummingbirds received at the park in many years (Ricord's Emerald, from Cuba) , the arrival of a whale-headed stork from Egypt, a new South American otter . . .

His interest in the society's educational goals had a very practical basis. *Of course* the Zoological Society was an educational as well as a scientific institution; everybody knew that. But was it *legally* educational?

The question had arisen in 1927 when the State of Ohio claimed an inheritance tax on the bequest of $1,000,000 that Anna M. Harkness had made to the society in a will probated in Cleveland. Ohio's Attorney General said the society was not primarily an educational institution, and therefore was not exempt from taxation under Ohio law; to be educational it would have to have a definite curriculum and staff of teachers.

Dr. Blair exhibited the charter and the society's technical and popular publications, told of school classes guided around the park by the curators, and so on. The Attorney General was not impressed, although the judge in the Court of Common Pleas was and ruled in favor of the society. The case went to the Court of Appeals and the society's position was sustained, but the challenge made the society take a long look at its status. Dr. Blair laid it on the line in a letter to Mr. Grant: "I feel that we have stressed the entertainment and recreation features of the Park and that we should now develop the educational and scientific fields which our collections afford."

He sought and got permission to look around for what he called a docent, some young man trained in biology and zoology who would make it possible for teachers and students

416

to get a great deal more out of their visits to the park. He found him in Claude W. Leister, then an instructor in the department of biology at Cornell University, where he was just on the point of getting his doctorate (his thesis was on the food of wild ducks). Dr. Leister joined the staff on October 1, 1929, at $3,500 a year, and the Zoological Park henceforth could proclaim itself a bona fide educational institution. Officially, Leister was assistant to the director and curator of educational activities.

There were other modifications of old ways and slight hints of a different personality in the director's office. Dr. Blair did not hesitate to refer to the Zoological Park as "the Zoo"—and to a newspaper city editor, at that! Indeed, in 1929 he wrote a book and titled it *In the Zoo*. It is a pity that Dr. Hornaday did not record what he thought about such looseness of language by his successor.

Blair even relaxed once—and as far as the record goes it was the only time since 1899—the rule against *anyone* taking photographs in the Zoological Park on Sunday. He made an exception in January of 1930 for the Boy Scout troop of the Kips Bay Boys' Club; the rule against Sunday photography, even for the staff photographer and the rare permit holders, was based on the annoyance it would cause on crowded days. Dr. Blair was willing to admit, as Hornaday was not, that a January Sunday is not likely to be a crowded day.

Nevertheless he maintained the rule against unrestricted photography in general and had a brisk exchange with a photographer named H. S. Schoenhals who had asked that his special permit be renewed. Dr. Blair wrote to him:

Since you are apparently no longer connected with a newspaper and it is against the rules of the Executive Committee to issue permits to private individuals, I regret that I am unable to renew your permit.

Schoenhals replied:

Dear Sir: Private individual hell—through the Asstd. Press &

N.Y. daily newspapers I make more photographs than perhaps any two newsmen in N.Y. City. Very Respectfully, Harry A. Schoenhals. I'm sore.

Dr. Blair could not let that pass:

I note that you claim to make more photographs than any two news men in New York City. I judge from your letter that you are overworked and in need of a good long rest, otherwise you may suffer a nervous breakdown.

I have at times also questioned the wisdom of the rules and regulations of the Executive Committee relative to the granting of permits for photographing in the Zoological Park but they seem on the whole to work fairly well.

Schoenhals had the last futile word:

Thank you for fatherly advice. Hope you'll learn the value of free publicity some day. I wonder if the men under you like you as well as I might if I were in their place. (Dr. Hornaday was a wise gentleman.)

Photographer Schoenhals did not get his permit renewed, but his barbed comments must have given Dr. Blair something to think about. Despite his press releases, the Zoo was not getting the great volume of publicity it had enjoyed in earlier years when Dr. Ditmars (Lincoln Memorial University at Harrogate, Tennessee, gave him a D.Litt. in 1930) was Hornaday's press surrogate. Ditmars was still an unfailing source of news stories, but they were not always the kind Dr. Blair wanted. He awoke on the morning of March 2, 1931, to read in the *Times:*

DITMARS TAKES COBRA AS PULLMAN COMPANION;
IN BAG, IT SHARES BERTH ON WASHINGTON TRIP

The headline told the whole story succinctly—except the ire of the Pullman Company, the embarrassment of the Zoological Society, and the reaction of at least one member of the society. The Zoo was making a gift of a king cobra, largest and most dangerous of the cobras, to the National Zoological

Park, and Dr. Ditmars thought the simplest way to transport it was to put it in a cloth bag and lock the bag in a stout leather traveling case, which he would himself carry to Washington. To keep the snake warm, he stowed the case in the foot of his Pullman berth. It made a good story and he told it to newspapermen in Washington, who of course loved it and spread it coast to coast. Unfavorable comments promptly bounced back to Dr. Blair's desk, including one from a member of the society who announced his resignation. Dr. Blair wrote to secretary Niles:

The facts are just as stated by Mr. Proctor [the member who resigned], and so far as I know there are no extenuating circumstances in connection with this exhibition of poor taste and judgment on the part of Dr. Ditmars. Ever since this story "broke" I have been expecting just such protests as Mr. Proctor's letter indicates. Mr. Proctor must know that it does not represent the kind of publicity the Society desires or sponsors. If Mr. Proctor only knew how embarrassing this story was to the Zoological Society, and to me personally, he would reconsider and withdraw his resignation.

Dr. Blair was not a humorless man, but he was not sympathetic to the offbeat stories that were the Ditmars specialty. He did not at all enjoy a headline in the *Herald Tribune* over the by-line of John O'Reilly, one of the greatest of that paper's feature writers:

DITMARS, BLIND

TO PUBLIC WEAL,

EATS ZOO FROGS

O'Reilly's story began:

Dr. Raymond L. Ditmars, curator of reptiles at the New York Zoological Park, the Bronx, has failed his public for the first time in thirty-nine years. The curator, who returned on Saturday after a trip to the tropics, wore a shamefaced expression yesterday when he admitted willful neglect of his public duty and tried to square himself with a lengthy explanation.

419

But the facts in the case were plain. Dr. Ditmars, the man who has devoted his life to instructing the public in things zoological, let his appetite for frogs' legs get the better of his scientific integrity. With the aid of certain gastronomic accomplices he ate a dozen fine specimens of frogs, Leptodactylus fallax, which were intended for exhibition in the reptile house at the zoo.

It ran for a column and was an amusing exercise in O'Reilly's ability to weave a good feature story. Dr. Ditmars had been making his annual vacation trip to the tropics, and in Trinidad had bought a dozen large local frogs, known as "mountain chickens" and much esteemed by the natives as food. He planned to exhibit them in the Zoo, but on the ship coming home one of them was found to have injured itself, and rather than toss it overboard, he had the cook prepare the legs for his table. One taste led to another, and presently all twelve *Leptodactylus fallax* went into the frying pan.

Dr. Blair had some sharp things to say about lack of judgment—he couldn't accuse his curator of reptiles of lack of taste, at any rate—but fortunately no members resigned.

Even the quiet and efficient Miss Grace Davall, who was secretary both to Dr. Ditmars and Curator of Birds Crandall, drew a rebuke from Dr. Blair for participating in a Ditmars effort to get publicity. A rotogravure photographer happened to be in Dr. Ditmars's office when he was unpacking a newly arrived boa and—as news photographers have a way of doing —sought a "different" kind of shot. Why not coil the snake around pretty Miss Davall's head?

Why not? The photographer made his shot and that was that. The photograph was not printed in New York, but it did have a good play elsewhere. Curator Crandall, at that time in Australia for the start of his bird-of-paradise expedition to New Guinea, saw it in a Sydney newspaper, was amused, and unthinkingly mailed it to Dr. Blair. The reaction was instant, in a letter from Blair to Ditmars:

The enclosed is an example of poor taste and from the stand-

420

point of the Zoological Society, an undesirable form of publicity. Please call Miss Davall's attention to this matter.

Miss Davall was crushed and brought to tears, but Dr. Ditmars was long accustomed to handling publicity-obtuse directors. He told her to forget it, and sent a letter back to Dr. Blair:

Miss Davall and I were as much horrified about the terrible picture as you probably were.

The photographer simply asked her to hold the snake, and it seemed that just at the moment the reptile slipped, the exposure was made, and the photographer considered it artistic. Miss Davall had no idea that he would use such a picture.

A newspaper photograph that distressed Director Blair—Secretary Grace Davall with a snake draped around her head. Dr. Blair thought it was "an example of poor taste." Maybe so, but it appeared in newspapers as far away as Australia.

Well, maybe not. The boa *had* been coiled around her head, and it *had* slipped at the moment of exposure, so that the head end draped across her face in a most rakish way. Actually it was a much more lively photograph than it would have been had the snake coiled evenly and demurely. Anyway, the Zoological Society got publicity in Australia—for whatever value that was to an institution in the Bronx.

For several years, even in Dr. Hornaday's time, Curator Crandall had been proposing that the Zoological Society send him to New Guinea to try for a big collection of birds of paradise. He thought he could make the trip in five months at a cost of $12,000, and in the spring of 1928 President Grant and Secretary Niles gave their assent. It was to be one of the most spectacularly successful expeditions the society ever sent out.

Crandall sailed from San Francisco on August 9, 1928, and returned on March 21, 1929, with forty birds of paradise of nine species and some two hundred other birds as well as a few Australian mammals. Accompanied by J. E. (Pop) Ward, of Sydney, an old hand in the New Guinea bush, he penetrated the Owen Stanley Range on foot with a train of native "boys" as carriers. Deep in the mountains Crandall and Ward engaged the local tribesmen (some of them cannibals) to

421

catch birds. It was surprisingly easy. As Crandall wrote in the society's *Bulletin* at the end of 1929:

I was quite unprepared for the abundance of birds of paradise in this region [Deva-Deva]. They were calling constantly all about us and were frequently seen flying from tree to tree. At first I was amazed at the evident ease with which the natives caught the commoner species, but later I realized that this was an essential part of their lives. In the bush, a native is as keen and sensitive as a hunting animal, to sound and smell. Nothing escapes his notice. In a given territory, he knows where each bird has its home—where it sleeps, where it feeds, where it displays. Except at certain seasons, when the birds are irregular in habits, he can catch them almost at will.

The commoner species came in in such numbers that the collectors could not take them all, but they paid for them in trade goods and then—what a pity!—the unwanted specimens accidentally slipped out of their hands and flew away. Shining trade axes inspired heroic efforts to capture the rarer species such as Prince Rudolph's blue bird of paradise and Count Raggi's with its filmy red plumes, and eventually the portable cages were all filled.

Four months to the day after leaving San Francisco, Crandall loaded his cages aboard the *Morinda* at Port Moresby and the expedition was essentially over, for he had no doubt about his ability to keep the collection in good health while at sea. Then the *Morinda* ran afoul of a coral reef from which she could not be pulled off, and everyone except a skeleton crew, Crandall, and Ward's son (who was to assist with the birds on the way to New York) was taken off the ship. Crandall and young Ward stuck by their birds, loaded them onto a relief steamer five days later, and reached Sydney on the day after Christmas for a rest and transfer to the vessel that would carry them to New York. Crandall's luck stood by him in Sydney. One morning the finest of the blue birds of paradise escaped from a small temporary cage. Five days later while Crandall was working in the storage aviary, he saw the missing blue clinging to the outside of the wire, evidently looking for a way to get in. A hastily rigged parrot trap did the trick and the blue rejoined the collection. Crandall reached New York without a single loss.

There had been only one really worrying period while the collectors were deep in the bush. Their food supplies were exhausted and they knew they would have to depend on local produce from villages along their route *if* there was any to spare.

They were crossing a part of New Guinea that had been only recently—and partially—redeemed from cannibalism, but when they came to a sizable village they were in no position to make distinctions. Mr. Crandall wrote about it in *The New York Times Magazine* after his return:

In spite of the scanty food supply our hosts were quite willing to share it with us in exchange for salt and tobacco. They even shouted to friends across the valley, who sent their women up to us with small nets of potatoes. I was touched by the friendly hospitality of these savages. One hardly expects to be fed by cannibals.

Going and coming, the expedition took a little over seven months rather than the estimated five, but the collection was conservatively valued at $18,000, while of the expense fund of $12,000 furnished by the society there was even a balance of $29.37 when the account was closed at the end of 1929. *And* the Zoological Park was able to put on exhibition the finest collection of birds of paradise ever seen in a zoo, and to share some of its duplicates with the zoos of Washington, Philadelphia, and Milwaukee. Crandall published an account of his expedition in *Paradise Quest* in 1931.

The society's interest in conservation of wildlife did not fade with the departure of Dr. Hornaday; it took other and less controversial routes than those Hornaday had usually pursued. In 1931 it gave $3,000 to the Society for the Preservation of the European Bison and pledged $3,000 a year for five years so that preserves could be set up in Poland and

One of the prizes of Curator Crandall's expedition to New Guinea in 1928–29: Count Salvadori's bird of paradise in courtship display.

Germany—with the stringent stipulation that there was to be no crossbreeding or hybridization between American and European bison, such as Dr. Lutz Heck was attempting near Munich in an effort to recreate the extinct aurochs.

Thanks in good part to those contributions, the European bison, or wisent, is thriving in preserves and zoos today.

In the summer of 1931, both Dr. Blair and Dr. Townsend of the Aquarium attended a conference in Matamek, Labrador, on fluctuations in wild-animal populations; it was a broad scientific (and certainly noncontroversial) subject in which the executive committee had been interested for several years. Largely as a result of the Matamek Conference, the society raised funds to enable Charles Elton of the Bureau of Animal Population at Oxford to search the journals and records of the Hudson's Bay Company and chart the fluctuations of fur-bearing animals over a period of some two hundred years. It found $5,500, too, for support of the International Office for the Protection of Nature in Brussels, working through the American Committee for International Wild Life Protection, which had been formed at the Boone and Crockett Club in January of 1930. Kermit Roosevelt, one of the society's trustees,* was its representative on the American Committee. From 1938 until the late 1960s the American Committee's official headquarters was in the Zoological Park. Dr. Blair, and later Lee S. Crandall, served as executive secretary. It is now in Washington.

The 1930s was a somnolent decade in the history of the Zoological Park. Curators supervised their collections from their own offices in their own buildings—Ditmars in the Reptile House, Crandall in the Bird House—and were summoned or sought conferences with Dr. Blair through Miss Franz in an outer office of the Administration Building; to give a curator access, she buzzed the director who in turn

---

* In 1930 the Board of Managers was redesignated Board of Trustees, that term being "deemed advisable as being more dignified and better describing the function and duties of those entrusted with the property of the Society and the carrying into effect of its objects as set forth in its Charter."

buzzed his own locked door. Dr. Blair, stately in a cutaway coat, lunched apart from his staff on the terrace of the Rocking Stone Restaurant in summer and at his special window table in winter. In the new department of educational activities, Dr. Leister was bringing order and continuity to the rather haphazard educational tours and lectures for school groups, creating sets of hand-colored lantern slides for school use, and even experimenting with the newest fad, 16-mm motion pictures. By the end of 1930 a 16-mm *Birds Through the Year* had been produced and was seen by 4,418 schoolchildren. Although he regretted this trend to narrow film—the old standard 35-mm film was better visually—Dr. Leister perforce went along with the times; most schools had discarded their 35-mm projectors. The single print of *Birds Through the Year* stood up reasonably well and was in such demand that in 1933 Dr. Leister ordered a second print of the same subject. Photographer Sanborn was not much interested in motion pictures and was glad to let Leister and the education department take over the filming and editing. By 1936 Leister had his own 16-mm Ciné Kodak Special camera and started building up a library of educational films. He also found time to write a seventy-four-page book, *Present Day Mammals,* which the society published in 1931 to give schoolchildren some idea of the relationships among mammals.

As the 1930s advanced, Sanborn slipped into a gentle neurasthenia and virtually abandoned any pretense of being the staff photographer; his flash-powder accident in the winter of 1926–27 was more traumatic than anyone had realized. At his request, Edward R. Osterndorff had been hired in 1928 to take over still photography, and although Sanborn continued to edit the society's publications, even this task proved too much for him, and in the spring of 1934 a former printer, John P. Fritts, was brought in to restore a regular publication schedule. Sanborn turned sixty-five in October, and the following month Dr. Blair offered him a choice of retiring on pension or taking a leave of absence without pay. He had already "resigned" twice, showing up a day or so later to make another effort to do his work, and the ultimatum could have been no shock to him. He went home to Norwalk and never again visited the park or kept up more than one or two of the friendships he had made there. He lived in lonely, withdrawn retirement until 1947.

A possible replacement was already at hand. On a dull Monday in December of 1933, the assistant city editor of the *Sun* dispatched an idling rewrite man to the Bronx Zoo to see if he could dig up a feature story or two. William Bridges found the Zoo virgin territory—newspapers had been paying little attention to it for a long time—and he returned with enough notes to write half a dozen column-length features. It was such a profitable investment of a reporter's time that Bridges was assigned to the Zoo once a week for the next year and when Dr. Ditmars made his annual tropical vacation-expedition to Trinidad in July, the *Sun* sent its Zoo specialist down two weeks in advance with Arthur M. Greenhall, Ditmars's unpaid assistant. Dr. Ditmars did get a bushmaster, the big venomous snake that was the pretext for so many of his trips, and the expedition was generously covered in the *Sun*. (It was not the *Sun*, however, that announced Dr. Ditmars's capture of "fertile ants." That was the exclusive scoop of the *Times* whose reporter, interviewing Dr. Ditmars, misunderstood his reference to a fer-de-lance, another venomous tropical snake.)

When Editor Sanborn retired, Bridges had been covering the Zoo for a little more than a year. Dr. Blair was concerned at that time about the society's dwindling membership and happened one afternoon to discuss it with the *Sun*'s reporter, who unconsciously said "we" in mentioning various ways of attracting new members. The following Monday the director casually remarked, "If you still feel 'we' can do something together, would you care to take over as curator of publications?" Bridges still felt that way and trudged through a two-foot snowstorm to begin work on January 1, 1935. He has since then sometimes pointed out that the incident illustrated the effectiveness of short, simple words.

Except when Dr. Ditmars let his enthusiasm for a good story run away with him, Dr. Blair maintained cordial but essentially aloof relations with his staff. William Beebe, of course, was in a special position: director of his own department of tropical research, quartered in the park when he was not in the field, an ally but one who went his own way always. As early as 1914 the society had built a small laboratory for him, a room added to the old winter house for eagles and vultures, and in 1931 it moved the eagles and vultures to less commodious but still adequate cages in the basement of the Aquatic Birds House and remodeled the remainder of the winter house so Beebe could spread out. He and Dr. Blair kept a wary distance from each other. They had nothing in common except the bond of the society, and Beebe's occasional attempts to bridge the gap usually fell short of closing it, as when Dr. Blair wrote to Mr. Grant:

> Mr. Beebe telephoned me last week that he was going to sail on Friday for London and would return about June 1. He sent for Mr. Crandall yesterday afternoon to come down to his studio about a letter he had received from you. Mr. Crandall did not tell me what he wanted to see him about but intimated that Mr. Beebe was coming to see me in a few days and would tell me the secret himself. I am sure that Mr. Beebe will not suggest anything not in the best interests of the Society and I am willing to assure him of my hearty cooperation before I know his proposition. With my well established reputation as an "easy mark" I cannot understand why anyone should hesitate to approach me with any sort of proposition.

As it turned out, Dr. Blair was not amenable to Beebe's idea, which was that the Zoo put on and publicize a series of special animal weeks, such as a Parrot Week one time, a Monkey Week the next. Dr. Blair felt the newspapers would turn the idea into a joke, although he assured Mr. Grant that he would not give the idea a harsh rejection:

427

I shall of course encourage Mr. Beebe in every possible way to take a renewed interest in the Park. If I live long enough perhaps I shall finally iron out some of the accumulated misunderstandings to which I fell heir.

Dr. Beebe (Colgate University gave him an honorary Sc.D. in 1928 and Tufts College gave him a D.Litt. in the same year) was not really geared to Zoo publicity, and it is a little surprising that he offered even such a mild idea. He was totally involved in his own departmental affairs, writings, and expeditions, for after a widely publicized trawling exploration of the Hudson Gorge off New York City in 1928, he had established a research base in Bermuda and made the first of his Bermuda oceanographic expeditions that culminated in his bathysphere dives in 1930, 1932, and 1934.

Dr. Blair evinced his goodwill toward Dr. Beebe to the extent of meeting him in Hamilton, Bermuda, on a vacation trip in 1930, but he could not spare the time to visit the Nonsuch Station and enjoy an underwater walk with a diving helmet—a treat offered to many of the distinguished visitors to the station. As the bathysphere dives continued, Dr. Blair became more and more dubious about them. In 1932 Beebe had gone down 2,200 feet with Otis Barton, the inventor of the steel ball with fused quartz viewing windows (Beebe had coined the name "bathysphere") and in 1934 was planning to try for considerably greater depths. To Mr. Grant Director Blair wrote:

I hope he will be successful but I am anxious about this stunt and its effect on the Zoological Society if any accident should occur. I cannot see much prospect of his obtaining any real scientific data from such a dive.

Dr. Beebe had no such doubts, however, and subsequently published descriptions and gave scientific names to abyssal creatures he had seen from the bathysphere—a procedure which did not meet with universal approval from more conventional ichthyologists at the time. (Since then several of

those deep-sea fish have been taken in nets, and Beebe's descriptions were found accurate.) In 1934 he and Barton descended to their greatest depth, 3,028 feet. That year's dives were supported by the National Geographic Society, and it was reaping a rich harvest of new subscribers as a result of the interest they generated. In the fall of 1934 Dr. Blair wrote wistfully to Dr. Beebe:

I too wish we might benefit by the success of your spectacular dives. We have not had a single new member since June 1. I am not envious of the Geographic's success but wish we also might have benefitted to some extent.

William Beebe, left, and Otis Barton, the inventor of the bathysphere, after their descent to 1,426 feet at Nonsuch, Bermuda, on June 6, 1930.

It was certainly not that Dr. Beebe was playing favorites and giving his most exciting news to the *National Geographic Magazine* rather than to the Zoological Society's publication. The last issue of the *Bulletin* in 1934 was devoted exclusively to the department of tropical research. It presented a graphic account by Beebe of what it was like five hundred fathoms down, John Tee-Van's description of the interior and equipment of the bathysphere ("In the year of 2034, the Zoological Society's bathysphere will be looked upon as we now gaze at Stevenson's 'Rocket,' for our descendants will be acquainted with super bathyspheres"), Jocelyn Crane's report on queer deep-sea creatures brought up in six net hauls, and Gloria Hollister's transcript of the telephone conversations between the bathysphere and the surface as the steel ball descended to 2,600 feet. There was even a color plate of twin-lighted lanternfish painted by Else Bostelmann, the expedition's artist. But somehow new members did not flow into the society the way abyssal fish drifted up to the bathysphere's windows—or new subscribers swam to the *National Geographic*.

The 1930s were not a somnolent era at the Aquarium. It could not match even the minor physical changes at the Zoological Park, of course—eight-foot-thick slabs of red sandstone cannot be expanded at will—but for the mind, stone walls do not a prison make, and Dr. Charles H. Townsend had some very good minds on his staff. They turned to research, not only because innumerable practical problems of fish-keeping had to be solved but also because other stimulating investigators wanted to use Aquarium material, adequate laboratory space was at long last available and—well, primarily because research associate Charles M. Breder, Jr., and pathologist Ross F. Nigrelli liked research.

Dr. Townsend took no part in their laboratory work, and actually very little in the day-to-day decisions about the management of the collection; his own research interests centered on whales and whaling and on Galápagos tortoises. (In 1931 he devoted almost an entire issue of the *Bulletin* to whales and tortoises, with an article on sharks and another on collecting freshwater fishes thrown in for good measure.) He had become interested in the giant tortoises during his examination of whalers' logbooks; they revealed the enormous number of tortoises that had been carried away from the Galápagos Islands for food. It was well known that the tortoises had been exterminated on most of the islands and that the remnants were threatened by introduced rats and goats, and in 1928 he resolved to establish protected colonies outside the islands in the hope of breeding. The *Albatross II* of the U.S. Bureau of Fisheries happened to be idle at that time, waiting on a new governmental appropriation, and Dr. Townsend persuaded the Zoological Society to finance a voyage to Albemarle (Isabela) Island, where there was still a chance of making a sizable collection. In about a month he collected 180 tortoises, ranging from four and one half-ounce hatchlings to big specimens approaching breeding age.

The Zoological Park played a minor role in the project. If Dr. Hornaday had still been director, Townsend certainly

24

The Townsend Era Comes to an End at the Aquarium

would not have felt free to call on the Zoo for help, but his relations with Dr. Blair were cordial and he cabled a request to arrange customs clearance and to house the collection until the tortoises could be sent to permanent homes. For some weeks the floor of the winter pelican house in the Zoo's service yard was paved with big and little tortoises. Eventually they were distributed to the Canal Zone, the Bermuda Aquarium, the San Diego, Houston, and New Orleans zoos, an arboretum in Arizona, and the Florida Keys. Two of the largest on Lignum Vitae Key disappeared in 1932 and Dr. Blair heard a rumor that one of them had shown up in the winter quarters of the Ringling Circus in Sarasota, Florida. He wrote to John Ringling that it would be "a great surprise and shock" to him to learn the provenance of his tortoise, but Ringling denied that there had ever been a giant tortoise at Sarasota and the matter ended there.

Dr. Townsend made another trip to the Galápagos in 1930 on Vincent Astor's yacht *Nourmahal* and collected eight more tortoises, this time on Indefatigable (Santa Cruz) Island. They were deposited at the Zoo.

His hopes for extensive breeding were never realized. He had thought they would breed so readily that they might become established as a food source in the Southern states, but apparently climate, food, and perhaps other factors were too critical. Over the years there has been some breeding, chiefly in the San Diego Zoo and in Hawaii, but by no means on the scale that Dr. Townsend envisioned. A more practicable scheme than Townsend's came along in the 1960s when the Charles Darwin Research Station was established on Indefatigable with protection and a breeding program among its objectives. It has been successful in both goals and in 1971 the Zoological Park sent to the station its oldest resident, a female Duncan Island tortoise, in the hope that she would contribute to the program. The society was already supporting a conservation officer attached to the station.

Beginning in the late 1920s, Dr. Townsend's "boys," as he

432

liked to call his staff, were contributing heavily to the society's scientific journal. Dr. Nigrelli had received his Ph.D. from New York University in 1936 and his thesis, "The Morphology, Cytology and Life-history of *Oodinium ocellatum* Brown, a Dinoflagellate Parasitic on Marine Fishes," was published in *Zoologica*. Despite the revelations he made about that organism, it is still a problem in public aquariums. Dr. Breder (Newark State College gave him an honorary Sc.D. in 1938) was writing voluminously on the reproductive habits and the locomotion of fishes, two specialties that have engaged his research interests for forty years, and reporting on scores of field and laboratory studies. He even found time to produce a *Field Book of Marine Fishes of the Atlantic Coast*.

Breder encouraged "outside" research men to work at the Aquarium and half a dozen might be pursuing their studies at any time. Among them were Dr. George W. Smith of Yale on cancerous growths in fishes, Dr. E. B. Gresser of New York University on the anatomy of the fish eye, Dr. Homer W. Smith of New York University College of Medicine on kidney function in marine fishes and lungfishes, and Dr. Richard T. Cox of N.Y.U. on physical characteristics of the electrical discharge of electric eels. During those years the Aquarium gained the research impetus that was to inspire the foundation of the Osborn Laboratories of Marine Sciences attached to the "new" New York Aquarium in Brooklyn. And it was in the summer of 1937, while Dr. Breder was assuming control of the Aquarium in anticipation of Dr. Townsend's retirement in the fall, that he hired a young Cornell graduate, James W. Atz, who was later to make a name for himself through his interest in the genetics and reproductive endocrinology of fishes. Many years later, when he was associate curator of the Aquarium, Atz and Dr. Grace E. Pickford of Yale wrote a 613-page book, *The Physiology of the Pituitary Gland of Fishes*. It was published by the Zoological Society in 1959.

Research might expand, but the Aquarium's exhibits could

only be rearranged for greater attractiveness and public interest. In 1930 Mrs. Alma C. Damon bequeathed $10,000 to the society, the income to be used to maintain an exhibit of small aquarium fishes. The gift was in memory of her husband, William Emerson Damon, who had been one of the original members of the society's aquarium committee in 1902. It enabled the Aquarium to enter what was essentially a new field for it: a display of freshwater tropicals in seventy-two small tanks around the balcony. Its management required a specialist, and one was found in Christopher W. Coates. A former broker on the New York Produce Exchange, he had long had a deep interest in small tropicals as a hobby and he was knowledgeable and enthusiastic. Eventually he produced a book, *Tropical Fishes as Pets,* and for thirty-three years he conducted a weekly newspaper column on tropical fishes and home aquaria.

When Coates started his column in the *Sun,* he asked Assistant Curator Breder's permission to do so. This was readily granted but with it went a warning that he must never mention the Aquarium or the society in his column; Director Townsend had strong feelings about "commercialization." Some years later this anonymity got Coates into trouble from a different direction. President Osborn noticed the column and demanded that he give credit to his organization. What was the matter—was he ashamed of the Aquarium and the Zoological Society?

Among Coates's assets was a publicity sense not equaled by anyone on the society's staff except possibly Ditmars. Aquarium stories came to be a staple of New York City newspapers, especially the *Herald Tribune,* whose John O'Reilly found in Coates a kindred spirit.

For some weeks in 1933 a Coates story had a runaway success and caused a certain amount of embarrassment. It concerned the "discovery" of a mysterious bacteriophage—bacteria eater—in the water of tropical-fish tanks. While he was research associate, Breder had for some years been interested in the phenomenon of tanks that were kept clear and habitable by fishes even though fish food decayed in the water and large amounts of bacteria were formed. Something was destroying the bacteria, and in 1931 he announced the presence of a lytic agent—bacteriophage—but did not publish further reports.

The Aquarium's tankmen were well aware that something was going on in the waters into which they dipped their hands so many times a day; working with glass as they did, they often got small cuts and these healed rapidly and without infection. To them it was just something that happened, but Coates sensed its news value and mentioned it to a reporter. The exact chronology of the story's development is confused, but according to newspaper accounts the bacteriophage's wonder-working properties were realized after Coates cut his hand and the wound healed in three days while being exposed repeatedly to fish-tank water in the normal course of his work. The *Times* wrote an editorial about it:

Strange tales come from New York's Aquarium—recalling the healing springs of medieval days. People afflicted with skin diseases beg for permission to dip their hands into tanks teeming with tropical fish. Dr. Coates's own festered hand healed wonderfully when accidentally brought into contact with aquarium-water bacteriophages. Cases of skin diseases have been similarly cured. With commendable caution further treatments are denied. A mystery must first be solved.

The commendable caution did not come a moment too soon. Scores of sufferers from undetermined kinds of skin disease had flocked to the Aquarium—which took the precaution of having them sign a form saying that the treatments were at their own solicitation and risk, and that if the expected results did not materialize the Aquarium would not be held responsible. The *Times* quoted Coates as saying that nineteen volunteers had tried the water "and in all of them the results could be described as encouraging." One man whose hand was so afflicted that he could not close it had reported that he was now able to grasp a golf club for the first time in twenty years.

Foreseeing that it was going to be swamped by sufferers and preferring less empirical tests, the Aquarium turned its "patients" away and passed the problem to a couple of New York City hospitals for proper scientific investigation. The results were inconclusive and the bacteriophage story died out.

In 1932 Dr. Townsend attained his thirtieth anniversary as director of the Aquarium, and the executive committee presented him with a bronze figure, executed by James L. Clark, of the fur seal he had discovered in 1892. He was then seventy-three years old, but had no thought of retiring. His health was reasonably good; his "boys" were looking after the collection, and if their research did not interest him very much, he had plenty of writing of his own to do. Breder was made assistant director in 1933 and relieved him of the chore of preparing the Aquarium's copy for the *Annual Report,* so he had time to work on an account of the fur seal of the Galápagos Islands, get his major work on the distribution of whales ready for the printer, and keep an eye on the growth of his colonies of giant tortoises, which he was to tabulate in 1937 as his final piece of writing for the society.

Even in those Depression years the Aquarium had an air of prospering. Dr. Townsend some years before had designed an emblem for the Aquarium, two inward-facing seahorses, and they were embodied in a plaque created by Gertrude Boyle Kanno which was installed over the front door. In 1933 Gertrude Chase Ward started painting a series of murals of underwater scenes that eventually ringed the public space. The next year Albert M. Vida telephoned the Aquarium one afternoon and offered a mudskipper, an interesting little fish that can spend more time out of water than in it. He had brought it back from South Africa on the American–South African Line motor ship *City of New York,* on which he was radio officer. It was the first of many donations from the ship's "Sparks" over the years. It became routine for the Aquarium's staff to save castoff clothing, which Vida carried back to South Africa and traded for fish, reptiles, birds, and small mammals. The Zoological Society made him a life member.

The 1930s were the years in which Dr. Beebe was engaged in his marine studies, and it is rather surprising that he and Dr. Townsend did not clash openly, for they might have been expected to have differing theories and opinions about the inhabitants of the seas. They certainly did not agree about sharks; Dr. Beebe always derided sharks as a menace to man and Dr. Townsend thought otherwise as a result of his long voyages in the *Albatross* as a young man. They never publicly fought over that matter, however. The one time they were supposed to have disagreed (in Dr. Blair's opinion) was on the subject of vampire-bat bites, of all things. Dr. Townsend published in the *Bulletin* a short article quoting an unnamed naturalist who had said that bloodsucking bats could not bite a human being without awakening him, and that the wound does not continue to bleed. Dr. Townsend commented that both of these propositions were contrary to his own experience in Honduras.

Dr. Beebe came back in the next issue with:

It is astonishing, in these days of wide exploration and keen observation, that any naturalist, such as the one mentioned by Dr. Townsend, could have made such absurd statements about the bite of vampires. For a quarter of a century I have been interested in and frequently bitten by vampires, and thought that the general facts were known to everyone.

The facts as seen by Dr. Beebe were that in four cases out of five, the victim did not awaken, and that the wound always bled if the bat used its "scoop" method of biting, never if it used its "bore" method.

To Dr. Blair this was unseemly. Perhaps he was abnormally sensitive to controversy, having lived so close to so much of it during his years with Hornaday, but in any event when he had

In the 1930s Dr. Townsend and Dr. Beebe disagreed mildly in the pages of the Zoological Society's *Bulletin* about the bites of vampire bats. This is a vampire bat, but it isn't sustaining either side of the argument—it is merely lapping defibrinated blood from a glass dish.

occasion to edit Photographer Sanborn's *Annual Report* copy he struck out several sentences and wrote to Mr. Grant that "I do not want him to get into the habit of carrying on controversy in our publications, like the objectionable matter between Dr. Townsend and Mr. Beebe in the Bulletin."

Dr. Townsend had not cited his own "experiences in Honduras," but by implication he took very much the same position as Beebe. So what? one might ask. Where was the objectionable controversy? But Dr. Blair was alarmed and thenceforth neither Townsend nor Beebe mentioned each other in the society's publications.

By the mid-1930s Dr. Townsend was at last beginning to think about retirement. His quirks—and they were many, of a kind perhaps more common among the great individualists in his day than in this—had ripened and provided much innocent amusement for his staff. Among other things, he was a "string saver," with all the hoarding tricks that phrase implies. Dr. Breder wrote of him (personal communication) :

From his office windows he could see floating trash in the harbor. When something caught his fancy, often some large timber, he would send some of the boys out in the redoubtable *Seahorse* to "rescue" it. This would go into the "attic," a capacious annular space that surrounded the skylight over the large center pool in the public area. Usually it took four or five men with a block and fall to get it up there. It usually was very heavy because of being waterlogged.

Building inspectors did not look with favor on the storing of heavy junk over a public area and periodically ordered it removed, to Townsend's great distress. Dr. Nigrelli, who was a kind of superintendent for a time in the intervals of his work on the pathology of fishes, recalled one massive housecleaning job he supervised. He piled the salvaged flotsam and jetsam outside the Aquarium's door to await the trash truck and a little while later saw Dr. Townsend inspecting it, picking up a few choice pieces and carrying them back into the building.

The director normally wrote his replies to correspondents on the back of their original letters, and much of the time he wrote standing up. He had two desks, one a normal office desk and the other an old-fashioned bookkeeper's desk intended to be worked at from a high stool.

Dr. Breder commented on it:

The only place I can recall seeing such a piece is in one of the illustrations accompanying Dickens's "Christmas Carol" showing Bob Cratchit at his daily stint. He once told me he could not sit long in his standard swivel desk chair because of what he called his "bone ache." This he claimed he got from staying too long in the Pribilof Islands on the fur seal project.

There may have been another reason why he preferred standing to sitting. When Dr. Breder inherited the office, he found that the desk chair's seat was so sprung that the occupant sat on the ironwork beneath. It had been that way for years, but Townsend was not a man to discard a chair simply because it was broken.

He was devoted to the sea and to ships, and it was a common belief among the men working at the Aquarium that anyone could get a job if he could splice a rope. He was disappointed because Breder did not know how to put in an eye splice, and Breder finally had one of the men teach him how to do it, just so his handicap would not bother the director so much.

Dr. Townsend retired in 1937, the year Dr. Hornaday died. He was seventy-eight and had served the Zoological Society for thirty-five years, five more than Hornaday. Under the severest handicaps of an ancient and inappropriate building and always inadequate financial support, he had made the Aquarium one of the showplaces of New York.

439

Fairfield Osborn (he shortened his full name of Henry Fairfield Osborn, Jr., after the death of his father) began to make himself felt as a forward-driving force in the Zoological Society when he became secretary in 1935. He was then forty-eight years old and had been a member of the board of trustees since 1922. Immersed in business affairs in Wall Street, he had taken little part in society matters except to make some desultory attempts by promotional letters and pamphlets to halt the steady decline in membership. In 1935 the Zoological Society became his career.

It was a natural, inevitable step. He had, as it were, grown up in the inner councils of the Zoological Society; as a boy of eight he had his private zoo when the society was founded in 1895, as a young man he enjoyed the friendship of the men who were dragging the Zoological Park into being, and as the son of Professor Henry Fairfield Osborn a high place in the society was almost his by inheritance.

The time to take up his inheritance came suddenly. Professor Osborn and William White Niles died in 1935, Madison Grant and Dr. Hornaday in 1937. The men who had determined the course of the Zoological Society for forty years were no longer there; at the Zoological Park Dr. Blair and Manager Mitchell were approaching retirement age, and so was Dr. Townsend at the Aquarium. Within the next five years there would be no one in high command who had been formed by the past and felt an obligation to the old ways and traditions. The institutions could not stand still and the son of Professor Osborn was eager to give them his own positive imprint, just as his father had done in the beginning.

The Zoological Society has long been addicted to surveys and plans, some of them extremely elaborate and expensive, and the first of them was made soon after Secretary Osborn took office. He was not inclined to rush into massive reorganization, however obviously needed, but he persuaded the executive committee to begin looking ahead. In 1936, the last year of his presidency, even Grant admitted the need for change. In the *Annual Report* he wrote:

25

Fairfield Osborn Breaks the Old Patterns

It is becoming more and more apparent to your Committee that the time is now ripe for a forward movement in various important services which the Society is rendering to the public. At both the Zoological Park and the Aquarium numerous plans have been formulated which, when carried out, will materially increase the educational and scientific values of these institutions.

W. Redmond Cross succeeded Mr. Grant as president from 1937 to 1940, and he too was thinking of change—small, perhaps, but in the right direction: "There is much iron fence in the Park which is so weakened by rust resulting from insufficient painting in past years that it must be soon replaced, and in some cases this could be better done by building moats."

Unfortunately, there was no money to do much of anything. The surveys made by such professional planners as Leonard Outhwaite and The J. G. White Engineering Corporation all seemed to call for even more study—and money. Dr. Blair noted in 1938 that "The plans which have been made for modernizing many of our buildings in order to provide more agreeable accommodations for our living exhibits will be carried out just as soon as funds become available."

Funds were not going to be forthcoming from the Zoo's visitor services; that was certain. The Zoo depended heavily on that income for the increase of its collections and improvement of the buildings and grounds, but profits from soda water and refreshments, automobile parking, the restaurants, boating, postcards, and riding animals had been shrinking for several years. The Outhwaite Report had been critical of the facilities operation, and Manager Mitchell explained that "In view of the decreasing volume of business during the past eight years we have not felt justified in the expenditure of sufficient sums to replace obsolete equipment or make long-needed improvements to provide better service." Then he underlined the obvious: "During the entire period since the Park was opened the policy in respect to Park privileges has been conservative."

Fairfield Osborn, conservationist and President of the New York Zoological Society from 1940 to 1968.

441

Change was coming, it had to come, but in the meantime the Zoo and the Aquarium were still going concerns and by no means abandoned by the public; attendance at the Zoo held steady at well over 2,500,000 visitors a year and at the Aquarium always above 2,000,000. Services to visitors might be at low ebb, but the animal collections held up and were sometimes spectacular, as when three giant monitor lizards arrived at the park on May 12, 1934, from the island of Komodo in the Dutch East Indies, where they had been captured by Lawrence T. K. Griswold and William H. Harkness. Although one died almost immediately and another was sent to the National Zoological Park, the third giant—more than eight feet long—survived until October, and long lines of visitors filed past its compartment in the Reptile House to shudder at it. The Zoo had exhibited two Komodo monitors brought back by the Douglas Burden expedition in 1926, but they lived only forty days; the Griswold-Harkness specimens at least did a little better than that. Grace Davall, in 1926 a secretary in the Reptile Department office, recalls that one afternoon before the Burden expedition's monitors were put on exhibition, Head Keeper John Toomey came in to ask if it was all right to show them to "some guy" who said he had come a long way to see them. Curator Ditmars was absent, but Miss Davall thought it would be all right. Later Toomey dropped a card on her desk; the "guy" was Vice-President Charles G. Dawes. Miss Davall hurried out just in time to see him leaving, smoking his famous underslung pipe. Toomey, an ardent Democrat, was not impressed.

History repeated itself in 1935 when Captain Bob Bartlett sailed into New York on the schooner *Effie M. Morrissey* with another baby walrus for the Zoo, almost twenty-five years to the day since he had delivered his first one, the celebrated Flip, to Dr. Hornaday in 1910.*

---

* Flip served the Zoo well on an April morning in 1912. For days keepers had tried to entice Silver King, a large and savage polar bear, into a shifting cage preparatory to moving him to new quarters. Finally someone had the idea of using Flip as living bait. Flip, who would follow his favorite keeper anywhere, casually waddled up to the barred end of the shift cage, mounted a

Captain Bob had named his new walrus Pee-uk, which was as close as he could come to the Eskimo word for "good." Pee-uk was everything his name implied, affectionate and eager to be petted by his keeper, always interested in the visitors who watched him playing in his pool. There had been some tense days before he arrived, however.

Soon after he was captured off Greenland, Pee-uk went on a hunger strike against the milk which the crew supposed was the proper food for a 140-pound baby walrus. A week later, when the walrus was obviously in difficulty, the *Morrissey's* radio operator happened to be chatting with an amateur short-wave radio station in Belgium, and mentioned that they had an ailing walrus aboard but that he had been unable to get advice because he could no longer raise the amateur station in New Jersey which had agreed to transmit the ship's messages. The Belgian operator had a solution; he had a radio pal at another New Jersey station, W2GOX, operated by J. E. Preston at North Arlington. This emergency would give him something interesting to talk about, and he would ask Preston to make a call to the ship. A few hours later Preston came through, and Bartlett asked him to telephone Dr. Blair at the Bronx Zoo and tell him: "Have a baby walrus on board which I want to bring to you. The little devil won't drink milk and we can't get him to eat, only by force. Can you suggest method of feeding. Best wishes."

After another few hours W2GOX called the *Morrissey* with Dr. Blair's reply: "Feed walrus shredded codfish six times a day. Mash fish until semi-solid. Start with small quantity and if he does not vomit increase until he takes four or five pounds per day."

The only codfish aboard was Captain Bob's personal supply of salt-cured Newfoundland cod, but he donated it, the salt was soaked out, and Pee-uk thrived as a guest at the captain's

soapbox platform, and began to grunt and gurgle in typical walrus fashion. Silver King could not bear to be mocked by his natural prey; he lumbered headlong into the open end of the shift cage, the exit gate dropped behind him . . . and Flip waddled back to his pool in front of the Reptile House.

table until the *Morrissey* laid in fresh codfish on the Labrador coast several weeks later.

The Zoo was delighted to have a walrus again, but Dr. Blair was not receptive to another offered attraction—a genuine, guaranteed "hoop snake" [the Eastern mud snake, *Farancia abacura*]. With pawky humor he closed off some weeks of voluminous correspondence with a would-be supplier in Pennsylvania:

It would be very interesting to have a hoop snake for exhibition in the Zoological Park, but as you say they are "very dangerous on account of sudden death if struck by one," I should not wish to endanger anyone's life in attempting to capture a specimen. Under the circumstances I would not want to order one for the Zoological Park.

In his *Annual Report* for 1937 Dr. Blair noted the sense of "lamentable and irreparable loss" the staff felt at the death of Mr. Grant on May 30, of Dr. Hornaday on March 6,* and of Dr. Charles V. Noback on January 6. They were not

---

* Dr. Hornaday's own ties with the Zoological Park did not relax after his retirement. In 1928 the executive committee made him director emeritus (and in that "official capacity" he undertook to cheer up Sanborn, whom he met, in a discouraged mood, one night in Grand Central Terminal), the society planted a white oak in his honor in the center of the Zoo in 1932, and the Borough of the Bronx gave his name to Hornaday Place, a short street near the Zoo. Perhaps it would be well to forget—or mention only for curiosity value—that in 1929 he had proposed to Mr. Grant that the *Bulletin* run a page of Western humor and drawings in each issue. He had just written a foreword for a book called *Desert Mavericks*, published at her own expense by a woman in California, and she was prepared to submit similar material. Reading the book, he had "laughed until I forgot my sciatica." Mr. Grant found the idea "somewhat startling" and never recommended it to the *Bulletin*.

Not did Dr. Hornaday relax his lifelong fight for wildlife. His obituary in the *Times* noted that "One of Mr. Hornaday's last acts was to write to President Roosevelt a week ago, asking the President to use his influence to save the remnant of wild life in the United States. He received a reply from the President expressing sympathy because of his illness and assuring him that he would do everything possible to carry out his request."

Like another Roosevelt, T. R., Franklin D. was an admirer of Dr. Hornaday. It was at his suggestion that in 1939 the U.S. Board on Geographical Names gave the name Mount Hornaday to a 9,900-foot peak in Yellowstone National Park at the head of Plateau Creek. It is visible from the northeastern entrance road to the park.

Dr. Hornaday's funeral services were held in Stamford, Connecticut, and in accordance with his wishes the choir sang "Home on the Range."

trite words, for the director had always worked closely and harmoniously with Mr. Grant, his ties with Dr. Hornaday were affectionate and of long standing, and he had himself chosen Dr. Noback as veterinarian in 1926. But if he sensed that these losses were a prelude to radical change, no hint of it appears in his writings for the remainder of his directorship.

One change that was to have many consequences for the society was a shift in its relationship with the New York City Department of Parks. Traditionally the society was a self-contained entity, having as little as possible to do with the city and the Department of Parks except to beg for more maintenance funds each year, but under President Cross and Secretary Osborn an era of active cooperation began. In 1937 the society willingly agreed to cede a strip of land on the Zoological Park's eastern border to Parks Commissioner Robert Moses to make room for the southerly extension of the Bronx River Parkway. It would mean the loss of the decrepit nursery buildings, where since the early days flowers, shrubs and trees, root vegetables, and white mice had been propagated for use in the park, but the city undertook to spend $80,000 on new nursery buildings and also handed over the section of the old Boston Post Road between 180th Street and Pelham Parkway which bisected the Zoo just west of the Bronx River. Thereafter, and especially after Mr. Osborn became president of the society in 1940, the society worked in harmony with the dynamic Mr. Moses.

"Dynamic" is a term that must likewise be applied to a new member of the park's staff. Dr. Charles R. Schroeder, who succeeded Dr. Noback as veterinarian, came back to his native New York from the San Diego Zoo, where he had been veterinarian for the previous five years, and immediately started to modernize the Animal Hospital and reorganize its functions with energy and enthusiasm seldom seen around the Zoological Park since the earliest Hornaday years. He set up an elaborate record-keeping system, organized a group of distinguished medical men to do research in cooperation with the Animal Hospital, charmed the executive committee into providing money for modern laboratory equipment, and proclaimed his goal as the practice of preventive veterinary medicine, with all that implied in the way of quarantine, close supervision of exhibition quarters, better diet, early recognition of disease, and so on. The report from his department at the end of his first year was a ten-page manifesto impressively sprinkled with tables and graphs, and he aimed high:

At our present stage of observation of mortality statistics in zoological parks, we conclude that a majority of deaths are preventable. Perhaps at some future date we may reach that utopian state when we will be able to retire the exhibited animal after a satisfactory active life spent in the park.

If Schroeder never actually turned any superannuated animals out to pasture in the next two and a half years (he returned to the San Diego Zoo as veterinarian in the summer of 1939, and later became its director), he certainly rejuvenated the practice of veterinary medicine in the Bronx Zoo. One vignette of Schroeder is still remembered there. On Christmas Eve of 1938 a late-working member of the staff passed the Animal Hospital on his way home, saw a light in the rear of the building, and entered to wish Dr. Schroeder a Merry Christmas. He found the veterinarian just outside the back door, a white apparition in the wet snow that had been falling since noon. He had the carcass of a camel suspended from a crane and was doing an autopsy all alone and softly singing "Stille Nacht, Heilige Nacht."

Dr. Leonard J. Goss succeeded Dr. Schroeder, and during the next nineteen years he instituted cooperative research in animal disease, set up a series of summer veterinary fellowships, and devised procedures and techniques and a system of close supervision of the collection that made him known as the country's outstanding authority on the diseases of zoo animals. As the country moved deeper into the war years, food for the animals became a tender subject which the staff were instructed to avoid. Goss was able to state, however, that "on no occasion have the animals been given food needed for human beings." For that matter, the animals themselves did not always get what *they* needed. Several times, one day's supply of horse meat had to be stretched over three days.

Dr. Goss left in 1958 to become director of the Cleveland Zoological Park, and Dr. Charles P. Gandal, his assistant since 1952, took over the Animal Hospital. He resigned in 1969 to enter private veterinary practice, and since 1970 Dr. Emil P. Dolensek has been the Zoo's veterinarian. Nearly a score of specialist consultants are now attached to the staff of the Animal Hospital, and grants and special funds have made it the best-equipped animal-care center in any zoo in the United States.

More than one old way was changing as the 1930s advanced. The Zoological Society became less resolutely social, and although Secretary Osborn was having negative success in attracting new members—the membership showed a monotonous annual decline to the low point of 1,282 in 1942 and did not go above 2,000 until Donald T. Carlisle injected humor and imagination into the campaign in 1945—there was a noticeable trend toward informality. By 1939 the spring garden party at the Zoological Park no longer had a receiving line of trustees, members of the ladies' auxiliary, and the staff. In fact, the ladies' auxiliary did not survive the 1930s. It had been formed in 1908 by Mrs. Henry Fairfield Osborn as a group of trustee wives with the quadruple purpose of adding to the endowment fund, attracting visitors to the park through a spring reception and garden party, forming a junior auxiliary of children of (well-to-do) members, and of presenting animals to the park. It was a valuable adjunct in the early years when the society badly needed the support of the wealthy and socially prominent people of New York, but the times had changed and now a broader and more democratic base was needed. Even so, it was not until the beginning of the 1940s that the midwinter members' meeting, traditionally held at the Waldorf-Astoria Hotel, ceased to be what the irreverent called "the penguin show," with the guests mostly in evening dress and the curtains of the ballroom stage closed until they opened to reveal twenty or thirty trustees, all in formal dress, sitting in a straight row. It was undeniably a social occasion but was seldom wildly entertaining.

If informality awaited a keynote, Pandora provided it. Pandora was the Zoo's first giant panda, a thirty-four pound black-and-white clown from the bamboo forests of the border between China proper and Tibet. An expedition led by

There is no doubt about a giant panda's ability to draw a crowd. This special enclosure was built for the Bronx Zoo's giant pandas, with graduated viewing steps.

448

Dean Sage, Jr., a trustee of the Zoological Society, brought her to the Zoo on June 10, 1938, and she instantly captured every heart with her antics. Giant pandas are now so familiar —a newspaperman remarked that "The giant panda looks very much like a large version of the familiar stuffed panda toy"—that her impact on Zoo visitors hardly needs to be stressed.

Princeton (not very seriously) tried to borrow Pandora for a scene in the 1939 Triangle Club show, *Once Over Lightly*. Robert M. McClung, who was to become curator of mammals at the Bronx Zoo in 1954, was a zoo buff as well as one of the three student writers of the show, and in one of his sketches a giant panda named Alice unearthed the original deed to Manhattan Island at the Zoo. The Triangle Club's publicity man sent out a story begging the Bronx Zoo and the Chicago Zoological Park (the only ones that had giant pandas) to lend an animal for the scene. Chicago's director sent back a stuffy reply explaining that the legislative act creating the Chicago Zoological Park required all animals to remain on the premises for exhibition purposes. Dr. Blair, surprisingly, went along with the joke and replied: "There are but two live giant pandas in captivity in the world and your suggestion that our specimen might be available for your Princeton Triangle Club tour of the East and Middle West raised my blood pressure to an alarming degree. You may have the loan of my wife's crown jewels but the panda is out of the question." His response was widely quoted in newspapers and *Once Over Lightly* had a good advance press. McClung himself played the part of the panda in the show, dressed in a remodeled bearskin.

When the Zoological Society went to the World's Fair in 1939 and 1940, Pandora went with it; she was, indeed, the chief element in the success of the society's exhibition building in the amusement area. Although there had been a giant panda (Su-Lin) in the Chicago Zoological Park since 1937, many World's Fair visitors were unfamiliar with the animal

449

and one, at least, believed that Pandora was a fake. No real animal could be as comical as this one, he insisted. "That's a man dressed up in some kind of skin." A sign alongside Pandora's air-conditioned compartment called her "The Flying Baby Panda," referring to the fact that she had flown from the interior of China to the West Coast, and from San Francisco to New York. That caused confusion, too, and a young man was overheard explaining panda flight to a girl.

"They don't have real wings, like a bird," he said authoritatively. "It's more like a flying squirrel, you know. They climb trees and take long jumps, and kind of soar."

Pandora was pure fun, but the other exhibits in the society's building were lively and imaginatively presented—electric eels, brilliant birds and fishes, fawns, giant tortoises, the bathysphere, dioramas of the Hudson Gorge, habitat groups—and since they were all "home grown" by the Zoo and Aquarium and department of tropical research, they were invaluable training for the creative efforts the staffs were about to be called upon to make in the Zoo.

Although he did not become president of the society until after the retirement of President Cross in June of 1940, Mr. Osborn had already assumed the vigorous leadership he was to maintain for the next twenty-eight years. In the spring of 1940 he wrote in the *Bulletin:*

A healthy restlessness has come upon the officers and staff of the Society. We are working upon plans for the future development of the Zoological Park. Last year, studies and drawings for a new Aquarium were completed. We are convinced that new techniques can and should be employed in maintaining and exhibiting our unique collection of living animals.

Change came swiftly. At a special meeting of the board of trustees on June 25, 1940, Mr. Osborn was elected president and Laurance S. Rockefeller became chairman of the executive committee. The new president made an "Announcement to Members of the Zoological Society" in the July-August issue of the *Bulletin,* in which he told of the retirement of

450

Dr. Blair on May 1, the interim appointment of Manager H. R. Mitchell as acting director (he too retired, on June 30), and the appointment of Allyn R. Jennings as general director of the Zoo and the Aquarium, and of Harry Sweeny, Jr., as assistant general director. Jennings had been general superintendent of the park department since 1936 and Sweeny had been with the park department since 1934. Neither was an "animal man," but they went to work on the Zoo with a sledgehammer anyway.

President Osborn rightly judged that the time had come to break up the old patterns. As chairman of the society's World's Fair committee he had been impressed by the response of people to educational exhibits so attractively presented that their message was absorbed unconsciously—and by the sheer enjoyment animals could give dwellers in a great and impersonal city. He wanted to give the Zoo's visitors a feeling of participating in what had always seemed to him a glorious thing—the wonder of animal life.

Away went the forty-year-old prohibition of cameras in the Zoo. (Dr. Hornaday had been the most vociferous defender of the society's monopoly of photography in the Zoo, but he was staunchly supported by Madison Grant. In 1937 there was a new outburst of agitation for opening the Zoo to amateur photography, and even on his deathbed Mr. Grant opposed it. Fairfield Osborn, then secretary of the society, called on him during his last illness. He could speak only in a whisper, but his greeting was: "Are we winning?") The uneconomical and poorly managed Rocking Stone Restaurant was closed and soon torn down. Vending machines dispensed packaged animal food and visitors were exhorted to "Feed the Animals." Dr. Ditmars became honorary curator of mammals and was asked to set up a new Department of Insects, Dr. Leister taking over his supervision of the mammals. A borrowed World's Fair tractor train began running in the Zoo. Special show followed special show—animal art and animals on postage stamps in the Heads and Horns Museum, exhibitions of amateur and newspaper photographers' work, a summer show of domestic cattle, young chimpanzees and orangutans being put through a series of simple tricks on a rustic stage outside the Monkey House.

On July 22, 1940, bulldozers went to work in what had formerly been the Bison Range in the southeastern corner of the Zoo, creating the African Plains exhibit where antelopes and zebras, ostriches and cranes, would bring "a spot of Africa" to the Bronx. (Trustee Marshall Field provided—anonymously—some $120,000 to build it.) On Christmas Day "Lion Island" was officially opened—it was a rocky plateau separated from the rest of the African Plains by a wide and deep moat—when five young lions were given their liberty on it. One promptly jumped into the moat and furnished a good show for spectators until he returned to the island by means of a ramp that had been installed for just such a contingency. The completed African Plains was dedicated on May 1, 1941, with speeches by Mayor La Guardia, Commissioner Moses, Bronx Borough President James J. Lyons, British Minister Sir Gerald Campbell, and Lowell Thomas. Mme. Frieda Hempel sang the national anthem. It was a spring day of the best kind New York can offer, and the following Sunday, May 4, 84,727 people came to the Bronx Zoo to see the new wonder of Africa-in-the-Bronx. It was the largest single day's attendance in the history of the park, and the entire year of 1941 was a record breaker, with a total of 3,320,313 visitors. President Osborn's instinct for change had been abundantly justified.

Innovations continued. Three weeks after the dedication of the African Plains, a Children's Zoo was opened south of the Lion House. First suggested by Dr. Beebe and designed by the assistant general director, it was immediately popular and drew 5,457 visitors on the first Sunday after its opening.

In the broader context of the society, the most momentous event of 1941 was the closing of the Aquarium. President Osborn had been told early in the year that plans for construction of the Brooklyn-Battery Tunnel would require the

A typical scene on the Bronx Zoo's African Plains.

closing of Battery Park for a long period and therefore of the Aquarium. He saw it not as a setback to the society's program but as an opportunity to build a new Aquarium embodying exhibits and techniques impossible in the old building, and had preliminary plans ready and waiting. The war in Europe might delay construction for a while, but he was prepared to wait if he could eventually get what he wanted.

Announcement of the impending closing and demolition of the building caused an astonishing uproar from those who wanted to preserve what they considered one of the city's precious historic sites. Commissioner Moses waded into the fray with a statement intended to demolish his critics as thoroughly as the building:

It seems that when this news broke there was not a dry eye at the Knickerbocker Club, all the shades were drawn at the Century Association and heart-rending sobs issued from the dusty diggings of the American Scenic and Historic Preservation Society.

Castle Clinton, which was a post-Revolutionary affair, has no history worth writing about. Various personages landed there, but the same distinguished people landed at many other places in the course of their careers.

In the new plan for Battery Park the Aquarium is an ugly wart on the main axis leading straight to the Statue of Liberty—a vista of which future New Yorkers some day will justly be proud.

We get down now to the only question which can possibly remain. What can be done with the present Aquarium, née Castle Clinton and Castle Garden, when the fish have departed for the Bronx? There will, of course, be an ancient, fish-like smell about the place compounded of the gunpowder of Castle Clinton, the lavender and old lace of Jenny Lind, the sweat of immigrants, and the mackerel of the Aquarium. No doubt this smell can be imprisoned and preserved in an empty, sealed building accessible to those to whom the faint aroma of the past is the very breath of life.

The commissioner's reference to moving the fish to the Bronx echoed an early plan to build a new aquarium in some hitherto unused area in the Bronx Zoo. But Mayor La Guardia was firmly opposed to that solution; he wanted to

454

give other boroughs a share of the cultural institutions. In late summer the executive committee reached an agreement with Commissioner Moses whereby the city would compensate the Aquarium for the loss of its valuable collection, pay the salaries of a nucleus staff and attendants for an "interim" aquarium in the Zoo, and permit distribution of unwanted exhibits to other public aquariums.

It was no simple thing to dispose of some ten thousand fishes, mammals, reptiles, and birds. The sea lions, freshwater reptiles and amphibians, and the penguins could be absorbed easily enough by the Zoo. The Damon collection of freshwater and marine tropicals was too valuable to let go and had to be taken to the Zoo, along with young tarpon from the Aquarium's tarpon research station on Palmetto Island in Florida, the popular electric eels and the blind cave fish Dr. Breder had collected on an Aquarium expedition to La Cueva Chica in San Luis Potosí, Mexico, in the spring of 1940. Everything else had to be given away to the aquariums at Boston, Philadelphia, and Washington, liberated in ponds and streams near New York City, or returned to the ocean. A dump-bottomed scow hauled several hundred marine creatures to Sandy Hook in mid-September and they were "liberated"—no doubt, as a newspaper suggested, to their great disgust at having to forage for themselves instead of being fed by the Aquarium.

Confident that there would be no hitch in the plans, the staff worked all fall to install tanks, water systems, and pumps along the west inside wall of the Lion House, and during the winter Mrs. Helen Tee-Van and Walter Addison painted appropriate murals on two hundred feet of wall into which the tanks were set. Officially the Aquarium had closed on October 1, 1941; actually it was not until November 12 that the last of the staff and the living exhibits rolled northward to the Bronx. On that day the pumps ceased to hum, sigh, wheeze, and gurgle, the iron-studded doors were closed and locked, and the shell of the old building was left to the ghosts of Jenny Lind and the immigrants.

Director Breder found laboratory space in the American Museum of Natural History, and so did Dr. Myron Gordon, the research associate in genetics, whose work on the genetics of melanomas in fishes was among the first to demonstrate that some types of cancer are heritable. There was simply no room for them in the Lion House. Aquarist Coates and Pathologist Nigrelli occupied rooms at either end of the exhibit panel, and the Aquarium's photographer, Sam Dunton (who was soon to become the society's general staff photographer and who now shares the duties with William Meng) set up shop in the Zoo's photographic laboratory. Smoothly enough, the staff and a small group of tankmen began coping with the familiar problems of exhibiting fish in unsuitable quarters. They had all had plenty of practice, and in any event they were glad of the chance to experiment with new labeling methods and exhibition techniques against the day when a real aquarium would be built.

That day was not coming soon. There were months of agitation about a possible site and the Bronx, Queens, and Brooklyn were strong contenders but in the end the mayor and Commissioner Moses, with the willing acquiescence of the executive committee, decided on city-owned land in Seaside Park in Coney Island, Brooklyn. Even so, the war years and postwar financial problems intervened, and it was not until 1957 that the Aquarium again had a home of its own.

The outbreak of the war in Europe had found the Zoo fairly well stocked, especially in the bird department. Even the effects of America's entry in the war were not immediately apparent, for Charles Cordier, a Swiss animal collector, arrived from Colombia on December 9, 1941, with eighty birds of twenty-four species—twenty-one species being new to the Zoo's collection. The greatest problem as the war years wore on was acceptable food substitutes; at one time beef could be fed to the meat eaters, at another horse meat was more readily available. The Zoo switched back and forth, and at each change had to overcome the reluctance of the carnivores to accept a kind of meat that they had devoured with relish perhaps only months before. Sweet potatoes were substituted for bananas, which became unobtainable except as dehydrated flakes.

After the spring of 1941 the Zoo no longer had a giant panda; the celebrated Pandora died on May 13 of an obscure disease of the central nervous system, although the foremost medical men of New York examined her near the end and tried to save her. Pan, a young male giant panda, had been brought out of China by Trustee Sage in 1939, but he never thrived and was gone by 1940. Then came an opportunity to get two giant pandas all at once. Mme. Chiang Kai-shek and

John Tee-Van and one of the young giant pandas he brought to the Bronx Zoo from China in 1941.

457

her sister-in-law, Mme. H. H. Kung, offered a presumed pair (two females, it turned out) to United China Relief, and that organization promised them to the Bronx Zoo. The only catch was that somebody would have to go to China, pick them up, and deliver them to New York.

John Tee-Van was available. Fishes were his specialty (he was editor in chief of a monumental cooperative work on *Fishes of the Western North Atlantic*), but he could turn his hand to anything and so on September 25, 1941, he set off on a journey of 34,868 miles by air, sea, and train to Chengtu and back. He and the pandas were at sea when the Japanese struck at Pearl Harbor and there were several anxious days in the Zoological Park until he reported safe arrival in San Francisco. Tee-Van had even more anxious days, for he had difficulty in getting supplies of fresh bamboo to feed his babies on the way home. However, they were in excellent condition when they arrived and they adapted immediately to their new home, a roughly semicircular walled and moated enclosure near the center of the Zoo.

Tee-Van kept a detailed diary of his journey and in it he referred to his charges merely by their sex symbols, ♂ for the supposed male, ♀ for the female. Eventually a commercial typist was engaged to transcribe the diary and when she questioned the meaning of the symbols, Tee-Van explained that ♂ was "the arrow of Mars" and ♀ "the mirror of Venus." Inevitably one day's entry came out in the transcript: "Mars was constipated, but Venus passed a good stool."

General Director Jennings had been engaged on July 16, 1940, for a term of three years, but on December 10, 1941, the executive committee made a "mutual termination" agreement with him, to take effect one month later. The assistant general director was given charge of construction and maintenance for a few months more and then he also was released. The first phase of President Osborn's modernization plan was over and the Zoological Society was ready to move in new directions.

When America entered the war, the Bronx Zoo did not form a home guard as Dr. Hornaday had done when he mobilized the keepers during World War I, but it did take note of the public uneasiness when air-raid sirens sounded practice alerts. The big cats were locked in their inner sleeping compartments at night and the elephants were chained. Some visitors asked what would happen if the Reptile House were bombed and the venomous snakes escaped, but they were easily reassured; it was midwinter, and no snake could survive very long.

For a few weeks keepers and maintenance men took turns sleeping in the Zoo, and in the spring of 1942 keeper teams with (unloaded) rifles impressed visitors with their readiness for any catastrophe when they practiced stalking escaped animals, running from cover to cover and crouching behind boulders. It made a nice break in the routine and got good newspaper picture coverage.

California was understandably nervous about bombing immediately after Pearl Harbor, and the California Academy of Sciences sent ten of its research flock of Galápagos finches to the Bronx Zoo for safekeeping. Charles Darwin had made those drab little birds famous for their contribution to his evolutionary theory after his visit to the Galápagos Islands in H.M.S. *Beagle* in 1835, and their deposit was an interesting dividend of the war, for the Bronx Zoo had never before exhibited the species.

Fears of direct attack on both coasts soon faded away, and apart from gasoline restrictions and rainy weather which cut Zoo attendance by almost exactly a million visitors in 1942 as compared with 1941, operations were still normal. Before the war was over, eleven trustees and sixty-two employees of the Zoo and the Aquarium had gone into the armed forces (two of the latter lost their lives), and for a couple of years young or elderly new employees had to be trained. The Zoo was not standing still, however; it even opened a novel new exhibit in July of 1942, the Farm-in-the-Zoo.

26

The Zoological Society's Role Expands

The strict Hornaday policy of exhibiting only wild animals had been broken only once before, in 1941 when a brief exhibit of domestic breeds of beef and dairy cattle persuaded President Osborn that there were many city people to whom "a Jersey cow is just about as strange and rare as a Malay seladang." Fortunately, before the war put a stop to almost all building, the city had erected a cluster of Normandy-type buildings in the northeastern corner of the Zoo, to replace the old nursery complex, and here was a great opportunity to bring the country into the city. Under the direction of Veterinarian Leonard J. Goss, himself a farm boy from Ohio, the Farm-in-the-Zoo was stocked with cows, horses, sheep, pigs, chickens, ducks, geese, goats, pigeons, and guinea fowl. Former State Senator Seabury C. Mastick contributed a hay wagon, and for a couple of summers thousands of New Yorkers took their first hayride, from the center of the Zoo to the farm, behind a team of plodding farm horses. Briefly the hay wagon had to mingle with automobile traffic on the

A hay wagon made round trips between the Zoo and the Farm-in-the-Zoo.

way to and from the farm, and it is a measure of the different pace of those days and this that the journeys were made without accident. A hay wagon on Pelham Parkway today would be on a suicide mission.

Authentic farmers may have scratched their chins when they contemplated the sturdy brick buildings with their slate roofs and copper gutters, but city dwellers loved the farm and as many as three thousand a day strolled or rode the hay wagon down the farm lane, perched on the "Sitting Fence" and chewed straws plucked from a supply thoughtfully provided by Dr. Goss. They may even have learned something about farm life, for Dr. Goss posted a series of advertisements at intervals along the farm lane. Reminiscent of the Burma Shave signs that were dotted beside rural highways in those days, the signs read:

> AT THE ZOO YOU SAW A GNU.
> AT THE FARM YOU'LL SEE A EWE.
> IF YOU THINK WE CANNOT SPELL
> YOU CAN JUST GO STRAIGHT TO

And then, after an especially long interval, the clincher:

> THE FARM GATE AND BUY
> A FARM DICTIONARY
> PRICE: 2 CENTS

The "Farm Dictionary," a sixteen-page booklet two and a quarter by three inches, was written by Veterinarian Goss and Curator Bridges and sold many thousands of copies before the Farm-in-the-Zoo was closed in 1963. Even H. L. Mencken ordered a copy—which was of course sent gratis as a courtesy between lexicographers.

The 1940s were a time of yeasty turmoil. At the beginning of 1942 the name of the society's magazine was changed from the *Bulletin* to *Animal Kingdom,* as being more expressive of the wider scope the society was assuming. (Dr. Beebe won a ten dollar prize in staff competition by suggesting the new name.) Jean Delacour, the great French aviculturist, joined

461

the staff as technical adviser on the many changes that were bound to come when the war ended. Wanting to immerse himself in Zoo affairs, President Osborn did not appoint a director but gave general operational control to John Tee-Van as executive secretary. After so many years in which there had been almost no staff changes and the familiar personalities of earlier years seemed almost immortal, there were abrupt breaks and a recasting of responsibilities. Dr. Ditmars died on May 12, 1942, the first death in the original Hornaday staff of 1899, and Dr. Townsend on January 28, 1944. Tee-Van added the reptile department to his other duties temporarily. At the end of 1943, Dr. Breder left the Aquarium to become chairman of the department of fishes at the American Museum of Natural History, and Christopher W. Coates succeeded him as curator and aquarist. Brayton Eddy, a Rhode Island entomologist, came in 1945 to set up a department of insects and soon thereafter to take on the reptile department. Gordon Cuyler became assistant to the executive secretary in 1947 and later, as membership chairman, greatly increased membership.

In the long view, perhaps the most important staff change was the elevation of Curator of Birds Lee S. Crandall to the general curatorship of the Zoo at the beginning of 1943, a title he held until his retirement on July 31, 1952. He knew birds better than any other zoo man in the world, and if he had never actually been in charge of a great collection of mammals, he had behind him three decades of close observation of the Bronx Zoo's mammals and a retentive mind stocked with management problems and practices in zoos everywhere; visiting zoo men naturally gravitated to him to talk about their animals—and after they had left, the significant residue of the conversations was always neatly penciled on an index card and filed away.

His memory was phenomenal. Writing in the 1960s of an echidna in the Philadelphia Zoo, he noted: "I saw this echidna first in 1909, a feat accomplished by inserting my

General Curator Emeritus Lee S. Crandall.

462

index finger through the cage bars and gently lifting the lid of the sleeping box. I repeated the act for the last time in 1951, the only noticeable change during the forty-two-year interval being the slightly increased resistance of the rusting lid hinges."

There was an even more astonishing example of his memory for individual animals. At the age of seventy-nine, turning through a new book on waterfowl, he questioned the color of a bird's eye in the artist's drawing. He had seen the species only once, on a visit to the London Zoo in the 1930s, but reference to the original technical description showed that his recollection was right and the artist was wrong.

Gentle and kindly by nature ("Oh, he's a very good sort of fellow, really," was a typical Crandall contribution to a conversation in which some erring zoo man was being dissected), he had the respect and affection of the men in all departments; after the high-handed and arbitrary administration of the 1940–41 interlude, it was good to have an experienced zoo man in charge again.

Crandall was very much in charge for the remainder of his active years and he had a quiet "behind the scenes" role for the rest of his life. During the ten years he spent writing *The Management of Wild Mammals in Captivity* and seeing it through the press (it was published in 1964), his knowledge and experience were continually called upon by the staff of the Zoo and some days he spent almost as much time in talking and advising as in writing. Eventually he moved his precious files of thousands of index cards into the old department of tropical research laboratory, carefully updating records of births and longevities, diets and new developments in the zoo world, and passing on a lifetime of zoo experience to a stream of visitors. He was, in fact, "active" in the Zoo five days a week until within six months of his death on June 25, 1969.

In the mid-1940s Dr. Beebe sent his research associate, Jocelyn Crane, to South America to "shop for a jungle" that

could be a new home for the department of tropical research. She went with two requirements in mind: the new station must be in a tropical rain forest, and there must be no undue prevalence of ticks; she calculated that if four research workers had to spend thirty minutes a day extracting ticks from their arms and legs, they would lose fourteen hours of scientific work a week. She found just what she wanted at Rancho Grande in Venezuela, a rambling concrete structure at an altitude of three thousand feet only three hours by automobile from Caracas, and with three hundred square miles of jungle around it. Rancho Grande had been built as a rural hideaway for Dictator-President Juan Vicente Gómez of Venezuela but was never completed before his death in 1935, although it had enough usable windswept rooms to

In 1949 the department of tropical research found a permanent home at Simla in the northern range of Trinidad. Dr. William Beebe is in the foreground with members of his staff.

464

make an ideal laboratory. It was the department's only tropical home until it found an even more ideal—and this time permanent—station at Simla in the northern range of Trinidad in 1949.

President Osborn had for several years been seeking a new role and purpose for the Zoological Society. It was far from moribund—the membership rolls were now climbing year after year—but it was not exerting the influence he felt it should have. As he settled into the presidency he began to shape the society into a force that would have been inconceivable to his father, preoccupied as he was with building a great zoo and lifting a handicapped aquarium by its bootstraps. The society of Professor Osborn and Madison Grant (and they *were* the society, as far as its policies were concerned) looked upon the well-being of the Zoological Park and the Aquarium as its chief concern. It did not disregard its charter obligations to what might broadly be called conservation, research, and education, but they certainly did not come first. Thus the Osborn and Grant names were inextricably linked with the Zoo and the Aquarium.

By the time Fairfield Osborn assumed the presidency, the Zoo and the Aquarium had long been prospering institutions. True, there was no limit to the innovations that might be made at the Zoo, and eventually a new aquarium must be built. But to concentrate on those well-worn and obvious paths was too easy. Fairfield Osborn had no intention of merely following in his father's footsteps; *his* Zoological Society would pursue the other goals so long kept in second place. "Protection of wild animal life" was a charter prescription and in earlier years the society had passed innumerable resolutions and granted generous funds to aid wildlife, but now the crises were more severe, and it was time to reorient the society. It would take up the old obligation of conservation and expand it to include forests and soils and water resources—the whole environment that made possible the survival not only of wild animals but also of human life.

465

In 1945 he declared himself. In an editorial in *Animal Kingdom* entitled "We Must Reverse the Tide," he wrote:

The tide is still running out. Forests are being depleted, soils and water resources are deteriorating. This is true not only in the United States but in many other parts of the world. If these primary natural resources continue to disappear, the gains that have been made in wildlife preservation will be forfeited. As for man himself, his world will become to an increasing degree a world of want.

Conservation is no longer a "side show"—it is the "big tent" of human existence.

It was a theme he was to speak about and write about until the end of his life, and which made him one of the most influential conservationists of his generation.

For a time it seemed that he would be able to demonstrate the interrelationship of forests, soils, waters, and wildlife in one neat package in the Bronx Zoo. He conceived the idea of a twelve-acre Conservation Exhibit in the sparsely wooded northeast corner of the Zoo, just west of the Farm-in-the-Zoo, and presented the idea so persuasively that the New York State Conservation Commission pledged $275,000 to build it. On July 25, 1949, Governor Thomas E. Dewey plunged a shovel into previous loosened soil in a ground-breaking ceremony and made an earnest speech in which he promised to see the venture through to completion. His promise was captured on magnetic tape in one of the Zoo's first experiments with electronic recording. The tape is still around somewhere, but the Conservation Exhibit was never built; funds were scarce and commissions and governors change.

Mass education in conservation was the new twist Fairfield Osborn wanted to give the society's old goal of direct protection of wildlife. The Conservation Exhibit failed of realization for reasons that had nothing to do with its value as a concept—and it *was* a good one—but he was triumphantly successful in a much more ambitious undertaking. That was the creation of the Jackson Hole Wildlife Park at Moran,

466

Wyoming, which was dedicated on July 19, 1948. Laurance S. Rockefeller, at that time a vice-president of the society, was closely associated with him in working out the philosophy and the management structure; indeed, the Wildlife Park lands were given by John D. Rockefeller, Jr., and by Laurance through Jackson Hole Preserve, Inc., and in its sponsorship the society was associated with the preserve and the Wyoming Game and Fish Commission.

It was a new kind of park. It had plenty of scenery, for a sweep of the eye could take in the sinuous Snake River, the shimmering waters of Jackson Lake, and the snow-capped Grand Tetons in the background, but that was incidental; the purpose of the Jackson Hole Wildlife Park was to show Americans, under natural conditions, the wild animals they were being asked to preserve. The Wildlife Park sprawled over fifteen hundred acres just east of Moran, and four hundred acres were fenced so visitors and even passing motorists could see herds of moose and mule deer, bison and pronghorn antelopes, or white-tailed deer now restored to the valley from which they had vanished before 1924. Coyotes howled, and black bears and an occasional grizzly could be seen ambling in the distance. Here in a vast reality was the kind of natural setting for big animals Dr. Hornaday had dreamed of re-creating in the Bronx Zoo so long ago.

It was more than a splendid showcase for wildlife. Outside its fence were eleven hundred acres of forest, stream, and slough where field naturalists could investigate the biology of the Rocky Mountain region, and with a little effort they could pursue their studies in another thirty-three thousand acres of untouched wilderness which John D. Rockefeller, Jr., had presented as a nucleus of the Grand Teton National Park. From the beginning the society administered and financed a biological research station in the Park. In 1953, however, it made an arrangement whereby the University of Wyoming took over the administration. The Wildlife Park was absorbed by the Grand Teton National Park, but the research station is still operating, with some support from the Zoological Society.

President Osborn had turned to writing as a means of conservation education during the war, when he edited *The Pacific World,* a volume distributed to servicemen in the Pacific theater and designed to tell them about the wildlife they would see. It was hoped that it would stop much random killing "just for target practice." Immediately thereafter he started gathering material for his most important book, *Our Plundered Planet,* a well-documented warning of what was happening to the natural resources of the world. (Dr. Beebe suggested the title.) The book came out in March and the National Education Association called it "the most important book of 1948."

By this time he was so vividly aware of the rapid increase of the world's population and the constant decline of the resource base that he felt the Zoological Society should become involved. Money was available; the society had received some $2.5 million from the estate of Mrs. Mary Clark Thompson after the death of her residuary legatee, Clark Williams. Both Mrs. Thompson and Mr. Williams had been interested in conservation, and some of the income from the bequest could appropriately be used to plan a long-range conservation program. Under the name of the Conservation Division of the New York Zoological Society, a small staff was gathered: George E. Brewer, Jr., Samuel H. Ordway, Jr., A. William Smith, and Robert G. Snider. They were charged with forming an affiliate that would have its own headquarters, staff, and financing, and would arouse public awareness of the threat to the whole environment in the United States. The result was the Conservation Foundation, chartered on March 30, 1948. Its purpose was:

To promote conservation of the earth's life-supporting resources—animal life, forests and other plant life, water resources and productive soils—and to advance, improve and encourage knowledge and understanding of such resources, their natural dis-

468

tribution and wise use and their essential relationship to each other and to the sustenance and enrichment of life.

Osborn became president of "Confound," as it was familiarly called by the society's staff, and he made it a significant force in the ever-growing conservation movement. Its staff turned out books, films, and special studies on such a variety of problems as underground water resources, pesticides, fire ants, flood control, population pressures in Jamaica, and Alaska's resources, and it shared with the Zoological Society the financing of studies of the bighorn sheep and the smaller mammals of the Western plains. Grants and special funds flowed into it, and its productivity was prodigious. It became, indeed, so well established and so specialized that in 1965 it moved out from the sheltering wing of the Zoological Society and took up a life of its own in Washington under the presidency of Russell E. Train.

Writing, speaking before conservation organizations, and presiding over the Conservation Foundation by no means absorbed all of the president's energy; he was deeply involved in planning for the future of the Zoological Park and the Aquarium. His frequent visits to the Zoo must have been, in fact, a kind of relaxation. In the mid-1960s the Gotham Chapter of the National Secretaries' Association chose him as President of the Year and its magazine said of him:

If there's one thing sacred in the Bronx Zoo, it's the tradition that bi-weekly staff meetings begin *exactly* at 11 o'clock. The President of the New York Zoological Society himself sits in the padded chair behind the big desk, and he expects everybody to be on hand when the clock strikes.

Except maybe Fairfield Osborn. He's the President.

Most of the time he gets to the meeting before anybody else, but now and then 11 o'clock comes and goes—and no President. He's over at the Lion House or the Sea Lion Pool or some other animal exhibit, with a clump of schoolchildren around him, and he's telling them about the animals. He loves it, and so do they.

Fortnightly staff meetings were an Osborn innovation and

an indicator of the new atmosphere of camaraderie and encouragement of initiative that came in with him. He was on a first-name basis with his staff, he was called "Fair" by everyone, and when he was in the Zoo his office door was always open. Ideas flowed freely at staff meetings and one of the happiest led to the creation of Question House in 1945. Staffed by the education department, it was a small and inviting room in the center of the Zoo where visitors could wander in, ask any question about animals, and get (generally) an immediate answer. If perhaps a third of the 10,000 to 15,000 questions asked every year were directional (Where is the nearest "bathroom"?) most of the rest were serious and thoughtful and sometimes called for all the expertise of the college-trained staff. Question House remained in operation until 1965, when the small staff of Curator Herbert J. Knobloch was too hard-pressed with other duties to keep it open. It is now the Safari Shop, a bookstore and souvenir center.

Knobloch, who retired in 1974, started as an attendant in the animal hospital in 1937. In 1948 he took charge of the education department and was curator of education from 1965 to 1972. Specializing in tape and film work, he was curator of audio-visual services and the Zoo's community affairs officer when he retired. James W. Waddick became associate curator in charge of education in 1973.

The Aquarium had settled comfortably into its restricted quarters in the Lion House. Although the staff fretted and wondered when, if ever, it would have a home of its own, it professed faith that someday the society and the city would be able to build a new aquarium at Coney Island. Plans, blueprints, and specifications, and the terms of a contract with the city, had been under study for many months when a telephone call to President Osborn on October 19, 1950, informed him that the Board of Estimate had ratified the contract and was willing to put up its half of the $6.5 million the building was estimated to cost. Rejoicing was premature, however; by

470

December the society's executive committee decided that this was not a good time to raise its share, $3.25 million, and in any event shortages of manpower and materials resulting from the Korean War would make construction impossible. Construction did not start until 1954 and it was three more years before the Lion House was emptied of Aquarium staff and its fishes.

The Lion House years were not wasted. They were a time to experiment with new types of pumps and filters, tanks, and labeling, to refine techniques that could be put to use later. Curator Coates pressed ahead with his studies of the electric eel, which had—it was revealed after the war—contributed to chemical-warfare research. Nobody talked about it at the time, but during the last two years of the war some two hundred electric eels lived briefly in twenty-two great wooden tanks in a hideaway laboratory in the basement of the Lion House until they were sacrificed so that their electric tissue could be used to measure the activity of a deadly gas, diisopropyl fluorophosphate, which destroys nerve activity.

Coates's interest in electric eels dated from his earliest years at the Aquarium. He knew that such great scientists as Galen, Henry Cavendish, Sir Humphrey Davy, and Michael Faraday had worked with electric fishes, and that Faraday had demonstrated that externally the eel's current flows from head to tail. But how powerful was the current? Coates tried running it through voltmeters, ammeters, and galvanometers —all of which either burned out or failed to register anything. The eels were giving off plenty of electricity, all right; many times he was knocked off his feet by discharges. But no combination of wiring would cause them to light up an ordinary electric bulb.

One Saturday afternoon in 1935 he happened to be testing a new kind of neon lamp, a small bulb of the kind now commonly used as a night light. Tired and getting careless, he made a connection that gave him a heavy shock, and as he was falling backward he saw the neon pip light up with an orange glow. He traced the wiring, found that the pip was in a simple direct circuit with the eel, and then he got repeated glows every time he stimulated the eel with a rubber-gloved hand. The explanation of earlier failures was simple: the lamps and electrical apparatus he had been using have a "warm-up lag," and the eel's discharge was too brief to actuate them; the neon pip's reaction time is instantaneous.

Since it takes at least eighty volts to excite a pip, he now had a crude way to measure an electric eel's voltage, and enough general knowledge of eel behavior to interest a specialist. He found one in Dr. Richard T. Cox, at that time professor of physics at New York University, and he contributed a portable cathode-ray oscilloscope to the experiments. With such sensitive instruments Coates and Cox recorded voltages up to 550 and found that an average discharge in water amounted to some forty watts. Dr. Cox was so enthusiastic about the studies that in 1937 he led an expedition to the mouth of the Amazon to study the electric eel at home, taking with him an "eel caller" devised in the Aquarium. It was a device to discharge five hundred volts in a thousandth of a second, a discharge much like the eel's natural one, and it was intended to lure electric eels into the vicinity of the electrodes where they could be captured. It worked.

As an outcome of his pioneering work, Coates hooked up a circuit connected with the tank of an electric eel on exhibition in the Lion House. At intervals during the day a rubber-gloved tankman stroked the eel until it discharged its five hundred volts, thereby causing a series of neon pips to spell out ELECTRIC EEL, a loudspeaker to crackle with static, and wavy blue lines to flicker across the face of an oscilloscope. It was a popular show, and it still is at the new Aquarium.

(The electric eel was supposed to have other esoteric properties besides producing real electricity. In 1909 a Pennsylvania man had written to the Aquarium: "Can you tell me where I can get an electric eel to be used for medicine to cure my brother of drinking. It must be put into a vial with

Christopher W. Coates of the Aquarium at work on some of his pioneering experiments with the electric eel.

the other ingredients until dead, then taken out and the medicine given.'')

The exhibition electric eel was not quite so popular with the Lion House keepers. Its tank happened to be directly opposite the compartment occupied by Dacca, the Zoo's prolific tiger mother. (She had thirty-two cubs between 1948 and 1959.) During several of her pregnancies she took a fierce dislike to the eel, watching it intently and clawing at the wire front of her cage when it rose to the surface to take a gulp of air. For the sake of Dacca's peace of mind, the eel tank was kept covered during the critical weeks.

The Bronx Zoo had its hundred-millionth visitor in 1947.

473

In those pre-computer days, mere telephone lines were kept open between the publications office and all entrance gates, incoming visitors were counted, and when the total reached 99,999,999, all gates were closed except the Fordham entrance. It was chosen because it was through that gate the official party had entered the Zoological Park on the opening day of November 8, 1899. Newspaper photographers gathered at the gate and at 12:55 P.M. on Friday, May 9, a sailor and his girl approached the gate, hesitated, then turned away. A moment later a fifteen-year-old boy entered. He was the hundred-millionth, and as a gate prize the society gave him a life membership. The only unfortunate thing about it was that he got his picture in the newspapers, and he was not anxious for publicity. On that particular day he was playing hooky from a nearby high school.

As Osborn's first decade as president neared its end, he could take satisfaction in much visible accomplishment. A special house for penguins was under construction, and for the first time the birds that "fly under water" could be viewed from below water level, swimming and swirling in a huge glass-faced pool. Better still the Zoo could now exhibit king and emperor penguins and several other delicate species in refrigerated and filtered air, free from the aspergillosis organisms that made it impossible to exhibit them in the open. A Great Apes House was being built, at long last giving the Zoo's gorillas and chimpanzees, orangutans and gibbons, the spacious and healthy home Madison Grant had wanted for them in 1914. It was formally opened on October 12, 1950, the first major exhibition building since the Zebra House was completed in 1914. Grant had suggested a solarium where the anthropoids could be exposed to the beneficial rays of the sun; President Osborn's architects went him one better and designed a series of open-air play yards where the apes could take the sun and at the same time be completely visible to visitors. The only flaw in their design was an outer moat filled with water three to six feet deep—

Even before the death of her companion, Makoko, the female gorilla Oka had a cordial relationship with her keeper, Michael Quinn.

474

an effective barrier, it was believed, to keep the animals from outflanking the high walls between the yards. Experience in other zoos had shown that chimpanzees, orangs, and gibbons do not swim, and it seemed logical that gorillas did not differ from their relatives. That an ape might accidentally fall into the water and, unable to swim, be in serious trouble seemed unlikely. The anthropoids are sure-footed; they wouldn't have that kind of accident.

On May 13, 1951, in sight of a huge spring Sunday crowd, Makoko fell in. He was a magnificent male gorilla which,

Makoko, an adult male gorilla, fell into the deep moat around his enclosure on May 13, 1951, and drowned.

with his female companion Oka, had come to the Zoo in 1941 —the first really healthy gorillas the Zoo had ever had.

He simply slipped while running along a twelve-inch ledge separating the play yard from the moat, and fell into six feet of water. Just on the off-chance of such an accident, General Curator Crandall had had a series of cables strung just below the water surface, and everyone expected Makoko to seize a cable and pull himself out. He didn't.

George Scott, the head keeper of birds, happened to be passing and—himself barely able to swim—dived in, found Makoko's hand, and tugged him to the surface. Another keeper, trained in first aid, gave emergency resuscitation treatment. The Police Department sent an emergency crew with oxygen bottles. It was no use. Makoko had simply drowned, without making the slightest effort to save himself.

His death was a sad blow to the Zoo's hope of being the first to breed gorillas in captivity, for an autopsy showed that Makoko was sexually mature. It did settle one point: gorillas cannot—or will not—swim. The play yards were immediately modified by extending the dividing walls to the perimeter, and the water area was regraded to make a gradual slope to a depth of only a few inches. Not all zoo men learned the lesson that an abrupt drop into deep water is the danger; in recent years four other gorillas in this country and Europe have drowned when they fell in over their heads.

In the 1950s President Osborn worked with an ever-shifting staff. The dedication that had kept a Beebe, a Crandall, a Ditmars, and a Tee-Van at their desks for forty or fifty years, despite inadequate pay, could no longer be taken for granted. Robert M. McClung, with a new master's degree in zoology from Cornell, became assistant in the mammal and bird departments in 1948, in anticipation of taking over on the retirement of General Curator Crandall in 1952. He resigned as curator of mammals and birds in 1955 to begin a highly successful career as a writer of animal books for young people, and thereafter mammals and birds had separate departmental heads. Dr. Richard H. Manville, who followed him in charge of mammals, left in 1957 to join the U.S. Fish and Wildlife Service in Washington. His successor, Dr. John L. George, also left, in 1958, for governmental work. Joseph A. Davis, Jr., thereupon became associate curator of mammals, leaving in 1966 but returning in 1967 as scientific assistant to the director. In 1965 Hugh B. House joined the mammal department as an assistant, becoming its curator in 1968. James G. Doherty, who was engaged as a student mammalogist in 1967, became associate curator in 1973.

Grace Davall, who had come to the Zoo as a secretary in 1923, linked both mammals and birds as assistant curator from 1952 until her retirement in 1970. Under William G. Conway's curatorship of the bird department, Joseph Bell moved from the keeper staff (which he had joined in 1942) into management as an assistant curator in 1963, associate curator in 1966 and full curator in 1973. Donald F. Bruning became a student ornithologist in 1967 and was made associate curator in 1973.

Brayton Eddy, curator of reptiles from 1945, died in 1950. Dependable Executive Secretary Tee-Van assumed his department until Dr. James A. Oliver was engaged in 1951. In 1958 Dr. Oliver became director of the Zoological Park but left the following year to become director of the American Museum of Natural History; he returned to the society in 1970 as director of the Aquarium. Dr. Herndon G. Dowling succeeded him in the reptile curatorship until 1966. Since 1967 Dr. F. Wayne King has been curator of herpetology. Under the Zoo's trainee system, John L. Behler was named herpetologist in 1970 and became assistant curator in 1973.

Dr. Oliver was the first professional herpetologist the Zoo had ever had; Dr. Ditmars had been a self-trained youth when Dr. Hornaday hired him in 1899, and Brayton Eddy was primarily an entomologist. Dr. Oliver undertook a complete remaking of the interior of the Reptile House, and when it was reopened in 1954 it was called "the most beautiful Reptile House in the world."

It is likely that there are some people to whom no reptile

Dr. James A. Oliver, curator of reptiles, then director of the Zoological Park and now director of the Aquarium, manipulating a snake during the filming of *The Locomotion of Snakes*. Staff Photographer Sam Dunton is using the camera.

and no reptile exhibit seem beautiful. This aesthetically stunted minority was in Dr. Oliver's mind when he designed the building; colored tile and subtly varying cage backgrounds, weathered driftwood, and natural and artificial planting pleased the eye; the reptiles were there, but they were not emphasized as they would have been in barren cages. There was even soft mood music to soothe the timid.

New Yorkers apparently are not repulsed by reptiles. Over the years many spot checks have shown that the Reptile House is the most popular single building in the Zoo. On the weekend after the debut of "the most beautiful Reptile House in the world," the Zoo had 116,164 visitors. It was perhaps twice the normal number, and traffic in the Reptile House was a serious problem.

The Zoological Society had extended a helping hand to European zoos after the First World War by sending shipments of animals; President Osborn sent a different kind of aid after World War II. In the summer of 1951 Jocelyn Crane attended the Ninth International Congress of Entomology in Europe, and returned home with enthusiastic reports of important new work being done in biology; as a postscript she added that it was a pity so many of her scientific colleagues in Europe were struggling with shortages of apparatus, experimental animals, and even recent scientific publications.

In 1949 President Truman had announced this country's "Point 4" program of technological aid to underdeveloped countries, and President Osborn conceived the idea of the Zoological Society setting up its own Point 4 program. He announced it at the midwinter members' meeting in January of 1952, to loud applause from the audience. The trustees approved a $5,000 "laboratory table" fund and letters went to twenty-two laboratories in twelve countries throughout Western Europe. Requests flooded back for living specimens of North American fishes and turtles and lizards, weasels for studies of their sexual biology, wire netting for confining experimental geese, an ultraviolet spectrophotometer, special thermometers, recent scientific books and journals, rare chemicals—a whole catalogue of research material and equipment difficult to buy in Europe but easily obtainable in America. The European biologists considerately limited their requests to essentials, and all of them were fulfilled within the first year. Some could be filled without cost. In 1934 Curator of Publications Bridges, then in Trinidad as a reporter for the *Sun,* disregarded instructions and collected a sackful of marine toads *(Bufo marinus)*. When he was finally persuaded that nobody wanted them, he turned them loose on the lawn of the beach house where he was staying. His host stepped on one in the dark and next morning Bridges was persuaded even more peremptorily to refill his sack and lug them back to the pond where he had caught them. In 1952 he was again in Trinidad, but this time the Max Planck Institute in Westphalia *wanted* marine toads, and Bridges joyfully supplied them.

As the 1950s progressed, the Zoological Society scaled down its grandiose plans for a $6.5-million aquarium; it was possible, with modification of the plans, to build in stages, and the minimum stage one might cost as little as $1.5 million. With generous gifts from Laurance S. Rockefeller and other trustees and foundations, the society's half of the money was raised and ground was broken at Seaside Park in Coney Island on the afternoon of Sunday, October 24, 1954. President Osborn ruefully commented in an *Annual Report* that "Getting an aquarium into successful operation is about as complicated and experimental as trying out an atomic submarine." After seemingly endless delays, the building was turned over to the Aquarium staff on September 27, 1956, and Curator Christopher W. Coates moved his office from the Lion House to a cramped basement room cluttered with blueprints, books, sections of experimental pipe, historic prints of Castle Garden, a chipped plaster bust of Dr. Townsend—a magpie accumulation perhaps intended to give him some feeling of continuity with the old aquarium that was now being reborn. For company, besides workmen and the tank-men creating decorative habitats for coral-reef fishes, he had two personable young walruses. Fishes and most of the marine mammals and birds would have to wait for warmer weather in the following spring. The last of the Lion House collections were trucked to Coney Island on March 13, 1957, and the Aquarium was opened to the public on June 6. Since then there have been minor alterations of the stage one design, the addition of outlying exhibits for marine mammals and penguins and additional tanks for fishes and invertebrates. But the fully envisioned $10-million structure (the original estimate of $6.5 million was revised) is still in the future and is not likely to be realized unchanged.

The emphasis on scientific work that Professor Osborn had urged on Dr. Townsend in 1902 now became even more central to the Aquarium's operations, vastly expanded as they were. Laboratories had come to be essential to aquarium management, and well-equipped rooms were provided in one end of the basement. Into them somehow was fitted a new branch of the society's scientific work under Dr. Ross F. Nigrelli: the department of marine biochemistry and ecology.

In the early 1950s pathologist Nigrelli had evolved a theory that there were antibiotics and other biological poisons among marine plants and animals. He and several research associates isolated from the common sea cucumber (*Actinopyga agassizi*) a substance they called Holothurin, a digitalis-like steroid saponin that appeared to have some anticancerous, anti-blood-coagulating, and heart-stimulating properties. The work was so promising that it justified creation of the new department.

Dr. Osborn (New York University gave him an honorary Sc.D. in 1955, the same year in which John Tee-Van received an Sc.D. from Rensselaer Polytechnic Institute. Eventually Dr. Osborn acquired six honorary degrees) took care that the scientific side of the society's work was constantly stressed in its publications; research, especially the kind that might

Dr. Ross F. Nigrelli was director of the Osborn Laboratories of Marine Sciences from 1967 until his retirement in 1973.

480

have a bearing on human well-being, he considered a powerful magnet to attract funds from individuals and foundations. Dr. Nigrelli's investigations of Holothurin and other "drugs from the sea" and Dr. Myron Gordon's studies of melanomas in fishes had his strong support. It was an appropriate recognition of his interest that the building which now houses the many phases of the Aquarium's research should be named the Osborn Laboratories of Marine Sciences. OLMS had indeed been a magnet for generous funds, $350,-000 from the National Science Foundation alone. Major contributions were made by the Health Research Council of the City of New York, the Rockefeller Foundation, the New York Foundation, the John A. Hartford Foundation, National Institutes of Health, the Atomic Energy Commission, the Scaife Family Fund, and some others.

Since 1973 **Dr. George D. Ruggieri, S.J., has been director of the Osborn Laboratories.**

The Osborn Laboratories, immediately adjacent to the Aquarium, were dedicated on September 28, 1967, and Dr. Nigrelli became their first director. Unhappily, Dr. Gordon did not live to see the spacious quarters allotted to the Genetics Laboratory; he died of a heart attack in 1959. Dr. Klaus D. Kallman succeeded him and is still carrying on the genetics studies that Dr. Gordon had pursued for 25 years. Dr. Nigrelli retired in 1973 into the working status of senior scientist and Dr. George D. Ruggieri, S.J., became director of the laboratories.

There were changes in the directorship of the Aquarium itself. Coates retired in 1964, to be succeeded by Paul Montreuil until 1966, when Dr. Nigrelli took over for the next four years. In 1970 Dr. Oliver became director of the Aquarium and began to expand its exhibits and its educational activities.

The Bronx Zoo's large collections had always seemed to Osborn an untapped source of studies in animal behavior, but as the years of his presidency rolled on he was having very little success in steering the curators into research; they were simply too preoccupied with the management of their animals. The solution was to offer research fellowships to competent graduate students; and a beginning was made in the summer of 1947. The Rockefeller Foundation made a grant for the planning of a long-term program in the Zoo, Dr. C. Ray Carpenter of Pennsylvania State College was engaged as coordinator, and research teams went to work on such problems as visual discrimination in primates, elephants, and Galápagos tortoises, color preferences in hummingbirds, the social behavior of gorillas, "handedness" in primates, and the like. The studies were so productive that in 1952 they were placed on a year-round basis under Dr. John V. Quaranta of Manhattan College, and he and various associates continued them for two years.

William Beebe retired—officially—in 1952, but his interest in tropical research was unflagging and for most of his ten remaining years before his death in 1962 he continued working at the Simla Station in Trinidad. (It was renamed the William Beebe Station for Tropical Research in 1963.) Dr. and Mrs. Tee-Van visited there in 1960 and Dr. Beebe commented in his departmental report:

They disproved a dictum of evolution, that it can never reverse itself, for within forty-eight hours they had changed from "houseguests" or "visitors," reverted to type and became valuable staff members. Soon Dr. Tee-Van was wading waist deep in the Arima River seining Guppies, cichlids and Armored Catfish. Then, while he wielded calipers and slide-rule, Mrs. Tee-Van sketched every species, just as in earlier days of the Department of Tropical Research.

Jocelyn Crane became director of the station in 1963 and continued her own work on spiders, butterflies, and fiddler crabs—the latter an interest that had absorbed her since 1941 when, in Panama to recover from an illness, she began watching fiddlers on the beach. She published the first of her many papers on them two years later and in 1970 sent to press the systematic section of a 400,000-word monograph on fiddler crabs she had studied all over the New and Old World tropics. The William Beebe Station for Tropical

Research was closed in 1971 after changing research emphasis and environmental and budgetary problems made its continued operation impractical.

North American wildlife was a special concern of the society, and in the course of a few years it supported or sponsored a great variety of field studies. Dr. Frank C. Craighead, Jr., produced *A Biological and Economic Evaluation of Coyote Predation* in 1951, and Dr. Carl Koford published *Prairie Dogs, Whitefaces and Blue Grama* in 1954. In the 1960s the society backed work by David Wingate, among the first to report the effect of chlorinated hydrocarbons on bird reproduction; by Dr. Tom Cade and his collaborators on the ecology and population status of birds of prey; surveys by Victor Cahalane of grizzlies, wolves, and mountain lions; by David Mech and others on the timber wolf; by Maurice Hornocker on the mountain lion . . .

A feeling was developing among conservationists that African fauna was approaching a critical time. An accurate report on the situation was needed, and in 1956 the Zoological Society sent a young naturalist, George Treichel, on an eighteen-thousand-mile tour of African wildlife parks and reserves. He was expected to write a handbook on the status of their animals, but midway in his tour he was stricken with poliomyelitis. Eventually he recovered, but the handbook project had to be abandoned.

African projects did not cease because of this setback. The society gave support or sponsorship to ecological studies by George Petrides in East Africa; Fraser Darling's work on the Mara Plains in Kenya and in the Sudan; experiments by Drs. Lock and Harthoorn on techniques to immobilize big animals; wildebeest and Serengeti-Mara studies by Lee Talbot; investigations of elephant ecology and behavior by Irvin Buss and Iain Douglas-Hamilton; John Goddard's work on the black rhinoceros in the Tsavo National Park in Kenya; development of radio-tracking techniques on the African plains.

These were long-range projects, and the stream of African

483

game administrators constantly flowing to New York for conferences or seeking financial help made President Osborn aware of the pressing, immediate needs. In 1959 he pledged the society's direct support for endangered African wildlife:

It seems to the New York Zoological Society that the time has come when action need, and can, be no longer delayed. As a Zoological Society with a long history of efforts on behalf of wildlife, we feel that we *must* take active responsibility in behalf of Africa's wildlife heritage—*our* heritage, the whole civilized world's heritage.

Through appeals to the society's membership he raised some $25,000 in 1959, and during the next three years, with new private contributions and the assistance of Hornaday's Permanent Wild Life Protection Fund of which the society was trustee, $150,000 was spent in Tanzania, Kenya, and Uganda for drilling wells and creating water holes in drought-stricken areas, training native wardens, on light airplanes for control of poaching, for studies of herd movements and the like. Between 1965 and 1968, $175,000 was expended from the society's African Wild Life Fund and help was given in creating new wildlife parks under government auspices or enlarging existing ones—specifically the Serengeti, Ruaha, and Tarangire Parks in Tanzania. The society's concern for the African fauna has not abated; in 1973 it and the government of Kenya signed an agreement whereby the society will help to provide water and forage for cattle of the Masai tribes now using a vital swamp area inside the 150-square-mile Amboseli National Park, thus removing a threat to the survival of the wild animals of Amboseli.

On still other fronts, the society was behind Robert Bowman's research in the Galápagos Islands, ecological and behavioral studies of the vicuña in Peru, of the Komodo monitor, South American crocodilians, Formosan pheasants, Japanese cranes, and the population ecology of flamingos.

Publications and conferences are a necessary supplement to field studies, and the Zoological Society has had its hand in a good share of them. It oversaw the development of the National Institutes of Health project out of which came Ernest P. Walker's *Mammals of the World,* contributed to the publication of the first *Red Book* of the International Union for the Conservation of Nature, supported the first conferences in 1965 and 1968 on the Availability of Primates for Medical Research, helped initiate and support the first International Conference on the Biology of Whales in 1971, and saw to it that scores of conservation-related papers were published or distributed.

An extraordinarily successful form of research was developed in 1965 with the creation of the Institute for Research in Animal Behavior as a joint effort of the Zoological Society and the Rockefeller University. The old Farm-in-the-Zoo buildings were converted to laboratories; Dr. Donald R. Griffin, who had been professor of zoology at Harvard, was made director, and a team of energetic young research men went to work. Dr. Richard L. Penney analyzed the sun navigation of Adelie penguins and other birds in a huge "air dome" that must have puzzled motorists who could see it from the Bronx River Parkway. Dr. George Schaller studied the Serengeti lions, Dr. Roger S. Payne the precise directional hearing of owls and, later, the behavior of whales. Dr. Thomas T. Struhsaker embarked on studies of the social behavior and ecology of primates in Africa, Dr. Ferdinand Nottebohm of the development of song in the European chaffinch. These and many other studies ran their course, and in 1972 IRAB was discontinued, with some members of the original research team continuing in a new Center for Field Biology and Conservation.

Nothing of significance can be made of the fact that the center has taken over William Beebe's old Department of Tropical Research Laboratory as its home in the Zoo; it was simply the only suitable building available. But surely there is a kind of inspired rightness about it. William Beebe created the tradition of field studies by the society. For many years while he was working in tropical forests or on tropical seas, the laboratory was the fixed base from which he left and to which he returned. Now a new generation of field men has inherited it. If there is a difference, it is that Dr. Beebe and his staff used to roast in summer, while the new men have air conditioning.

The society, the Zoological Park, and the Aquarium all took on larger dimensions during President Osborn's regime. Perhaps he considered his creation of the Conservation Foundation and his efforts to awaken the public to the threats to the ecology as his most important work; certainly those aspects were stressed in tributes to him at the time of his death on September 16, 1969. But deeply and basically he was interested in animals and he left a mark on the Zoological Park and the Aquarium as distinctive and personal as any made by his distinguished predecessors, his father and Madison Grant.

Fidel Castro came to New York in 1959, and after an out-of-towner's tour of the high spots he passed judgment: "The Bronx Zoo is the best thing New York City has."

What does one say in reply to extravagant praise of one's possessions? An embarrassed "Thank you, *we* like it," is one of the standard responses, and essentially what President Osborn said in an editorial in *Animal Kingdom:* "Although not competent to judge his views on other matters, we can easily be persuaded to go along with him on his opinion as to the place the Zoo holds in the affections of the public."

The Bronx Zoo *was* high in public esteem; it put on a good show. With 2,939 animals, of 1,078 species, on exhibition, it was approaching its all-time record for sheer variety of animals and constantly spicing the collection with great and well-publicized rarities. In the Reptile House you could see the only tuatara in the United States; true, it was a twenty-inch creature that might be mistaken for an ordinary iguana at a glance, but the sign explained that it was actually a rhynchocephalian from New Zealand, the only living representative of an order that flourished a hundred million years ago. At the Antelope House you could see (and if the wind was from the right direction, catch a whiff of) a takin from Burma, a distant relative of the musk-ox and the first one seen alive in the New World. (Her name, incidentally, was Gracie, for Grace Davall, who had spent weeks finding transport on an airline that did not object to the musky takin odor.) With patience you might catch a glimpse at the Pheasant Aviary of two survivors of the seven Congo peacocks that Charles and Emy Cordier had brought back from what was then the Belgian Congo in 1949—special prizes among the many "first time exhibited alive" birds in the collection.

The Cordiers deserve more than the brief mention that has been made of them, for Charles Cordier has the reputation of being the best bird collector in the world and to him the Bronx Zoo owes many of its greatest rarities. As a boy he had run away from his home in Switzerland to pursue a dream of

27

A Future Without Limits

sometime "seeing a free, wild monkey in a jungle tree," and at the outbreak of World War II he was in South America on a collecting mission for Jean Delacour's aviaries at Clères in northern France. The war stranded him and the Zoological Society thereupon engaged him as its own collector. He "worked" South America for the society during most of the war years and afterward made two other South American trips for it. From his journeys into remote rain forests and mountain valleys came such spectacular "first time" birds as the scarlet cock of the rock, the bare-necked umbrella bird, the long-wattled umbrella bird, and the three-wattled bellbird. From a valley eleven thousand feet high on the eastern slope of the Andes he brought back the extraordinary sword-billed hummingbird, which uses its five-inch beak to probe for nectar in angel's trumpet blossoms (*Datura* sp.).

In 1947 the society sent the Cordiers to the Congo with a long list of desiderata, with the little-known and never-ex-

488

hibited Congo peacock (*Afropavo congensis* Chapin) first among the birds. It expected them home in 1948, but unfortunately Charles broke his leg while two days' deep in the forest in Congo peacock territory; he had to be carried out lashed to a pole on the shoulders of his native helpers, and spent months in the hospital at Stanleyville. But he and his wife (who maintained the base camps while he was in the bush) did come home in June of 1949 in a DC-3 so crammed with mammals, birds, reptiles, and even fishes that Head Keeper of Birds George Scott had to be flown to Stanleyville in advance to help with the feeding, watering, and cleaning en route. No airplane had ever before carried such a varied and valuable cargo of wild animals. Among them were a mountain gorilla, an okapi, a giant pangolin, tree pangolins, pottos, spectral galagos, Emin's giant rats, Torday's elephant shrew, a Cameroon finfoot, a black guineafowl, and, of course, the Congo peacocks—no less than 252 specimens of eighty-two species or subspecies. The Cordiers collected sporadically for the Zoological Society in later years and finally settled in Bolivia as a base from which to supply South American animals to zoos, mostly those in Europe.

Zoos have traditionally depended upon professional dealers for most of their animals, but the do-it-yourself collecting expedition is an old New York Zoological Society tradition. It may be said to have started with ex-Mammal Curator J. Alden Loring's trip to Alaska in 1901 (he brought back two bears), continued through a Beebe-Crandall collecting visit to British Guiana in 1909 and Lee S. Crandall's collections in Costa Rica in 1914, and culminated in the Crandall expedition to the interior of New Guinea in 1928 to bring out birds of paradise.

Head Keeper of Birds Scott repeated the bird-of-paradise quest in 1953, but with a considerable difference. It had taken Crandall seven months by boat and afoot, and he had to capture the birds and carry them out of the mountains; a quarter of a century later it was incomparably easier. Scott traveled

489

by air, and after eleven weeks he came home with seventeen birds of paradise of ten forms as the Bronx Zoo's share of a presentation made to the zoos of San Diego, St. Louis, Chicago, and New York by Sir Edward Hallstrom, chairman of the Taronga Zoological Park Trust in Sydney, from birds in his aviaries at Nondugl Station in the Wahgi Valley of New Guinea. It should be added that while travel was more agreeable on the second bird-of-paradise expedition, the work and worry of bringing the birds home in superb condition were just the same.

In the economics of the zoo business, individual zoos have not ordinarily sent staff-led expeditions to collect, say, elephants, zebras, antelopes, or almost any of the large mammals; the international trade in wild animals was so well organized that it was cheaper to buy them from dealers or arrange a trade or purchase from other zoos. Now that situation is changing, and the time may be coming when a consortium of zoos will do their own collecting and transporting. Birds are (or were) * an exception that the Bronx Zoo has frequently made—partly because its exhibits have an insatiable need for specimens and perhaps because birdmen *like* to get into the field, study exotic birds in the wild, and capture them. If the goal is some great rarity, it is likely to be a great deal cheaper to mount your own collecting expedition than to commission a dealer to make a special, limited trip.

In the unrestricted days of 1959 and 1960, Curator of Birds (later Director) William G. Conway made two historic collections. The first was his capture of the mossy-throated bellbird of Trinidad and northern South America. Georges Cuvier had described the bird in 1817 but not much more was known about it until 1954, when Dr. Beebe recorded its nest for

* Bird collecting outside the United States ended in August of 1972 when an outbreak of Newcastle disease that affects poultry caused the government to place an embargo on all wild-bird importations except of the Anseriformes, Galliformes, and Columbiformes, for which quarantine facilities exist in this country. Presumably it will eventually be lifted, perhaps after importing zoos have built their own quarantine stations, but until that happens even once-common birds are going to be in short supply.

the first time; it was a flimsy platform of interlocking Y-shaped twigs, and Beebe found it in the northern mountain range not far from his Trinidad laboratory. Except for one feature, the bird is not particularly distinguished: in size somewhere between a robin and a pigeon, it has a light silvery-gray body, black wings, and a cap of chestnut feathers. What makes it extraordinary is the long, dense, bushy, black beard of fleshy strings depending from its throat, giving it the alternative name of bearded bellbird.

It had never been exhibited alive, and when Conway planned a collecting trip to Trinidad in 1959, naturally it was high on his list. He could reasonably hope to snare tanagers, honeycreepers, hummingbirds, manakins, maybe woodpeckers and jacamars, but the mossy-throat—well, as he noted in *Animal Kingdom,* it was hard not to be superstitious about a bird that had eluded capture for 142 years.

He found it almost too easy to collect the lesser prizes. In a single day's "set" of his mist nets—black silk or nylon nets with a three-quarter-inch mesh—he took almost forty manakins and hummingbirds. But Trinidad was having an abnormally dry spell, and for the first two weeks no bellbirds were calling. Then the rains came in thunderous downpours, the rain forest steamed, and everywhere across the valleys bellbirds were clamoring: an explosive "kokk" followed by "kong kong kong kong kong kong kong."

Conway trailed them through the forest, spied on them with binoculars, noted their flight paths, and at last was ready to stretch his nets from trees and extensible aluminum poles. By this time he knew the routine path of one bird so thoroughly that he was confident of catching it. Then a female came along and the male began an ardent pursuit, but always over, under, or between the almost invisible nets. Two hours went by and then at 1:30 in the afternoon the male shot between the two lower nets and disappeared. But:

We scarcely had time to feel disappointment when a fearful growling came from our highest tree net. We charged down the mountainside, brushing through razor grass as though it was eider down and leaping over fallen trees with a speed that would have done credit to a herd of Impala. Hanging neatly, but far from quietly, directly in the center of the net was the bellbird.

Geoffrey Hellman wrote an account of Conway's exploit for *The New Yorker* and summed it up thus: "Moustached Curator Catches Bearded Bellbird after Hair-raising Chase." It was the Bronx Zoo's most important bird acquisition of 1959, and as far as the Bird Department knows it is still the only mossy-throated bellbird that has been exhibited alive. It lived in the collection for seven years, three months, and two days.

Capture of the mossy-throat was a mere holiday diversion in comparison with Conway's expedition to Laguna Colorada in the Bolivian Andes the following year. Again his quarry was a bird that had never been exhibited alive, James's flamingo.

Conway and Bates Littlehales, a photographer for the *National Geographic Magazine,* left New York in January of 1960, and in Chile they were joined by Luis Peña, the Chilean entomologist who had guided the American ornithologist-artist Roger Tory Peterson to Laguna Colorada in 1958. A truck carried them through a mountain pass at 16,000 feet, and by the end of the month they were camped on the shores of the lake at 14,800 feet. It was exactly as Peterson and Peña had said it would be: a vast shallow lake ringed by mountain peaks, the waters stained blood red by minute algae on which the flamingos fed. And there were thousands of the birds feeding and bathing and nesting far offshore.

It was obvious why so little was known about James's flamingo. Laguna Colorada was remote, Indians in the neighborhood were sometimes hostile, the air was thin and cold. Temperatures rose to seventy degrees Fahrenheit at noon and burned the skin without warming; at night they fell to five degrees and even the salty lake was covered with a skim of ice.

William Conway, now director of the Zoological Park, with one of the James's flamingos he captured on a cold, blood-red lake at 14,800 feet in the Chilean Andes in 1960.

In New York the most practicable device for catching flamingos had seemed to be a cannon net trap which worked well for capturing ducks. Three small tubular "cannons" would be implanted on the edge of an area the flamingos habitually used, and from a blind a charge could be set off to fling a net over the birds in a high arc. The trouble was that

493

the cannon net trap did not work in Laguna Colorada. Violent winds swept a "wind tide" across the shallow waters from west to east, submerged the bases of the cannons, and weighted the nets with salt crystals. It was brutally hard work to flounder through icy mud to retrieve the nets, wash them, and reset the cannons. Then the local Indians showed up to raid the flamingo nests for fresh eggs, and the birds avoided the area where the cannon net was poised.

Burned by the sun, always half frozen, with some of the helpers coming down with altitude sickness and sheer exhaustion, the expedition seemed liable to fail. Conway resorted to his last trick. Just on the off-chance that primitive measures might be necessary, he had brought along a spool of stout fishing line. He knotted hundreds of slip nooses and anchored them underwater where the flamingos were accustomed to bathe in the freshwater streams that flowed into the lake.

They worked. Before breakfast next morning two James's flamingos had stepped into the loops, entangled their feet, fluttered and complained for a minute or two, and then simply stood there.

Conway returned with twenty James's flamingos and a few weeks later Peña captured two Andean flamingos and shipped them to the Zoo. For the first time all six forms of flamingo were on exhibition: James's, Andean, greater, lesser, West Indian, and Chilean.

The Aquarium also had its collecting triumphs. It had long been accustomed to catching many of its own fishes, either by sending the wellboat *Seahorse* to Sandy Hook or other local waters, or making more colorful collections among Bermuda's coral reefs. Now it wanted white whales, or belugas, for its new and very large oceanic tank. One had been captured in Alaska in 1958 and another in Quebec in 1960, but both survived only briefly; the Aquarium now believed that better capture and transportation techniques would ensure success.

At certain seasons the white whales come to feed in the

shallows at the mouth of the Kvichak River, just above the point where the Aleutian chain drifts off from Alaska. While they are in the shallows and on a falling tide, they are vulnerable; they can be herded by a speeding motorboat, the immature gray calves can be isolated, and with luck and brawn they can be seized and wrestled into a boat and cushioned on foam-rubber mattresses. That is the theory—and, as it turned out, the practice—of white-whale catching.

In August Associate Curator Carleton Ray, Senior Tankman Charlie Young, and *National Geographic Magazine* photographer W. Robert Moore flew to Alaska and were joined by Seward Johnson, a motion-picture photographer.

A tankman at the New York Aquarium feeding a beluga underwater.

Strenuous but discouraging days followed; either no whales came to feed, wind caused a chop that made it impossible to follow movements under the water, or calves simply refused to be herded into the shallows. But a day did come when the boats were returning from Dead Man's Flats and an 800-pound female was spotted. In half an hour she had been maneuvered into three feet of water and one throw of the net entangled her. Somehow the men rolled and hoisted her onto the mattresses aboard a low skiff and reached the beach—only to find that the tide was at dead low and the whale would have to be dragged three hundred yards uphill across sand and mud to the holding pool. It took more than an hour to move her there on an improvised skid; when the motion picture of the operation was shown at the Zoological Society's members' meeting the following January, the audience cheered when the skid finally reached the top of the beach.

In the end Ray and Young and their local helpers captured two 800-pound belugas, Charlie and Bertha II, and a 450-pound youngster they named Alex. They even caught a bonus beluga, a 1,600-pound female, but all their combined strength could not slide her into the skiff and she was released.

Twenty-three days after they left New York, Ray and Young flew back with their three white whales bedded down in a converted B-17. All three adapted readily to the oceanic tank and as they matured lost their calfhood gray and became snow-white monsters. Other white whales were brought from the mouth of the St. Lawrence in later years to replace losses, and the oceanic tank has continued to be the Aquarium's most impressive exhibit.

Despite new buildings and the renovation of old ones, expeditions and rarities, the abundant testimony to the popularity of the Zoo and Aquarium, the Zoological Society's broader interests—that is to say, President Fairfield Osborn's —were dominant in the 1950s. He was making the society a truly international force. From it, money and encouragement and assistance in setting up basic wildlife research flowed to many parts of the world; a map insert in *Animal Kingdom* picked out in red thirty spots in North and South America, Spitsbergen, Finland, Europe, Africa, and remote Burma to illustrate "The Far-flung Interests of the Zoological Society."

The Zoo was, by contrast, self-centered. Under the directorship of John Tee-Van and in 1958–59 of Dr. James A. Oliver, it was busily and happily absorbed in being and proclaiming itself the biggest zoo in the world—or at any rate, when the San Diego Zoo occasionally surpassed it in the number of species on exhibition, the *best* zoo in the world. It was nevertheless losing some of its parochialism. For many years the Bronx Zoo had the reputation of keeping aloof from other zoos, participating minimally in the affairs of the American Association of Zoological Parks and Aquariums (which Hornaday had looked upon as an association of inexperienced upstarts) and, while always cordial to other zoo men who came to marvel at the wonders of the Bronx, not much interested in going visiting itself. Naturally outgoing, President Osborn was responsible for the beginning of the change, but it picked up momentum after 1956 when William G. Conway came to run the Bird Department.

His was just one of several staff changes announced by Dr. Osborn at the end of the year. John Tee-Van assumed the title of general director of the Zoo and the Aquarium, which he was to retain until he retired in 1962; Christopher W. Coates became director of the Aquarium; and Charles B. Driscoll stepped into the superintendency of construction and maintenance after the death of Quentin Melling Schubert, who had been responsible for $2,000,000 worth of new building and renovation during the past twelve years.

Conway was a mere stripling of not quite 27 when he was recruited from the St. Louis Zoo, where he had been curator of birds. He was the youngest man on the staff but was thoroughly experienced in keeping birds under zoo conditions. Most importantly, he was a professional zoo man. New departmental heads there had been aplenty in late years, but they came with academic, field, or research backgrounds which they had to learn to apply to zoo exhibition. Conway had grown up, as it were, in a big and important zoo. He was self-confident to the point of brashness and he brought with him a salutary freshness of viewpoint. President Osborn saw in him a young man with imagination and energy to match his own, and in four years advanced him to associate director and then, in 1961, to director.

The director's section of the printed *Annual Report* distributed to members of the society was usually a bland recapitulation of the highlights of the year. Conway took occasion in his first *Annual Report* to expound a philosophy and new goals:

Zoo visitors should have the opportunity to learn something about each animal's environment through natural habitat displays, to explore the mystery of wild animal behavior, to be informed by special displays of nocturnal species, of burrowers, of strange animal courtship rites and of curious creatures of camouflage. Techniques are available to reach these goals.

The justification for removing an animal from the wild for exhibition must be judged by the value of that exhibition in terms of human education and appreciation, and the suitability and effectiveness of the exhibition in terms of each wild creature's contentment and continued welfare. Man's works and his proliferating population impose new stresses upon the wild species, and those stresses demand greater responsibilities from the zoological parks of the world.

For more than half a century *Annual Reports* had been the dusty repositories of the hopes of directors and curators; some had become realities, of course, but after how many years of delay and setback and compromise! Conway asked for a department of exhibition capable of preparing illustrative and educational material and natural habitat displays.

He wanted an exhibit of nocturnal animals to be called the World of Darkness, a radical new kind of bird building to be called the World of Birds, more realistic polar-bear and Alaskan brown-bear exhibits, a South American continental exhibit. In less than ten years he got them all, and more.

The first year of his directorship was not without stress. Three years before, in the spring of 1958, Zoo employees had stopped work twice, for one day and then four days, to demonstrate against the city. There were prolonged labor negotiations, but eventually they broke down. On Easter Sunday of 1961, Zoo and Aquarium employees, members of Local 1501 of the American Federation of State, County and Municipal Employees, AFL-CIO, walked out and this time remained on strike for nearly seven weeks, during which the Zoo and the Aquarium were closed. Wages, hours, and working conditions were little involved, since they are prescribed by the city, but the major stumbling block was the society's demand for a guarantee of safety for the animals. It refused to recognize a "zoo union" which would not give such a guarantee. The animal keepers did perform their routine duties of feeding, watering, and cleaning during the strike, but it was not until May 9 that the union gave up on its principle of total withdrawal of the keepers, and what was called "the zoo world's Magna Charta" in labor relations was signed. It provided that:

The parties agree that the animals in the custody of the Society at the Bronx Zoo and at the Aquarium should never be deprived of food, drink, sustenance or needed care by reason of any controversy or disagreement which might arise between the parties.

The Union agrees that it will at all times oppose concerted action to deprive said animals of food, drink, sustenance, or needed care.

This agreement to continue in full force and effect as long as the Union claims to represent or seeks to represent, any of the employees of the Society.

The Zoo rapidly returned to normal after the strike ended,

although attendance had fallen off by some 400,000. Director Conway sensed "educational and social pressures" on the Zoo:

Generations are growing up without *any* natural contact with wild creatures; a new public opinion concerning wildlife and wild environment is arising unfettered and unguided by fact or experience. Except at the Zoo, the opportunities to know or even become interested in wild creatures are largely vicarious ones for many city dwellers. The opinions of these people will shape the future of wild lands and wild creatures.

In numerous small ways the Zoo began to stress its educational function; in signs and graphic displays it began to explain why animals behaved the way they did, where they fitted into the whole environment, what was happening to the wildlife and the environment—and why. It began tagging exhibit labels of endangered species with a special red warning symbol keyed to another eye-catching sign:

DEAD AS THE DODO

Once there were vast numbers of Dodo birds. "Civilized" man killed them all—not one remains alive. Hence the expression, "Dead as the Dodo."

Many other animals may be as dead as the Dodo unless we protect them. This red symbol calls attention to endangered species. Look for it around the Bronx Zoo. And think about what it means—the final emptiness of extinction.

Oddy enough, the Bronx Zoo was the first to call attention to vanishing species; now the "endangered species" symbol of an antelope skull has been adopted by the American Association of Zoological Parks and Aquariums and is displayed in many zoos.

Director Conway got his chance to test the public's receptiveness to disguised education with the opening of the new Aquatic Birds Building in 1964. It was the oldest building in the Zoo, the scene of the opening-day ceremonies in 1899, but for several years it had been a mere shell and winter storage place for water birds. Conway conceived of it as a

500

series of exhibits showing where birds live and their varied ways of life, and the architect, Harmon Goldstone, worked with him enthusiastically. Boat-billed herons nested in treetops inside the building just as they do in the wild—the trees growing in sunken cages so that only the tops were at eye level. Shore birds skittered and ran and nested on a sand dune washed by mechanically impelled waves so realistically coordinated with a recording of actual surf that many visitors declared they smelled salt air. Birds lurked among rocks and fallen trees and lush tropical vegetation in a Jungle Stream exhibit, and no one could have known that the massive boulders were fiber-glass replicas molded by Designer Jerry Johnson and his new department of exhibition. There was a cliff where tufted puffins and Inca terns and guanay cormorants swooped and dived and swam underwater, swamps with gigantic cypresses hung with Spanish moss . . .

As a means of calling attention to our disappearing wildlife, the Zoological Society annually sets up this "graveyard" of extinct species on Baird Court in the Zoo.

The public loved it; educational it was, but above all it was a novel and spectacular way of exhibiting birds in a zoo.

Since 1961 the northern half of the old Small Mammal House had been given over to experiments in the diurnal exhibition of nocturnal mammals. Associate Curator of Mammals Joseph A. Davis, Jr., had conceived the idea of lighting the cages with red fluorescent light by day—a color the eyes of nocturnal animals could not perceive, so that they remained active as they naturally would be at night—and flooding them with white light after the Zoo closed, thereby creating the "daytime" when the animals would normally go to sleep. Such experiments had been carried on elsewhere, mostly using blue light to create an illusion of darkness, but Davis's red-light idea had a more scientific basis; it worked remarkably well, and visitors who had been accustomed to seeing a kinkajou, a galago, or a civet as mere balls of fur curled up asleep at noon now found them alert and active.

It was a show worthy of wider application, for there are many nocturnal birds and reptiles as well as mammals. Conway had proposed a World of Darkness in 1961; he got it on June 12, 1969, in a building that "pioneered a new sophistication in the exhibition of wild animals." It was a huge circular structure whose exterior walls were panels of black conglomerate, and it crowned a hilltop with its entrance oriented to the ice-age Rocking Stone a few yards away. The Vincent Astor Foundation and the city's capital budget put up the $660,000 construction cost, and the society spent another $100,000 for preparation of the exhibits. Money, it seemed, could always be found to match dramatic new ideas.*

Director Conway was not lacking in still other dramatic new ideas. The doors of the World of Darkness were scarcely open before bulldozers moved in to start an even more strik-

The World of Darkness in the Bronx Zoo, opened in 1959. Morris Ketchum, Jr., and Associates, Architects. Photograph by Alexandre Georges.

The World of Birds in the Bronx Zoo was opened in 1972 and has been spectacularly successful. Morris Ketchum, Jr., and Associates, Architects. Photograph by Alexandre Georges.

* Sizable sums are involved in the Zoo's operations; its cash flow is $8 million to $10 million a year, depending on what projects are in hand. The financial administration is in charge of the comptroller; Herbert F. Schiemann was comptroller from 1946 to 1966, and since then Walter Lerchenfeld has had that responsibility as director of finance and administration. He is also assistant treasurer of the society.

502

ing exhibit: the World of Birds. It had been six years in the planning and was to be the supreme culmination of ideas and techniques for which the Aquatic Birds Building and the World of Darkness were in a sense preparatory. Its opening on June 16, 1972, was triumphantly successful. Ada Louise Huxtable, who reports on architecture for the *Times,* wrote: "There are no flies on New York's Bronx Zoo. It entertains, instructs and proselytizes, and it uses the tool of architecture to do so with singular skill. The World of Birds . . . is surefire drama and painless education. And fun."

There are and will be other spectacular exhibits in the Bronx Zoo, but for many years the World of Birds will be the *one* building that visitors feel they must see, whatever else they miss. For the record, let it be said that the concepts and organization were Director Conway's and that by his side throughout were Curator Joseph Bell and Associate Curator Donald F. Bruning of the bird department, Superintendent of Construction Charles B. Driscoll, Jerry Johnson and his exhibitions department, and architects Morris Ketchum, Jr., and Associates.

And that Mrs. Lila Acheson Wallace paid for it: about $3.5 million. A house for birds was the first building opened in the Zoological Park in 1899. *This* house for birds, almost three-quarters of a century later, is a world away from the first one in concept and philosophy, but the men who went before would have found it a glorious realization of their own dreams.

To have been pedantically exact, this history of the first seventy-five years of the New York Zoological Society should have broken off with whatever had been accomplished by May 7, 1970, exactly three-quarters of a century after the incorporators met in 1895. But there is another seventy-fifth anniversary on November 8, 1974, which is of more popular significance and must be accounted for: the opening of the Zoological Park in 1899. Since pedantry and wild animals do not mix, both exact terminal dates will be ignored for the sake of generalizing about the point at which the society has now arrived and about the future of the Bronx Zoo and the Aquarium.

From the very beginning the society set an example to the zoo world of what such specialized institutions could do for the conservation of wildlife, for research, and for education; that until lately few followed the example is beside the point. It was simply ahead of its time, but it did help to create to-day's more responsive climate. It is still leading and setting an example. Fairfield Osborn expanded the society's involvement, and it has not lessened under the succeeding presidencies of Laurance S. Rockefeller and, since 1970, of Robert G. Goelet. Indeed, men working out of the Center for Field Biology and Conservation in the Zoological Park are going further afield than ever they did in the Osborn era. More significant still, the society has on its staff a greater number of biologists than all the country's other conservation organizations put together.

If there was at some periods an apparent dichotomy in the relationship of the society and the Zoo, it has long since disappeared. Their interests and many of their aims are identical. To put it in its simplest terms, a broad goal of the society is to preserve the fast-vanishing wildlife of the world; the *insistent* goal of the Zoological Park is to do the same thing within the practical confines of its own fences and (eventually and very probably) in wildlife breeding reserves under its management elsewhere.

In earlier years the Bronx Zoo (like all zoos) considered that its function was to display as many kinds of animals as possible. A zoo collection was a living catalogue of the animal kingdom, and the larger the catalogue, the greater the zoo's pride. Today more and more zoo directors are realizing that they have other responsibilities toward their animals, and that their zoos *are actually refuges, perhaps the only safe refuges, for hard-pressed species.* Take two examples:

505

The time is probably not far off when the Arabian oryx will exist only in zoos. Many years ago it was in the Bronx Zoo's collection, but no efforts were made to establish a breeding herd. Replacements could always be made from the wild. But is it possible today?

Or take Siberian tigers. There are nine in the Bronx Zoo and their breeding record is good. There are perhaps 180 left in the wild, another 250 in scattered zoos. How are Siberian tigers going to survive unless zoos extend a sheltering wing?

The trend today is toward keeping fewer species and keeping them better. The management technology, the veterinary skills, are available, and one of the glories of the Bronx Zoo is that it has hammered this message home in innumerable conclaves of zoo men.

Exhibition merely for the sake of exhibition is no longer a primary aim of the Bronx Zoo; it has moved into concern for conservation that makes it a vigorous partner of the Zoological Society.

What of the immediate future?

The New York Aquarium will not reach its seventy-fifth anniversary under the society's auspices until 1977, but in its seventy-second year it is flourishing—self-supporting and with its opportunities limited only by the imagination of its staff.

Dr. Hornaday's concept of the Zoological Park was rounded out with the opening of the Heads and Horns Museum in 1922. Today no one would be foolish enough to say or even think, "When such-and-such is built, the Bronx Zoo will be complete." There will always be new ways to interpret wild-animal life to people who must understand the natural world in order to save it, and themselves.

Changes in the Zoo are already on the way. An enormous complex to be called Tropical Asia is in the blueprint stage. It will be spread over wild acres in the southeastern corner of the Zoo. Baird Court, once thought of as the exhibition heartland of the Zoo, is now conceived of as a vast classroom.

In 1973 an aerial tramway, the Skyfari, began to operate in the Bronx Zoo and has been immensely popular with visitors. The circular building in the background is the World of Darkness.

Present animal buildings will become indoctrination centers from which visitors will radiate to the living exhibits, all but unconsciously prepared to understand and appreciate them far more than ever before. Even the hundreds of mounted heads in the Heads and Horns Museum can be combined with graphic exhibits to make them mean something to a generation more concerned with saving the "big game" of the world than in shooting it. The building will, in fact, become the educational services headquarters of the Zoological Park.

It will take time, and money. But there are vital ideas behind the changes that are coming, and in the seventy-five-year history of the New York Zoological Society great concepts have had a way of being realized.

Gracie, the Zoo's first takin, makes a cautious acquaintance with a young male at the left.

508

Index

513

518

74 75 76 77 78 10 9 8 7 6 5 4 3 2 1